D1521921

**From Stereotype to Metaphor:
The Jew in Contemporary Drama**

SUNY Series in Modern Jewish Literature and Culture
Sarah Blacher Cohen, Editor

From Stereotype to Metaphor
The Jew in Contemporary Drama

Ellen Schiff

State University of New York Press
Albany

Published by
State University of New York Press, Albany

© 1982 State University of New York

All rights reserved

Printed in the United States of America

For information, address State University of New York Press, State University Plaza,
Albany, N.Y., 12246

Library of Congress Cataloging in Publication Data

Schiff, Ellen
  Fom stereotype to metaphor.

  (SUNY series in modern Jewish literature and culture)
  Bibliography: p. 261
  Includes index.
  1. Drama—20th century—History and criticism. 2. Jews in literature. I. Title.
II. Series.
PN1861.S29   809.2'935203924   82-761
ISBN 0-87395-621-4   AACR2
ISBN 0-87395-622-2 (pbk.)

093567

For Mort

The word *Jew* has no neutral connotations in drama.
—Derek Cohen

Contents

Illustrations

Preface

This study was prompted by the extraordinary prominence of Jewish characters in drama since the second World War. Inasmuch as the Jew made his debut on the Western stage in the twelfth century, his enormous recent popularity is no overnight success story. A number of factors have contributed to his fame, and in these pages I have tried to account for them. Before an inquiry into the Jew on the contemporary stage could get underway, however, there was an important preliminary. Determining the focus of the investigation led smack into two issues as knotty as they are fundamental: Who is a Jew? What is a Jew?

In terms of the theatre alone, the first question invites a profusion of answers. Often we understand that people in a play are Jews because of their names, speech patterns or values. Although a playwright's decision to endow his characters with ethnic background is doubtless as calculated as other artistic choices he makes, it is prudent to avoid exaggerating or distorting his intent. Since drama typically makes inference and implication work hard, the suggestion that someone is Jewish may serve as little more than a shorthand explanation for the way he responds. For example, the Jewish tendency to be excitable and articulate helps two playwrights to make opposite comments about characters we take to be Jews. In *The Kitchen*, Arnold Wesker gives the only long speech to Paul, an otherwise undistinguished pastry chef. Paul passionately deplores the lack of mutual respect and support among workers who suffer many of the same woes. An antithetical effect is achieved by Michael Weller in *Moonchildren*. Here the tight rein which the sensitive student Bob keeps on his feelings emphasizes his alienation from the world of his emotional Uncle Murry. Coding a persona as Jewish in order to set off associations that enrich the characterization is a splendidly efficient device in dramatic literature. But because the practice works through allusion, it indicates Jews only superficially. This study required an index to characters of definite Jewish substance.

At the risk of preferring the obvious to the subtle, I have adopted a twofold standard as a uniform, workable method of identifying Jewish personae. The criterion draws upon the wisdom of Ben Gurion's statement that a Jew is anybody who says he is, and the logic of Sartre's "The Jew is one whom other men consider a Jew"[1]—a perception perhaps even more valid in art than in life. Consequently, the present investigation is limited to plays whose protagonists proclaim their Jewish identity, whether by boast, lament or resignation. The Sartrean part of the test resulted in the selection of works where the reactions of gentile characters to Jews, or of Jews to one another, acknowledge their Jewishness.

If the application of this two-part standard of Jewish self-awareness confirmed in the eyes of others permits the consideration of a large number of personae, it excludes others who may be Jews. For instance, critical argument has been advanced for the Jewishness of the Loman family in Arthur Miller's *Death of a Salesman*[2] and for the mother and son in Harold Pinter's *A Night Out.*[3] The identifying principle operating here refuses these characters. However, the same formula recognizes the unequivocally Jewish figures in Miller's *The Price* and Pinter's *The Birthday Party.*

One of the most interesting consequences effected by this method of identification is the mandate to scrutinize characters who, though they are not Jews, insist that they are and are taken at their word. Such is the case, for example, with Marguerite Duras' Parisian hippy in *Destroy, She Said* and Arthur Miller's Catholic Count von Berg in *Incident at Vichy.* Not unexpectedly, plays like these furnish some of the most original and thoughtful interpretations of the word *Jew.*

However, to consider various meanings of *Jew* is to arrive at the question of the "what" rather than the "who," a determination much less likely to yield to pre-established criteria. In the last five decades the theatre has devoted itself with conspicuous vigor and imagination to an eight-century-old tradition of showing what a Jew is. To give the reader a sense of how far the Jew has come and where he has come from, the introductory chapter traces his career from medieval drama to the early twentieth century.

The very concept of *Jew* was forever revised by Hitlerism, which contrived the destruction of an entire people, and by the establishment of the State of Israel, which gave it a homeland for the first time in two thousand years. Dramatists in the United States, England and France, a fair number of them Jewish, have been mining recently introduced notions of the Jew to generate a highly diversified and unfamiliar breed of dramatis personae. The contemporary versions fall easily into two general categories. The first perpetuates some aspect of the established stage Jew, usually by updating or overturning time-honored assumptions and practices. The second includes a heterogeneous assemblage perhaps most appropriately called the New Jews. One of the few things they have in common is that they do not appear in Western drama before the century's critical Jewish events and its enhanced appreciation of ethnicity. Together the reworked and fresh images demonstrate an unprecedented period in the evolution of one of the theatre's veteran personae. It is hard not to be impressed with the staying power of Jews on stage and with the versatility they have exhibited in the last few decades. There is no arguing with the candid self-assessment of one of the recent prototypes who really speaks for the many. "I have," he observes, "amazing skills."

Acknowledgments

Writing a book provides, among other things, a sobering demonstration of one's dependency and, more hearteningly, of the generosity of human nature. I am indebted to a great many individuals I
know only as helpful voices on the telephone, faithful mailers of
information, and knowledgeable retrievers of material in archives and
libraries.

I wish to thank Sarah Blacher Cohen without those confidence the
project would not have been undertaken. Rabbi Arthur D. Rulnick
was never too busy or amazed to answer even the most eccentric
question. I am grateful to North Adams State College, particularly to
Vice President for Administration and Finance Thomas M. Jones and
to Director of Library Services Charles A. McIsaac. I am especially
thankful to Geraldine Krumholz for her perceptions, patience and
loyalty.

Arnold Wesker most graciously lent production photographs of *The
Old Ones* from his own files. I acknowledge with appreciation the
permission of the Editors of *The Massachusetts Review* to reprint in
Chapter Six material which appeared in the Winter 1980 issue, as well
as that of the American Jewish Historical Society to include passages
from an article in the September 1980 issue of *American Jewish History*.

All happy families may resemble one another, but not every one
has a daughter who offers excellent editorial advice, a son who restores perspective and humor, and a husband willing to spend an
inordinate amount of time in the theatre. I treasure the support and
devotion of Stacy, Gary and Mort.

1

Introduction:
The Tradition of the Stage Jew

I

In his famous "Hath not a Jew eyes?" speech, Shylock means to justify his claim on Antonio and at the same time to argue the similarities between Christian and Jew. His plain logic is still compelling, even for audiences far better acquainted with Jews than were those at the Globe. Yet the degree to which the Shakespearean sense of humanity is original becomes more readily apparent when Shylock's hypotheses are applied to the Jew as he had appeared on the stage since the middle ages. For early European drama relied heavily on Jewish types whose life force was not blood, but legend.

Though the Jew on the medieval stage was ubiquitous, his role there had very little to do with his having "hands, organs, dimensions, senses, affections, passions" of human proportion. On the contrary, his greatest value to the playmakers of the era was that he was different from all other men, a quality which illuminated all his idiosyncrasies. The popularity of the Jew in mystery and morality plays can be attributed to the medieval taste for juxtaposing extremes. The processions of "devils, executioners, tryants, bawdy fellows, Jews, side by side with saints and the pious" illustrate that "the Jew was, in the ideas of the time, perfectly suited to the role of the foil."[1] Moreover, there was intrinsic drama in setting the nobility and beauty of Christ against the impotent rage of those hostile to him. Most important, the inclusion of despicable, risible types in Church drama, which naturally proscribed ridiculing the sacred, allowed for the introduction of the comic.[2]

A remarkable example is provided by the thirteenth-century Benediktbeuern nativity play. In the prologue, a band of Jews led by the melodramatically named Archisynagogus is seated to the left of Au-

1

gustine. On his right, by contrast, are Isaiah, Daniel, the Sybil, Aaron and Balaam. As the representative of the unbelievers, Archisynagogus mocks the prophesies by behaving ridiculously, "striking his companions, shaking his head, acting like a Jew generally [imitando gestus Judaei in omnibus]."[3] Subsequently, he displays his ignorance further in a debate with Augustine, a disputation whose didactic thrust was aimed well beyond the Jews on stage, for it was introduced into the Benediktbeuern play "for no other purpose than to suggest that Archisynagogus' ridicule of the paradox of the virgin birth can be adequately met only by the great Church father."[4] The leader of the Jews is made to appear foolish in this scene and sinister in the next where he gives guileful advice to Herod who, having acted on it, promptly succumbs to a horrible death in full view of the spectators.

Along with Herod, Pilate and the devil, the Jew was regularly dramatized as the stiff-necked enemy of Christ, especially in the mystery plays, or as the diabolical tempter or sorcerous undoer of Christians (e.g., the various versions of Theophilus' pact with the devil through the agency of a Jewish conjurer, of which Rutebeuf's thirteenth-century Miracle of Theophilus is perhaps the best known). Bringing Jews into the Christian faith offered one of the most dramatic demonstrations of the glory and the power of the Church. Indeed, the disputation between Augustine and Archisynagogus in the Benediktbeuern play is followed by a poem which cites prophetic justification for proselytizing the unbelievers. There is an abundance of drama in which Jews, visited by personal miracles or bested in a debate with a Christian, directly present themselves for baptism.[5]

Two important distinctions were made by the medieval mind as it dealt with the children of Israel. The first is a certain ambivalence, bordering on open distrust, toward the Old Testament venerables like Abraham and Isaac who "belonged to the brotherhood of saints traditionally haloed on the stained-glass windows."[6] The reverence paid the patriarchs stemmed from typological exegesis of the scriptures wherein the Old Testament served to prefigure (e.g., Isaac as the sacrificed Christ) or announce (e.g., the prophesies of Isaiah) the advent and promise of Christianity. Brought down from the cathedral windows to the stage in the parvis, Israelites were sometimes dramatized in ways which suggest that they were not as entirely "idealized, lacking all ethnic nature" and ennobled as one commentator observes.[7]

The suspicion evident in the stage treatment accorded these prototypes betrays a far from neutral recognition that biblical Hebrews were Jews. For instance, the stage directions for the twelfth-century Ordo de Ysaac et Rebecca required Isaac and his sons to wear "pilea

Judaica,"[8] the identifying pointed caps of the Jews, which in later plays gave way to Oriental turbans, along with gold and silver belts and tassled purses.[9] The title page of the sixteenth-century interlude of *Jacob and Esau* specifies that those players who are to be considered Hebrews should be attired as such,[10] which presumably meant that they were outfitted with contemporary attributes like the special hat and the yellow badge.

A certain unwillingness attached to the receiving of sacred testimony from a Hebrew. In an early prophet play, Isaiah is tartly rebuked, "*Isayas verum qui scis,/ueritatem cur non dicis?* (Isaiah, you who know the truth,/Why do you not tell the truth?)".[11] In the twelfth-century *Jeu d'Adam*, "the prophets are solemnly escorted back to hell after the delivery of their testimony,"[12] while Adam and virtually all the other patriarchs await the advent of Christ there at the end of *Le Mystère d'Adam* (thirteenth century).[13] In a number of mystery plays, it is the Hebrew language itself that is caricatured when the litany solemnly chanted by stage Jews is patently gibberish.[14] On the medieval stage, the men of the Hebrew Bible tended to be conceptualized somewhere between the saintly New Testament antitypes whom they prefigured and the stigmatized contemporary Jew who, the internal evidence argues, must have descended from them.

A second discrimination made by the theatre of the middle ages affected the portrayal of Jewish women. While the Old Testament matriarchs were depicted reverently, the repellent male Jews—whether Judas, Annas and Caiaphas or the more contemporary *mauvais sujets*—have no female counterparts. In the study *Portrait of the Jewess in French Literature* (*Portrait de la Juive dans la littérature française*), Luce Klein observes, "[The Jewess] is neither the wife of Judas, or the devil, or even, it would seem, of the usurer or the sorcerer. If, in medieval literature, she is sometimes seen associated with the cruel, greedy, aggressive, hard-hearted or opinionated man who is her husband, it is at the precise moment when she is severing this association."[15]

To be sure, the matriarchs also played typological roles in church drama. Rachel lamenting her inconsolable children represents the *virgo mater* both in dramatizations of the coming of the magi (*Officium Stellae*) and the slaughter of the Innocents (*Ordo Rachelis*, both eleventh through thirteenth centuries). Perhaps the most interesting Jewish female image on the stage of the middle ages is the personification of the allegorical and iconographic[16] Synagoga. A young woman whose bandaged eyes symbolize her blindness to the truth of Christianity, Synagoga almost always appears in contraposition with Ecclesia. Her attributes vary. Often she is a figure noble in defeat carrying a broken lance or standard and losing the Tablets of the Law (much as she appears on the façade of the Strasbourg Cathedral), though occasionally she is given some of the gross caricatured traits more commonly applied to the male Jew.[17]

When Synagoga enters the twelfth-century *Libellus de Antichristo* she is with a band of co-religionists decrying Christianity. They are offset by Ecclesia attended by Mercy, Justice, the Pope and his clergy, and the Roman Emperor and his soldiers.[18] Synagoga is singled out for attention. She is subdued by Antichrist, then converted by Enoch and Elijah who for their troubles are slain with her. The death of the three Hebrew figures serves as a reminder of "Christ's Passion, the sacrifice destroying the power of the Princes of Darkness."[19] Synagoga's lot is no happier in the fourteenth-century play presented for the Feast of the Blessed Virgin Mary. Here, "after a tearful lament, Synagoga is pushed down the west steps of the stage by Gabriel and Raphael, lets fall her banner and the tables of the Old Law, and flees crying from the Church."[20] Though the episode is meant to demonstrate the inaccuracies of Jewish belief, it is worth noting that Synagoga's exit was greeted not with compassion, but laughter.[21]

The trials of the allegorical Synagoga notwithstanding, there seems little question that the Jewess was treated with less frequency and with much less fierceness than the Jewish male in the early theatre. Klein theorizes that this amnesty from opprobrium reflects "Christianity's initial ambivalence toward Judaism in which love combines with hatred and the recognition of a bond mingles with the violence of a rejection."[22]

Something of the durability of that perception can be gauged in the reason offered by Chateaubriand in 1836 to explain the distinctive beauty of Jewish women. Unlike their men, he wrote, they are blameless. There was no Jewess in the crowd who humiliated and punished Christ. "The women of Judea believed in the Savior, loved him, followed him, comforted him with their goodness, soothed him in his afflictions." Concludes Chateaubriand, "The reflection of some magnificent beam must have remained on the forehead of the Jewess."[23]

The conception of both male and female Jew in the middle ages announces and doubtless explains the fascination this "dual image"[24] will exercise in subsequent ages. The polarization into gender of positive and negative qualities associated with Hebrews manifests itself in a pair of characters who become a conspicuous literary motif, the beautiful Jewess and her repulsive father. The idealization of feminine virtue in a creature whose bloodline is nonetheless disposed to perversity gives rise to another literary stereotype, the *belle Juive*. We shall meet them again in these pages.

One of the medieval Jew's most conspicuous distinctions is his

virtual absence from the societies in whose drama he figures so color-
fully. William the Conqueror brought Jews to England specifically to
serve as "engines of finance." Despite humiliations, special taxes and
various types of discrimination, their restricted existence was toler-
able until the persecutions and massacres of the twelfth century.
Edward I's act of expulsion in 1290 drove 16,000 Jews out of the
country and put an end to a 225-year span in which Jews inhabited
England, always as aliens.[25]

By contrast, Jews had lived in France since the first century C.E.
Along with periodic persecutions due to the exigencies of a king or
nobleman or the zealousness of Crusaders, the recurring threats were
forceful baptism, restrictions on occupations and religious practices,
and discriminatory taxes. The southeastern Jews were the least vulnerable due to the limited reaches of royal command and the protection of prosperous, enlightened nobles. But in 1229, when the region
from Carcassonne to the Rhone was annexed to the crown, all French
Jews suffered worsening persecutions. Philip the Fair's Edict of 1306
confiscated the real and personal property of France's 100,000 Jews
and expelled them, an act Cecil Roth interprets as spelling "the end
of the ancient and glorious traditions of French Jewry."[26] Many of
the exiles found temporary refuge just across France's borders or
in provinces not yet part of the kingdom (e.g., Lorraine, Provence,
Dauphiné), where they were hardly more immune to periodic banish-
ment. Writing of the expulsions from Provence in 1498 and 1501,
Bernhard Blumenkranz observes, "In France as elsewhere, the Jewish
middle ages lasts until the Revolution."[27]

While the notion of the Jew as undesirable alien is thus rooted in
fact, the depiction in dramatic literature of his sinfulness and peculiar-
ities is hardly reportage. What is significant is that the figure of the
Jew as outsider, long an accepted dramatic convention, became a
literal reality at the very time that amusement began to rival edification and glorification as prerogatives of the stage. Its sensationalism
unchallenged, the theatre expanded its Jewish types into forms and
shapes limited only by the human imagination.[28]

The Jew is cast everywhere along the gamut of malevolence, from
the simple foil who provokes laughter by ludicrous contrast with the
faithful, to the wicked perpetrator of cruelty conceivable only by a
mind possessed of the devil. Fostered by a climate of ignorance and
superstition, exploited by the zeal of Christian apologists and pros-
elytizers, frequently inspired showmen, the figure of the Jew could
not possibly have become other than an increasingly spectacular personification of evil.

Yet in its portrayal of the Jew as a creature accursed and apart, the early theatre reflected not only religious, social and cultural postures, but the assumptions that lay behind them and made them possible. These are primitive, emotionally charged premises that have very little to do with what people see and everything to do with what they need to believe. In his fascinating study of medieval mentality, Joshua Trachtenberg writes that "everybody knew that the devil and the Jews worked together. This explains why it was so easy to condemn the Jew a priori for every conceivable misdeed, even if it made no sense. . . . The catalogue of alleged Jewish crimes is long and varied indeed, and wholly unreasonable, unless we accept the self-evident fact, in medieval eyes, that as Satan's agents, nothing was beyond the depraved and evil nature of the Jews."[29]

Paradoxically, although the stage Jew often appears to be constituted of elements foreign to human nature, like all successful villains he acts out fantasies beyond the reach of ordinary men, but not by any means beyond their yearning. Jonathas, the Jew of *The Croxton Play of the Sacrament* (c. 1470), is a fine example. He gloats over his fabulous wealth which, almost better than being inexhaustible, accrues from traffic with far-off, exotic places rather than from the sweat of his brow. Not only does he have the curiosity and the audacity to challenge the doctrine of transubstantiation, he also has the means to acquire the host for his personal examination. Who but a Jew would dare? It is difficult to miss the transference of guilty feelings at work in *The Croxton Play*. Moreover, since Jonathas is patently an ancestor of Barabas, Shylock and Isaac of York, he helps demonstrate that the myth of the wicked Jew responds to the human need to avow and be punished for baseness, a requirement not at all peculiar to men of the fifteenth century.

So indelibly was the Jew's moral fiber stained that he deserved to be cheated and humiliated even when he comported himself with uncommon magnanimity, as in the morality play *The Three Ladies of London* (1584). Four years later, as Barabas (Marlowe could hardly have chosen a more inflammatory name) the stage Jew attains diabolical apotheosis:

As for myself, I walk abroad o' nights
And kill sick people groaning under walls;
Sometimes I go about and poison wells;
And now and then, to cherish Christian thieves,
I am content to lose some of my crowns,
That I may, walking in my gallery,
See 'em go pinioned along by my door.
Being young, I studied physic and began
To practice first upon the Italian;

There I enriched the priest with burials,
And always kept the sexton's arm in ure
With digging graves and ringing dead men's knells:
And after that, was I an engineer,
And in the wars 'twixt France and Germany,
Under the pretence of helping Charles the Fifth,
Slew friend and enemy with my stratagems;
Then, after that, was I an usurer,
And with extorting, cozening, forfeiting,
And tricks belonging unto brokery,
I filled the gaols with bankrupts in a year,
And with young orphans planted hospitals;
And every moon made some or other mad,
And now and then one hang himself for grief,
Pinning on his breast a long, great scroll
How I with interest tormented him.
But mark how I am blest for plaguing them;
I have as much coin as will buy the town.
      (*The Jew of Malta*, II, 3, c. 1588)[30]

Even an overachiever as remarkable and lucid as Barabas shares with his less accomplished stage brethren characteristics that are constants in the theatre through the sixteenth century. Whatever his form, the male Jew is a wretched, stiff-necked creature incapable of recognizing truth, unrepentant (if he is at all aware) of his crime of deicide, and—worst of all—tenacious in his inscrutable ways.

Having noted the special qualifications of the Jew to become everybody's boogeyman and the circumstances of history that have cooperated in making him one, it is important to account for his unflagging popularity as a villain in the theatre, even considering the medium's hospitality to stock figures in general. How is it that even at the end of the eighteenth century, author Richard Cumberland could make his character Sheva observe, "If your playwriters want a butt, or a buffoon, or a knave to make sport of, out comes a Jew to be baited and buffeted through five long acts for the amusement of all good Christians" (*The Jew*, I, 1)?

One clue is provided in the transition from life to dramatic literature of a cherished legend—that all usurers were Jews. While many European Jews had become moneylenders in the thirteenth century, curiously the usurer does not appear in French drama until the sixteenth century, despite "Carnival games and . . . scenes . . . in some mystery plays where Jews haggle with Judas over the price of his betrayal."[31] The English stage presents quite another picture. Jews were expelled from the country in 1290, shortly after Edward I discovered he could rely on Italian bankers. Yet of Tudor England, Modder records, "What the average playgoer expected to see, and did see, in the stage Jew was the incarnation of all the evil and unsocial traits of the medieval moneylender and tax-gatherer."[32]

Which medieval moneylender? Laws against usury in England were enacted both before the Norman conquest and the subsequent influx of Jews and in 1341, 1487, 1546, 1552, and 1571, that is, long after the expulsion and well before the readmission of Jews in 1655. The multiplication of anti-usury measures in the sixteenth century bespeaks an obviously exacerbating problem for which it was illogical to hold the Jews accountable. Still, *The School for Abuse* (1579), a tract on secular immorality by Stephen Gosson, actor and playwright turned preacher, refers to a play entitled *The Jew* (unrelated to Cumberland's later work by the same title mentioned above), which exposed "the greedinesse of worldly chusers and the bloody minds of usurers."[33] M. J. Landa indignantly remarks, "At that time there was flourishing in London a notorious Christian usuer, Hugh Audley. . . . Whilst the apocryphal Shylock has given his name to the whole fraternity, who ever heard of a moneylender being termed an 'Audley'?"[34] Despite, or more likely because of the actual practitioners, usury was regarded as un-English (hence foreign); there is no question it was un-Christian (hence immoral). In short, an identity ideally suited to the Jew.[35]

The emergence of the Jewish usurer as a stock type goes a long way toward illustrating the versatility and endurance of the nefarious stage Jew. The caricature was accessible, it was infinitely adaptable to any sort of base role, and it was credible, especially to a beleaguered and superstitious public. In an age where money, credit and banking brought daily woes, the Jew made a wonderful scapegoat. Although as we have seen, it was not the Jew who was running up the rate of borrowing, it was he who was represented as maniacally obsessed with acquisition. Furthermore, the culpability ascribed to the Jew attached not only to draining men of their resources, but to consuming their very lives. The image of the usurer who mulcts his creditors is of a piece with that of the scoundrel who poisons wells to spread the plague, and both are consonant with—indeed, derived from—the figure of the deicide. The myths of the Jew as vampire and as cannibal prospered, as myths always do, because they met a need. The Jew could be blamed for general catastrophe and held to account for the inexplicable. The transference of guilt for practicing usury in defiance of Church law pales beside the transference of the fascination with bloodshed which fuels the dire and apparently indelible myth of the Jew whose ritual requires Christian blood.[36] Lurking behind the Jewish usurer is an even more baleful figure, no doubt descended from Abraham, the first Jew of all—the Jew with the knife. And these two images are fused in Western drama's most illustrious malefactor, Shylock.

The archetypal usurer, humanized by Shakespeare, advances to a new position among dramatis personae, a position from which he exercises in *The Merchant of Venice* (and only there, for several centuries more) an unaccustomed function. In 1597, Shakespeare moved Shylock out of that vague "Jewrye" from which his predecessors had been summoned only long enough to work their mischief. He placed him in the same society and subjected him to most of the same pressures and demands as the other characters. And he used him to articulate the fears and concerns of that society as it grapples with the vexations of a common problem—competition. It is hardly remarkable that *The Merchant of Venice*, like *The Jew of Malta* and *The Jew* which served Stephen Gosson as an example, should deal with usury when excesses in lending and forfeiture were gouging Englishmen. Similarly predictable is the use of the reprehensible Jew to set off the generous, merciful Christians. But rivalry serves as a far more important theme in *The Merchant of Venice* than usury or moral commentary. The unexpected and unprecedented lie in showing the Jew as equally subject to competition—in business and personal life—as the rest of the characters.

Through the figure of the Jew, Shakespeare makes other kinds of distinctions. The Christians dissimulate (note the priority given Portia's attributes in Bassanio's "In Belmont is a lady richly left,/ And she is fair, and fairer than that word,/ Of wondrous virtues;" note the relaxed fervor of Antonio, the Christian gentleman, whose mercantile concerns have been satisfied: ". . . that, for this favour/ He presently become a Christian"). Shylock, by contrast, displays his ignoble human sentiments nakedly:

I hate him for he is a Christian;
But more, for that in low simplicity
He lends out money gratis, and brings down
The rate of usance here with us in Venice.

And again, stung and outraged by Jessica's treachery, "I would that my daughter were dead at my foot, and the jewels in her ear!"

Shylock's most shocking confessions have a way of transcending his particular situation to express more universal concerns. Such is the impotent rage of the individual at cross purposes with his society:

If you deny me, fie upon your law!
There is no force in the decrees of Venice.
I stand for judgment. Answer—shall I have it?

Such the loneliness of the man suddenly bereft of all he holds dearest:

Why, thou loss upon loss! the thief gone with so much, and so much to find the thief, and no satisfaction, no revenge, nor no ill luck stirring but what lights a' my shoulders, no sighs but a' my breathing, no tears but a' my shedding.

As a stage Jew, Shylock incorporates a new dimension. His behavior reveals truths "better" men dissemble. Not only has he "senses, affections, passions," they constitute a range of feelings broader and more poignant than those of any other character in the play. For the present author, Shylock is far more convincing as a human being than as a Jew. His impoverished family life, his lack of ethics, his misanthropy bespeak the very antithesis of Judaism. As a Jew, he is fabricated of mythic malevolence and hellishness. But as a villain, he embodies authentic human capacity for greed, resentment and retaliation. The interworking of these distinct aspects of Shylock, rarely considered separable before the present century, may account for the unflagging appeal *The Merchant of Venice* has enjoyed for four centuries with actors, theatregoers, playwrights and literary critics.

Although it is never astonishing to discover that Shakespeare is as relevant to modern audiences as he was to the Elizabethans, it is noteworthy that with the complexity of Shylock, he prepares the vastly modified role and image of the Jew in the twentieth century more surely than almost any other intervening playwright. Paradoxically, it is Shylock's vulgar attributes rather than his nuanced individuality that made him and his play towering prototypes throughout the ensuing centuries. Edgar Rosenberg sees Shylock's first line ("Three thousand ducats, well") "as a piece of stage logistics . . . in which the Jew's entrance binds him at once, without fuss, to his cash-nexus."[37]

However, it is not exclusively as a moneyman that the Jew is henceforth cast. The most cursory review of the many Bible-based plays of the late sixteenth century[38] points up the need to distinguish between Old Testament and extra-scriptural (one cannot reasonably say "real-life") stage Jews. The Bible proved an inexhaustible source of inspiration for dramatists both in France, despite the Paris Parlement's ban on religious plays after 1548, and in England, where Cromwell's closing of the theatres in 1642 instituted a period of almost three centuries during which no biblical drama appeared on the professional stage. While I shall discuss in the next chapter those Old Testament plays which fall into the chronological purview of this study, the number and importance of religious dramas prior to 1945 where Jews play significant roles are too vast to pass in review in a summary such as this.[39]

What is relevant here is the radically new direction biblical dramatization takes in the Renaissance. The trend is well exemplified by *Abraham Sacrificing* (1550), whose author, Théodore de Bèze, was Calvin's successor in the chair of theology in Geneva. Bèze wrote a play about Abraham because he identified with the patriarch whose career seemed to the Renaissance man to parallel his own. In so doing, Bèze heads a long line of dramatists who, feeling a kinship with Old Testament Israelites, regard them as representatives of contemporary man rather than as prefigurations of New Testament personages. The Protestant tendency to view moderns as embodiments of scriptural Hebrews derives largely from the Reformation's fresh exegeses of the scriptures and its recourse to rabbinical commentaries on them. As a result, various Christian sects, notably the Baptists and the Puritans, became markedly more appreciative of Jews and Judaism. Indeed, English identification with Israel manifested itself in the sixteenth century when Lyly likened God's favoring of England to that "of a new Israel, his chosen and peculiar people."[40]

In dramatic literature, one of the most successful fusions of poetic messianism and Christian identification with an Old Testament figure is *Samson Agonistes*. Murray Roston observes:

> Of all the biblical drama composed during the [sixteenth] century, none overcomes completely that barrier of sanctity which prevents total identification between author and character. Bèze may feel deeply the similarity between his own exile and that of Abraham, but the analogy is confined to one restricted aspect of the patriarch's life. Similarly Udall's identification of Henry VIII with Hezekiah is intended as little more than a graceful compliment to the king. But in *Samson Agonistes* Milton has so immersed himself in the biblical character that the drama is, in a sense, a catharsis for Milton even more than for the audience.[41]

Although the uncertain date of composition of *Samson Agonistes* renders impossible a precise catalogue of the ways in which Milton identified with Samson, some substantial affinities are obvious: blindness, bitter disillusion in relationships with women, the success and hostility of enemies. Roston notes that "above all both were obsessed by the need to reconcile their suffering with the doctrine of divine justice."[42]

Milton's Samson acknowledges his own guilt again and again. Still, he is not above the Old Testament hero's characteristic contumacy, lamenting that God has punished him too severely and repeatedly questioning divine wisdom. While sincere in his desire to expiate, he is far from humble and worries about his image:

Am I not sung and proverbed for a fool
In every street, do they not say, "How well
Are come upon him his deserts?"

The pitch of Samson's rage in the scene with Dalila reveals his thoroughly human outrage and jealousy, underscored by his shame that he had given in to her, a degree of insightfulness Milton adds to his biblical prototype:

Of what I now suffer
She was not the prime cause, but I myself.

Samson's passion bursts forth when Dalila begs to touch his hand:

Not for thy life, lest fierce remembrance wake
My sudden rage to tear thee joint by joint.

Yet he is forced to acknowledge the truth of her defense, agreeing that he had been false to himself before she betrayed him. Like Job, to whom he is often compared, Milton's Samson seeks to penetrate the divine reasons which explain how he has brought such misery upon himself. He ends like Job, reaffirming his faith in an unfathomable God. The giant who atones by bringing the pagan temple down upon himself and his enemies is, like the Old Testament original, passionately extravagant to the end.

Samson Agonistes differs most from his biblical antecedent in his sensitivity and introspection which dignify him and ultimately raise him to tragic stature. For all his newfound depth and breadth of character, however, Milton's protagonist retains his Judaic authenticity. At the same time, it is impossible to miss in this seventeenth-century dramatic poem the immediacy of the anguish, the frankness of the tortured senses and the incisiveness of the questions directed to God. Like Shylock, Samson comes through his work as a recognizable human being. Both figures are patently the forefathers of those Jews on the twentieth-century stage who, while remaining faithful to their own particular identities, come to have a resonance and an applicability that transcend them.[43]

The human intensity of Milton's Samson is thrown into relief by comparison with the more numinous and fabulous Hebrew personae that Jean Racine depicted somewhat contemporaneously. Milton studied the Bible and the commentaries as an unorthodox Protestant; Racine, as a Jansenist whose morality was based on the notions of divine grace and predestination. In preparing to write Esther (1689) and Athalia (1690), Racine read widely in the Hebrew Bible and in

Jewish history.[44] There are textual borrowings from the Old Testament in both plays. Although the plot lines are entirely dissimilar, central to each play is a challenge hurled at Jehovah by ruthless human beings. In *Esther*, the treacherous Haman plans to rid the earth of the chosen people. In *Athalia*, where, as critics like to point out, "God is the principal character,"[45] Baal worshippers led by Jezebel's daughter Queen Athalia almost triumph over the House of David. Both *Esther* and *Athalia* are concerned with the breaking and re-establishment of the Covenant between God and His people.[46] Indeed, the representation of the Divine is of central importance, for the god in both these plays is the terrible God of the Old Testament who gives the law and whose power makes itself manifest even in the hearts of apostates and idolaters.

Despite their specifically Hebrew source, the dramatis personae in both works acquire levels of identity that tend to surpass their Jewishness altogether or to impose a codified Christian view upon it. The first claim is especially substantiated by the eponyms of the plays. Racine takes more liberties than Milton with the human nature of his Israelites, endowing them with traits borrowed from the Greco-Roman tradition. While Esther and Athalia retain many of their scriptural qualities, they also bear the hallmarks of the talent responsible for some of the most unforgettable women in French dramatic literature. Racine's genius in animating psychology is superbly illustrated when the bedazzled Esther makes a lightning recovery from her audience with the overwhelming Ahasuerus, then adroitly maneuvers to undo Haman and save her people. Again, the dramatist's extraordinary skill fashions the arrogant Athalia's surprised discovery and wavering indulgence of her emotional vulnerability before Joash. In this climate of internal turmoil and restabilization, there is scarcely room for ethnic considerations. It is small wonder that both Bettina Knapp and Roland Barthes perceive the struggles that rage both within these women and between them and their antagonists as mythic conflicts of masculine and feminine forces.[47]

There is one noteworthy exception to the supra-Hebrew women in these plays. She is Jehoshabeath, the wife of the high priest in *Athalia*. Her minor role allows us a glimpse of the compassionate materfamilias who dares acts of courage but bends her will to her husband's, an image reminiscent of the "woman of valor" in Proverbs.

Of course these women are not the only Jewish characters in their respective plays. In fact, it is in the delineation of Mordecai, Jehoiada and Joash, all of whom serve as spokesmen for God the Father, that the Jewishness of the Racinian personae is most Christianized. We must not forget that the Jansenist-educated poet was writing for the edification of the young ladies at Saint Cyr. The male Jews in these plays are Old Testament figures conceptualized and esteemed by an ardent Catholic. Mordecai, the stubborn seer, Jehoiada, the prophetic, manipulative priest, Joash, the noble child pretender to the throne of Judah attest the Church's position that redemption comes through a Hebrew figure. It is no coincidence that the savior figures belong to the House of David from which Christ descended. In the dramatic conclusion of the first act of *Esther*, the heroine prays to the God who has sworn a holy alliance with her people. At the exact middle of that prayer, Racine, whose attention to symmetry was meticulous, has Esther remind God of "the saint whom you promise and whom we await."

While the riches of the biblical plays, especially the complex *Athalia*, demonstrate that Racine achieved far more than his royal patron asked for,[48] they constitute preeminently apologia of Christian doctrine. Paradoxically, at the heart of *Athalia*—a play where changes in human fortune are both enacted and predicted—lies a tenet common to Jansenist theology and to Judaism: only those men are just and triumphant whom God chooses to be just and triumphant. In much different fashion, but no less than Milton, Racine found in his Jewish characters the embodiment of his own passions and persuasions.

By the end of the seventeenth century then, several theatrical conventions were firmly entrenched. On stage, the Jew never doffed the cloak with which he had been fitted out when he made his debut in Church drama, a reversible mantle of source and curse. Through the middle ages and the Renaissance, theological attitudes engendered two groups of stage Jews. On the literal level there were the scriptural Israelites who, as we have seen, underwent modification during the Reformation in response to its unorthodox notion that the Old Testament figures represented not the antecedents of the New Testament, but contemporary Christians. The second prefabricated image of the Jew is more symbolic but no less rooted in Christian ethic. Grotesque and treacherous, stereotyped Jews provided on the stage "an indispensable reference group, enabling Christians to know themselves as Christians and to incarnate good by contrast with evil."[49] The oddity about these sturdy roles and images is that they flourished for hundreds of years in the very countries from which Jews had long been exiled. If the theatre from medieval times through the end of the seventeenth century holds a mirror to nature, its dramatization of Jews—the exalted and the infamous alike—reflects not external reality, but human nature, certain of whose primal needs were satisfied by myths about the Jews.

II

During the Age of Reason and the early nineteenth century, the theatre turns away from church and court and blossoms into an exuberantly social institution. The triumph of the middle class is everywhere apparent—from the exaggerated modes in acting and costume, to lively exchanges between spectators and actors, to the rise to supremacy of the actor-manager. The plays themselves are typically long on spectacle and intrigue, while almost without exception, dramatis personae have the depth and intensity of pasteboard. Despite isolated skirmishes between classicists and romantics, the boards become increasingly the domain of the well-made play, a crowd-pleasing confection at which nineteenth-century dramatists like Eugène Scribe prove uncommonly adept and prolific. As theatre grew more and more popular and lucrative, there was an insatiable demand for plays. The absence of copy- or stageright laws permitted a deluge of French plays in England, where they were eagerly translated, performed and imitated (William Archer referred to the early nineteenth century as "the winter solstice of English drama"). Nor was that the end of it. An account of plays on the American stage from 1752 to 1821 shows that New York, Boston and Philadelphia audiences might just have well attended the theatre in London or Paris.[50]

But we are getting ahead of the story, for while the well-made comedies of the late eighteenth and nineteenth centuries were liberally populated by Jews, as we shall see, the era begins on quite a different note. The vast social, economic and political changes which radically altered the fortunes of European Jews—recall and resettlement, emancipation (Jews were first granted full citizenship in France in 1791), increased social mobility—seem to go all but unnoticed in dramatic literature. Indeed, at first Jews are conspicuous by their absence, particularly in France. It is surprising, for example, that there is no Jewish character in Lesage's *Turcaret* (1709), a comedy built around the universal need for money and unscrupulous, heartless means of getting it. And it is nothing short of astonishing that Voltaire's prodigal vilification of Judaism does not spill over into his plays.[51]

M. J. Landa records a similar phenomenon on the English stage. He suggests that Charles II's protection of the small number of newly returned Jews may have dissuaded playwrights from acknowledging their resettlement (1655) as the theatres reopened. Restoration plays were nonetheless much more apt than their French contemporaries to contain disparaging references to Jews, as well as slight but abusive caricatures which are patently formulaic rather than a matter of intentional maliciousness. So one finds the routine slurs and disagreeable bit roles in plays by Webster, Marston, Beaumont and Fletcher, Dryden, Congreve and Colley Cibber.

The conspicuous disjunction between the roles of the Jew in society and on stage is particularly evident in the relatively tolerant American colonies. The very first Jew to appear on the American stage was Shylock, in a 1752 production of *The Merchant of Venice* in Williamsburg, Virginia. The first American play to contain a Jewish character, Susanna Haswell Rowson's *Slaves in Algiers* (1794), had him describe himself "as a forger and a crook, as one who cheated the Gentiles because Moses so commanded."[52] Shown in New York, Philadelphia, Hartford and Boston, Rowson's play evidently "satisfied theatregoers' predilections for Jews as stage-villains."[53] The early American stage accepted without question European plays and their freight of attitudes and stereotypes.

Yet surprisingly, the essentially undistinguished theatre of the late eighteenth and early nineteenth centuries did contribute to modifying traditional roles and images. The most promising development was the stage's very gradual responsiveness to Jews in society, eventually including those in the audience. Of major importance is evidence that dramatists saw and cared that their depiction of Jews was not only inaccurate, but offensive.[54] Smollett countered his negative image of the Jew in *Roderick Random* (1748) with the incredibly altruistic and generous Joshua Manasseh of *The Adventures of Count Fathom* (1753). Sheridan's *The Duenna* (1775) made sport of a sly apostate, Isaac Mendoza, tricked into marrying the titular governess whose highest praise for Mendoza was that he is "so little like a Jew, and so much like a gentleman." But the following year in *The School for Scandal*, Sheridan's moneyman Moses earned the favor of Sir Oliver Surface and of the audience as he guided the former through the labyrinth of high finance so he could redeem his misguided nephew. The best known volte-face was Richard Cumberland's. Having created a disagreeable Jew in *The Fashionable Lover* (1772), he overcompensated with Sheva, protagonist of *The Jew* (1794). Cumberland's effort is noteworthy in that he consciously sought to rehabilitate the image of the Jew "according to the new doctrine of human perfectibility . . . and the sentiment of universal tolerance associated with the era of the French Revolution."[55]

The popularity of *The Jew*, both in England and in the United States, bespeaks a growing tolerance of the sympathetic stage Jew. Unfortunately, the impossibly good Sheva rings no truer—either as a human being or as a Jew—than his opposite number, Barabas. Cumberland's endeavor demonstrates that it was as possible to create a character without any Jewish depth in a society where there were plenty of models as where there were none.

Cumberland's play is one of many which reflect the spirit of Lessing's *Nathan the Wise* (1779). The German work, translated into English in 1780 and French in 1783, was iconoclastic not only in its enlightened and generous Jewish protagonist, but in its view that the best religion is the one which forms the most virtuous men. The fact that Lessing modeled his Nathan on Moses Mendelssohn adds another reason to believe that the Jew in society was beginning to project his image on the Jew in the theatre. It is heartening that the benign Jewish characters began to prepare the way for others in the drama of succeeding decades. Although benignity is not the same thing as dimension, apparently the Jew had to show he could be nice before he was entitled to substance and versatility.

Playhouses during the rather extensive period under consideration here were not by any means monopolized by contemporary works. The classical repertory provided an ideal showcase for changing concepts of characterization. For that reason, the fortunes of Shylock at this time serve as some index of the ambivalence which continued to cling to the image of the Jew. In 1741, Charles Macklin broke the mold which had turned out decades of comic Shylocks. Macklin's masterful reinterpretation of the role stunned audiences unacquainted with Shylock's depth and strength. His performance, which ranged from melancholy through malevolence to agitated silence, won the acclaim of audiences and critics, wringing from his initially opposed theatre manager the concession, "Macklin, you *was* right."[56] Macklin's "rightness" served as the foundation for subsequent moving and more sympathetic portrayals of Shylock by Edmund Kean and Henry Irving.

It is instructive to compare how Shylock was faring on the continent. Of the many French reworkings, it is the adaptation Alfred de Vigny wrote, almost ninety years after Macklin's breakthrough, that compels our attention. Vigny's version is important partly because of his literary eminence, and partly because of his attitude toward Hebrews. Like all the Romantic poets, he was drawn to Old Testament subjects. Unlike the others, Vigny felt such an extraordinary affinity with the patriarchs that in major poems written between 1820 and 1839, he depicted himself as Jephthah, as Moses and Joshua, and as Samson. However, Vigny's Shylock, created right in the midst of that period, is a throwback to the sixteenth century. The poet diminished both the play, which he rewrote in three acts, and its Jew. Shylock is rendered petty (he bites his lips when he fears Antonio will not conclude the loan in the first place) and mean (he refuses Bassanio's repayment on an absurdly flimsy alibi).[57] Although Vigny's work went into rehearsal at the Ambigu-Comique in 1830, it was not performed, a setback attributed to two other updatings of *The Merchant of Venice* for which Paris audiences were having difficulty restraining their derision.[58] Alfred de Vigny's perpetuation of the stereotyped image must not be regarded as exceptional or superannuated. It is essential to note the deathlessness of the Jew-villain even as we record the embryonic amiable types springing up just outside his shadow.

A couple of ostensibly superficial techniques adopted in this era deserve credit for furthering the development of the stage Jew. For one, the Jew acquires a dialect. If one recalls the gibberish which passed for Hebrew on the medieval stage, that may appear more a revision than an innovation. True, in the eighteenth century, the accent and the jargon continue to mark the Jew as alien and ridiculous. The broken speech does not invariably defame an already sullied reputation however, for there are plays like Desaugiers's *Jew* (1823) which sets forth an honest and charitable character who "talks funny." Still it is in itself an unbecoming attribute and one easily understands M. J. Landa's denunciation of it. In describing O'Keefe's *The Young Quaker* (1783), to which Landa imputes "the most repugnant stage Jew of the century," the exasperated theatre observer barely contains his wrath at the play's use of cant. Landa's anger is fully justifiable, yet a late twentieth-century perspective invites us to wonder if the stage dialect at this time, unlike its medieval antecedent, was an exaggeration of the actual difficulties Jews resettling in England and France had with their new language. The introduction at the end of the eighteenth century of special speech patterns to characterize the Jew on stage, however clumsy and offensive initially, begs to be viewed in retrospect as a notable harbinger. The gimmick will be refined into an art in the twentieth century, practiced by none more skillfully than by Jewish entertainers who based their funny patter on authentic Yiddish phonetics and cadences.

Disguises were a second bit of stage business that caught on with great success in the stylized theatre of light comedy and farce. Among them numbered many variations of the gentile who passes himself off as a Jew. The subterfuge was first employed by John Webster in *The Devil's Law Case* (1618) where a Christian adopts a Jewish identity the better to accomplish his nefarious deeds. But in the eighteenth and early nineteenth centuries, the tactic gains a whole repertory of uses, provoking a gamut of responses. The first is predictable. When the respectable gentleman of Hannah Cowley's *The Belle's Stratagem* (1780) goes to a masked ball as a Jew, he is promptly maligned as a ragman and moneylender. Jewish masquerade serves an unusual and equivocal function in Henry M. Milner's thoughtful *The Jew of Lubeck* (1819). The eponym is not a Jew at all, but rather an Austrian aristocrat who, having been denounced for treason, adopts the guise so as to escape his past. Gentile characters in this melodramatic universe also assume Jewish disguises in order to assist a maiden's escape, remain undetected as a responsible guardian, and frequently and most ironically, to gain admission where they otherwise would be barred.[59]

The Jewish disguise figures among the many contrivances employed in these platitudinous entertainments. While neither the artifice nor the plays in which it appears have great artistic value, the distinctly modified attitude which made possible the use of the masquerade impresses this writer as a milestone in the evolution of the stage Jew. It would be excessive to interpret as philo-Semitic the gentile's willing adoption of a contemporary Jewish identity; nonetheless, until the Age of Enlightenment, the practice would have been unthinkable. When we read, for example, that an ambitious hero type, learning that servants of his inamorata have orders "to admit only an old woman, a rustic and a Jew, impersonates all three characters,"[60] it is clear that the Jew has been accepted as a type among types. However ambiguous his image, he has moved into society. On stage he is still unique—and so he will remain, for that is his value to drama. But he is no longer an abstraction.

Masquerading as a Jew must be seen in a new light. As the practice was employed in the eighteenth- and nineteenth-century theatre, it perpetuated the tradition of the Jew as deceiver and wrongdoer, albeit on a vastly reduced scale. That is not to imply that it is somehow preferable for the Jew to be depicted as a smuggler than as a poisoner of wells. However, the gentile who does in Jewish guise the mischief that he and everybody watching him knows he is perfectly capable of doing without the masquerade openly acknowledges that the Jew represents impulses that, however guilty, are nevertheless universal. Or as Victor Hugo's surprised blackguard puts it—in grudging admiration—when his self-serving motives are easily penetrated by a Jewish moneylender, "You are my conscience dressed up like a Jew."[61] Behind the mocking, mimicking and misrepresentation in the roles and images of Jews on the eighteenth- and early nineteenth-century stage, one can dimly but unmistakably discern the silhouettes of genuine human beings. That is a giant step forward.

III

While the gradually humanized stage Jew continues to develop through the nineteenth century, it is his antipodes who command center stage. By mid-century, two monstrous newcomers had slunk from the pages of popular novels to theatrical renown. Between them, Isaac of York (*Ivanhoe*) and Fagin (*Oliver Twist*) resuscitate virtually every medieval myth connected with the Jew—the ubiquitous, scorned Isaac with his inexhaustible store of wealth and cunning (and his beautiful daughter, of whom more presently), Fagin the trafficker in stolen goods and feeder on the innocence if not the blood of little boys, a villain whose evil eclipses the mere bestiality of a Bill Sykes. The theatricality of Scott's and Dickens' novels is confirmed by the impressive number of stage adaptations they inspired and the prestige of the actors drawn to animate the Jewish roles, among them John Ryder and Beerbohm Tree, Fagin, and Edmund Kean, Isaac.[62]

With Fagin and Isaac as pacesetters, the odious Jew makes a triumphant return engagement in the second half of the nineteenth century. He is the bad conscience of the man who murders him for his gold in *Le Juif polonais*, a huge success at its Paris première in 1869 and a starring vehicle for leading actors in London and New York where it was known as *The Bells*. He is the bad conscience of his people in countless dramatizations of the wandering Jew. And he is the importunate infidel, spectacularly depicted in *Torquemada* (1882) by the Hugolian flair for juxtaposing antitheses:

> Through the door at the back, wide open, come a frightened and ragged crowd between two rows of halberds and pikes. They are the deputies of the Jews, men, women and children, all covered with ashes and in tattered clothes, barefooted, with ropes about their necks. Some, mutilated and enfeebled by torture, drag themselves along on crutches or stumps; others, deprived of their eyes, are led by children. At their head is the Grand Rabbi, Moses-ben-Habib. All have the yellow badge prescribed for their race on their torn apparel. At some distance from the table, the Rabbi stops and falls on his knees. All behind him prostrate themselves. The old men strike the floor with their foreheads. Neither the King nor the Queen looks at them. They seem to be gazing at vacancy, above all these heads.[63]

The contemporary Jew was scarcely more sympathetically delineated. Gyp, in her "Smart Set" sketches, spins him out into multiple, ludicrous caricatures.[64] He becomes the venal writ server called Solomon Isaac in Boucicault's *London Assurance* (1841) and the unctuous purveyor-of-all-goods of identical character traits in Zola's *The Rabourdin Heirs* (1874). He belongs to the fraternity of Jewish fences who spring up in Fagin's wake, like Melter Moss of Tom Taylor's phenomenally successful melodrama, *The Ticket-of-Leave Man* (1863). More soberly, he is the Baron de Horn in Lavedan's *The Prince d'Aurec* (1892). The Baron is a millionaire, of course, whose faults do not include lack of self-assurance. He makes the mistake of voicing his conviction that "times have changed; today we are the true aristocrats" within ear-shot of more traditional nobility who spare themselves nothing to shove the arrogant Jew's words down his throat.[65]

There can no longer be any question about ingenuousness in the use of stock types. Authors knew exactly what they were doing—and why. Dickens explained to the woman who voiced a protest about Fagin that

> he is called "The Jew," not because of his religion, but because of his race. If I were to write a story, in which I pursued a Frenchman, or Spaniard, as "the Roman Catholic," I should do a very indecent and unjustifiable thing; but I make mention of Fagin as the Jew, because he is one of the Jewish people, and because it conveys that kind of idea of him, which I should give my readers of a Chinaman by calling him a Chinese.[66]

Dickens' point is abundantly clear. Other men (except the Chinese) are endowed with race, nationality and religion, but a Jew from any angle is a Jew, a fact which, at least in literature, transmits all one needs to know about him. Alexandre Dumas *fils* is even more specific; he records as a given that "it is agreed that a Jew in the theatre must always be grotesque,"[67] a prescription he himself took pains to ignore.

In 1886, preparing to lecture to the learned Society for Jewish Studies on "The Jew in Theatre," author Abraham Dreyfus asked Adolphe d'Ennery, a boulevard favorite, if he had written any plays with Jewish characters. D'Ennery responded:

> No, and the reason for it is very simple. I believe that in the theatre one must not fight public opinion. The first duty is to please the audience, that is, to respect its tastes and habits. If I had put a Jew on stage, naturally I would have been obliged to make of him a usurer or a crook or a traitor, or some sort of nasty type. I would have found that disagreeable, since I am myself of Jewish origin. So what did I do? I completely eliminated the Jew. You won't find a single one in my plays. By contrast, you will find in them a number of Catholic missionaries who throw themselves into the midst of fires to rescue children in peril.[68]

America's first Jewish playwrights, Mordecai Manuel Noah, Jonas B. Phillips and Isaac Harby responded to the axiom Dumas cites in much the same way d'Ennery did, avoiding the depiction of Jewish subjects. No rehabilitated Jewish personae came from the first Jewish playwrights in England (e.g., Leopold Lewis, Alfred Sutro, Charles Salaman) or from d'Ennery's colleagues in France (e.g., Georges de Porto-Riche, Catulle Mendès).

Instead, Alphonse Daudet's adaptation for the stage of his novel, *The Kings in Exile* (1879), demonstrates the production of stage Jews from formulas, both old and new. The novel's Catholic second-hand dealer turns into a Jewish rag peddler on stage. His daughter Sephora, who has inherited her mother's Semitic charms, becomes, unexpectedly, the novel's resolute immoralist. Given full Jewish pedigree in the playscript, Sephora's exotic allure and pernicious determination define her as an exemplar of a new theatrical type, the *belle Juive*. She is a creature irresistible but troublesome, at the very least, to the men (usually Christian) who love her.

The *belle Juive* makes a triumphant debut on the late nineteenth-century stage where she undergoes an interesting development. Often she is named Rebecca, inevitably recalling the heroine of *Ivanhoe*, that majestic paragon whose beauty of face and person melted the most hardened bigot.[69] In 1873, some fifty years after Scott's novel which had inspired numerous stage adaptations, Alexandre Dumas *fils* wrote a play entitled *Claude's Wife*. Significantly he named his Jewish protagonist Rebecca. The characterization of Dumas's Rebecca sheds light on Scott's heroine and, in the process, on the new sorority of *belles Juives*.

Dumas's play concerns the love between the gentile Claude, one of theatre's most wretchedly mismarried men, and the virtuous daugther of his associate Daniel. Since legal and religious considerations deem that nothing can come of this unhappy state of affairs, the playwright packs Daniel and Rebecca, who are fortunately early Zionists, off to Palestine. (Although he solved the lovers' problem, Dumas created one for himself; his play brought down upon his head the wrath of nationalistic French Jews, while simultaneously inflaming the anti-Semitism of Edouard Drumont.) Thereon ensues a crucial moment. As she leaves France forever, the heroine is permitted to declare her love for Claude in a speech that manages to be simultaneously chaste and passionate. She assures her beloved that although she could not be his wife during this lifetime, she will be so in eternity. Then she ends on a very curious note: "My religion does not authorize such hopes, but my heart goes beyond it and I know things will be thus."[70]

In Rebecca's confident assertion about the attainability of contradictory goals lies one of the values that inform the *belle Juive* whom she announces. A venerable tradition of contrarieties attaches to the Jewish woman. She is a virgin mother, the Mother of God, but she belongs to a deicidal race. She is a worshipper of Christ, if we are to believe Chateaubriand, but one who does not live by His word. Out of these prototypical polarities develops a more generalized and earthy ambivalence. The Jewess as virgin temptress begins to represent the desire for mutually exclusive goals of which the most intriguing is the longing to possess while preserving the desired object intact. That is quite literally the image we see both in *Ivanhoe* and in *Claude's Wife*.

In both works, marriages which are made to look irresistible if not inevitable do not, in fact, materialize. The Rebecca in each case instead devotes herself to an idealistic cause loftier than matrimony. No doubt Scott's Rebecca, who will sublimate her feelings in missionary work, is meant to personify the perfect faithfulness and purity of the Virgin. Dumas's heroine is up to something rather more mundane. She hypothesizes in glowing detail the conjugal life she and Claude would have shared, ending with the conviction that it will all still come true. The ambivalence surrounding the earlier Rebecca—untouched but yearning, untouchable but yearned for—reflects the Christian ethic. In Dumas's play the ambivalence associated with the Jewess is translated into psychological terms. It is not just the wish to attain contradictory goals that we see here, but the faith that such a desire can be fulfilled. Dumas suggests a sort of *folie à deux* in which the participants believe they can solve their dilemma through the agency of the Jewish woman. How Rebecca is to bring this off the playwright does not say, but it is clear he wants us to think she can. Rebecca is, after all, a name associated biblically with proven managerial ability.

What is important is the shift of role and image ascribed to the Jewess in *Claude's Wife*. The enigmatic icon of positive and negative values gives way to the woman who shares and even implements the universal desire to have things both ways, a notion that sticks to her in the popular mind.[71] Significantly, as far back as the Old Testament, the inherent ability of the literary Jewess has been rooted in her spunk and her healthy libido (e.g., Esther, Judith, Jael). While the *belle Juive* makes the most of those established attributes, her enormous energy and appeal have little to do with the idealized virtue that once attached to the Jewish woman.

The *belle Juive* evolves into a bold, proud and occasionally vulgar woman, sometimes more accurately described as a *Juive fatale*. Invariably handsome, she turns exploitative, canny about money and determined not to be done out of it, as in Léon Hennique's *Esther Brandès* (1887) and Edmond de Goncourt's *Manette Salomon* (1896). She is reworked from the Bible, again simultaneously alluring and destructive in Darzens's *Christ's Lover* (1888), Wilde's *Salomé* (1893) and, later, Giraudoux's *Judith* (1931). She embodies an extreme form of the Shavian New Woman—spirited, willful and often unprincipled in getting her own way, like Rachel Silberchatz in Ghelderode's *Pantagleize* (1929) and Judith in Donnay's *The Return from Jerusalem* (1903).

The Return from Jerusalem[72] is the unrelenting dramatization of Donnay's conviction that what he calls Aryan-Judaic relationships are unworkable. To make his point, the playwright shows how an accomplished and arrogant Jewess manipulates the lives of the Christian men who fall in love with her. Although she has converted to Catholicism as an expedient, Judith remains devoted to Zionism. When her lover leaves his wife for her, Judith sees the opportunity for a trip to Jerusalem. Palestine galvanizes the heroine's Judaism which, upon her return to Paris, becomes the center of her life and foyer, leaving precious little room for her hapless gentile lover. He, predictably and not unjustifiably, objects. What is neither predictable nor justifiable is the scope and fervor of the "Aryan's" scathing indictment of the entire Jewish people. Of course Donnay is playing with loaded dice by demonstrating the incompatibility of two people who would be constitutionally unsuited to one another regardless of their ethnic backgrounds. Nonetheless, the play contributes to a genuine turning point in the tradition of the Jew in the theatre. Here are four acts which put the Jewish heroine center stage, developing her character, probing her psyche, displaying her strengths as well as her wickedness, four acts which also afford her gentile victim ample reason and opportunity to vent his resentment of her and what she represents. Clearly, something radical has happened to the prescribed image of the Jew and the accepted understanding of how the stage may, to use Donnay's own term, "talk about the Israelites."

The Return from Jerusalem cannot stand alone as a landmark work. Rather it forms part of a representative group of turn-of-the-century plays which treat Jews and Jewish topics in an entirely new light. The consequence of works by dramatists like Donnay, Ancey, Savoir and Nozière, Bernstein, Pinero, Jones and Zangwill transcends their modest artistic value. They are the vanguard of modern drama about Jews. That *The Return from Jerusalem* and some, though by no means all, of its contemporaries are blatantly anti-Semitic will come as no surprise to students of the Jew in drama.[73] Yet even the overt prejudice with its topical accusations is symptomatic of a transformation in theatre. For the depiction of Jews in *The Return from Jerusalem* et al. emanates not from conventional cultural attitudes, but from the actualities of the epoch. Donnay and his colleagues wrote in the highly charged climate of the years 1894–1906. Essentially they were all treating one of the most perplexing questions churned up by the Dreyfus Affair—Jewish assimilation. It is thoroughly understandable that opinions about assimilation were running high; however, to discover dissenting, passionate, contemporary points of view providing the conflict in drama is unprecedented. Donnay's play and its coevals signal a theatre that has begun to reflect its society and to comment on it. That breakthrough demands an explanation. It is unlikely that the time-honored or recently modified roles and images of the Jew gave way to more authentic imitation as the result of higher Jewish visibility in society and in theatre audiences. In his 1886 lecture, Abraham Dreyfus emphasized the point that theatregoers' enslavement to convention was a matter of habit absolutely unrelated to their personal sympathies and antipathies. The gentile spectator, he said, would be astonished to see that a Jew in an adjacent seat did not share his hilarity at a standard maligning reference from the stage.[74] Nor is there reason to credit the emerging group of Jewish playwrights with the remodeling of Jewish characters and subjects. For example, Israel Zangwill's characterizations in *Children of the Ghetto* (1899) provoked this assessment from Max Beerbohm:

> When the conflicts come—a conflict between a young man and the old man whose daughter he loves, a conflict between the young man and the girl—one does not care twopence about them because none of the conflicting characters has drawn one breath of life or contains one drop of blood. The young man, we know, is a millionaire and a lax Jew; the old man is a strict Rabbi; the girl accepts the hand of the young man. But that is all we know about them.[75]

The emergence of verisimilitude and psychological substance in Jews on stage is, rather, one result of the energizing revolution in theatre which blazed up in the last decades of the nineteenth century. The iconoclastic dramaturgy and often shockingly truthful subjects of Ibsen, Chekhov, Strindberg and Shaw loosened the strangleholds of conventional plot and characterization and undermined countless entrenched attitudes toward the theatre and its role in society.

The turning point in the representation of the Jew on stage was not the emancipation of the Jew, but the emancipation of the theatre. In the plays of the first generation of iconoclasts, the focus was trained on social issues and ideologies. In the plays of those dramatists who followed in their wake and treated Jewish subjects, the emphasis was on those topics relevant to societies where Jews lived among gentiles: nationalistic sentiment, integration, assimilation, intermarriage, the conflict between generations, and the psychology of the Jewish bourgeoisie.

As the plays previously mentioned indicate, integration provoked numerous works espousing varying points of view toward the conviction widespread among gentiles and Jews alike that the most expedient way for Jews to get on in society was to disappear into it.[76] In *The Baptism* (1907), Savoir and Nozière explore the motivations and for-

tunes of the four members of the Bloch family who convert to Catholicism, each for a different reason, and the two who do not. There is
no question that Jews in *The Baptism* are treated satirically. So are the
Catholics who seek to exploit them. Savoir and Nozière, who professed the influence of Ibsen, invite audiences to see Jews as people
among other people and to observe that "the Jewish middle class is
afflicted by a certain number of faults and absurdities more or less the
same as all middle class people."[77]

Arthur Wing Pinero treats assimilation from the point of view of
the Jew as social climber and parvenu. His characters, sketched out in
Iris (1902) and *Letty* (1904), are important primarily because they rein-
force the new stage image of a *young* Jewish man and, in the process,
pave the way for Galsworthy's *Loyalties*.

The related question of intermarriage animates a large number of
plays, thereby giving voice to an even larger number of attitudes.
This exchange about the genealogy of H. A. Jones's practically perfect
young minister, Judah Llewellyn, speaks eloquently for one point of
view:

Jopp: Welsh, isn't he?

Papworthy: A Welsh father and a Jewish mother.

Jopp: Celt and Jew! Two good races! Just the man to give England
             a new religion, or to make her believe in an old one.[78]

René Fauchois's *Exodus* (1904) makes a "vehement defense" of Judaism as well as an earnest appeal for casting off old prejudices. Its
idealism can be gauged in the dénouement where a young couple who
have decided to intermarry are asked by her Jewish father whether a
child they might have will be Christian or Jewish. "Neither," responds
the daughter, to which her fiancé adds, "A man"—a retort echoed
almost verbatim in 1968 by the assimilated Alexey in Elie Wiesel's
Zalmen, or The Madness of God.

The varying reactions to plays about assimilation permit some idea
of how faithfully the stage was reflecting public opinion. It is useful to
contrast the receptions of Heijermans' *The Ghetto*, presented in London in 1899 and in Paris in 1901. This is an early problem play in
which a Jewish boy defies his orthodox father and marries their gentile maid. M. J. Landa sniffed that the play, which ran in London only
a fortnight, "is not a play to appeal to English audiences, or to English Jews; its themes are religious revolt and intolerance."[79] Max Beerbohm, who hated the play, loved what it had to say: "Here, surely,
we have the makings of a most fascinating conflict—the conflict of
youth and passion with the patriarchal idea; the old theme of father

against son, intensified and made more poignant by the fact that it is a Jewish son against a Jewish father."[80] By contrast, Émile Faguet wrote that in Paris, *The Ghetto*

> . . . not only interested, but captivated and gripped the public. . . . It is the victory of youth and love over the old racial and religious hatreds, something like a *Romeo and Juliet* that ends well.
>
> It is the escape from the ghetto, no longer physical, but moral, and I don't know if that responded to latent aspirations in the auditorium, but the success was enthusiastic, the applause frequent and unanimous. . . .[81]

A comparable difference in opinion greeted Israel Zangwill's dramatized conviction that America would provide the climate of tolerance in which intermarriage would produce "peace to all ye unborn millions." That is the curtain line of Zangwill's *The Melting Pot* which had a long run in the United States after its Washington première in 1908. In London, where it appeared first in Yiddish (1912), then in English (1914), Zangwill's easy acceptance of mixed marriage provoked a torrent of protest and denunciation.

In the innovative productions of the first independent theatres at the close of the last century and the beginning of this, there appears the promise or the embryo of characters destined to play major roles in the twentieth century. Pierre Wolff's *Jacques Bouchard* and Louis Mullem's *A New School* shared the bill at Antoine's Théatre Libre in Paris on May 2, 1890. While there are no Jewish personae in these plays by Jews, they are shot through with a self-conscious mordant irony and cerebral humor as unmistakable as those in the works of Proust, Kafka or Bellow; they announce the figure of the Jew as comic and as artist. *Ahasverus*, another Heijermans play also produced by Antoine, features a young man who by accepting baptism escapes the pogrom that annihilates his family, but who must thereafter live with his father's curse and the survivor's guilt. In 1906, the Court Theatre in London staged Shaw's *The Doctor's Dilemma* whose Leo Schutzmacher, freely accepted by his colleagues, distinguishes himself from them chiefly by his inability as a Jew to imitate the Englishman's unreliability in financial dealings.[82]

Alongside the special types—George du Maurier's Svengali (*Trilby* came to the theatre in 1894), who even as an updating of the Jewish sorcerer must be considered *sui generis*, and Shaw's Mendoza (*Man and Superman*, 1903), who declares himself "an exception to all the rules"—the Jew on the popular stage remains, reliably, the moneyman. Shylock has become a parvenu. Sidney Grundy's eponymous *Old Jew* (1894) controls his world by the simple expedient of buying as much of it as he can lay his hands on. Paul Claudel, writing from and ostensibly about America, invents the enterprising Thomas Pollack Nageoire (*The Exchange*, 1894). Audiences clucked their tongues at the arrogance of arriviste financier Isidore Lechat (*Les Affaires sont les affaires*, 1903, presented at the Haymarket as *Business Is Business*, 1905, and then in countless spin-offs in the United States), whose ethnic traits are so hackneyed that Mirbeau does not bother to make a single explicit reference to Lechat's Jewishness.

As the Preface to this volume points out, playwriting relies heavily on the inferences packed into a character's ethnic heritage. The focus of this study does not permit more than the simple acknowledgment of the fact that the Jew is but one of the theatre's stock characters. One of the reasons that the personification of the Jew stands out is that it has travelled indefatigably over so many centuries. By the time the Jew reaches the modern stage, his image is surrounded by a great accumulation of baggage. Even when he does not open it, the simple fact of it, communicated by his identity, bespeaks his history of endurance, of wandering, in short, of uniqueness.

IV

The theatre of the twentieth century has received warmly the rich legacy of the stage Jew, finding imaginative ways to use his characteristic differences and alienation as universal metaphors. In the process, the Jew has been transformed from object to subject. From the Jew, a persona defined even as late as in Dickens' England by the conventions attached to his clanhood, he is with ever more frequency and variety cast as the Jew who . . . , a definer of convention, or whatever. As we have noted, Shylock was the first stage Jew to experience and articulate the worries troubling the society in which he lived. By the turn of the present century, the Jew as a humanized, sympathetic protagonist, still a rarity in Europe, had made a modest but promising debut on the American stage.

An example is provided by George H. Jessop's *Sam'l of Posen*, a silly melodrama about a group of rascals. Sam'l, one of the mob, is comic because he is overdrawn and irrepressible. He is also kind, scrupulously loyal and honest, traits that rarely typified the stage Jew. Jessop's play was a tremendous hit when it opened in New York in 1881. Apparently its appeal was not limited to audiences at the Fourteenth Street Theatre, for it was revived over and over again and triumphed from New York to San Francisco. Sam'l provided a starring role for one M. B. Curtis, who "took the audience by storm in his Jew garb . . . and moved the risibilities of the audience at will."[83]

In London, *Sam'l of Posen* opened—and closed—on July 4, 1895. Landa explains, "Samuel Plastrick, as played by Mr. M. B. Curtis, that puzzling afternoon in 1895, was beyond the grasp of London's playgoing *cognoscenti* and *intelligentsia*. . . . Not that Sam'l was absolutely novel. But it was still a law in the theatre that people were to laugh *at* the Jew behind the footlights, not *with* him."[84]

One of the surest ways to teach audiences to laugh *with* the Jew was to make certain they understood he was laughing at himself. That was something he was very likely to be doing in variety shows and music hall sketches. The impressive number of Jewish comedians and comediennes, first in vaudeville, later in radio, who "moved the risibilities of the audience at will" handily accomplished the necessary audience conditioning. The resounding success of the Jewish entertainer is an early indicator of the magnetism of the modern theatre for Jews, who make their mark in every aspect of show business in the twentieth century.

Audiences changed too. After the enormous waves of migration westward from Poland, Austria-Hungary and Russia, Jews were more prevalent than ever in Western societies. Like the other arts, the stage of the early twentieth century reflected the tastes and concerns of the newcomers, perhaps functioning more effectively as a mirror of society than it ever had. Notwithstanding, we need to bear in mind Murray Roston's astute observation that "the depiction of the Jew tells us more about the latent emotional patterns of his creator than about the historical circumstances of the contemporary Jew."[85]

Roston's comment is one of the elements that figures in the way we assess Jewish characters as they are increasingly created by Jewish dramatists. One cannot dismiss the significance of the fact that Jews are finally making plays about Jews, even though for Jewish authors, the stage—with the notable exception of the Yiddish theatre—has not served the same function as the novel where Jews have been, from the start, compulsive chroniclers of their own hypersensitivities and nightmares. However, to the attitudes toward Judaism which color the creative imagination, one must add the "latent emotional patterns" of Jews in the audience who are apt to take personally the works of Jewish playwrights and to see themselves judged on stage. Hence even popular comic characters as innocuous as Abe Potash and Mawruss Perlmutter and the Jews in *Abie's Irish Rose* have been variously dismissed as specimens of the offensive "stage Jews, with hooked nose, flapping hands, singsong English and Yiddish expletives,"[86] and praised for being "traditionally Judaistic in mood because of their preoccupation with achieving decency in the face of life's brutalities."[87]

While the evolution of Jewish images on the modern stage is largely the work of Jewish playwrights, there are at least two assumptions which must be resisted. The first is that Jewish dramatists have a built-in advantage in characterizing Jewish personae. However likely that preconception may appear, it proves unreliable. Jewish authors have demonstrated that they are entirely capable of spawning shallow types with no ethnic substance. By contrast, one of the most sensitive and fully developed portraits of a Jew in contemporary drama is that of Sidney Brustein, the creation of black playwright Lorraine Hansberry.

A second erroneous supposition is that Jewish playwrights will present Jewish characters in a positive light. Henry Bernstein's *Israel* (1908) provides an early example of the fallacy of that expectation. Here a rabidly anti-Semitic young aristrocrat insists on challenging a banker named Gutlieb to a duel purely because he wishes to make a statement about the encroachment of Jews on French society. Improbably, Gutlieb turns out to be the young man's father, a revelation Bernstein uses not to broaden the son's tolerance, but to motivate his melodramatic suicide. His inability to cope with his heritage comes as no surprise, as one of the longest scenes in the play has been devoted to his eloquent recital of grievances against Jews, a catalog worthy of Drumont. What is especially intriguing in the published script of *Israel* are the specifications of dialogue the author wished suppressed in performance. The cuts are lines that either reflect poorly on the play's anti-Semitic priest or flesh out the figure of Gutlieb. Whatever Bernstein was attempting in *Israel*—one suspects it was to appeal to the box office at a time when opinions about the Affair were still running high—kept him from developing strong Jewish characters. Neither Gutlieb nor his son demonstrate sufficient psychological truth to be convincing in their patently fascinating situation. Bernstein's play invites reproach at least as much for that lack of substance, which betrays the author's disinterest in his own characters, as for its ostentatious display of anti-Semitism.

Clearly, Bernstein's *Israel* is not in the vanguard of twentieth century approaches to characterizing the Jew. Rather, both Jewish and gentile dramatists tap with frequent success the possibilities for fresh and interesting Jewish personae. In our pluralistic century, the potential for such creation becomes virtually inexhaustible. These are the riches which are to be explored in the pages that follow. While observations about authors' backgrounds are offered when they seem relevant, this book has no all-embracing theories to defend or debunk about the ethnicity of playwrights and its influence on their characters.

Rather, the focus is on the diversity of Jewish roles and images, a diversity which already distinguishes the theatre by the third decade of the century. Juxtaposing works from that era which depict Jews forcefully helps make the point that the authenticity of the stage Jew and his pertinence to the role in which he is cast have little to do with whether or not his creator is Jewish. Three exemplary plays, written within an eleven-year span in disparate parts of the world, are *Loyalties*, *Chronicles of Hell* and *Awake and Sing!*

John Galsworthy's *Loyalties* (1922) is the landmark play *The Return from Jerusalem* was not, a fair-minded study of problems in Jewish integration into gentile society. It portrays Ferdinand de Levis, "young, rich and new," in his quest for acceptance into the *haut monde*. By the end of the first scene, we know how achingly new de Levis is. The son of a carpet dealer, he already belongs to three exclusive clubs and is knocking on the door of the most select, the Jockey Club. At the country estate where he has been invited for a weekend, he exhibits a naive candor and pride that, along with his garish dressing gown, offend even the butler. De Levis' determination to make his way as a Jew among the elite preoccupies him entirely. The upper-class Britishers, for their part, seem ready to receive him. His host expresses the prevailing sentiment, "I like Jews. That's not against him—rather the contrary these days."[88]

Yet the Jew's upward mobility forces the gentry to reckon with a threat he unintentionally but inevitably poses to the establishment's values and loyalties. Galsworthy's balanced scenario includes spontaneous outbursts of the conventional, barely dormant anti-Semitism which feeds de Levis' paranoia, as well as the genuine bewilderment of the ruling class which accepts the validity of the young man's efforts, even as it resents his "getting on so." Nonetheless, his aggressive social climbing widens many a narrow-minded view. Even a mindlessly prejudiced society girl, Margaret Orme, comes to see a reality she never before imagined, in this conversation with a lawyer:

> Margaret. There are more of the chosen in Court every day. Mr. Graviter, have you noticed the two on the jury?
>
> Graviter. No: I can't say——
>
> Margaret. Oh! but quite distinctly. Don't you think they ought to have been challenged?
>
> Graviter. De Levis might have challenged the other ten, Miss Orme.
>
> Margaret. Dear me, now! I never thought of that.[89]

Galsworthy's keen perceptions and even-handedness enable us to empathize with sharply conflicting points of view. In one of the most painful moments in the play, a ne'er-do-well who has always been ferried through his peccadilloes on the unquestioning faith of his peers finally must confront his immorality which has victimized de Levis, among others. It is a tribute to the incisiveness of the characterizations that we can appreciate how richly deserved is this facing up, and how much more humiliating, having been brought about because of a Jew.

The figure of the Jew in *Loyalties* functions on several levels as an *agent provocateur*. The play accepts as a given de Levis' right to move up in a society that prides itself on fair play. As he looks for reparation of the wrong done him in the process, de Levis, like Shylock before him, "craves the law"; he asks only for justice and, again like Shylock, wonders, "Shall I have it?" In the course of the action, the dean of celebrated attorneys learns that his first duty lies not to friend, client or even to England, but to the law. *Loyalties* also accepts as a given de Levis' loyalty to Judaism, while demonstrating that the Jew's seeking entrée among the privileged throws into question many of their allegiances—class, professional, social, marital and personal. De Levis' bid provokes a re-examination of the very warp and woof of that stratum of society. In the Jew's pursuit of acceptance, he asks for no more than he has earned a right to expect. He never tries to appear to be what he is not. The play shows that however painful the process, those who consider themselves superior may do well to emulate that example. At the same time, *Loyalties* suggests to the upward bound Jew, for surely de Levis is intended as a representative figure, that *noblesse oblige* is for him, no less than for those born into the ruling class, a matter of patience, tolerance and good will.

While *Loyalties* reflects the society for which it was written, Michel de Ghelderode's *Chronicles of Hell* (1929) looks rather like a page snatched from Rabelais or a scene extracted from Breughel or Bosch. This frenzied one-act "tragedy bouffe" which assaults all the senses takes place in a decaying palace in "bygone Flanders." It depicts the chaos and corruption raging in the district of a recently murdered bishop and the struggle for power among the degenerate churchmen responsible for his death. In what appears the least likely spot for a Jew, Ghelderode makes one the center of attention.

He is Simon Laquedeem, a renegade who has risen in the Church to become an auxiliary bishop. The contradictory connotations of his name befit him ideally. In fashioning this priest who stands over and above the other ecclesiastics, Ghelderode twists together strands of numerous Jewish images. Laquedeem is doubtly alienated, an apostate feared and detested by his fellow clerics. He is a colossus of strength and determination, the only one who intrepidly challenges the resurrected bishop Jan in Eremo and literally tries to wrestle his power from him. Nowhere does Laquedeem embody the Old Testament more directly than in his historical consciousness. He alone has witnessed the entire bizarre career of the triumphant impostor, Jan in Eremo, from its mysterious inception. As much as the other priests revile Simon, they beg him to tell Eremo's story.

In a highly unusual, if scatological, innovation, Ghelderode uses the body of his Jewish protagonist as a metaphor. The subtext of *Chronicles of Hell* concerns the accumulation and the passing on of power. This motif is introduced by the rumbling of a thunderstorm and the snarling of a threatening crowd which persist throughout. Jan in Eremo has been choked by a poisoned host which is stuck in his throat; he struggles mightily against swallowing it. Simon Laquedeem suffers from digestive difficulties. The terms he uses to describe his malaise augurs its role, "My stomach! . . . Calvary of a stomach! . . . The thorns, the nails, and the lance in it."[90] Simon is not crucified, of course, but at the end, the function of his intestine serves as the ultimate metaphor for the elimination of the heretical bishop and for the evacuation of the depleted.

By any standards, Simon Laquedeem's is a unique role and an uncommon image. Whatever repugnance *Chronicles of Hell* may inspire, it would be an error to underestimate the indispensability of its Jewish protagonist. And it would be impossible not to respond strongly to the sight of him as the curtain falls, crouching in his cassock, "his rabbinical face expressing demoniac bliss."[91]

The only possible parallel between the decaying palace in bygone Flanders and a certain modest apartment house on Longwood Avenue in the Bronx is that both are inhabited by Jews. Values diametrically opposed to Ghelderode's are incorporated into the plot and personae of Clifford Odets' *Awake and Sing!* (1933),[92] the earliest quintessentially Jewish play outside the Yiddish theatre. It bears the unmistakable stamp of authenticity, exactly what one would wish from a Jewish dramatist writing a slice of Jewish life problem play, now forever associated with the great Jewish actors who brought it to life in 1935: Stella and Luther Adler, John Garfield, Morris Carnovsky and J. Edward Bromberg.

Five decades after its première, *Awake and Sing!*'s excellence still resides in its large cast of Jewish personae, a compelling mix of stereotypes (Hennie, the *belle Juive*; Uncle Morty, the pleasure-loving moneyman) and its introduction of characters just acquiring literary identity. At the head of the list is Bessie Berger, indefatigable dispenser of seltzer and sensible advice, and prototype of that gorgon of subsequent American-Jewish fiction, the *Yiddishe momma*.

By endowing his characters with historical depth, Odets suggests that the matriarch's extraordinary capabilities may have compensated for the ineptitude of the bewildered immigrant or first-generation male, less prepared than the shtetl-bred woman to cope with "life in America." As Bessie reasonably puts it, "If I didn't worry about the family, who would?" In the Old World, men like Jacob and even Myron Berger and Sam Feinschreiber, spiritually attuned to change-less values may have filled the role of the patriarch. In America, their idealism withers into a source of impotence and frustration. Myron tries to become the American equivalent of the Talmudic scholar: he goes to law school. Although he abandons his studies for clerking in a haberdashery, he remains the incurable dreamer for whom the Messiah will surely come in the form of a hair restorative or a winning sweepstake ticket. The opportunism professed by Moe Axelrod, crippled physically and emotionally by wartime combat, is the transparent façade of his quest for genuine human warmth. And the play's young rebel, Ralph, takes his place in the vanguard of the disgruntled, ambitious intellectuals in the exodus from Longwood Avenue to Yama Yama, the rigors of which will be detailed more frequently in Jewish-American novels, and in films based on them, than on stage.

This ill-assorted trio of plays is deliberately put together to argue the preferability of taking Jewish characters on their own terms, a consideration to which the ethnicity of the playwright is, as we see here, of variable relevance. "Why is this character Jewish?" is a more feasible and profitable question than "What does this author's background indicate about his portrayal of Jewish characters?" The first query leads to Galsworthy's choice of the Jew to represent one of the forces responsible for provoking a re-examination of English conscience and values, an assessment he obviously supported. The same question leads to Ghelderode's reworking of the monstrous Jew to foil the equally corrupt but less dynamic personae in *Chronicles of Hell*. There is less chance that we would pose the question of *Awake and Sing!* since Odets, writing a Jewish story, uses Jewish characters literally, not figuratively, just as Sean O'Casey, writing a remarkably similar play a decade earlier, used Irish personae in *Juno and the Paycock*. Since in all three cases the Jewish images are aesthetically solid and integral to the success of the play, there seems little reason to probe the writers' personal biases for a response to the second question. By and large, considering together works as diverse as these three is less rewarding than grouping plays thematically so as to contrast the dramatic treatments of the Jew in a given role. The latter organizing principle operates in the chapters to follow.

Strikingly, in both the proliferation of contemporary images and the updating of stock figures in the drama of our century, the original nonconformity of viewpoint, values and allegiance that particularized the Jew on the medieval stage continues to distinguish him. Only the manifestations and the dramatic uses of the differences which mark him off have changed prodigiously. The most convincing documentation lies in the persistence—indeed, in the multiplication—of Jewish roles in modern drama, roles which depend upon those differences. That basis for literary identity was conceded by Abraham Dreyfus, who understood, even if he could not accept, the logic of the traditional posture that "if the theatre represented Jews who were indistinguishable from Christians, these Jews would not appear to be Jewish. . . . Indeed, why would they be Jews?"[93]

The revolution and evolution of Jewish roles and images, already in flux in the early decades of this century, were galvanized by history. Particularly since the Holocaust and the establishment of the state of Israel, the word "Jew" has earned unfamiliar and indelible connotations. Since the second World War, dramatists in the West have been especially ingenious in reshaping the tradition of the stage Jew. Their innovations can be considered in two large categories: updatings of time-consecrated images, and newly minted ones. In the chapters to follow, we explore the range of these modified and fresh images. Both groups demonstrate how in the last four decades, the Jew on stage has become not only a recognizable human being, but with ever greater frequency, a representative of contemporary mankind.

In 1949, Leslie Fiedler provoked a lively debate with an essay in *Commentary* about the persistent stranglehold of the legendary Jew villain on Western literature. He proposed loosening his grasp through the dissemination of more pertinent "myths," reflecting more contemporary realities:

> In all the countries of the West, and pre-eminently in America, we [Jews] have been passing in the last three or four generations from the periphery to the center of culture; more and more, the myths of the Jew will be the handiwork of Jews or of Gentiles whose sensibilities have been profoundly conditioned by ours.
> Indeed, in this apocalyptic period of atomization and uprooting, of a catholic terror and a universal alienation, the image of the Jew tends to become the image of everyone; and we are perhaps approaching the day when the Jew will come to seem the central symbol, the essential myth of the whole Western world.[94]

This is a book about how splendidly Fiedler's prophecy has been fulfilled.

PART ONE

Updating Traditions

2

Modern Heroes of Biblical Drama

Although the Scriptures continue to stimulate modern religious drama (e.g., Yeats's *Calvary*, Ghelderode's *Miss Jairus*, MacLeish's *J. B.*; the list is a long one), they also appeal to the twentieth century's penchant for irreverence. The consequence has been a desanctification of the Bible and a demythologizing of its heroes and heroines. In an age where the Exodus has been filmed in Panavision, technicolor and stereophonic sound, and Jesus Christ, catapulted to superstardom on stage, screen and records, the Bible is plainly contributing something besides divine inspiration to the performing arts.

The Old Testament was the first to be profaned for several reasons. In the Christian world it was apparently regarded as less inviolable than the New Testament. Since there are no saints in the Jewish Bible, the adaptation of a Hebrew patriarch into an up-to-date type perhaps seemed iconoclasm without blasphemy. Moreover, such streamlining develops the precedent established by sixteenth-century Protestant dramatists like Théodore de Bèze who used Old Testament figures to mirror the personality or plight of contemporary man. By contrast, as late as 1952 Beckett was able to mine shock value in the tramp Estragon's rejoinders in *Waiting for Godot:*

Vladimir. But you can't go barefoot.

Estragon. Christ did.

Vladimir. Christ! What has Christ got to do with it? You're not going to compare yourself to Christ!

Estragon. All my life I've compared myself to him.[1]

Finally, history has gone to work to verify biblical facts, psychology, to analyze superstitions, and science, to explain miracles. Today's rationalism defies the traditional respect accorded the Old Testament,

39

a deference held in certain quarters to be based on myths which obscure the Scriptures' fundamental truth. The point is made rather tartly by Laurence Housman in the preface to his *Palestine Plays* (1942):

> Sound moral feeling quite as much as intellectual scepticism, has caused modern thinkers to regard as no longer worthy of respect a system of miraculous intervention which turns God into a showman performing tricks for the delectation of a small favoured tribe, providing it with short cuts to victory over its enemies, and special visitations of plague, pestilence or famine whenever its rulers behave badly. Such a process of alternate coddling and bullying is no true education for man or nation. . . .[2]

On the twentieth-century stage God becomes not necessarily less holy or even less powerful, only infinitely more approachable. Sholom Aleichem's Tevye the Dairyman unburdens himself by chatting man to man with the Lord, occasionally questioning His decisions. André Obey's Noah likewise carries on a running conversation with heaven over some sort of private intercom system. An on-stage God engages in dialectic with all the characters in Arthur Miller's *The Creation of the World and Other Business*. Marc Connolly's *The Green Pastures* depicts heaven as a nonstop fish fry conducted by a Negro God. And God is a Puerto Rican attendant with a remarkable vocabulary in Bruce Jay Friedman's *Steambath*.

The ironic treatment of scriptural figures typically results in good-natured humor. James Bridie's Tobias, a plump, balding character in *Tobias and the Angel*, bumbles to success in his mission thanks to the tutelage of Raphael, who looks human enough but insists on swimming privately because of "a slight abnormality in the region of my shoulder blades." In A. P. Herbert's *The Book of Jonah (As almost any modern Irishman would have written it)*, Mrs. Joner explains to a suitor how she became a widow:

> It was the sailors of the ship that did be saying they would sail the ship no longer when they found himself was in the Post Office, and him travelling for the Government. And there was a great storm and the ship tossing the way you wouldn't know she was a ship at all, or a cork that a boy throws in the water out of a bottle; and the sailors said it was the English Government—and why would it not be?—and they cried out against himself, and he rose up out of his bed and "Is it sinking the ship I would be?" he said, and he threw himself over the side into the water—and that was the way of it.[3]

Modern playwrights have given Mrs. Joner sisters whose existence in the Scriptures is even better substantiated but whose behavior has recently undergone extraordinary modification. Murray Roston notes the similarity of "Biblical suffragettes" to incipient feminists: "During the first quarter of the century, some dozen plays appeared on the themes of Judith, Jezebel, Esther, Vashti, Salome, and Mariamne, in each of which the female character dominated the drama by her independent spirit and bold determination."[4] The titular heroine of David Pinski's Yiddish play *Abigail* loyally defends her husband Nabal, all the while batting her lashes madly and heaving passionate sighs at David. An even less demure Judith does a belly dance in T. S. Moore's 1916 play. Giraudoux's *Judith* traces the transformation of its protagonist from proud virgin to heroine who "becomes at the same time saint and prostitute."[5] The biblical heroine, like the patriarch and the prophet, has come a long way.

The heroes of the seven plays to be discussed in this chapter all have their origins in the Old Testament. All are Jews, even Noah for the duration of Clifford Odets' *The Flowering Peach*. That is almost all they have in common. A spectrum of diverse Jewish images is ambitiously delineated in Marcel Pagnol's *Judas*. Contrasting characterizations are a prominent feature in most of these works; one is struck both by the differences among the images within each play and by the variations between them and their scriptural antecedents. Most of the plays present an essentially average human being called on to perform the extraordinary deeds originally associated with him. Even though the modern biblical heroes are diminished in stature, the reduction is not evenhanded. A few retain something of their prototypical grandeur, like Fry's Moses and Kalisky's David; others command a modicum of respect for a dignity rapidly fading, like Abel's David and Kalisky's Saul. Some are rough men, like Odets' Noah and his three sons, and others, like Mankowitz' Jonah and Chayefsky's Gideon, are frankly designed to make us laugh.

Because there are no major roles for women in these plays, there are fewer important female images. Nonetheless, a variety of female personae are depicted. Odets picks Noah's grumbling wife out of medieval legend and makes of her a *Yiddishe momma*. Fry refashions the prophetess Miriam into an embittered pessimist. Both David plays draw on the charms of the *belle Juive*. In *Dave at the Sea* Kalisky invents a neurotic wife for Saul and has Jonathan observe of his svelte mother and sister that they "give the lie to the legend of the heavy but beautiful Jewess."

Even the language that these stage Jews speak runs the gamut of possibilities. The Fry play is in blank verse; the characters in *The Flowering Peach* tend to use hackneyed Yiddish speech patterns; Abel's people often sound like philosophers; Chayefsky's, like television personalities. The fact that it is all but impossible to generalize about the

Jewish images in this group of plays itself makes a statement about the difference between them and the biblical Jews once portrayed on the Western stage.

Noah in a Prayer Shawl

For reasons that are not altogether apparent, the Noah of Clifford Odets' *The Flowering Peach* (1954) is a Jew. Perhaps Odets associated the relationship between the Jewish Bible and the New Testament with the story that mankind descended from Noah and his sons after the Flood. The anachronism does lend the characterization some convenient references. Having learned of God's plans for him in a dream, Noah sends for his sons, using the approach of the Sabbath as his excuse. Where Noah's Jewishness is theatrical, it is cliché-bound. For example, when his Sabbath prayers for renewed strength are answered by a miraculous rejuvenation, his hair turns from white to red. In a distortion of both Scripture and stereotype (the Jew has a reputation for sobriety), Noah is a heavy drinker.[6]

Yet behind the melodramatic façade, there is evidence of a human being who can be understood as Noah, the father of mankind. He reveres God and he has "found grace in the eyes of the Lord." Unlike the Noah of Genesis but in the manner of many other Old Testament figures, Odets' protagonist questions God's choice of him. He feels unworthy, and for good reason: he knows nothing about boats, he cannot manage his sons, he is afraid people will laugh at him, and, most important, age and drinking have sapped his energies. Despite his reservations Noah's piety and stubbornness give him the strength to follow God's specifications for the ark. Once aboard, however, his authority fluctuates. Disheartened by his children's refusal to demonstrate the worthiness befitting chosen survivors, he disappears on a nine-week binge. Even sober, Noah is essentially a lonely soul who has difficulty sustaining rapport with any of his family, including his wife of sixty years.

During his experiences on the ark, which in this version last for a year, Noah slowly learns to respect the validity of other people's responses to life. What is more, he understands that God accepts the wordliness of man, a perception that faithfully reflects the concessions to human nature God makes in Genesis. The rainbow at the end of the play serves to reconfirm Noah's faith in God and in himself as a man God spared. Giving thanks for his newly found humility and comprehension, Noah declares, "Now it's in man's hands to make or destroy the world."[7] The Noah with whom God makes a covenant speaks in this play, and he does in Genesis, for all mankind. Yet Odets, by making him a Jew, melds Noah into the image of Abraham, whose covenant with God involved only Israel. What results is uncertainty as to what the image of the Jew is intended to contribute to *The Flowering Peach*, a question that is complicated, as we shall see, by the figure of Shem.

Noah's wife, unnamed in Genesis, is here called Esther. She is an amalgam of the medieval comic images of Mrs. Noah, the ill-tempered nag, and a Sholom Aleichem momma, sensible, long-suffering and gruffly loving. Except when she is in the middle of a squabble herself, Esther arbitrates. *The Flowering Peach* is more concerned with personality differences than with the story of the Flood. Once the family is shut up in the ark, the rigors of living together render its members all but mindless of the destruction outside. Fierce arguments grow out of their incompatible viewpoints.

The eldest son, Shem, is an indefatigable entrepreneur. He had infuriated Noah by selling his land and orchards before embarking and trying to avoid paying his taxes besides. His wife Leah wears a large bunch of keys at her waist. The dangerous tilt that the ark develops is traced to the manure Shem and Leah are hoarding against the day they can sell briquettes for fuel.

Ham, the second son, is a dedicated sensualist. He shares his father's taste for liquor. With practiced flair, he seduces Goldie, the fiancée of his younger brother Japheth. Ham has only taunts for his own wife, who has been in love with Japheth for five years but has nonetheless remained faithful to Ham.

To get his youngest son on the ark, Noah has had to knock him unconscious. Japheth would prefer to die as a protest against what he sees as the brutality of a vengeful God he had been taught to love. Later he rebels against the authority of his father whom he also loves. Japheth wants to equip the ark with a rudder. The rudder becomes a bone of contention between the pious Noah, who objects that it would signify lack of faith in God who never specified they were to steer, and the determined Japheth for whom the rudder represents self-reliance. Japheth's insistence on human resourcefulness earns the respect of his customarily antagonistic brother Shem who tells their father, "I'm very ashamed to say it . . . but your youngest son is a better man of God than you" (p. 74). Noah's ultimate acceptance of Japheth's steering the ark is one of the lessons in tolerance the patriarch masters; it foreshadows his assertion at the play's end that he has learned "to walk in humility. . . . And listen, even to *myself* . . . and to speak softly, with the voices of consolation" (p. 85).

In dramatizing the shifts in alliances within the family Odets makes implications that transcend the turbulent relationships of eight willful people compelled to live together in close quarters for a year. Noah's children will, after all, repopulate the earth. Their experiences in co-existing on the ark announce the interaction of their descendants who, in Noah's final words, will "make or destroy the world." In view of that prediction and of what the biblical table of nations purports to explain about the origin of the races, it is interesting to examine the traits with which Odets endows the progenitors.

Ham, the sensualist, is to procreate the African peoples. Japheth, the sympathetic, high-minded son, who respects but still dares to challenge established authority, is the forefather of the Indo-Europeans. Shem, the businessman, becomes the ancestor of the Semites.

Shem is composed largely of stage-Jew bromides which are apparent to a lesser degree in Noah. Where father and son share a quality, the device works well. For instance Noah anticipates Shem's reluctance to leave off harvesting his olive crop and commands his youngest son, "You'll tell Shem a big building proposition came up! The Customer is very important, can't wait, understand? Needs an estimate right away, hear me?" (p. 8). But when Shem's single-mindedness is countered by a Noah whose vision is larger, the dissonance is confusing, as here:

> Shem (ruminating)—Did you ever realize, Poppa, when we land—granting all goes well—that the whole world will be ours?
>
> Noah (with a dour chuckle)—Ours? Awright whatever you'll grow with your own hands, it's yours. People you can't hire no more to work for you.
>
> Shem—Yeah, that's what worries me . . .
>
> Noah—The whole world stinks of ruined bodies an' rotten grass. And today, Shem, on this sacred wood, your head's fulla business . . . ? (p. 56)

No doubt we are to understand that fathers are sometimes wiser or more moral than their sons. More problematic are the implications in Shem's being the forebear of the Jewish people. The play seems to suggest that Shem's descendants are to be typified by his monomaniacal commercialism. That formula is as absurdly simplistic as those which would have to apply to the lineage of the equally single-dimensional Japheth and Ham. To complicate matters, there is the added problem of Noah. The play runs into difficulty with its scriptural givens precisely by making him Jewish. That liberty raises unanswerable questions: Why is Shem more obsessed with business than his

Jewish father? Why does Shem inherit and transmit a tradition which bypasses Ham and Japheth?

The contrasting portrayals of the Jew in the figures of Noah and Shem update two medieval conceptions: the patriarch of the Old Testament and the bizarre contemporary type. While contributing color and entertainment value to a Broadway show, the two images are not fused into any unified version of the Jew that might illuminate this retelling of the Noah story. Because it is so difficult to forget the wonderfully authentic Jews Odets created in *Awake and Sing!* The *Flowering Peach* leaves us asking the wrong question. Instead of "Why did God pick this family?" we wonder, in terms of working with Jewish characters, why did Odets.

Moses: "I Heard My Blood Weeping"

In *The Firstborn* (1946), Christopher Fry dramatizes the events preceding the Exodus. To Moses' stature as patriarch the playwright adds the nobility of the tragic hero and the sensitivity of the introspective man. The play develops the conflicting loyalties implicit in Exodus 11:3: "Moreover the man Moses was very great in the land of Egypt, in the sight of Pharaoh's servants, and in the sight of the people."

Since his disappearance after killing the Egyptian taskmaster ten years before, Moses has become a legend. "Egypt loves and hates you inextricably," he is told.[8] Now the Pharaoh Seti urgently needs Moses' proven military and diplomatic skills against Libyan invaders. Considering Moses' upbringing, it is not unreasonable for Seti to count on his allegiance. The Jew's ties to Egypt are stronger than he himself realizes in his present distraction with a growing sense of mission to Israel. Though his messianism is not pressed on him by a voice from the burning bush, the play suggests it is divinely inspired. Moses' zeal to liberate his people has evolved slowly from the crisis of identity provoked a decade earlier when he killed the Egyptian whose Hebrew victim somehow reminded Moses of his long-lost mother. Indeed, the two major themes of Fry's play are affirmation of identity and the resolution of conflicting allegiances.

What Moses is and what he makes himself are closely bound up with the Pharaoh's eighteen-year-old son Rameses. The (or the most important) firstborn of the title, his life comes to stand for the price Moses must pay for his people to "become themselves,/ By reason of their own god who speaks within them" (p. 49). The significance of that price is manifest on two levels. Personally, Rameses is a beautiful figure. He is drawn instinctively to the returned Moses whom he senses he ought to recognize, but can't. Apprised of his long-lost "uncle's" identity, he strives to close ranks with him, opposing his father's harsh policies. Rameses is the promise of youth, painfully aware of adult responsibilities which beckon. On a figurative level Rameses represents the boyhood Moses had as a prince of Egypt. The Pharaoh's sister lavished love on the baby she had rescued. Like Rameses, Moses had spent his spare time after lessons, military exercises and social obligations "fowling down at the marshes." Small wonder Rameses' appeal to Moses to serve his country against the Libyans awakens past loyalties, at the same time forcing the Jew to confront the irreconcilability of the two causes. How could he "clank to Egypt's victory in Israel's bones?"

The indulged boyhood which Rameses came by honestly, but to which Moses now feels he himself had no right, contrasts vividly with that of Moses' true nephew Shendi. Miriam's son leads the life Moses might have led had he grown up as a Jew in Egypt. Embittered by forced labor, maddened by oppression, Shendi aspires to a single goal: to wield the whip. When, through the intervention of Rameses, Shendi rises suddenly from slave to officer, he has no problems of identity or questions about justice. Easily accepting his new status, he goes off to earn the approbation of the Egyptian overseers by driving the Jews even harder than they.

If Shendi is callous and opportunistic, he perhaps reflects the values and attitudes of his mother. Hardly the biblical prophetess who sings of Israel's deliverance, the Miriam of Fry's play pledges loyalty only to subsistence. She keeps her tent shut against the outside world. Miriam supports her son's apostasy feeling that Shendi has the right to profit from the opportunity to escape a fate he never deserved. She is daunted by guilt, her regret for Shendi's miserable life being only a part of a larger, more oppressive sense of responsibility. Moses' sister has lost faith in herself, her people and God. Scornfully recalling the early years when she visited the child Moses at the palace, she scoffs, "Israel! Israel's the legend I told you in the nursery./ We've no more spirit to support a God" (p. 30). Reduced to collaborating with her own despair, Miriam regards her Jewish identity merely as source and repository for the guilt of the oppressed.

Miriam's resignation and Shendi's treachery seem meant by the playwright to characterize the unprepossessing people whose freedom Moses is determined to obtain. Like Moses, they are not susceptible to being galvanized until they understand what being a chosen people entails. That recognition breaks softly over Miriam when the

water turns to blood in all but the Jewish wells. Shendi's reconciliation with Judaism comes in an epiphany. He feels the angel of death
pass him by:

> The wings were right over me and I was wrenched by a hand
> That came spinning out of them. I'll not be sent into a grave.
> I'll be what I was. I am Shendi, a Jew. (p. 84)

Identity and ideology are not problematic for everyone in *The Firstborn*. Like his opposite number, the Pharaoh, Aaron knows exactly
who he is and what he must do. Aaron also recognizes that the
moment is ripe for a leader of Moses' talent. In a third parallel with
the resolute Egyptian, Aaron's dedication to his cause leads him to
pragmatic insensitivity to ideals. He values his brother as a soldier.
He somewhat enviously respects Moses' ability to forge unity among
the people in preparation for the Exodus, leading "man upon man
into consciousness." The straightforward Aaron's reluctant admission
that his brother "has me by the scruff of the heart and I ask/ No
questions" is eloquent testimony to Moses' inspired persuasiveness.

The essential difference between the two Jewish leaders is underscored at the moment of Moses' anagnorisis. Transported by his own
zeal, he has come to think of himself as "only a name and an obedience" to the God of the Hebrews. It is just when Moses is most
responsive to his Judaism that he becomes the most murderous. In
announcing the imminence of the final plague, Moses realizes in a
rush of horror his own role in the inevitable death of Rameses. He
rejects the image of himself as assassin and casts about for some way
to save this firstborn whose dearness quite overwhelms him. But the
obdurate Aaron reminds him that this is the way wars are fought,
that Moses well knows how to "grieve and advance, uninterrupted."

It is as an anguished human being rather than a disciplined soldier
or a driven prophet that Moses bursts into the palace to do battle with
the ineluctable. In forging a new existence for his people, he fears he
has lost himself. "I followed a light into blindness," he laments moments before Rameses falls dead. Aaron's announcement that the Jews
stand assembled for his command to leave Egypt restores Moses'
perspective, though he accepts with difficulty the unavoidability of
sacrifice.

What sustains Moses finally is the hope of finding personal wisdom
during his wanderings. His sense of unfinished mission as he leaves
Egypt brings Fry's Moses quite close to his scriptural antecedent. At
the same time the shock of self-actualization and the painful resolution of conflicting allegiances endow him with tragic nobility. Having
to meet the demands of justice and to pay the price of freedom cause

this Moses to surpass an exclusively Jewish identity. He is broadened into a representative of men who feel chosen to lead and exemplary of those for whom conscience is a sobering part of valor.

The Affirmation of Gideon

Disregarding for a moment the copious liberties Paddy Chayefsky takes with the biblical text, the basic situation in his *Gideon* (1961) is an accurate if stylized rendering of the verses in Judges that repeatedly report that "the children of Israel did that which was evil in the sight of the Lord" by worshipping false deities. Even after divine punishment in the form of subjugation by Canaanite tribes, the Jews resisted permanent reform. Their obstinacy in defying the Law of Moses was matched by the Lord's persistence in saving them from themselves. So in the opening scene of this light-hearted play, an angel of the Lord watches unnoticed as a group of misguided elders botch a sacrifice to Baal whose protection they are asking against the imminent menace of the Midianites. Chayefsky underscores the inanity of the ritual by having the elders plod on with it without really knowing what they are doing, ignoring their women's more practical demands for immediate protection.

The angel greets another bystander, Gideon, an individual of modest intelligence who is astonished to hear the salute from the Scriptures, "the Lord is with you, O mighty man of valor." In doubtless unwitting conformity with the biblical custom that the appointed of God question his credentials for being designated, Gideon challenges the angel. The black-robed figure, visible only to Gideon, claims the obedience due "the Lord your God who brought you out of the house of Egypt." But unlike his scriptural antecedent, this Gideon lacks any personal appreciation of what he has heard of God's favors. Yes, he remembers the old men talking of Yahweh whose importance has diminished before other gods the Hebrews have revered. Gideon's own demands of a deity are moderate. He asks only "the natural increase in things, no special favors." Even so, he has been disappointed. A Hebrew's life, he says, has always been hard. As a result, he's stopped believing in gods.

The tension between Gideon's recalcitrance and the Lord's determination to make a leader of him is dramatized as Gideon is empowered to marshal his astonished but relieved fellow Abiezerites and to summon reinforcements from their neighbors. However, the victorious Gideon makes no pretense of understanding the military tactics he has been told to employ. A ridiculous figure chafing under his dependence on the angel's unrevealed strategies, as well as under the cuirass and corselet he donned without the proper undergarments, he is ill-prepared for the implacable angel's warning that he must not play the prince.

The angel's fierce resolution to restore all the Hebrews' lost faith in God's miracles is nicely served by the incident the playwright borrows almost unaltered from Judges where Gideon is instructed to reduce his forces to three hundred men and rout the enemy hordes by frightening them with loud noises and eerie lights. However, the post-victory interlude between the angel and the triumphant Gideon has no scriptural precedent. Here the new leader finally proclaims his love for the God whose favors can provide him with fortune and esteem which, in spite of the modest aspirations he earlier professed, he now admits he always wanted. Still, he is abashed that the angel can offer no special reason for him to have become God's favorite and wishes with all his heart that the source of his success were personal merit. But the angel reproves him:

> Do not presume to matter, Gideon, for in the house of God you matter not. . . . You are a meaningless thing and live only in my eye. I shall make you great, Gideon, because I love you; but it is merely my caprice. If you displease me, I shall destroy you in a whim of temper. To love me, Gideon, you must abandon all your vanities. They are presumptuous and will come between us.[9]

Gideon is only temporarily chastened by the angel's prophetic words. In the victory celebration that follows, he resists the temptation to leave uncorrected the inflated stories of his valor in battle. He reminds his disappointed well-wishers and crestfallen son that the glory of their triumph is rightly the Lord's. But shortly they are off to yet another fray, and the angel hears disapprovingly the war cry, "For Gideon and the Lord" which so recently had been, "For the Lord and Gideon."

That rallying cry undergoes one further transformation. Gideon begins to question whether his allegiance belongs properly to man or to the Lord. His dilemma is deepened when he finds himself in situations where he must try to evaluate human life as God, not man, sees it. He simply cannot obey God's order to kill the seventy-seven elders of Succoth who had denied his followers bread, however richly they may deserve retribution. He argues with the tyrannical angel to spare that "piteous lot of senior gentlemen" and cannot believe the celestial reassurance that "death changes nothing."

Moreover, Gideon is frankly seduced by popular ovations. While in the book of Judges he refuses a proffered kingship, Chayefsky's man is more responsive to the honor. Though he again hesitates on the threshold of the monarchy, he fails to dissuade his chiefs who welcome the chance to restore Israel's unity and, one senses, to improve their own fortunes. Gideon's last sincere effort to control personal ambitions by subordinating them to the role the Lord has designated for him falters precisely at the point where he is incapable of slaying the elders of Succoth. He understands then that he is more capable of loving man than of loving God:

> I tried to love you, but it is too much for me. You are too vast a concept for me. To love you, God, one must be a god himself. I did not kill the elders of Succoth, and I shall tell you why. I raised my spear above their heads, but in that moment I felt a shaft of terror that chills me even now. It was as if the nakedness of all things was exposed to me, and I saw myself and all men for what we truly are, suspensions of matter, flailing about for footholds in the void. . . . I cannot love you, God, for it makes me a meaningless thing. (pp. 127–28)

The angel thunders forth the ire of God, threatening awesome punishments in a fury which perhaps befits the Old Testament God of wrath and jealousy better than his earlier displays of long-sufferance. But the divine anger also ennobles the persistence of Gideon, who leads off his proud, rejoicing family.

In a curtain speech more reminiscent of Roman comedy than the twentieth-century American stage, the angel, left alone, recites a volteface in verse, suggesting that Gideon's rebellion may have persuaded God to accept less than total submission:

> God no more believes it odd
> That man cannot believe in God.
> Man believes the best he can,
> Which means, it seems, belief in man.
> Then let him don my gold ephod
> And let him be a proper god.
> Well, let him try it anyway . . . (pp. 137–38)

Along with its slickness Gideon is full of the affirmation so characteristic of Chayefsky's theatre. The play says that the look of pride on a son's face, even when the son may himself become the victim of a vengeful deity, is worth a father's risking his own chances for heavenly exaltation. It asserts that the values of life are in life, perceptible to all men. And it suggests that God is tolerant of—perhaps even amused by—man's resistance to being shaped by divine schemes rather than by his own.

To these purposes, the playwright has made a felicitous choice in the story of Gideon. Since the regal lifestyle of the biblical figure and the gorgeous sanctuary he erected at Ophrah, where the gold ephod was kept, are understood to be significant deviations from Mosaic religion,[10] it is not unlikely that this Gideon is meant to exemplify man who stubbornly prefers earthly gratification to eternal glory. Chayefsky's *Gideon* declares the characteristically, though not exclusively, Jewish belief that life is for the living. Finally, the play asserts that once made aware of his God-given abilities, man will better himself in accordance with his own ideas. Or as Gideon tells God, probably without surprising Him too much, "My Lord, it is elemental in me to aspire to be greater than myself. This is your doing, for you gave me the passion that I might raise myself to you" (p. 128). That, says Chayefsky's play, is a vanity worthy of respect.

David, Then and Now

The reworkability of biblical accounts itself furnishes the subject of two iconoclastic plays about King David. Both René Kalisky's *Dave at the Sea* (*Dave au bord de mer*, 1975) and Lionel Abel's *Absalom* (1956) are devoted to reshaping and reinterpreting personae who challenge the books of Samuel. The French play, which modifies I Samuel, is by far the more daring.

For Kalisky, the revision is a means of liberating playwright, players and theatregoers through the use of a text already part of the collective subconscious. Kalisky wants actors and spectators alike to let their imaginations work on the story of David and Saul, prying it loose from its original historical and behavioristic moorings so that the forces operating within the story are freed to serve the informatory function of myth. The author's dramaturgical goal grows out of his metaphysical stance which holds that there is no chronology man cannot overturn.[11] The biblical subject of *Dave at the Sea* lends itself ideally to the playwright's principle that "for the Jew, present, past and future meet" (p. 219).

The point is made with stunning clarity in the opening *tableau vivant* of *Dave*. From four oversized Chiricoesque forms which support the remains of ruined cities emerge the four members of the emphatically contemporary Kish family, Saul, his wife and two children. The strains of Handel's Saul Oratorio fade into a popular Hebrew song. The scene gives way to the luxuriously furnished terrace of Saul's ultramodern seaside villa in Israel. While the scantily clad Jonathan and Michal play Ping-Pong, Saul cools off with a battery-operated fan, while his wife Achi, one of Kalisky's inspired fictions, coats herself with suntan lotion. They are waiting for David. He makes his appearance in bathing trunks and a T-shirt bearing a yellow Star of David on the chest. Despite their mod appearances, these personae are not caricatures.

On the contrary, each character incorporates several identities. The opening scene presents the first: the larger-than-life images suggested by I Samuel. Next there are the contemporary human beings whose memories of a recent past are perhaps even more familiar to the modern audience than their biblical dimension. Third, although the characters in *Dave* are conscious that they are playing roles circumscribed by Scripture, except for David himself, each is determined to modify the parameters of his legend. These three levels of identity correspond to the Jew past, present and future. Small wonder Jonathan is fond of singing snatches of the Gershwin song which makes specific reference to David's killing Goliath, "It Ain't Necessarily So."

The play manipulates time and space in another way. It expands the quarrels between Saul and David to include other differences currently creating factions among the Jewish people. The Saul ben Kish of *Dave* slipped into British-occupied Palestine with his wife Achi. He has made a fortune, first in import-export, then in real estate. He and Achi take pride in having hewed a modern state out of the wilderness, and in their children who are sabras. They look down on diasporic Jews who return to the Promised Land only now that the hardships of building it are less formidable. That is one charge Saul levels against Dave, an emigrant from Brooklyn who, it turns out, had earlier been smuggled out of his native Lodz in a cardboard box, the only member of his family to survive. To Saul's taunts about his being a Johnny-come-lately, Dave responds pointedly that Saul spent the war years in the safety of his hideaway in Palestine.

Other disagreements between the modernized scriptural kings feed on updatings of their original situations. Saul criticizes David, whose instrument here becomes the double bass, because he only makes music about the battle Saul and Jonathan have actually fought against present-day Philistines. David countercharges that his Israeli hosts don't get along with their neighbors; they exploit their Arab laborers and disdain their countrymen who look or smell different.

Decades in Israel have failed to alter the East European patterns of the Kish family's lifestyle. Food is a constant preoccupation. Increasingly irritated by David's presence, Saul eats gluttonously throughout the play. After a particularly stormy argument in which Dave rejects the renovated images the latter-day Saul and Jonathan have of themselves, the lean, Coke-drinking Dave is force-fed until he vomits.

Even when the visitor from America sits down to break bread peacefully with his Israeli hosts, there is a profound gulf between them. Dave will not join the pre-meal blessing; he will not even say amen. Perhaps recalling his life in the cardboard box, he remarks, "Since my childhood, I don't pray anymore."

Underneath these representative images of contemporary Jews reside the prototypical identities of Saul ben Kish and David ben Jesse. Many events in the play arise from the scriptural accounts of the ambivalent relationship between the two kings. Neither Saul nor David knows exactly why Saul has summoned Dave to Israel; the reason seems to have to do with Dave's musical ability. He has brought a tape recording of his performance in Handel's Saul Oratorio which exercises a calming effect on the irascible Kish. Yet Dave has not really come to Israel to be a musician. He hopes to find other work, a goal encouraged by Michal, a pragmatist who has done her compulsory military service. However, Dave's options are restricted, if not by scriptural specifications, then by contemporary Israeli realities.

The playwright works the past into the present most ingeniously. As Dave picnics with the Kish family, word comes over the radio of a terrorist attack and atrocities in Beth-shan. The bulletin uses exactly the gruesome details which the Bible reports accompanied the death of Saul and his three sons after their defeat at Gilboa. This is but one of numerous allusions that agitate Saul's seething fury against Dave. From the first, something in the sight of the young man—his natural grace, his physical beauty, and especially his red hair of which the play makes a great point—has provoked in the older man an almost irrational fear, exacerbated of course by his knowledge of the past they share. He sees David as his nemesis. This time, however, he is determined that things will go differently. Grabbing Dave around the neck, he tells him with mounting vehemence:

> This time I will win. This time I feel it, I know I will please the Eternal One, blessed be He. There is no more legend. The legend is dead. You made it up. You're going to put an end to your legend here in Israel. . . . And our people whom you deceived will recognize that Saul is their true king, their first king, the one who responded to their will and who never failed. (pp. 133–34)

The supremacy vaunted here by Saul goes beyond personal, historic rivalry. It asserts as well the distinction claimed by those who developed modern Israel when it was crucial to do so.

Saul is not the only character inflamed by Dave. Jonathan, whose soul is knit to David's much more reluctantly here than in I Samuel, opposes him vigorously before resigning himself to seconding him.

Michal, in bikini and carefully applied makeup, almost succeeds in seducing Dave under the eyes of her still lovely mother, also physically attracted to him. Dave is the provocateur of passions he himself does not experience. He is strangely distant. He does not fight back when Saul, encouraged by the other exasperated Kishes, beats him mercilessly. Instead, when Saul is exhausted, David gasps, "You've ruined your comeback." Although Saul reviles Dave's sang-froid, he finally sees that it is one source of his greatness. In the explosive climate of modern Israel, cool heads must prevail. "It is for that reason," admits Saul reluctantly, "that all Jews ought to resemble David and forget Saul" (p. 179).

Yet unlike Jonathan and Michal, Saul cannot reconcile himself to his prescribed lesser role vis-à-vis David. He resolves to rewrite history by first humbling, then shooting his rival. But Saul's harassment of David is interrupted by news bulletins of further terrorist activities, then terminated by a raid on the Kish villa. Jonathan and Michal fall victims. As the raped Achi cradles the wounded Saul's head in her lap, Dave escapes by means of a rope improvised from prayer shawls which afford him physical rather than spiritual sustenance.

Dave disappears from the action almost as mysteriously as he arrived. Although the play's ending is inconclusive, another kind of finality attaches to it, a strong hint that the opportunity to repeat and revise the past is running out. Several times in the course of the work, Saul remarks that Israel's enemies would turn her Jews out into a world which is "all Hitler and Cossacks." The setting of the play in Eretz Israel serves as a literal reminder of the Jewish past which has become, triumphantly, the Jewish present and the mainstay of its future. At the same time, the sea motif stated in the title and reiterated throughout inevitably rings echoes of Arab threats to drive Israel into the sea, a threat made manifest in *Dave* by raiders dressed as frogmen who arrive by rubber raft. The refurbished David of Kalisky's play retains much of his scriptural stature, resilience and composure. But his image is modified by the understanding that this David must exercise his inspiration, charm and muscle in a reduced kingdom peopled by Jews who do not all hail him, and perched precariously at the edge of a menacing sea.

In his quasi-existential *Absalom*, a reworking of the later chapters of the story of David, Lionel Abel's reach is more modest than Kalisky's. "All the modern mind can add to the old story is reflection," Abel wrote in 1963 about Archibald MacLeish's *J. B.*[12] The observation applies to what Abel had done seven years earlier in his own play,

Absalom, a work which illustrates its author's subsequent definition of metatheatre, his artistic goal: "Metatheatre glorifies the unwillingness of the imagination to record any image of the world as ultimate."[13] Appropriately, that declaration anticipates René Kalisky's belief in the ability of the imagination to overthrow chronology.

Abel's choice of protagonists suggests that his interest lies in demonstrating that the value of human endeavor is not in the accomplishment but in the effort. David's story in II Samuel is a concatenation of his struggles with time, his own nature and a God steadfast in forgiving him despite his transgressions. Absalom's defiance of his devoted father is analogous with David's opposition to God. Unlike the personae in *Dave at the Sea,* the figures in *Absalom* derive their entire identities from the givens of their scriptural legends. All the playwright leaves himself to work with in the figure of David is the Kierkegaardian "anguish of Abraham," the unrecorded pain that patriarch must have felt in confronting the sacrifice of Isaac. Hence Abel's David says to his scribes, "You can tell me what must be done, but not how I may do it."[14] If there is a little more room in the play for a reinterpretation of Absalom's intrigues, it is because that character is at first unaware, then scornful, that his fate is foreordained.

The action of *Absalom* hinges upon the senescent David's naming his heir to the throne. The outcome of the choice is already known to the king's scribes who represent the revealed word of God. David reacts to their information by rebelling. He will thwart fate as well as the expectations of three of the pretenders, his sons Jonadab, Adonijah and Solomon, by refusing to announce any decision. In addition to rejecting the notion of predetermination, David is loath to abandon his search for a way to name to the throne Absalom, his personal favorite. Giving him the kingship would provide the ultimate proof that David had pardoned Absalom for killing his own older brother for the rape of their sister Tamar. Yet David cannot exercise this preference because, in expiation for *his* sin, he had promised God to make Solomon, his son by Bathsheba, his successor.

The urgency for a decision rekindles David's memories of the circumstances in which his promise to God about Solomon was made, memories of a heightened sense of reality. The scribe recalls the guilty king's moment of reckoning before the prophet Nathan:

> And when Nathan said to David, "Thou art the man," and it was David who had no word to answer, but sat stricken with astonishment at the meaning of his own act brought home to him by another, ah, I tell you, David drank in all the pain of it with the utmost voluptuousness. He, David, was in error. He, David, had sinned. Then it was real, the world. . . . (Turning to David) Remember David, what it means to be fortunate,

remember what it means to be loved of God, it means that your very sin and suffering from sin build the reality in which you triumph. (p. 170)

The relived wondrousness of that moment prompts David to restructure his present reality by sinning again, even more seriously. The temptation to name Absalom pushes him to the limits of his own legend. He has already wondered, "But how can I break a promise to God? How can I do that? Would I even be David if I did that? . . . Can I be someone else, at this point in my life?" (p. 149).

He cannot be someone else. His only alternative is to do nothing in the expectation that death will carry him off before he can fulfill his oath to appoint Solomon. Although David wants the satisfaction of having made a decision, he knows he need not really exert stronger influence on the scales of justice because God has already set them in his favor. However, no such divine protection is afforded Absalom for whom the issues of justice and reason are arguable and, he thinks, negotiable.

The son who forces David into confrontation has every reason to demand the crown: the law of primogeniture, personal popularity, ambition and talent for leadership, the support of Tamar and even of Solomon's grandfather, Achitofel.[15] It is a challenge for Absalom to learn he is *not* the man. He will act as if he were. Undaunted by his father's warnings that justice is decided by God, not man, that the greatness Absalom wants is given, never earned, he determines to wrench from life what he thinks he merits. He seizes the crown.

It is not only David that Absalom defies. Heeding Achitofel's argument that "God does not like the man who counts on the goodness of his case. For if a man's case is good, he will count on that and not on God" (p. 183), Absalom decides to ruin his case. He will commit the very act for which he murdered his brother. His plans are almost foiled because Tamar is more than willing to make love with him. Learning the real motives for his interest in her, she stabs herself. Absalom urges the scribes to record his responsibility for Tamar's death as well as that of Achitofel, a suicide for the shame of abandoning Solomon. The rebel dictates a conversation he claims to have had with God, in which he earned approbation by asking for the "one thing no man can give himself, the right to be implacable." But the scribes rebuff this attempt to tamper with the Scriptures.

Absalom is not utterly alone in his final defiance. He seems to have aroused his father. Although David already knows his men will slay Absalom in battle the next day, he insists on meeting with his son to try to dissuade him from fighting. However, Absalom too has had a vision. He has seen his own death; he describes the ignominy of it.

He regards this revelation as a favor from God which "I wrested from Him by sheer force of my desire to have it." Of course Absalom's success does not come in a victory over David that the Scriptures will record. Rather, the favored son here becomes his father's master by absorbing, and with his own death destroying, that part of David that wanted to sin in order to shape destiny. "Nothing of you will remain to obscure, delay or soften the extreme designs of God," Absalom tells David before the final battle. "You will be *His* plaything, *His* puppet even. But the self [David's] that sympathized with me yet blocked my way, the self I can never think better than myself, that must be annihilated with me" (pp. 221–22).

By dint of creative energy and indomitable will Absalom becomes an existential hero in the sense that he does the battle with God for which David lacks everything but the desire. There is divine confirmation of his victory. After the death of Absalom, God, to punish both father and son, lightens David's heart so that he is unable to grieve. Hence we never hear David utter his famous lament which would have been imbued with such a different meaning in the context of Abel's play, "O Absalom, my son, would to God I had died for you."

We do not need David's reinterpreted lament to see that the struggles of father and son in *Absalom* are one-sided because David lacks the *disponibilité* of the existential hero. He is not free to offer serious resistance and to shape his own destiny. The basic weakness of the play is that David and Absalom contend with God in separate arenas: Absalom in metatheatre, which concentrates on the possibilities of human aspiration; David, in tragedy, which assumes an ultimate order in which man is bested by superior forces. While Absalom makes a convincing metatheatrical hero, David demonstrates neither the depth nor the vitality of the tragic protagonist. By contrast, when David and Absalom do battle with one another, they are in the same sphere of conflict and their positions are more satisfactorily defined. David becomes the rock Absalom rolls uphill. Absalom's situation is the kind described by Sartre in "Forgers of Myth": he is free in the circle of his own situation.

The philosophic aspirations of *Absalom* are regularly set off by low-key humor in the characterization of scriptural Jews: David's ingenuousness, Tamar's inopportune voluptuousness, the scribes' insolence, and the clumsiness of David's less fortunate sons, though Abel does slyly insert evidence of Solomon's incipient wisdom. The inversion of both scriptural and literary antecedents to portray the success of a resolute Absalom against an ineffectual David and an inexorable God is highly original. In reinterpreting the Scriptures, Abel draws on the tradition of flamboyant, active resistance associated with figures like Gideon, Judah Maccabeus and Samson in order to fashion a hero who, failing to reverse his legend, finds a way to transcend it.

Both Kalisky and Abel are ambitious in reinterpreting the events and personae of I and II Samuel in terms of their post–1945 relevance. While the dramatists take vastly different routes to their destinations, and while it is next to impossible to recognize in the troubled old king of *Absalom* the vital adventurer of *Dave at the Sea*, it is noteworthy that both plays present a David whose most essential attribute, nobility, survives. Kalisky's Saul and Jonathan and Abel's Absalom are entirely transformed into figures of not much more than ordinary human proportion; the women in both works are *belles Juives*. But David, however diminished in *Absalom*, even clad in imprinted T-shirt in *Dave*, manages to retain something of the aura of majesty which proclaims that "the Spirit of the Lord came upon [him] from that day forward."

An East End Jonah

Like the Book of Jonah on which it is based, Wolf Mankowitz' *It Should Happen to a Dog* (1956) is short and spirited. Fast-paced and parodic as well, the play weaves anachronism, slapstick and dollops of the broad humor of popular theatre into an appealing, lightweight coat for the earnestness beneath.

Jonah, the son of Amittai, becomes J. B. Amittai, an unspectacular itinerant salesman who, after thirty years of travelling, has no sooner found a "good pitch" than his life is disrupted. As he tells a customer who has come for a quarter-ounce of his Archangel Gabriel tobacco, he has a recurring dream in which a bird chirps that the end of the world is at hand. What he doesn't tell his customer is that the bird also says, "Arise Jonah, arise. Go to Ninevah [*sic*], that great city and cry against it."[16]

Mankowitz does not draw upon any scriptural explanation for the prophet's unwillingness to go to Nineveh, an omission entirely appropriate to the modest stature of the play's protagonist. This Jonah is reluctant for no reason other than that the trip is an inconvenient detour from a promising commercial territory. To try to escape the mysterious command, he books passage, tourist class, on a ship bound for Tarshish, the wrong direction. When a storm blows up, all the passengers are asked to make a sacrifice. Jonah casts a beautiful if slightly nibbled meat pie into the wind with the promise, "Here God. And remember, I'm catching the first boat from Tarshish. All right?"

(p. 282). Naturally the pie comes straight back into his face. Spotting the refusal of the sacrifice, the sailors advance menacingly on Jonah who falls overboard.

It had never entered Jonah's mind to associate the end of the world with the odor of a fish shop. But if the whale's belly isn't the end of the world, he would like another chance to go to Nineveh. Seconds later he is on the path to the city. The immediacy of God's response bewilders the reluctant prophet who, like Chayefsky's Gideon, is not distinguished for his intelligence. Nonetheless, he pluckily enters Nineveh, only to find himself before the king, charged with vagrancy and suspicious behavior, inanely repeating that the end of the world is at hand and adding, "chirp, chirp." The last quirk prompts the king to remark that he himself has been perturbed by bad dreams about a bird. In a scene slightly reminiscent of Joseph with the Pharaoh, Jonah interprets the king's dream, but as if he were delivering a singing telegram:

> The Lord saith: Cry out against Ninevah, that great city, for their wickedness is come up before me. Stop. Yet forty days and Ninevah shall be overthrown. Stop. The end of the world is at hand. Stop. Repent lest ye perish. End of message. (pp. 283–84)

The monarch is astute enough to perceive truth in Jonah's improbable explanation that the source of his information is that a little bird told him. Certainly that is the very bird of the royal dreams. The king orders national repentance, speaking unchanged the verses of Jonah 3:7–9. Verse 9 is a hopeful question: "Who knows whether God will not turn and repent, and turn away from His fierce anger, that we perish not?"

The Ninevites are forgiven and lose no time in declaring a national holiday. Jonah sits on a rock under the broiling sun, sulking that he has become "the biggest bloody fool in the Middle East." Evidently he is too preoccupied by jubilant voices singing "Jonah, Jonah—he pulled a boner" to take pleasure in the role he played in obviating disaster in Nineveh.

As in the book of Jonah, the final scenes in the play are the most important. In both cases, God supplies accouterments for the prophet's personal comfort, here a coat-stand palm tree, laden with zippered coconuts filled with cold milk. All is forthwith destroyed. Jonah once again shows what a common man he is; the reservations he had earlier voiced about the unpredictability of God's favor to the Ninevites are no consolation when *he* is the frustrated party. He rages at the abrupt disappearance of the tree which he regarded as his due and is answered by an angel who comes to paraphrase the scriptural verses which ask Jonah to measure his regret for the tree with God's pity for an entire city. But the confused prophet doesn't get the message. If God wasn't going to destroy Nineveh, why all this "expensive business with whales and palm trees?" Though the angel remonstrates, "You mankind, you can't see no further than your nose," he is scarcely less benighted than the prophet himself. "You think it is such a wonderful thing to be an angel and do a few conjuring tricks? It *should* happen to a dog" (p. 287).

In a burlesque routine, Jonah and the angel puzzle out the answer for themselves:

Jonah: On the other hand, come to think of it, whose dogs are we?

Angel: We are the dogs of God.

Jonah: So . . .

Angel: Nu?

Jonah: Whatever happens to a dog . . .

Angel: . . . must happen to us, eh? (He chuckles with admiration.) (p. 287)

They realize that God's favor is available to everyone, even to the "dogs," that is, those not especially well regarded by a prophet or an angel or, for that matter, even by audiences to whom this Jonah is made to appear as something of a *schlimazel*. The play does not mention that the Ninevites whom the scriptural Jonah helped save were longstanding enemies of the Hebrews. In the Bible that fact broadens the allegory's message about the availability of divine grace to all who acknowledge God and ask Him for it. The omission of this significant dimension in *It Should Happen to a Dog* narrows the focus, training it on a thoroughly ordinary individual who is not too obtuse to appreciate a wonderful lesson. Jonah is chosen to learn to regard other men not as potential customers, but as brothers whose well-being is worth his personal commitment.

The play thus implies that it has become more difficult for man to earn consideration and concern from his fellow man than from God. In a prefatory note, Mankowitz writes, "As to the message of the story—'Why should I not spare Nineveh?' This is, one hopes, how God feels about Man—unlike Man who is less tolerant of himself" (p. 275). It is not unlikely that Wolf Mankowitz knows that the Book of Jonah is read at services on the Day of Atonement. In interpreting its scriptural scource, the play reflects the holy day's reminder of the impossibility of escaping God's presence. It echoes as well Yom Kippur's appeal for inner change and the opportunity it offers man

to strengthen his relationships with God, but first of all with his fellows. Mankowitz' *It Could Happen to a Dog* is a Haftarah chanted by
vaudevillians.

Judas: One Contemporary View

Several modern playwrights have been attracted to the story of the
disciple who betrayed Jesus.[17] Marcel Pagnol's *Judas* (1956) is especially
relevant to the present consideration, first because it portrays a Judas
who has much in common with Old Testament figures entrusted with
onerous responsibilities, second because the play presents an uncommonly broad range of Jewish images.

Pagnol uses characterization skillfully to create ambience and to
suggest dimension in his array of personae. The entire first act, for
example, is given over to depicting the mores and mentality we are
meant to understand as typical in Jerusalem in 32 C. E. The Roman
soldiers who search Jewish farmhouses are even less enlightened
than their terrified victims about one object of the search, "a blond,
bearded rather skinny type who talks all the time . . . a name like
Nesus."[18] The Romans know only that Jesus is the leader of a band of
troublemakers who has pushed the authorities beyond patience by
proclaiming the imminent destruction of Jerusalem and the Temple.
The search party is looking as well for the eldest son of one of the
farmers. They think it likely he has returned home for Passover.

For different reasons, the farmer Simon also regards his son's companions as troublemakers. They have filled his head with new ideas
and taught him to speak as convincingly as a rabbi—talents unnecessary for the potter he once was. Worse, three years earlier, the son
had substituted for the money he'd been sending home the message
that he was going to spread the Good News to mankind. Simon freely
discusses his disappointment and resentment with his Roman inter-
rogators. He is eager to appease the search party, even at the expense
of paternal devotion and personal dignity. Part of his willingness to
risk humiliation could be cowardice, or perhaps concern for the rest
of his large family. One has the impression that Simon feels somehow protected in the situation, convinced that the Lord will keep
faith with him. Like his family and neighbors, he perceives God to
be very close, constantly making His will known in man's everyday
affairs. Simon's allegiance to the faith of his fathers comes through
his speech patterns, although they occasionally border on the ostentatious (he addresses his grandson as "son of my son, hope of my
race"). His vanity about the family secrets for producing a panacean

ointment from camel's milk, among other necessities, makes him slightly risible. However, that very pride also rivets the old man to the values of the Jewish past. Hence his concern for his eldest son is expressed in terms of the boy's current standing with the Temple priests. If he has committed sacrilege, Simon does not ever want to see him again.

The renegade turns up just after the Romans leave. His return has been protected by a stranger named Ebion who introduces himself in the time-honored role of the traveller seeking hospitality. Ebion represents another kind of Jewish mentality.* He is the only one who listens sympathetically as Simon's son describes the three years he has spent as Jesus' follower. While his brothers, who welcome him home, agree that the Temple needed to be purged of commercial traffic, they are provoked to incredulity and finally to anger as they discuss some of Jesus' teachings which run counter to Jewish beliefs and practices. Even more inflammatory are the young man's plans to share the impending Seder with Jesus rather than with his family. Forgetting that he has only just made a similar discrimination in which ethical values prevailed over family loyalties, Simon orders his son to report Jesus' whereabouts to the Romans and come home to stay. The vigor of the disciple's horrified refusal ("How happy [Satan] would be . . . if an apostle handed over the Savior! That would be the crime of crimes!" [p. 66]) confounds his brothers to whom a father's commands are sacred. However, Ebion, who has grasped the essence of the contradiction, persuades Simon that the betrayal he urges breaks with Mosaic law and the demands of friendship.

Simon's eldest son is, of course, Judas. Pagnol does not confirm our suspicions until the first act curtain. The delayed disclosure heightens dramatic impact. It further permits a balanced exposition of the character of Judas throughout the first act. He is portrayed as the most responsible of the apostles. His role as keeper of the communal purse is probably intended to foreshadow the fatal bargain. However, the Judas who supervises preparations for the Passover supper, chooses the campsites, makes Jesus a pillow fragrant with moss and thyme and throws his own cloak over him to ward off the cold desert night, is unmistakably the reliable firstborn son of the struggling family we see in the first act of Pagnol's play.

"So, you are the chief of the apostles for terrestrial matter," Ebion

---

*The reference is to the Ebionites, a sect of Jews which derives its name not from an individual, but from the Aramaic root for "impoverished person," the source of its ranks and an accurate description of the character in Pagnol's play. Equally apt is that character's frequent designation as The Stranger, for the Ebionites were at home neither with traditional Judaism nor with the tenets of Christianity.

gently encourages the bewildered Judas who returns home after the Seder in order to ponder his role in the inauspicious turn of events. Ebion tries to help Judas penetrate the two fearsome sentences Jesus had pronounced: "One of you shall betray me" and "What thou must do, do it quickly." Although like much else in Pagnol's play, the meditative scene between Judas and Ebion has no scriptural basis, it is an inspired idea to imagine the first painful struggle with the paradox that lies at the core of all Judas inquiry: why did Judas betray Christ? Despairing, Judas prays to God for a sign of His will. The answer comes in the form of a search party led by Caiaphas.

Wily and self-assured, Caiaphas plays on the youth's family loyalties to induce him to reveal Jesus' location. He argues the logic of permitting the Temple tribunal to hear Jesus explain his own doctrine. He turns Judas' trump card to his own advantage; if Jesus is the Messiah, why shouldn't Judas tell where he is waiting to destroy or convert them? The contrasts among four dissimilar Jewish characters are vivdly set forth as the resourceful Caiaphas produces 2,000 deniers of gold. Old Simon Iscariot is overwhelmed and reaches for the rare treasure. Judas sternly forbids his father to touch it. And Ebion observes that in order to fulfill the scriptural prescription he attributes to Jeremiah the price has to be thirty pieces of silver. However, Ebion's citation does not convince Judas that he has been shown a providential sign:

> Caiaphas, I'll tell you one last time: I am a Jew and I want to save the children of Israel. Have you reflected carefully? Have you considered your responsibility? You who would put your hands on the Messiah, aren't you afraid of the vengeance of the Eternal One? (pp. 113–14)

The single-minded high priest replies self-righteously that he has always served God faithfully, indeed, he believes he is serving Him by involving Judas in the intrigue to capture Jesus.

These struggles within and among the Jewish characters are thrown into relief by concurrent events in the palace of Pontius Pilate. Pagnol brilliantly captures the amused Roman superciliousness toward non-Roman religions that one finds recorded in Tacitus and Pliny the Younger. The palace scenes create the high life, high-risk environment inhabited by Herod whose appearance—languor by Wilde, costume by Beardsley—betrays his awareness that he is a figurehead. Though peace in Judea depends upon bringing Jesus to judgment, Herod yields that responsibility to the province's proconsul or the priests. Confessing his personal sentiment that Jesus should die, Herod counters Pilate's taunt, "But he's a Jew like you!" with his own narrow concept of Jewishness: "No. Not like me. He doesn't love Jews enough since he also loves those others" (p. 149).

Trapped between the effete tetrarch and the enraged priests who come to announce that the Sanhedrin has already condemned Jesus, Pilate is forced to reconsider his opinion that Christ has not transgressed Roman law. He sends for Judas. At first the apostle's reasonableness deepens Pilate's awareness that Christ presents his greatest threats to minds closed against him. The proconsul hesitates on the verge of defiant reaffirmation of Jesus' legal innocence. Then Judas makes a tactical blunder. Carried away by his own zeal, he tries to proselytize the Roman on the spot, warning him that "As you treat Jesus, so will you be treated." The threat is more than Pilate's pride can absorb. He strides resolutely off to the Temple.

The Calvary scene in *Judas* makes excellent use of the dramatic device Ghelderode adapts from Flemish painting in his play *Barabbas*: the scene is played at the *bottom* of the hill. This view allows Pagnol to add bizarre touches that also testify to the influence of the Belgian playwright. There is an influx of tourists: sightseers carrying well-provisioned picnic baskets; pious old men giving their grandsons lessons in life ("When there's no execution," explains one of these sages, "I take them to the slaughterhouse"); a delegation from the provinces which bribes the soldiers for places close to the crosses. The repugnant caricatures are balanced by sketches of Jews touched by grace. Simon Iscariot confides to his shuddering son that he has prayed that Jesus' soul will be saved. Rebecca, once Judas' fiancée, tries to respond to the ritual summons for testimony proving the condemned's innocence. She steps forward (thereby illustrating Chateaubriand's theory about the origins of the blessed Jewess), only to be told that women don't count.

Judas, made to view the Crucifixion whose raw physical cruelty is stressed, cannot contain his horror and disbelief when Jesus is pronounced dead. He genuinely believed that someday "Heaven was going to split in two and God the Father was going to descend in His glory to install His Son on the throne of the world" (p. 226). Judas did not realize that Jesus could die. Flinging the thirty pieces of silver at the priests, Judas retreats into soul-searching that later helps him argue eloquently with the apostles praying near the tomb. It is as a Jew seeking justice that Judas reminds them how he had risked stones, dogs and rebuffs to beg while they stayed near the Master and preached to the crowds. He accounts for each coin in the communal purse. He tries to explain that he took the thirty pieces of silver because he believed he was fulfilling a prophecy, the kind of obligation, he reminds Peter, that Judas was not the only apostle asked to undertake. But the eleven spurn Judas. They flaunt the fact that there is no room for him in the Church that Jesus founded in Judas' absence after the Last Supper. That disclosure hardens Judas' conviction that there is nothing left for him on earth. Were his character less carefully developed, his final prayer would ring theatrical instead of genuinely moving:

> My memory will be accursed from century to century; the kindest will refuse me a prayer; never will a little child be baptised in my name. . . . Thou charged me with incarnating the ugliness of men, Thy will be done, and if I can still serve my Master by confessing to the crime of crimes, I will confess it. Yes, Judas betrayed Jesus Christ for the price of thirty deniers. But now consider that my task is done. I am the broken tool that can serve no longer. (pp. 231–32)

Pagnol's play ends on another prayer uttered by a centurion who had stood at the foot of the cross. In an exemplary gesture of brotherhood, the Roman soldier offers the three drops of Jesus' blood that had fallen on him to redeem the soul of Judas. He asks forgiveness for him "who no doubt misunderstood his orders, but who believed he was obeying you."

It is significant that this important request comes from a gentile. The centurion's prayer to which Peter adds a final amen seems unmistakably to recommend the revision of conventional attitudes toward Judas. Pagnol's play does not go as far as others, like Carlo Suares' *The Passion of Judas*, in exculpating the betrayer by showing him to be the instrument of Christ's will. However, Pagnol's nuanced, sensitive portrayal of the man and his origins, his struggles with his people and with himself, compels us to regard Judas more nearly whole, as a human being who accepted a superhuman challenge.

In dramatizing the story of Judas, Pagnol neither whitewashes Jews nor tars them all with the same brush. Instead he draws unusually fine lines on an extraordinarily wide canvas. He depicts a heterogeneous people, including the traditional paterfamilias Simon Iscariot, the opportunistic Caiaphas, the sympathetic Ebion, and finally Judas, for whom Judaism no longer exerts an exclusive appeal. Pagnol's discernment and broadmindedness in 1956 anticipate the enlightened climate in which the Vatican Council announced eight years later:

> What happened to Christ in His passion cannot be attributed to the whole Jewish people. Besides, the Church held and holds that Christ underwent His passion and death freely because of the sins of all men and out of infinite love.[19]

The images in these seven plays demonstrate the value of biblical Jews to the post–1945 stage. Since it is the humanity of the scriptural figures rather than their supernal attributes that contemporary playwrights look to depict, the original nature of biblical Hebrews makes them eminently suitable to today's theatre. For if one could venture a single generalization about the unhaloed hero of the Bible, it would be his ordinariness. Typically he is surprised, even reluctant to be selected to do God's will. The Old Testament rarely claims that the chosen are innately superior, only that they have found favor in the Lord's eyes, an inscrutable matter in biblical times as in our own. Often dramatized without whatever divinely inspired eloquence or prowess he has in the Scriptures, the erstwhile hero turns up in the modern theatre not only without grandeur, but in cases like Chayefsky's Gideon and Mankowitz' Jonah, without conspicuous wit. Some of the authors do not even permit their personae the dignity of bygone manners. The dramatis personae here are recognizably our contemporaries, homines not always sapientes, with all their warts and weaknesses (e.g., Noah's drinking and Ham's concupiscence, Saul's hot temper and Michal's lasciviousness). Their very lack of distinction qualifies them for the contemporary stage where the common man reigns supreme.

In one respect only the renovated biblical personae retain a measure of their original uniqueness. Their legends are extraordinary because they include a confrontation with the Lord. It is noteworthy that the theatre of our sophisticated age has not changed that. An established Jewish way of thinking about God is based on obedience, the fundamental idea of the Decalogue. The traditional Jewish injunction to obey, with its related idea of imitating God by adopting the moral values associated with Him,[20] lies at the heart of the Mankowitz, Pagnol and Chayefsky plays. The question of obedience animates the works of Abel, Fry and Odets as well. Significantly, each of these plays affirms God's acknowledgment of human behavior (e.g., indulgence for Gideon, promises held out to Noah and Moses, punishment for Absalom). Although the popular theatre is not the most likely place to look for such a demonstration, God's responsiveness to the protagonists in these works reflects the Old Testament concept of the kind of concern God and man have for one another.

From man's vantage point, that regard is tempered—and in Kalisky's script, overshadowed—by his need to exercise self-reliance. Gideon and Absalom celebrate man's irrepressible urge to surpass himself. Fry's Moses play concentrates on Jews galvanizing Jews to assert themselves against their oppressors. René Kalisky's reworking of the David and Saul relationship makes an issue of precisely the same consideration in terms of present-day Israel. Finally, while the roles and images in these works are by definition bound to specifically Jewish situations, their emphasis on man's responsibility both to God and to man knows no religious exclusivity. Odets' Japheth speaks a universal truth when he insists on steering because "a rudder is vital to the health of the ark."

3

Myths and Stock Types

One may call Shylock the brother or successor of the Wandering Jew. In the latter a Biblical myth became part of the medieval consciousness: in the former the medieval image passed over into a modern conception. They belong to each other because they are the only two Jewish characters of significance in European literature. The curse that drove the one to eternal wandering had, in fact, driven the other into the Ghetto. They are burdened with a sense of "foreignness" and, therefore, eternally suspect.

—Hermann Sinsheimer

Scarcely less venerable than its scriptural figures are the theatre's stereotypical Jewish images and stock roles. The introductory chapter of this study notes how the medieval stage barely concealed the unsavory silhouette of the contemporary Jew behind the Old Testament patriarch, a device that served as a transparent façade for the prevalent attitude toward Jews. The standard attributes of the legendary Jew are repeated down through the centuries with a dreary regularity that betrays the tenacity of the myths which shaped his image in the popular conscience. In every respect, the Jew is alien. He worships false gods, of which the most important is gold. His ritual requires the blood of little children. He is universally despised, rejected and put to flight, yet he persists, omnipresent. Satan whispers secrets into his ear. It is difficult not to see that the stock figure of the sneering Jew with knife and moneybag is nourished by the quintessential Jewish merchant and deicide, Judas Iscariot.

As we have earlier seen, medieval representations of the Jew ultimately polarized around two models: the usurer and the sacrilegist. Those two images in turn became codified in the colossal figures of Shylock and the Wandering Jew, whose origins "are far vaguer and more elusive than the myth which begat the Jew-villain."[1] Between them, these paradigms incorporate virtually all the myths associated with the Jew through the centuries.

The long shadows of Shylock and the Wandering Jew, or more

68

precisely, that part of them which spreads over post-1945 plays, provide the subject of this chapter which has two goals. Certainly we want to see what the two archetypes are like by the time they arrive on the contemporary stage. But since both master spirits embody such an assortment of myths, it seems useful to investigate first how their components have been "fleshed" out into modern versions of stock personae. For modern playwrights have adroitly appropriated the constituent features of the legends to fashion new-style money men and villains, victims and wanderers.

The Jew whose identity derives from his money appears in Jean Anouilh's *Invitation to the Chateau* and in Arthur Miller's *The Price.* Wealth also accounts for much of the Jew's importance to both works. The Anouilh character's fortune is as inexhaustible as that of Barabas or Isaac of York, but infinitely less treasured. Miller's man, like his Shakespearean ancestor, is portrayed in the act of making his profits, albeit under circumstances in no way reminiscent of the Rialto. There are many other variations of established stock types. On the modern stage, for example, the Jew-villain drives up in a big black car to practice his terrible sorcery at a ritual celebration. But Goldberg in Pinter's *The Birthday Party* does not skulk back to the ghetto or swamp or end up in boiling oil once his dreadful work is done, for he is as entrapped as his quarry by higher powers of malignity. Contemporary Jewish characters also become victims from whom a sacrifice is required in order to right the lives of others. That is true of Miller's money man in *The Price,* and even more dramatically, for Sammy Goldenbaum, the unfortunate military school cadet in William Inge's *The Dark at the Top of the Stairs.*

All these characters trail after them a prior history that ranges from the unusual in the instance of young Goldenbaum to the genuinely astonishing· with Miller's Gregory Solomon. Their biographies inevitably include wandering. Anouilh's Messerschmann has roamed the face of Europe, part of the time with his beautiful daughter. The Wandering Jew himself appears in Rabi's *Judas* to play a most unusual role. We see him young and beardless, a commentator on the first century events that launched his career on which, anachronistically, he already has twentieth-century perspective. Finally we come to Arnold Wesker's antipodal Shylock, the very antithesis of the archetypal wanderer, usurer and misanthrope.

Clearly, it makes good sense and good plays to draw on the mythic roles and characteristics that have been assigned to Jewish types for centuries. Yet the best-established stock character must have something to offer besides his long and monotonous curriculum vitae. Those considered here most assuredly do.

Of eighty-nine-year-old Gregory Solomon making his initial appearance in *The Price* (1968), Arthur Miller observes, "In brief, a phenomenon." There is no hyperbole there. Compounded of several stock types—the usurer, the ole-clothes man, the entrepreneur, the wanderer—Solomon still manages a degree of originality. He is a thoroughly delightful character whose wit and wisdom provide the most successful part of Miller's play.

Solomon is a used-furniture dealer. After sixty-two years, he has been trying to get out of business. The habits of a lifetime, however, prove to be even more persistent than his outdated yellow pages listing which attracts Victor Franz, who needs to dispose of his late parents' household effects. Though the old man has almost cleaned out his shop, he lives in the back of it; he could no more refuse to answer Victor's call than to "lay down and die." What he cherishes in doing business is not the opportunity to make money, but the challenge to exercise his considerable abilities. Even before he decides to take on the Franz furniture, a "big bet" for him, since disposing of it could take over a year, his whole manner betrays the model salesman. He strikes exactly the right balance between exhibiting confidence and inspiring it. His complimentary banter with Victor's wife Esther ("Sweetheart, all the girls like me, what can I do?") and his way of sizing up the customer and the merchandise demonstrate his amazing vigor as well as one of the sources of it: "The trouble is, I love to work." The very terms in which Solomon expresses his decision to take a chance on surviving this undertaking ("I'll have to live, that's all, I'll make up my mind") indicate another source of his energy, perhaps the primary one. He loves life. He knows what to do with it.

As the play supplies some of the details of Solomon's biography, it exploits yet another myth, the Jew as vagabond. Solomon claims to have struggled in six countries, to have smoked, drunk and "loved every woman who would let me," to have married for the fourth time at seventy-five. He was the man on the bottom in a family acrobatic act that played on the same bill with Gallagher and Shean. To prove his birthdate, Solomon produces his discharge certificate from the British Navy. He needs no documents to validate his boast of having recovered from four bankruptcies dating back to 1898. His ability to bid on the extensive Franz furnishings verifies that claim, simultaneously setting Solomon up as the antithesis of Franz *père*, a millionaire who never recovered from the crash of '29.

The household belongings which Solomon has been invited to buy temporarily hyphenate his future to Victor's and to that of his estranged brother Walter. "The price of used furniture," the merchant warns them, "is nothing but a viewpoint."² Appropriately named, Solomon is given to making sensible remarks like this one. Indeed, his insights contribute at least as much as his money to the action of the play. His holistic, reasonable attitude toward life runs counter to that of the alienated Franz brothers.

Walter's hard-headed pragmatism enabled him to ignore their bankrupt father and to drive himself to a successful medical career which eventually devoured his marriage and his health. Sobered by his failures, he is trying valiantly but unconvincingly to show real concern for others, especially his brother. Victor renounced his own youthful career aspirations because he genuinely believed that their ruined father could not afford his education. Regarding his twenty-eight years on the police force as "a long, brainless walk in the street," Victor nonetheless feels he made the right decision. Walter's shocking revelation that their father had purposely refused Victor tuition money from a secret hoard, valuing his own security more, horrifies Victor without making him regret his choice.

Victor still needs to believe that his father loved and needed him, that he couldn't have deliberately held out on him. Walter's demonstration that there was neither love nor loyalty in their home does not alter the fact that Victor had acted as if there had been both. Walter wants to clear his own conscience by making his brother question the human instincts that had kept him steadfast to their father long after Walter had walked away. That is a price Victor is unable to pay. He needs to trust people.

When Victor tries to mask his innate belief in others, he appears defensive, a pose Solomon penetrates early in the play. Although it is as a merchant that Solomon insists that their business can be transacted only in the spirit of mutual confidence, he sounds more like a father lecturing a son on the indispensability of faith:

> Mister, I pity you! . . . Nothing in the world you believe, nothing you respect—how can you live? You think that's such a smart thing? That's so hard, what you're doing? Let me give you a piece advice—it's not that you can't believe nothing, that's not so hard—it's that you still got to believe it. *That's* hard. And if you can't do that, my friend—you're a dead man! (p. 37)

At first the old Jew tries only to get the dispirited Victor to admit he has faith in something. After Walter's arrival, Solomon pursues a more specific goal, one which draws on the implications of his name. Physically absent during much of the second act of the play, Solomon in his periodic appearances is bent on keeping the brothers on the track of their search for something solid to believe in. Thus he brings them back to themselves when they seem about to drown their differences in an emotional wave of nostalgia, and again when Victor is tempted to accept a job Walter can get for him, even though they both know he is unqualified for it. Solomon insinuates himself for the last time just as the Franzes have reached an impasse. They have nothing left to bargain with; they have found nothing to build accord on.

Several times during the family quarrel, Solomon had been unable to restrain his indignation at how Victor's wife and brother were tearing him to pieces. As he performs his marvelously comic counting-out ritual to the badly shaken Victor at the end of the play, the merchant makes a beautiful gift to forestall Victor's now tearing himself apart. He shares an intimate lesson he has learned in the pointlessness of guilt and self-recrimination:

> I had a daughter, should rest in peace, she took her own life. That's nearly fifty years. And every night I lay down to sleep, she's sitting there. I see her clear like I see you. But if it was a miracle and she came to life, what would I say to her? (p. 114)

Finally alone with his massive purchase of household goods, Solomon impulsively puts a party laugh record on the phonograph and gradually succumbs to its infectiousness. This nonagenarian shaking with laughter and delighting in life at the end of *The Price* really has only one thing in common with earlier stock Jews: he lacks verisimilitude. In Gregory Solomon's case, that is largely because such an emphatic commitment to life is, in every sense of the word, fabulous.

A much different reworking of the Jewish money man appears in Jean Anouilh's *Invitation to the Chateau* (*L'Invitation au château*, 1948).[3] Anouilh actually adapts here the durable stock duo of the rich Jew and his beautiful daughter. As we have seen, this mythic pair traditionally translated Christian ambivalence toward Judaism. The fundamental wickedness of the Jew, typically a usurer, plays off against the redeemability incarnate in his daughter, who also represents the mother of religion. She is not only irresistible, but generally enamored of a Christian for whom she will eventually forsake her father and, of course, Judaism.

The formula admits many variations. The Jew is not always a moneylender or even remarkably affluent (Daniel in Dumas *fils' Claude's Wife* is an inventor's associate), nor does his daughter invariably abandon faith and father (Rebecca in the same Dumas play perpetuates the tradition of the namesakes of Walter Scott's heroine by giving up her heart's desire to remain constant to her origins). Even when the *belle Juive* does marry outside her faith, the act is not necessarily a defiance of her father (Ali Habernichts in Claudel's *Crusts* gladly consents to Sichel's union with a Christian nobleman). Nor is it inevitably the old man rather than his daughter who is the disagreeable member of the pair (e.g., *Kings in Exile*, discussed in Chapter One; in addition, this theatregoer has never been able to summon much admiration for Jessica in *The Merchant of Venice*, though that clearly has not been the prevailing opinion of audiences).

Some of these variants figure in Anouilh's portrayals in *Invitation to the Chateau*. Prodigiously wealthy financier Romuald Messerschmann is sometimes comic, sometimes pathetic and constantly more sympathetic than his daughter Diana who is thoroughly preoccupied with social climbing. This *belle Juive* is the target of an elaborate game which constitutes much of the action of the play.

The plot grows out of the machinations set up by the aristocrat Horace to open the eyes of his sentimental twin brother Frederick (another stock pair) to the unavoidability of heartbreak should Frederick marry his fiancée, Diana Messerschmann. Horace is a young rebel interested in flexing his muscle by meddling with what he disdains as "the normal order of things." To make his point, Horace decides to reverse the expected march of events by interfering with his brother's engagement. Horace's choice of target betrays the fact that he is far less indifferent to Diana than he would like to appear. He flatters himself that she has accepted Frederick as a surrogate for Horace himself with whom, he says, she fancies herself in love. As a matter of fact, he is quite right. Now Horace prides himself on his inability to really love anyone, a trait which he recognizes in

> that Diana [who] certainly is not lacking in attributes. Her race gives her something more than our kind of rich girls. She is harsh, she is capricious, but her very egoism is amusing. (p. 404)

This speech constitutes the only acknowledgment by any of the aristocrats that Diana is a Jewess. It is curious that her Jewishness serves both as the source of that *je ne sais quoi* that distinguishes her from all other rich women for Horace, and at the same time the lure that makes Horace attentive to her other scheming qualities which are, in fact, so like his own. In an unusual inversion of the beautiful daughter of the wealthy Jew motif, however, Anouilh's young man does not declare himself until he thinks Diana's fortune is gone.

Horace's taste for manipulation parallels Messerschmann's. One view of the tycoon's stance vis-à-vis the world is displayed in his attitude toward his daughter's marriage. *Père* Messerchmann asks nothing better than to buy Diana's happiness at any price. What is more, he is sincerely convinced he can. Having been hurt by Horace's meddling with her engagement to Frederick, Diana comes to vent her frustrations on her father who refuses to be dissuaded from his belief that money has the power to make dreams come true.

The scene between indulgent father and his spoiled little rich girl acquires depth by reversing the heartless "O my ducats! O my daughter!" tradition and by drawing upon the prior history of this Jew and his daughter. When Diana comes whimpering to Messerschmann to salve the wounds inflicted by Horace, she asks, "Can you still do everything like when I was a little girl?" She recalls how they travelled interminably from border to border, huddled together in third-class compartments, and how magnificent Messerschmann was when he invaded the forbidden territory of the first-class dining car to buy oranges for Diana with his last sous. Horace's plot against Diana reawakens the pain of past humiliations. She is newly aware of a vulnerability for which her father's millions provide no defense and despises his amused awareness of the terms of their admission to high society. The more Messerschmann tries to soothe her by offering to ruin whoever stands in the way of her happiness, the more he alienates her:

> They are stronger than we, Papa, with their dusty portraits and their decaying houses. They are perfectly willing to take our money to pay for the repairs, but that's all. Oh! I hate you, I hate you for being your daughter! I would so much have liked to be like them! (p. 331)

Nastily, Diana taunts her father with the scorn he too attracts, particularly from his faithless mistress, Lady India. But Messerschmann is wryly acquiescent:

> I *am* old and ugly, my dear daughter. That's my business. Moreover, I'm not upset with the way she treats me. She thumbs her nose, she struts about, she tells me I'm a nasty old Jew, but I have her by her string of pearls and she always comes back to me. What's more, it's a fact that I am a nasty old Jew. Every night I scratch at the door of her room and Lady India, the most beautiful woman in the English court receives me, covering me with contempt, because every night she has something she wants to ask me for. That's a rather nice feeling for a nasty old Jew—the scorn included. (p. 326)

The image of the capitalist Messerschmann emerges as a novel revision of the stereotyped Jew as moneyman. Like Shylock et al., he recognizes exactly what authority his great assets command. He is reconciled to being identified in terms of his millions and fully aware that they alone constitute his entrée into the *haut monde*. But unlike the fraternity of stock Jewish moneymen, Messerschmann is not rapacious or obsessed with acquisition, or the least interested in revenge on those who force him into the social role he occupies. Strangely, he accepts himself much as others accept him, deriving his self-respect entirely from his Midas touch. A flat figure in this respect, it seems exactly right that Messerschmann subsists on nothing but plain boiled noodles.

Yet there turns out to be another, unexpected aspect of Messerschmann—the wanderer who has nowhere else to go. It is likely that he resides among the scornful aristocrats to please his daughter who is much dearer to him than his ducats. Outside the carriage set, his money would be an embarassment (it is of course useless to speculate why a secondary character in a popular play couldn't just endow a hospital). Messerschmann knows the world, the power of money, and himself, and he is not happy because despite what he tells Diana, he too wants what money cannot buy. In his most affecting scene, he tries to give an enormous sum to a young idealist who refuses it because she doesn't believe in money. He bellows his frustration:

> But I don't believe in money either, Mademoiselle. All it gives me is dust, smoke, nausea, vomit. I have liver trouble anyway and my life is restricted. I eat noodles, I drink water and I get absolutely no pleasure out of having that icy woman every night. . . . I don't want anything! I am only a poor little tailor from Cracow and the only true joy I can recall is the first garment I made successfully when I was sixteen. It was a priest's jacket, it fell nicely, and my father said, "Jonathan, you did well this time, you know your business." And I was happy. Since, I have never succeeded at anything except earning money, more and more money, and money never brought me anyone's love, not even my daughter's— not even the love of money itself. (pp. 385–86)

Thereupon follows a madcap scene in which the financier at last derives real pleasure from his money. He and the young idealist reduce wads of bills to confetti, revelling in designating all the material things it will never buy. Yet in the midst of their hilarity, they are struck by the futility of what they are doing.

Comparing himself with the unfortunate, ridiculed Samson, the Jewish magnate determines to pull the whole temple down, that is, to dump all his holdings on the international market at a tremendous loss. Messerschmann's plans to ruin himself and the economy are aborted in a comic reversal. Investors, suspecting a stock market maneuver, gobble up the securities he sought to devalue, making him twice as rich as before. Instead of returning to Cracow to open a tailor shop, he will have to find the stamina to carry on in the world of high finance and high society. In a final grand gesture designed to flaunt his determination to demand more of himself, he orders his boiled noodles prepared, just this once, with a little salt.

Messerschmann and Gregory Solomon offer contrasting and successful updatings of one of the sturdiest Jewish stereotypes. These contemporary moneymen are wittier than their antecedents, and infinitely more benign. At the same time, the new characterizations incorporate an affective dimension, appropriately overdrawn as a caricature's traits should be. Although Solomon and Messerschmann play secondary roles, they are portrayed at least as incisively as the protagonists of their plays. Oddly, the very works that expand and modify the myth of the money man preserve a stereotyped view of him within his society. The American becomes a hard-working independent businessman; the French financier, who profits as effortlessly as he breathes, lives on the fringes of a self-indulgent elite, always needy of Jewish money.

A milieu just as familiar although much less readily accepted provides the setting of The Birthday Party (1958). The apprehension which pervades the play arouses the suspicions of imminent menace that everybody harbors. To evoke that foreboding, Harold Pinter exploits a number of myths and clichés. He crossbreeds strains from a variety of stock Jews to produce a hybrid, noxious boogeyman, Nat Goldberg. And he pairs Goldberg up with Dermot McCann, a smaller-scale mosaic of conventional Irish types. The figures of the Jew and the Irishmen synthesize silhouettes representative of the Old and New Testaments, literary antecedents such as the Devil and Vice, Shylock and Launcelot Gobbo, Bloom and Dedalus, and characters out of a barroom joke run amuck.

Goldberg and McCann are sinister from the start. Their role is to corporealize the primitive dread which is the real destroyer in The Birthday Party. The play's most terrible fear, that things are not what they seem to be, has made itself felt long before the entrance of the bad men at the rundown boarding house where Stanley, an artist on the run from society, has taken refuge with a middle-aged couple. Early in the play, Stanley, who never goes out, projects his most alarming dread onto his landlady, Meg:

Stanley (advancing): They're coming today.

Meg: Who?

Stanley: They're coming in a van.

Meg: Who?

Stanley: And do you know what they've got in that van?

Meg:	What?
Stanley:	They've got a wheelbarrow in that van.
Meg (breathlessly):	They haven't.
Stanley:	Oh yes they have.
Meg:	You're a liar.
Stanley (advancing upon her):	A big wheelbarrow. And when the van stops they wheel it out, and they wheel it up the garden path, and then they knock at the front door.
Meg:	They don't.
Stanley:	They're looking for someone.
Meg:	They're not.
Stanley:	They're looking for someone. A certain person.
Meg (hoarsely):	No, they're not!
Stanley:	Shall I tell you who they're looking for?
Meg:	No![4]

Enter Goldberg and McCann. At first, Goldberg cunningly displays some of the hallmarks of the patriarch. Chosen by a higher power to do its bidding ("I mean naturally they approached me to take care of it"), he has been entrusted with what he refers to as a mission. Because he has earned "position," he was able to request McCann as his partner. He leads his associate to their destination with an assurance that belies the fact that he has never been there before; he did not even need to look for the house numbers.

Goldberg loses little time in discerning the particular susceptibility of Meg and Stanley to the ultimate authority represented by the assertive paternal figure. Both residents of the boarding house are vulnerable in distinctly childlike ways.[5] The calculating Jew turns their defenselessness to his own purposes. He charms Meg by flattering and encouraging her. When he learns that it is Stanley's birthday, he insists there be a party and assumes responsibility for all the preparations.

The grim irony, of course, is that the birthday celebration Goldberg plans for Stanley commemorates his destruction. Unsurprisingly, the fiendish Jew knows exactly what rites have to be performed. The ritual includes a brutal interrogation during which Goldberg, ever the father figure, makes accusations and passes judgment. However, during the procedure, we begin to see how the bragging, confident Jew is not all he seems to be. For one thing, Goldberg is a hypocrite. As he

McCann and Goldberg grill Stanley in Printer's *The Birthday Party*. New York 1971. Photograph by Martha Swope, New York.

and McCann harass Stanley with often nonsensical questions, Goldberg persists in accusing him of sexual profligacy, an unlikely charge given Stanley's paranoia. Yet at the party which follows the cross examination, it is Goldberg himself who loses no time in taking advantage of Lulu, the neighborhood nymphet.

In important ways, the Jew is less unassailable than he first appeared. At the end of the interrogation scene, although Stanley has beeen reduced to babbling confusion, he has just enough strength to retaliate. He kicks Goldberg in the stomach. The morning after the long night of torment, the Jew complains that, odd as it may be for him under the circumstances, he feels "knocked out." Perhaps to reinvigorate himself, he launches into a blustering inventory of his achievements, commending his personal self-improvement program to McCann. Abruptly he runs out of conviction. And thereupon follows one of the play's most stunning reversals. Goldberg begs McCann to revive him by blowing into his mouth. The New Testament thus breathes life into the Old. On another, ironic level, the Christian (McCann at one point even impersonates a father confessor) resuscitates the failing Jew so he can carry on with his diabolical business.

Unlike most Pinter personae, Goldberg has a history. Although the details of his biography, assuming they are accurate, shed little light on the action of *The Birthday Party*, they do enrich the characterization by endowing Goldberg with a variety of attributes that attach him to scriptural tradition among others. Goldberg's memories go back long before "Shabbuss" at Brighton to a time when he was called by another name and bid by a dying patriarch to observe a distorted Decalogue:

> My father said to me, Benny, Benny, he said, come here. He was dying. I knelt down. By him day and night. Who else was there? Forgive, Benny, he said, and let live. . . . I lost my life in the service of others, he said. I'm not ashamed. Do your duty and keep your observations. Always bid good morning to the neighbours. Never, never forget your family, for they are the rock, the constitution and the core! (p. 78)

The specter of another familiar Jewish image is raised by Goldberg's complaint that having devastated Stanley, he feels "knocked out." The lament echoes Shylock's exit line, "I am not well." Where Shylock cherished the jewels of his late wife, Goldberg, then known as Simey, rhapsodizes over his deceased wife's rollmop and pickles. Like Shylock, Goldberg entrusts his money to his child. But the strongest parallel lies in the enormous egoism these two Jew-villains share, an egoism that leads them to play games with other men's lives and to operate beyond the limits of accepted morality.

Yet another mythic facet is added to Goldberg by his affability which is occasionally oleaginous. He wills himself to appear good-humored, like a nervous newcomer or a merry old gentleman, a term Dickens repeatedly applies to Fagin and which, Edgar Rosenberg reminds us, is a euphemism for the devil. Indeed, Goldberg does have ruinous powers at his command ("The nerves break. There's no guarantee how it's going to happen, but with certain people . . . it's a foregone conclusion"). One catches a hint not only of Barabas and Svengali, but those Jewish priests in medieval legends (e.g., the Theophilus legends) whose pacts with the devil entitled them to magical resources.

Goldberg's unctuous compliments, his braggadocio, his opportunism with Lulu all mark him as thoroughly common. His vulgarity is an appropriate veneer for balefulness in demonstrating the play's premise that danger resides in the ostensibly ordinary. Goldberg represents the ineluctable menace peeking out from behind the commonplace: "If we hadn't come today, we'd have come tomorrow. Still, I'm glad we came today. Just in time for his birthday" (pp. 32–33).

Nat Goldberg, evil wearing the Jew's mask, barges into Pinter's 1958 play from the middle ages, with this important difference: Traditionally, having done his nefarious work, the Jew disappears altogether or, more frequently, he is brought to retribution. But in *The Birthday Party*, the fires or boiling cauldron that once dispatched the Jew, righting the balance in the name of Goodness or Justice are, as Goldberg himself would say, neither necessary or probable. This Jew-villain, for all his cockiness and potency, is simply an organization man. He is subject to the same command that decrees Stanley's ruination, a higher authority fittingly if cryptically called Monty. Monty works through Goldberg just as, for so many centuries, the Devil was supposed to have worked through the Jew. But in the menacing theatrical universe of Harold Pinter, the force that undoes is not infernal, but internal. The characters' worst dreams do come true, and we have already had a glimpse of Goldberg's nerves beginning to break. Scattering a potpourri of mythic references, the Jew-villain works beautifully as the instrument of a nightmare's every threat to identity, security, sanity. But this Jew is not all he seems to be, and that very unreliability makes him an extraordinarily formidable boogeyman.

The obverse of the Jew singled out to work evil is the Jew selected for martyrdom to a cause that has little or nothing to do with him. As history grimly certifies, this phenomenon is even more common as fact than as literary device, though of course the same myths operate in life as in art. Twenty centuries of history have been blackened by the staggering aggregate of social and economic problems which have been considered soluble in Jewish blood.

It is essential to distinguish between literal and figurative approaches to the representation of the victim in contemporary drama. Holocaust plays work with a concept of the Jew as victim which has no precedent in literature. These plays are considered in Chapter Seven. The present focus is on updatings of the traditional, emblematic Jewish victim, a notion which, for example, stains the characterization of Gregory Solomon who, his optimism notwithstanding, has taken upon himself the disposal of the burden of other men's lives. A more fully developed Jew-as-victim motif appears in *The Dark at the Top of the Stairs* (1945), where it is used by William Inge in order to

> divert the audience from the main story so as to bring them back to it at the end of the play with a fresher viewpoint. In the play, I try to explore some of man's hidden fears in facing life and to show something of the hidden fears that motivate us all.[6]

The "main story" of *The Dark at the Top of the Stairs* has to do with the Flood family's problems staying in touch with reality and communicating their needs and concerns for one another. Rubin Flood, stubbornly trying to sell harnesses despite the advent of the automobile, has walked out on his family. His wife Cora is hard put to manage their neurotic children. Sonny manifests an unresolved oedipal complex and an aptitude for fearful temper tantrums. Reenie is excruciatingly shy. Although she spends a lot of time being sick to her stomach over it, she has managed to strike up a friendship with her polar opposite, a girl suitably named Flirt. The crisis of the play develops when Flirt arranges a blind date for Reenie with a friend from a nearby military school.

The cadet is Sammy Goldenbaum and the subplot to which he is central is intended by Inge "to show something of the hidden fears that motivate us all." Significantly, Inge, like Pinter, shows the Jew stirring up universal fears that, whatever their genesis in notions of deicide, mutilation or plague-spreading, have long been generalized into the dread of the unknown—like the dark at the top of the stairs. On the literal level, there could scarcely be a more apt embodiment of the unfamiliar than a Jewish adolescent in a dress uniform who comes to take out a gentile girl in a small Oklahoma town. Like so many hapless Jews, Sammy unwittingly makes his way into a climate of ignorance and superstition. Reenie, queasy with nerves, asks, "Mom, what's a Jewish person like?"

Cora: Well, I never knew many Jewish people, Reenie, but . . .

Flirt: I've heard that some of them can be awfully fast with girls.

Cora: I'm sure they're just like any other people.

Flirt: (dancing coquettishly about room): They don't believe in Christianity.

Cora: Most of them don't.

Reenie: But do they act different?

Cora: (Not really knowing) Well . . .

Flirt: My daddy says they always try to get the best of you in business.

Cora: There are lots of very nice Jewish people, Reenie.

Flirt: Oh, sure! Gee whiz, of course.

Reenie: I don't know what to expect. . . . Mom, I feel sort of scared to go out with someone so different. . . .

Cora: Now Reenie, I'm sure that any friend of the Givens boy is nice, whether he's Jewish or not. And besides, his mother's a movie actress. (pp. 238–39)

Regardless of his advance notice, the seventeen-year-old Sammy who comes to call for Reenie is far from disconcerting as he waits for her with her family. His bearing befits the panache on his shako. He demonstrates enormous poise and an uncanny flair for making the most appropriate responses. An especially big hit with Sonny, he talks him out of a temper tantrum by sharing his own sense of being an outsider ("You have to be a good boy before people ask you to parties. Even then they don't always ask you"). Sammy's empathy with the uncertain latecomer who craves assurance stands him in good stead when Reenie finally makes her entrance. Suavely, he makes her feel like a lady. His choice of subject for small talk could not be more felicitous: "I always worry that maybe people aren't going to like me when I go to a party. Isn't that crazy? Do you ever get a kind of sick feeling in the pit of your stomach when you dread things?" (p. 270).

Like the Flood children, Sammy has lived with the problems of an absent father, including the resultant aggravation of an oedipal attraction to his actress mother who, having no place for Sammy, keeps him in boarding school. He tells the Floods:

I guess every boy thinks his mother is very beautiful, but my mother really is. She tells me in every letter she writes how sorry she is that we can't be together more, but she has to think of her work. One time we were together, though. She met me in San Francisco once, and we were together for two whole days. She let me take her to dinner and to a show and to dance. Just like we were sweethearts. It was the most wonderful time I ever had. (p. 271)

Triply isolated as a Jew in a completely gentile society, as a loving son all but orphaned, and as a warm human being thwarted by the "hardboiled" generals whose pictures fill his military academy, Sammy Goldenbaum poignantly, if melodramatically, incorporates the unabashed appeal for human love and acceptance that penetrates Inge's play.

The Jew in The Dark at the Top of the Stairs is intended less to inspire fear than to experience it. Sammy furthers the play's argument in behalf of the critical role of sympathetic response to basic human needs. He is there to demonstrate what happens when neither the individual's private fears nor the generosity of spirit he offers others earns the response it merits. The dance to which Sammy takes Reenie proves crushing for him. Roundly insulted by the anti-Semitic remarks of his drunken hostess, Sammy then discovers that Reenie has left alone, ashamed that nobody has cut in and afraid Sammy would think himself stuck with her. His limited experience hardly equips him to understand that the hysterics of a society matron or the disappearance of his overwrought date are not personal attacks, but distress signals from people themselves unable to cope with their situations. The hostess's bigotry and Reenie's timidity are presumably meant as manifestations of those "hidden fears that motivate us all." Sammy unfortunately and unwittingly triggers both. His self-esteem destroyed, he returns to his hotel and jumps to his death.

Although Sammy is the victim of strangers in a strange place, his death could hardly have a more pertinent significance for them. Learning how Reenie had abandoned her escort, Cora finally sees and rejects her daughter's hypersensitivity as selfishness. Reenie shares this insight and is overcome with remorse. In chiding Reenie, Cora herself comes into a new appreciation of other people's need for reassurance. That both Cora and Reenie have learned a valuable lesson is demonstrated in their revised attitudes toward the rest of the family. Rubin returns home to a daughter who offers to play the piano for him and take her brother to the movies, and to a wife who, for the first time, understands his fear of striking out in a new direction.

For Sammy's drama to relate meaningfully to the main plot about the Floods, it must be assumed that he dies because he misunderstands and is misunderstood. His death is not gratuitous since it does awaken understanding and compassion in those who are indirectly responsible for it. Yet although Inge suggests that "maybe I was drawing a little on Christian theology to show something of the uniting effect human suffering can bring into our lives" (p. ix), Sammy's death is too circumstantial to be likened to that of a conscious martyr. In the end, he stands as yet another in the endless line of Jews whose death serves a scheme from which they are excluded.

Since Goldenbaum is, by the playwright's own admission, a contrivance to help him make his point, one does not look for much depth or psychological truth in his characterization. A genuine stereotype, he is too good to be true. His suicide is barely plausible. It is worth noting in passing that Inge has drawn on scriptural antecedents in fashioning him. He resembles Joseph as the beautiful boy cast into a pit. He recalls his namesake in that this Samuel's upbringing is also entrusted to others by his mother. Like the biblical prophet, Sammy is a seer who reveals truths to other people. And like him too, finally, when they sought him, he could not be found. The date of composition of *The Dark at the Top of the Stairs* is telling in retrospect. Perhaps only in America in 1945 was there sufficient ignorance of the fate of European Jewry to render workable on stage the device of sacrificing a Jewish youth to the domestic problems of an unremarkable family.

Sammy Goldenbaum's rootlessness allies him with Gregory Solo-

mon, Goldberg, and Messerschmann *père et fille* as outcast and vagabond. They call forth the notion of the Jew as one who strays off
course, with innuendoes of alienation, guilt, self-reproach and the desire for expiation, all of which are in fact characteristics of the legendary Wandering Jew, Ahasuerus. As a literary persona, the Wandering
Jew amalgamates several versions of the story of an affront adminis-
tered to Christ.[7] In the thirteenth-century account, a Roman who
struck Jesus was condemned by him to abide until the second coming. By the time the fable resurfaced four centuries later, the offender
had become a Jew named Ahasuerus who refused Christ succor on
the way to Calvary and was, for that reason, condemned to nomadism
until the arrival of the Messiah. Thus Ahasuerus still roams the face
of the earth. As he cannot die, he becomes "a walking moral, a
perpetual embodiment of Sin in the process of being punished."[8]

   The scholar quoted in the epigraph of this chapter provides
Ahasuerus with an alternate, more favorable genesis, even while
seeing him as Shylock's brother in blackness. Hermann Sinsheimer
gives the Wandering Jew an authentically Jewish ancestry, tracing
him back to Elijah.[9] In Jewish folklore, the prophet travels endlessly,
witnessing and judging the affairs of men. "The transformation of the
Jewish conception of the holy wanderer with Messianic features into a
Jewish figure burdened with the curse of the Christian Messiah is a
characteristic fact of medieval mythology," writes Sinsheimer.[10]

   Over the centuries, the Wandering Jew is typically depicted as accursed and exiled, in the nineteenth century as often by his Faustian
aspirations as for having insulted Christ. What makes him such a
wonderful literary device is that he is as close to organic as a fictional
character can be. His sole fixed attribute is the awesome longevity he
has earned, and all that it implies. He is magically able to turn up
anywhere, at any age, in any guise. He can give testimony about
events he has witnessed which have transpired before the memory of
another living soul. Curiously, although Ahasuerus is much more
specifically tainted than Shylock with the guilt of rejecting Christ, he
sometimes travels through literature without the burden of assorted
wickedness that is always associated with Shakespeare's villain. As
Rosenberg puts it, "A study of the Shylock story down the ages involves little more than a knowledge of the prototype, but the Wandering Jew can mean all things to all men and all ages."[11]

   The restless, prophetic alien who plays a major role in Rabi's *Judas*
does not borrow traits from the mythic wanderer like the other no-
mads examined here. He *is* the Wandering Jew, a forceful allegory in
the context of a thesis play penetrated by the spirit of objective inquiry. Doubtless the tone of the work reflects the fact that Rabi (the

pen name of Wladimir Rabinovitch) is a lawyer and a judge as well as a writer who, in 1961 at the age of fifty-six, described himself as one "committed for three decades to the existence of French Judaism both as fighter and observer."[12]

In *Judas*, Rabi's purpose as playwright is decidedly not to dispute the gospels. Aside from minor elaborations of rôles and a few liberties with names, Rabi adds to his scriptural givens only the delineation of motives and emotions that might well have figured in the opposing points of view he portrays, a method similar to Lionel Abel's in *Absalom*. The evenhanded retelling functions as support for the inquiry into the lessons taught by Judas' betrayal. For the play exists to explore a significant question: Given that the events of 33 C. E. transpired because men at the time were subject to passions and prejudices we can still recognize as valid, what perspective on them do the subsequent two thousand years allow? Since the printed script indicates that *Judas* was written between October 1942 and April 1944,[13] we must consider the play's investigation in terms of the relevance of its events to a historical moment calamitous for the personae the work links together, Jesus, Judas and the Wandering Jew.

Rabi makes a felicitous choice of guide to that perspective. Who is better qualified to attest to twenty centuries of human history than the Wandering Jew? We meet him at the very beginning of a career launched not by the legendary insult to Christ, but by his blood bond to Jesus and Judas. The mythic Jew whose presence contributes in many ways to the action of *Judas* is nonetheless distanced from that action; to extend Cocteau's famous distinction, he is a character *of* the play rather than a character *in* it.

He is sometimes the judge-interrogator whose questions are all the more provocative for being ignored as if unheard by the personae to whom they are addressed, such as when he asks Jesus how he feels about the stubborn refusal of his own people to acknowledge him as the Messiah. He is sometimes the poetic narrator, as when he describes the entry of Jesus and the disciples into the expectant ambiance of Judea. Later, seated on either side of the proscenium, tragic masks around their necks, the Wandering Jew and Mary Magdalene narrate the Gethsemane scene mimed by its protagonists. Here the Jew is not only commentator, but interpreter. He sees Judas and Jesus as inseparable. He argues the indispensability of the disciple to Christ, the Church and redemption: "There is no resurrection if there is no sacrifice and death. There is no Jesus if there is not, beside him, a Judas who betrays" (p. 52). As he watches Judas approach, he perceives that the very hand that holds the thirty pieces of silver holds "the hope of mankind and the salvation of nations." Even as he observes the exchange of loving glances between the Master and his disciple, the Jew understands it to reflect their privileged glimpse of divine will, "the unique human mystery of the gospels to which Jesus and Judas alone possess the secret" (p. 61).

Although the interrelation of Jesus and Judas is central to Rabi's defense of the disciple, the drama is enriched by the addition to that relationship of the Wandering Jew. He sees himself united with Jesus and Judas because of their humanity, their Judaism, their martyrdom and the impact all three have had on civilization. Rabi supplies a third explanation of the origins of the Wandering Jew. He maintains that the mythic figure's plight, which stands for anti-Semitism in all its forms, had its genesis in Judas' betrayal of Christ. So when Judas leaves Caiaphas' palace with the purse of silver deniers, the Jew immediately falls into step with him, already recognizing what the consequences are to be:

> And I will walk at your side from continent to continent, I shall cross lands, seas and centuries. We will play our role, actors in the vast drama of the world, struck by God whom we cast into the shadows. (p. 52)

Although the Wandering Jew maintains the necessity of the betrayal, he acknowledges its implications. Judas' act did indeed liberate idolatrous men from the fear of the unknown. Since Jews refused Jesus' message of humility and submission, they excluded themselves from the hope which Jesus brought to the Christian world. Yet having long observed that troubled world from his unique vantage point, the Wandering Jew now challenges it:

> So what have you learned from your suffering? In the course of these twenty centuries, what has the good news yielded you? The sword and not peace. (p. 88)

That accusation hangs heavy in the atmosphere of investigation created by the play. Human rationality and dispassion are alternately implored and called into question. The wanderer implies that his co-religionists need to remember that Christ was a Jew, a human who was anguished by human pain, and the last of the Hebrew prophets. He predicts that Jesus' face will be obscured by scribes, doctors and pharisees of the new law. The play builds a compelling indictment against the intolerance wrought from distorted interpretations of Christ's death. As the Wandering Jew watched Judas' betrayal, he foresaw that the act would represent the last great love of man for man. His prophecy materializes almost immediately. The assailed Judas prays to Christ before his suicide, "Destiny marked us both with the same destructive love" (p. 90).

The unique perspective of the Wandering Jew is thus used to show how Judas has served simultaneously as the instrument of Christian redemption and the provocateur of centuries of calumny and persecution of his people. Although the action of the play is largely given over to demonstrating the first idea, the second is developed from the very beginning of the play by a smooth-cheeked, robust Wandering Jew who explains that he is unrecognizable because "I am not yet acquainted with Christian nations and their twenty centuries of high civilization, numberless expulsions, endless flights, the yellow star and the sealed railroad cars" (p. 15). By the end of the play, we understand that like the wanderer, Jews will continue to seek a rectification of Christian conscience as long as they endure. "We are the people who prevent the world from sleeping," the Wandering Jew declares.

The Jew's final assertion in *Judas* prevents the play from slipping into apology or accusation. The play escapes both by emphasizing the respect for rationality and the potential for fraternal love which are, as a matter of fact, themes that run throughout the work. The point is made forcefully in the curtain line, given to the Wandering Jew, which makes an undisguised allusion to the historical moment of the play's composition: "The gods have passed," he declares. "The way is open for the race of men" (p. 91).

In common with more conventional versions of the Wandering Jew, Rabi's persona seeks conciliation. What is totally fresh is his appeal to Christianity to ask forgiveness instead of granting it. He looks to co-exist, receiving from the Christian world respect commensurate with that which he is ready to offer. Rather than a figure "spiritualized by the penalty Christ inflicted upon him,"[14] Rabi's Wandering Jew is a figure deeply humanized in the crucible of inhumanity. His indestructibility having been demonstrated, he asserts his optimism, listening, even in the night for "the song of upright and courageous men."

By contrast to that of the Wandering Jew, the image of Shylock is rigidly defined as the archetypal Jew-villain. As the first chapter of this study observes, it would be more accurate to see him as the quintessence of evil embodied in the form of a Jew. The unflagging fascination of the character for audiences and for the theatre's greatest actors[15] provides perhaps the most persuasive argument that Shylock spellbinds not because he is Jewish but because he is fiendish. That the two attributes have been so long considered indivisible makes Shylock a terrible embarrassment for Jews.

Mendel Kohansky records how when, in 1936, Habimah announced a production in Palestine of *The Merchant of Venice*, virtually the entire

Sydney Walker as Shylock in Ellis Rabb's contemporary *The Merchant of Venice*. New York 1973. Photograph by Martha Swope, New York.

Shylock Kolner and his friend Antonio Querini toast one another in Arnold Wesker's *The Merchant*. Washington 1977. Photograph by Martha Swope, New York.

press denounced the undertaking and public protests were orga-
nized.[16] Every present-day production of *The Merchant of Venice*—and
the post-1945 stage has seen some iconoclastic versions, among them
Jonathan Miller's laid in the financial circles of Victorian England,
Ellis Rabb's in which Shylock, in homberg and pinstripe suit looked
like "a bad dream being dreamed by Bernard Baruch," and George
Tabori's, which used thirteen Shylocks and was set in a concentration
camp, echoing the performance of *The Merchant* commanded by the
Nazis at Theresienstadt—arouses vigilant monitoring and vigorous
criticism from the Jewish community. The response could not con-
ceivably be otherwise.

For modern Jewish dramatists working with Shakespeare's play,
updating it has been largely a matter of rehabilitating Shylock, or, at
the very least, explaining him. A notable early example comes from
Tristan Bernard, a popular French author. Despite his own origins,
Bernard did not regularly treat Jewish themes or create Jewish personae. Nonetheless, in 1936 he wrote a script for stage and screen
entitled *The Jew of Venice*.

The adaptation does not moderate Shylock's infamy; however it
introduces David, an old friend who serves as Shylock's confidant.
David functions also as a sort of public relations man on a level
between Shylock and those who observe him on both sides of the
footlights. So, for example, when the betrayed Jew reacts to Jessica's
flight in his "O my ducats!" speech, David unsays him. Shylock, he
asserts, really entertains far more appropriately paternal emotions,
but has gotten used to exhibiting only false sentiments within earshot
of gentiles. Finally, however, Shylock's intransigence with regard to
Antonio's bond depletes even David's good will. His explosion is in
part an apologia of the entire Jewish people, obviously intended for
ears other than Shylock's:

> Wretch! Miserable Jew! I defended you in front of these people because I
> am a Jew like you, but you are the greatest enemy of your race. If we are
> scorned and hated, it's not only because of maliciousness of men, it's
> because of Jews like you who debase our great Jewish family. . . . Really
> my supreme duty in the interest of the race would be to abandon people
> like you. But there is in me as in other Jews an instinct for mutual
> protection which rises above all reason . . . [17]

Some forty years after Bernard, another Jewish playwright, Arnold
Wesker, stung by the anti-Semitism of *The Merchant of Venice*, set
about a radical reworking of the play. *The Merchant* (1977) holds out
no antidotes to prejudice; in fact, it ends on a sardonic note of victory
for the play's fuzzy-thinking young bigots. What *The Merchant* does

do thoroughly and satisfyingly is to destereotype Shylock. It strips him of his formulaic attributes and reshapes him into a dimensional human being, richly endowed with a life abounding in Jewish values.

Wesker begins by giving his Jew a full name, Shylock Kolner. He installs him in a ghetto which, for all its restrictions and taxes, bears a distinct resemblance to a crowded city university campus teeming with music, lectures, visiting intelligentsia. However, there are also Jewish artists and scholars fleeing the Inquisition, for the year has been moved back to 1563. The first time we see Shylock, he is revelling in unpacking a huge collection of precious books he has saved from the autos-da-fé. Quite literally a man of the book, Shylock has a mania for his library: "I am a hoarder of other men's genius," he confesses. "My vice, my passion. Nothing I treasure more, except my daughter."[18] Nor are the books an empty vanity. Shylock loves interpreting, disputing, honing his mind. A perennial schoolboy with an impressive command of the history of man and of ideas, he is eagerly anticipating the arrival of his personal scholar.

The family life of Shylock Kolner is decidedly truer to Jewish life than that of his Shakespearean prototype. Since his wife is dead, Shylock's sister serves as the hostess in his house. A sensible, plain-spoken woman, Rivka sometimes mediates in the quarrels between her brother and her niece, Jessica. Shylock's adoration of his daughter shows in the way he has educated her and indulged her in "all the things I couldn't have." But Jessica has little patience with what she sees as her father's book fetish and with the stern control he exercises over her. One of the most touching shortcomings of this Shylock is his constitutional inability to tell Jessica of the tenderness and pride he feels for her. Though he refuses to praise her or credit her opposed but intelligent points of view, when she runs off with Lorenzo, Shylock heartbrokenly reacts with much more insight than he knows, "You must be so lonely. So lost and lonely." The estrangement between Jewish father and daughter is one manifestation of a major theme in *The Merchant*, the bitter irreconcilability of generational differences.

Despite her disagreements with her father, Jessica Kolner could never complain, "Our house is hell." The Kolner house is instead an oasis for refugees and a mecca for artists, dignitaries and travellers whom Shylock dispatches all over the world to buy books. Rivka grumbles contentedly that she never knows how many there will be at the table. A frequent dinner guest is the same man with whom Shylock shares his delight in cataloguing those rare books, Antonio Querini. The close friendship which has grown between the two brokers over the last twenty years is fueled largely by Shylock's ebullient, bottomless *joie de vivre* which warms the cockles of Antonio's melancholic, disenchanted heart.

Shylock's exuberance forms part of a trait which rounds out his Jewish nature. Over and over again, he perceives evidence in life of a soul-satisfying "scheme of things" which inevitably triggers his quasi-comic tag line, "I love it!" Shylock associates that "scheme of things" rather instinctively with his religion and the demands it makes on him. "Even those of us who don't believe in God have dark suspicions he believes in us," he explains to Antonio, recounting how Abraham had inspired Hebrews with the concept of an unseen God who had chosen them. Henceforth, he continues, Jews became

> a nationhood that had to be better than any other, and, poor things, all other nations found them unbearable to live with. What can I do? I'm chosen, I *must* be religious. (p. 11)

This generously proportioned Shylock is the major achievement of Wesker's play. In 1977, Joseph Leon brought the character to life on stage with great distinction. It is appropriate to note that Zero Mostel was first cast in the part, which he did not live to play, because the suitability to the role of the widely known Mostel persona—warm, zestful and multi-sided—stands as an emphatic measure of the distance between Wesker's Shylock and virtually all of its antecedents.

Having made a *mensh** of Shylock, the play is off to a running start frustrating audience expectations with a series of frequently ironic reversals. The infamous bond, for instance, is contracted only after Antonio persuades Shylock that it is dangerous for a Jew to flout the law which states that the terms of indemnification for default must be prescribed whenever a contract is drawn between gentile and Jew. It is to mock the law that Shylock, who would prefer to lend Antonio the three thousand ducats gratis, specifies the pound of flesh bond. Touching irony ends the Act I curtain scene where Shylock, having magnificently demonstrated his erudite respect for the past and his prophetic sense of the present, has to respond to the ringing of the curfew bell by donning his yellow hat and rushing back to the ghetto. And while the patrician Antonio grows increasingly disillusioned with the lack of "holiness and light" in the city where he is an unencumbered administrator, Shylock, restrained by the walls of the overtaxed ghetto and the strict laws of his native city, declares passionately that he loves Venice because "it's a city full of people living."

Shylock does not need to hear Rivka's reminders of how alien and

---

*A Yiddish word for "man," *mensh* connotes a human being with admirable qualities. See p. 122.

despised are the Jews of Venice. *The Merchant* plays off against Shylock and Antonio the arrogant, conflicted and amazingly prejudiced coterie of Bassanio, Graziano and Lorenzo. The latter is the most outspokenly anti-Semitic, which naturally sharpens the irony that it is he who wins Jessica's heart. In the trial scene, Wesker puts the "Hath not a Jew eyes?" speech into the mocking mouth of Lorenzo. Hearing the bigot defend his humanity finally unleashes Shylock's fury and drives him into the speech which must be regarded as one of *The Merchant*'s most significant reversals. The new Shylock justifies himself not as a man with "senses, affections, passions," but as a Jew:

> Jew! Jew! Jew! Jew! I hear the name around and everywhere. . . . Dear God of Abraham, will your mindless hungerings for *our* flesh ever be satisfied? There's nothing we can do is right. Admit it! You will have us all ways, won't you? For our prophecies, our belief in universal morality, our scholarship, our command of trade, even our ability to survive. If we are silent we must be scheming, if we talk we are insolent. When we come we are strangers, when we go we are traitors. In tolerating persecution we are despised, but were we to take up arms we'd be the world's marauders, for sure. Nothing will please you. . . . (p. 62)

For all his virtues, Shylock Kolner finishes not much better off than his prototype. The State must confiscate all his goods. Antonio sadly observes, "You take his life when you take his books." Shylock's last line also echoes the Shakespearean original; it is certainly more moving. His "I am not well," becomes here, "I am so tired of men." He goes off to Jerusalem, which may be a final irony. Theatregoers familiar with Arnold Wesker's trilogy will recognize Jerusalem as the code name for an unattainable paradise (see p. 143).

Strikingly, the more Jewish Shylock becomes, the more individual he is and the less representative of the Jew. There is no paradox here, rather, a reiteration of the point that the original Shylock, so long considered the exemplar of Jews, his very little Jewish substance at all. Shakespeare envelops his character in a cloak striped with the most sensational hues of Jewish iniquity, then allows the creature inside to display exactly enough genuine humanity to guarantee his becoming the most provocative and magisterial stereotype in English literature. Almost four hundred years later, the mighty cloak of evil has been shredded and the remnants passed over the ghetto walls where they become the veils of prejudiced attitudes with which some of the Venetians cover their faces as they pass by. Because Wesker concentrates on the human flesh and the Jewish blood in his protagonist, he accomplishes an entirely different result. His Shylock is a unique individual who stands out even among his co-religionists in *The Merchant*. "Shylock Kolner" will not pass into the language as a generic term in the way "Shylock" has become a stock synonym for loan shark or heartless creditor. In short, Wesker has thoroughly inverted the myth, negating its negativity by returning wickedness to its proper source, and giving Shylock not only hands, organs and passions, but fingerprints.

The other updated stock types we have looked at here have also been modified in ways which tend to individualize them by blunting or reversing their conventional characterization and behavior. The money men are not obsessed with greed. On the contrary, each makes a sincere effort to divest himself of his earning capacity. The Jewish evildoer is himself victimized. The solitary Wandering Jew does not travel alone. Even the victim Sammy Goldenbaum is given his moments of chivalry and heroism. Moreover, all but one of these plays lack the symbolic isolation associated with the Jew and the sharpening of the archetypal threat into its traditional representation, the knife. Except for the one in Messerschmann's name, where it probably underscores his financial acumen, there is a knife only in *The Merchant*. It provides Shylock with a brief opportunity for retribution as he presents it to Lorenzo and his confederates, "There! For you! *You* need it. You've no wit to draw blood with your brains or tongues, take this" (p. 63).

For all that their stereotypic traits may be watered down or offset with redeeming qualities, these personae nonetheless retain many attributes of the stock Jew. A certain woodenness or implausibility, the earmark of stereotypes, clings to them. When they are comic, it is in the Bergsonian sense of the mechanical veneered to the human (e.g., Solomon's periodic popping out to deliver his wisdom to the arguing Franz brothers, Shylock's oft-repeated "I love it!," Messerschmann's regularly increasing worth). Vestiges of the awesome powers traditionally associated with the Jew linger in Gregory Solomon's indestructibility as well as Messerschmann's being in the improbable position of controlling the stock market in London, New York and Vienna. Family ties are made out to be enormously important; since these are highly articulate characters, those bonds evoke passionate outbursts (the Wandering Jew), sentimental apostrophe (Messerschmann), expressions of loyalty (Sammy, Goldberg) and, inevitably, feelings of guilt (Solomon, the Wandering Jew). Exoticism figures in their portraits (Sammy's dark beauty, Diana's *je ne sais quoi* that gives her the edge over French heiresses), as do cliché properties (briefcases, souvenirs of the past, Yiddish or stage-Jew speech patterns).

Naturally, all of these qualities, added to the characters' mythic and legendary resonances, enhance their value to playwrights.

That stock types are indispensable to the theatre and readily acceptable to audiences is demonstrated not just by modern revisions of venerable images, but also by the spate of new Jewish stereotypes, a development treated more fully in the introduction to the second part of this volume. The causal relationship between myths and the new formulaic images is rendered problematic because so many of the latter have been created or popularized by Jewish authors. While the twentieth century figures are scarcely more flattering than their traditional ancestors, they are surely less poisonous, e.g., the Jewish mother, the libidinous hustler, the Jewish-American Princess. Rather than manifest long-cherished hostility toward Judaism, they ridicule idiosyncratic behavior considered typically Jewish. That is hardly reason to rejoice. Plautus and Molière teach us that however funny, the stock type is, at base, an aberrant, frequently ugly human being.

Myths and the stereotypes they nourish are, of course, far from an exclusively Jewish problem. In recent years, the theatre has drawn stock figures from an ever widening circle of ethnic groups. It is next to impossible to prove that the updated conventional Jewish types or the freshly minted ones have any more propagandistic or emotive value than the hot-blooded Hispanic or the finger-popping black. And it is certainly a sign of our times that Pinter's Jewish boogeyman is paired with another equally malicious ethnic. One might infer that that odd kind of parity reflects the way Jews are perceived vis-à-vis other ethnic types.

There are two other observations to be ventured about stereotyped Jews on the post-1945 stage. The first is the possibility that the reworked, humanized conventional images demonstrate that the infamous myths which sustained the archetypal Jew monsters may finally be attenuating in an age plunged into a sober understanding of the calamitous consequences such myths can bear. As Leslie Fiedler, surely referred not just to the Holocaust, points out, "It is impossible to forget that men have died of our myth."[19]

A final conclusion needs be far less tentative. Some of the formulaic Jews who thrive on the stage as in the other arts faithfully mirror the world they live in. Jewish stock figures who are guilt-ridden or alienated, victimized or wandering have come to represent contemporary myths restricted neither to literary stereotypes nor to Jews.

4

The Jew as Other

Stereotypes rest on the supposition that Jews are so alike that, say, any moneyman is interchangeable with any other. A concomitant premise holds that Jews not only resemble one another, they are different from everybody else. The effectiveness of stock images on stage often proceeds from the belief prevalent on both sides of the footlights that Jews are *sui generis*. Since the generally accepted "otherness" of Jews can be shaped into characterizations that go beyond stock types, it has been immensely valuable to dramatists.

As a synonym for "other," "Jew" is impressively functional. Fundamentally, it provides a label people use to distinguish that which is different, though not necessarily separate, from whatever they perceive themselves to be. Rather than designating a portion of mankind, "Jew" can be applied to a component of the individual, typically an aberrant, latent part capable of revealing itself with persuasive force. (One thinks of the outraged Parisians who, after a synagogue was bombed in 1980, demonstrated with placards reading "We are all French Jews.") That which is other threatens to the extent that it is perceived as a challenge to received ideas or established norms. Since giving things a name confers an elementary sense of mastery over them, it is a step in the right direction to call the other a name. "Jew," with its connotations of perdurability and inscrutability, is an especially apt choice. A great range of roles and value judgments resides in the use of "Jew," either literally or figuratively, as representative of the other. They vary from cardboard to fully dimensional, and from repellent to enchanting.

One of the many functions of "Jew" is to refer to that part of himself the individual seeks to deny. Erckmann-Chatrian's 1896 play *The Bells* (the original title, *Le Juif polonais*, is even more explicit) furnishes a noteworthy example. The death of the titular Polish Jew does not silence the jingling of his sleigh bells in the memory of his murderer. Consequently, the mere appearance of a second, totally unrelated Polish Jew years later suffices to wrench a confession from the guilty party, certain that truth has caught up with him at last. What is especially intriguing about the figuration of the Jew here is the way the indomitability of conscience is blended with the notion of the Jew as repository and revealer of truth.

In some contemporary plays, even Jewish characters associate "Jew" with a terrifying or repugnant element within themselves they try to isolate or control. The self-possessed neuro-psychiatrist in Victor Haïm's *The Visit* (*La Visite*, 1975) falls victim to an intruder she could easily outwit were she not erroneously convinced that he had discovered the secret whose concealment she obviously sees as fundamental to the person she has made herself: she has never been able to reproach her mother for denouncing her Jewish father to the Nazis.

In Mart Crowley's *The Boys in the Band* (1968) where self-loathing is a dominant theme, the most hostile and tormented homosexual defines himself as "a thirty-two-year-old, pockmarked Jew fairy." The ethnic slur attracts attention because Harold is the only one of the eight men brutally attacking one another's psyches who vituperates his Jewishness. Being Jewish is for him a supreme reason for despising himself and he perversely exaggerates it, just as he deliberately enlarges the pores in his scarred face.

Another conscious but very different sort of distancing one's Jewish otherness occurs in Murray Schisgal's *The Old Jew* (1966). The eponym delivers a lengthy monologue to imaginary neighbors, cataloguing his loneliness and helplessness, then his guilt and anger. Reaching the depths of despair, the Old Jew tears off his wig to reveal a young actor down on his luck. He has adopted the subterfuge to work out his frustrations and failures, projecting them into what he takes to be experiences more appropriate to a sixty-year-old immigrant without family or friends to sustain him.

It is not always part of oneself that becomes the estranged Jewish other. Reduced to its lowest common denominator, "Jew" is a term people give to the other who is not like them. This distinction is invariably pejorative, the creation of spite foraging for a target. As Sartre put it, "If the Jew did not exist, the anti-Semite would invent him." An extreme illustration is Harvey Perr's one-act play *Jew!* (1968) where "Jew" is the ultimate in a series of epithets exchanged by quarrelling, gun-toting neighbors of unspecified religion. Not only does "Jew" prove so much more inflammatory than "Communist," "Nigger lover," "Fag," and "Southern Baptist" that it impels the offended party, Curly, to fire his rifle, but when Curly's wife inadvertently runs into the line of fire, the taunter persists in repeating "Jew!

Jew! Jew!," as if wife-slaughter were yet another constituent of the term of abuse. In the Perr piece, "Jew" is a name fraught with such threat that the party insulted by it needs a bullet rather than a word to retaliate. It is a name freighted with such malevolence that the accused takes on its menace while in the act of repudiating it.

A far more subtle use of "Jew" as a term of vilification occurs in Jean-Claude Grumberg's Feifferesque *Michu* (1965). The comic strip protagonist of this very brief play unquestioningly absorbs all the identities laid on him by his bigoted office colleague Michu. For example, he must be a Communist if Michu says he is for believing that everyone on earth should have enough to live. Moreover, he reports each new denigration to his equally impressionable wife who tries bravely to adjust in the hope that her husband will improve if he "watches himself." Trying to stay on the right side of Michu, the milk sop takes him some chocolates. Unhappily, the boss, Mr. Schmol, thinks the candy is for him and offhandedly asks Michu his opinion of the friendly gesture. "Normal between Jews," replies the obdurate Michu. Obediently, the little man reports to his wife that now he's a Jew. That is the irreparable blow to their marriage; no home remedy will cure Jewishness. But Grumberg neatly inverts the destructive value of name-calling. The real Jew, Schmol, promotes the little man, thereby providing an authentic way for the protagonist to redefine himself, by contrast with Michu's accumulation of baseless smears.

However tiny Schmol's part in *Michu*, it is not anomalous that his is the voice of common sense. The figure of the Jew as other has been admirably prepared by history to serve as the repository for wisdom or insight. By virtue of the Old Testament, the Jew's credentials include extensive service as prophet, seer and divinely inspired spokesman. His erstwhile segregation or virtual absence from society made him a mysterious stranger, endowed with the reputation for consorting with nefarious supernatural powers. In modern plays, where the Jew is typically a less spectacular outsider living within the society depicted, he is unlikely to be attuned to celestial or diabolical voices. Instead, his otherness affords him perspective, his foreignness yields insight. The Jew sees things differently from the "insider" figures in the play. He is often privy to perceptions or information withheld from the other personae. His role is to disseminate the wisdom of the outsider. Discharging that duty, however, is rarely self-serving or even gratifying.

The revelations the Jew makes seldom engender auspicious consequences either for him or for those his life touches. Sometimes the enlightenment of the outsider earns him contempt. Abraham Kaplan, the one-man chorus who comments from his window on the economic sources of human wretchedness in Elmer Rice's *Street Scene* (1929) is derided by his neighbors. The scholarly, compassionate Esdras in Maxwell Anderson's *Winterset* (1935) scoffs at the ineffectiveness of his own vast knowledge as counteragent to fear, guilt and injustice. "It's a useless wisdom. It's all I have,/ but useless," Esdras reproaches himself.

In contrast with these Jews who are ill-served by their own sagaciousness stands Esther Brandès, eponym of Léon Hennique's 1887 play. Esther's function is to ferret out and dispense like slow poison the information that incriminates or destroys all the other characters in the work, a fate they mostly deserve. Like Esther Brandès, Ferdinand de Levis in Galsworthy's *Loyalties* (1922) alone figures out all the facts pertaining, in this case, to a significant theft. The characterization of de Levis illuminates the source of one kind of wisdom or understanding possessed by many Jews on stage. What they know derives less often from personal advantages, such as native intelligence or education, than from the collective unconscious, their historically alienated position which has allowed them to develop what one observer has aptly termed "an amazingly intuitive comprehension of the plight of the lonely, the scorned, the insulted and injured, the 'possessed,' the martyred."[1] The Jew in literature frequently comes by his insights because he is quick to recognize familiar misfortunes or inadequacies plaguing non-Jews. De Levis, for example, knows just how far an ambitious man will go to compensate for the lack of resources considered essential in the society where he chooses to belong. The Jew's own jockeying for admission to the "right" places puts him on to the thief's motives and methods for replenishing his funds.

In the case of Ferdinand de Levis and Erckmann-Chatrian's Polish Jew mentioned earlier, the Jew not only points to the damaging truth that a character must finally admit about himself, he is perceived by that character as the representative of that truth. In this role, the Jew may not only be informed because he is the outsider, he may be outside because he is informed, hence rejected as incompatible with the other character's view of himself. The prevalence of the Jew viewed as the embodiment of that which men seek to avoid recognizing is affirmed by the Jewish psychiatrist in Arthur Miller's *Incident at Vichy* (a work discussed in Chapter Eight), who observes, "Each man has his Jew; it is the other. And the Jews have their Jews."

However unwelcome the knowledge associated with the figure of the Jew as "other," it typically attaches to life's most perplexing concerns. In the plays to be considered more closely here, these include man's tolerance of truth, the challenges to loyalties provoked by the demands of citizenship and religion, and the assertion of a new-found identity.

In Sidney Kingsley's *Detective Story* (1949) and Morton Wishengrad's *The Rope Dancers* (1957), the Jew is cast as an outsider involved with unlocking a secret in other people's lives. Although in both cases the Jew's intentions are benevolent, the revelations in which they play a major role have drastic consequences.

Detective Story's Joe Feinson is an idealistic police reporter in the tradition of the American comic book and radio adventure of the 1940s ("Could be some shooting," he warns, tucking a gun into his belt, "Wait for me, baby"). A City College graduate working for a New York daily, he hangs around the squad room of the 21st Precinct. The human comedy played out at the police station appeals to Joe's fascination with tolerance as a moral principle as well as to his conviction of the relativity of justice. The station offers him proof of the workings of democracy which for him is a system that makes sure that "nobody gets too big for his britches."

Another magnet that draws Joe to the 21st is his friendship with crack detective Jim McLeod. They feud constantly, mostly in jest, though they really are opposite numbers. In a reversal of the attitudes typically associated with the Old and New Testaments, Feinson's respect for tempering justice with mercy and for "a little heart" contrasts with McLeod's passion for absolutes and unswerving standards. Fuming at one of Joe's burglary stories, McLeod demands, "Why don't you print the truth for once, [Joe]?"

Joe: Which truth? Yours, his, theirs, mine?

McLeod: *The* truth.

Joe: Oh, that one? Who would know it? If it came up and blew in your ear, who would know it?[2]

The detective's inability to relax his rigid principles wreaks havoc with his personal life when he stumbles upon a truth he cannot ignore or accept. Before he met his wife, she had had an abortion. Mary had never been able to tell Jim about it because she sensed, correctly, that his adoration of her was based on an idealization that equated perfection with purity and left no room for failures. McLeod is governed by his incapacity to settle for less than a paragon of virtue and his disdain for any kind of softness. In an effort to broaden Jim's perspectives and help him see his crisis in clearer focus, Feinson discloses that he has known and worshipped Mary for years:

I met Mary years before you did. The spring of '41—I was on the Newark *Star*. She didn't remember me. I never forgot her, though. It's one of those faces you don't forget. She's one in a million, your Mary. . . . She could have had anything. She chose you instead. Why? What'd you have to offer her? Buttons!—These crazy hours, this crazy life? She loves you. You don't know how lucky you are. I know. I'm little and ugly—and because I'm a lover of beauty, I'm going to live and die alone. But you? . . . The jewel was placed in your hands. Don't throw it away. You'll never get it back again. (pp. 131–32)

The subdued and enlightened detective's attempts to effect a reconciliation with his wife come too late. Obsessed by his view of things as black or white, intolerant of any degree of deviation from his impossible standards, McLeod has already demonstrated a pitiless need for vengeance that horrifies Mary. She leaves him. Although he is not likely to derive any satisfaction from it, Joe Feinson proved his point: "If [truth] came up and blew in your ear, who would know it?" While Feinson's truth—human fallibility, the redeeming value of tolerance and humility, the relativity of justice—fails to save McLeod's marriage, it does open the detective up to more humane possibilities within himself and to the imperative to cultivate them.

A comparable result is effected in Wishengrad's play, again through the discernment of the Jew who views a perturbation from his marginal position. One of the principal rope dancers to which the play's title refers is a neurotic eleven-year-old named Lizzie Hyland. The only child of a young Irish couple who can neither live together nor stay apart, Lizzie is kept home by her high-principled mother Margaret on the pretense that she is too sickly to go to school. Each time a truant officer catches up with them, they change address, a maneuver Margaret also uses to throw her ne'er-do-well but thoroughly charming husband James off their trail.

Jumping rope is one of the rare components of normal childhood which Lizzie is allowed. Even her style of dress is unique. She wears only white dresses, with a large pocket into which she frequently thrusts her mittened left hand with its six fingers. The child's disfigurement, slight as it is, obsesses her mother. She regards it as "the finger of God's wrath," His punishment for the circumstances in which Lizzie was conceived. It is the extra finger more than Lizzie's consitutional frailty which keeps her out of school. Similarly, it is the guilt the finger represents, more than James's irresponsibility that alienates the Hylands.

A surprise visit from James, eager to prove that Margaret's latest move cannot keep him from his daughter, and the subsequent arrival of yet another truant officer provide more excitement than the little girl's nervous system can endure. She suffers a first attack of Saint Vitus' Dance. Over Margaret's objections, a doctor is summoned. Lizzie is terrified. Confused by Dr. Jacobson's gentleness and his calm acceptance of her deformity, she runs "weeping with hopelessness" to James:

Lizzie:	Pa, make him understand that my name is Elizabeth Pamela Ursula Hyland and I have six fingers.
Jacobson:	My name is Isaac Jacobson. I am a Jew.
Margaret (whispering it):	No, Dr. Jacobson, not the same thing.
James:	We have kept her covered for eleven years.
Jacobson:	What a waste of life! We all wear a glove over something. . . . It's hard for us to come into the presence of another and stand naked. Elizabeth, you have nothing to be ashamed of.
Margaret:	Evil is on her hand.
Jacobson:	Evil is in the mind.[3]

This exchange, followed by Lizzie's second seizure, convinces Jacobson that her malady results from sheer horror on the superfluous finger. He prevails upon the Hylands to let him perform then and there the simple surgery to remove it, the child already being deeply anesthetized to control her convulsions.

Dr. Jacobson's response to the situation bespeaks the perceptivity of the sensitive outsider. However, his forthright action bears consequences far different from those he must have anticipated. For while the compassionate Jew penetrates the source of Lizzie's fear that "makes her mind so afraid, her body tries to run away," he does not realize how accurately he simultaneously diagnoses the basis of Margaret's feelings about James. The removal of the accusatory finger wrests from Margaret the confession that she had seen Lizzie's phallic defect pointed at her, a reprimand not of James, who had been drunk at the time of Lizzie's conception, but of Margaret, for her enjoyment of sex. Because she has been unable to freeze James out of her life, she now tries to repel him, as she revolts herself, by flaunting her unabated desire for him. His gentle refusal of that tactic opens Margaret's eyes. "You are such an innocent in your sin and I am such a whore in my virtue," she realizes.

Margaret and James reach a fresh understanding of one another only seconds before Lizzie's death is discovered by a stunned Dr. Jacobson. From her newly found grasp of reality, Margaret finds the strength to assume responsibility for having deformed Lizzie so severely that she was unfit to live a normal life. If the child's death makes any sense, it is as the necessary condition to a reconciliation between her parents and to their determination to adopt a more pragmatic view of their marriage. In a complete inversion of the stock image of the Jew with the knife, Wishengrad's play presents the Jew as the sympathetic stranger who comes forth to practice a science which prepares the way for conscience.

Sometimes the business of the Jew as "other" is not to open vistas and possibilities to others, but to occupy a perspective which he then invites them to share. Gabriel Marcel's *Rome Is No Longer in Rome* (*Rome n'est plus dans Rome*, 1951) treats a theme dear to this playwright and, historically, to many of his countrymen, namely, the kind of allegiance Frenchmen owe to France. At the center of Marcel's work is a prominent Parisian writer, Pascal Laumière. He has published anti-Communist sentiments which, now that the Party has gained power in France, put him in danger of reprisals. Indeed, he has already received anonymous warning letters. Yet he is not ready to cede to his wife Renée's wishes that they seek refuge in Brazil. Their vigorous disputes over immigrating to South America arouse Renée to a display of uncommon determination which puzzles Pascal. His query about its genesis leads to the following exchange, with its reference to an unseen character whose sole function is to foreshadow the role of the Jew in this play as the keeper of patriotic faith. Renée explains to her husband that it is precisely *his* intensified resolution that has heightened her own, then turns his question back to him:

> Renée: My conviction comes from you. I speak with your voice, a voice that comes from the deepest part of you. . . . (A silence. Then, in a changed tone) Indeed, how do you explain your faithful soul, your unusual expression? Where do they come from?
>
> Pascal: (after hesitating) A schoolmate I recently came across again. A Jew.[4]

Pascal Laumière's difficulties with both the prospects and the actuality of expatriation are given their fullest exposition in the long discussions he has with his wife's half-sister, Esther Peyrolle. Though Esther and Renée, daughters of the same father, were not close as girls, a rapprochement has taken place since the war. Esther, having adopted the religion of her Jewish mother, suffered cruelly. Because her husband was deported, she came to rely heavily on Pascal in raising her son Marc-André, the more so after her brother Robert's affiliation with Communism led to a rupture between him and Esther. Pascal's attachment to his sister-in-law is easily understood. They are spiritually and intellectually in tune. Whereas Renée is so convinced that the move to Brazil is the logical solution that she cannot comprehend her husband's scruples, Esther thoroughly appreciates his reluctance to leave the France he loves and wants to serve. So dependent does Laumière become upon Esther and Marc-André that finally he refuses to leave for South America without them.

The company of sister-in-law and nephew turns out to be the only solace for Pascal in San Felipe. To his intense gratification, Marc-André blossoms from the first. Laumière's daily discussions with Esther have never been more fortifying. But he shortly runs afoul of the clerical watchdogs of morality and political opinion whose approbation he needs to assure his university post; then he offends the spurious rectitude of his South American hosts. Already remorseful over what he now recognizes as an imprudent and irreversible move, Pascal suffers further pangs of conscience because he is committed to broadcast to France messages of assurance that French patriotism remains energizing no matter where it is transplanted.

Meantime, Esther receives word that her brother Robert is a victim of political assassination and plans to return to France to take care of his young son. The mission represents the opportunity she has been longing for. Marc-André is already assured of excellent prospects as a citizen of the New World, but Esther sees her own life as an émigrée lacking in purpose and moral value. She belongs to France. Once Pascal had declared that Esther was the only person in the world who could sway his thinking. Now her course of action in returning to their homeland emboldens him to correct whatever misinterpretations his leaving it may have stimulated. Courageously, he begins his broadcast by denouncing himself as a deserter. Contradicting the sentiment Corneille put into the mouth of Sertorius, "Rome is no longer in Rome, it is wherever I am," Laumière asserts, "The illusion that one can take his homeland with him can only be born of pride and the wildest presumption" (p. 148). As he pleads earnestly with his countrymen and, simultaneously, with himself to muster fortitude for whatever menaces threaten, Pascal is felled by a heart attack.

While drawing on Esther as the "other," both as a Jew and in terms of her status in the Laumière household, Marcel's play works with what might seem the anomaly of the Jew setting an example of patriotism for the well-established Parisian. Ironically, the Cornelian "illusion" that one can take his country wherever he goes, the position Laumière ultimately rejects with strength borrowed from Esther, is precisely the one that has sustained the Jewish people through centuries of wandering. But Esther is not a homeless Jew. She is a French Jew, and that is a special identity. Esther serves as spokesmen for two centuries of French Jews who have never taken for granted the emancipation and freedom offered by their country. While Jews in

France may be far from unanimous in the primacy of their loyalty within the famous "double allegiance"—do they consider themselves French first and Jewish after, or the other way around?—they rarely underestimate the heritage of French civilization and culture. As a recent study indicates, "Jews in France have a better opinion of France than other Frenchmen."[5] Marcel's play illustrates this phenomenon by transposing the role of the "other." Esther Peyrolle, the most steadfast in her loyalty to the national patrimony, becomes the "insider" whose values inspire her gentile compatriot.

Esther Peyrolle could be related to Barney Greenwald, the Navy lieutenant and lawyer who wins his case in Herman Wouk's *The Caine Mutiny Court-Martial* (1954). Barney shares Esther's patriotism completely. To the degree that each persona typifies the attitudes of his respective countrymen, a comparison of them suggests a substantial cultural difference. Esther is more French than Barney is American. One can never be surprised when a Frenchwoman announces her love of country, for French pride in France is part of the national character that finds frequent and natural utterance. There is no real American equivalent. With the possible exception of Kate Smith,[6] an American would be embarassed to proclaim his love of country as joyfully and ingenuously as a Maurice Chevalier, a Charles Trenet, or a Georges Moustaki.

While doubtless as chauvinistic as the French, Americans salute the United States differently, sometimes by insisting on the superiority of national institutions. One of these that rarely comes in for praise, however, particularly among well-educated Americans, is the armed forces. Hence it is surprising to hear Barney Greenwald, a Georgetown Law School graduate and, in civilian life, a successful Washington attorney, confess to his client that he's not looking forward "to twisting the Navy's arm one bit," not because he is scared, but because he is respectful. Barney's deference has less to do with his being American than with his being a Jew and thereby endowed with a point of view apparent to no one else in the matter.

Greenwald conducts a clever defense of his client Maryk, brought to court-martial for having seized control of the mine sweeper *Caine* because he considered its commanding officer Queeg psychologically incapacitated. In order to clear Maryk, Greenwald has to show that Queeg, a career officer, is indeed a disturbed, disoriented man. The demonstration succeeds dramatically, winning Maryk's release and for Barney, the respect of the court. However, the lawyer cannot exult in his victory. Instead, he feels sullied by it. The only way he could defend his client was to destroy Commander Queeg. As richly as Old

Yellowstain, as his men dubbed him, may have deserved what happened to him, Greenwald sees him as far more worthy than the others do. He explains to the celebrants at Maryk's post-hearing party:

> . . . the reason I'd make Old Yellowstain a hero is on account of my mother, little gray-headed Jewish lady, fat. Well, sure you guys all have mothers, but they wouldn't be in the same bad shape mine would if we'd of lost this war. See, the Germans aren't kidding about the Jews. They're cooking us down to soap over there. . . . So, when all hell broke loose and the Germans started running out of soap and figured, well, time to come over and melt down old Mrs. Greenwald, who's gonna stop 'em? Not her boy Barney. Can't stop a Nazi with a lawbook. So, I dropped the lawbooks, and ran to learn how to fly. Stout fellow. Meantime, and it took a year and a half before I was any good, who was keeping Mama out of the soap dish? . . . Old Yellowstain, maybe? Well yes, even poor sad Queeg. . . . a lot of them sharper boys than any of us, don't kid yourself, you can't be good in the Army or Navy unless you're goddam good. Though maybe not up on Proust, 'n' *Finnegan's Wake,* 'n' all.[7]

Like Sgt. Nathan Marx in Philip Roth's "Defender of the Faith," who is "a veteran of the European theatre and consequently will take no shit," Barney Greenwald understands that the American uniform makes special demands on the American Jew who wears it, particularly in a world infected by Hitlerism.

The calling into question of a loyalty at least as deep-rooted as patriotism animates plays about intermarriage. As the fictional cases of Esther Peyrolle and Barney Greenwald indicate, it is possible to meet the demands of being devoted simultaneously to religion and to country. However, the hyphenating of two cultural identities in intermarriage almost inevitably ends in compromise of one or both. A thriving phenomenon in our day, intermarriage churns up dilemmas of ethics and identity. And, where Jews are involved, yet another version of the "other." For the obverse of the proposition that "Jew" is a name other people give to that which is not like them, is that Jew is the name Jews use for what is uniquely theirs. The basic connotation of "otherness" still obtains, of course, and with no less emotional overtones.

In Yvonne Mitchell's *The Same Sky* (1952), a play from the Nottingham Repertory Company, Jewish characters confronted with a mixed marriage come into a new wisdom. They share their insights with the very personae who, at the beginning of the play, consider the Jews the "others" and are regarded by them in exactly the same way.

The Same Sky opens with a fist fight, a repeating motif. It involves two thirteen-year-olds, George Smith and Manny Brodsky, or, as they refer to one another, the "goddam Goy" and the "dirty Jew." Manny cautions his sister who tries to break up a scuffle, "Don't touch him, Esther, he's not one of Us." George counters, "How would you like to have dirty Jews sitting next to you in class?"[8] In an animosity no less bitter than that which raged between Montagues and Capulets, George's brother Jeff and Manny's sister Esther have fallen in love. Their families' reactions are predictable. Momma Brodsky argues:

> That is what your children would be, Esther; between two [races], belonging nowhere. And when you first quarrel, hm? Maybe about the children, maybe about nothing big, maybe because from a cheese-cake or a button, what do you think the first thing your Goy will say to you? He'll call you "dirty Jewess," you wait. And every time you don't agree, it will be in his mind because you are Yiddisher. Even if he don't say from such things he will think them. (p. 264)

If Mrs. Brodsky is more articulate in her objections, Mrs. Smith nonetheless makes herself unmistakably understood. "My Mum says she won't have nothing more to do with Jeff if he marries you," George reports to Esther. When Esther suggests to Jeff that she might placate his mother by "changing the name" of her religion, Jeff sensibly responds, "Christian and Jew, they mean more than names".

Esther: To her? What more then, if it's not religion?

Jeff: I don't know. It's deep but I don't know what it is. . . .

Esther: She makes you feel guilty, loving me, I know.

Jeff: No, not guilty . . .

Esther: No, not guilty, something near it though. I feel it with Momma and Poppa. Guilty of not feeling guilty when they think I am . . . (p. 260)

The playwright makes us see that the biases so carefully cultivated by the Smiths and the Brodskys are meaningless to the young couple who only want to marry before Jeff's unit ships out. Their defiance asks to be viewed in the context of the relaxation of accepted values and moral principles wrought by emergency situations. It is unlikely that a girl still living with her close-knit, orthodox Jewish family would otherwise speak so lightly of "changing the name" of her religion. Similarly, Jeff's demonstrated integrity is sorely challenged when they discover that his embarkation leave will expire before their marriage license can be issued.

Fortunately, Yvonne Mitchell is up to more than demonstrating the predicament of a couple alienated from both family homes who spend a premature honeymoon in a room over a shop, or the futility of regret when, months later, the dreaded War Office telegram arrives as Esther is leaving for the maternity ward. Were the dramatist interested in the melodramatic for its own sake, she would not probe so sensitively the crisis provoked in the conscience of the parents. The Brodskys and Mrs. Smith learn their responsibility in a situation that can be resolved neither by teenagers' stubbornly perpetuating learned hatreds in street brawls nor by young adults throwing their moral code to the winds. They make a genuine effort to root out the sources of their prejudiced thinking.

Notably, the initial and most intensive search is made by Poppa Brodsky who was implacable in his objections to the marriage which to him represented Esther's turning her back on God. Poppa allowed Esther to live at home after Jeff went to the front, but refused to speak to her. As Esther struggles for her life after a difficult childbirth, Poppa reflects:

> I believe in the belief of my fathers. The chosen people. God asks my people to multiply among themselves, not to marry with people who worship strange gods, but only Him. But in the night when the heart is breaking I hear Esther's voice telling me from far back, "Isn't a good man a good man no matter if his parents was chosen or not?" and when I let myself listen to the voice of mine child, I tremble in front of God, because He forbids me to listen. Yes, our God is a jealous God. He will take mine Esther from me the night I first listen to her. I am weak, and I say to God, "I want to open mine heart to a baby whose father is not Your chosen, and in mine weakness I will do it." And I pray to God to forgive me, because I can do no other. (p. 308)

Brodsky laments his lack of strength to emulate Abraham who ignored Isaac's pleas and listened to God instead. For the first time in his life, he finds the will of God inscrutable by contrast to the clear, irresistible demands of his own nature. When Momma brings the news that Esther is out of danger, Mr. Brodsky's first thought is to send word to Mrs. Smith. She responds by sending George to ask permission for her to visit the Brodskys soon. "Tomorrow," insists Poppa.

The Same Sky is noteworthy because it makes room in a familiar dramatic situation for parents to reassess how their principles impinge upon the lives of their children in a vastly changing society. It seems especially important that the inquiry into tolerance of "renegades" and "outsiders" alike is seen here from the point of view of the Jew who is, in this play, both outcast and ostracizer. The double focus lends Mr. Brodsky's re-evaluation a broader relevance, underlined by Mrs. Smith's response. Furthermore, Brodsky's redefined sense of responsibility transcends his family's immediate situation to address larger concerns posed by the play's historical moment. "What do we do for our children when they live?" he asks himself. "We make a mess. Are we going to make a mess with the new life, with the baby?" (p. 312).

The interrogative mode is entirely fitting here, for Brodsky's plea for enlightenment acknowledges the formidable challenge to traditional creeds for answers to problematic contemporary issues, of which intermarriage is a capital instance. For Judaism, the matter is, of course, critical. At stake is survival. *The Same Sky* makes a convincing case for compassion and open-mindedness, but stops short of answering Poppa's question, "Are we going to make a mess with the new life?" The question really amounts to asking the Jew to what degree he can in good conscience continue to insist upon his "otherness."

A somewhat similar set of conditions in Paddy Chayefsky's *Middle of the Night* (1956) elicits a different set of questions and a more emphatic answer. In this work, Jews and gentiles also perceive one another as threats to long-established values. While differences in religion kindle controversy, a more acute issue is the June-and-January complexion of the romance.

The husband that gorgeous Betty Preiss walks out on in *Middle of the Night* is in almost every way the opposite number of the boss with whom she is about to fall in love. Despite what her mother has told her, there must be more to marriage than sex, Betty unexpectedly finds herself telling her employer. Manufacturer Jerry Kingsley has stopped by to pick up some sales slips Betty hadn't brought to work. His observation, "You seem very distraught. Is there something I can do?" unleashes the torrent of Betty's troubles. As she pours her heart out, one can guess at the contrast between the fifty-three-year-old widower who sits for several hours, listening, and Betty's husband who associates gentleness with weakness, and so asserts his masculinity by being tough.

The warmth of his sympathy for a beautiful, overwrought employee is the last thing that Kingsley anticipated feeling. A few hours earlier, he's been persuading his sister Evelyn and his daughter Lillian that he was going through change of life. Nevertheless, Jerry comes alive in the romance that blossoms between him and Betty. He tells the disapproving Evelyn, "It's important to me that a young girl finds me attractive. . . . It's been a long time since anybody needed me. My kids are all grown up, with children of their own. I'm a man who has to give of himself."[9] And to his possessive and scandalized daughter, who is about Betty's age, "All right, so who's perfect? Apparently I'm attracted to childish women." Betty represents a challenge to Lillian and Evelyn; she upsets a comfortable image they have of Jerry and poses a rivalry where they cannot hope to compete. They advance some valid objections to the marriage, but know their cause is lost when Evelyn's trump card, the imperative of the "other," ("Is she Jewish?") is dismissed by Jerry's, "Does that matter in this day and age?"

Kingsley's Jewishness does matter very much to Betty's mother. Appearances count heavily for Mrs. Mueller. Though she forewarns a curious neighbor who drops by to see Betty's boyfriend for herself, "He's a Jewish man, you know," she is embarrassed by her certainty that the whole neighborhood is buzzing about Betty's "sugar daddy." Her objections to Jerry are also fueled by her own experiences. A Catholic, Mrs. Mueller refused her husband a divorce sixteen years earlier. Her façade of self-righteousness does not quite cover the resentment she harbors at having had to raise two daughters alone despite her lack of real affection for them. Betty's mother reveals her basic objection to Jerry as an outrage to her in every way when she declares that she's not going to let Betty marry "a Jewish man like that."

It is telling that Mrs. Mueller labels "Jewish" all the negative feelings stirred by the prospect of her daughter's remarriage to a gentle, well-off man "old enough to be [her] father." Her displaced protest finds its parallels in the demurring of the other women in Kingsley's life. His maiden sister Evelyn, who moved in with Jerry after his wife died, now thinks of herself as her late sister-in-law's replacement. Lillian remarks to her husband, "She [Evelyn] resents me a great deal. Every time my father and I sit down for one of our talks, she always finds some way of breaking in. She resents any woman my father likes. It's frankly a little incest, that's what it is" (p. 92). Lillian is not quite so perceptive about her own feelings for her father which a contrived buddy attitude ("How's your sex life, Pa?") does not really cloak.

The regard of all these women for Jerry and his responses to them contribute largely to characterizing him. The nonchalance which marks his attitude toward marrying outside his faith contrasts with the figure he cuts, for Kingsley is a typical middle-aged Jewish widower. He has all the assets and liabilities, including the hovering bevy of designing Jewish widows. He lives by the Jewish ethics of brotherhood and tsedakah,* giving freely of himself in his genuine concern with other people's welfare and emotional needs. That is how he got involved with Betty in the first place.

*Tsedakah is a biblical term applied generally to helping others and specifically to lightening the burden of the needy.

Jerry and Betty never discuss the differences in religion which loom so important to everyone else. Paradoxically, that fact works to enhance Jerry's cultural identity and to demonstrate the perception referred to here as the wisdom of the Jew. Falling in love with Betty presents him an opportunity he could no more have foreseen than he could have, before Betty, imagined himself married to a gentile. In terms of Kingsley's life, the fortunate encounter comes not in the middle of the night, but at sunset. He recognizes it for what it is, a turning point in his life, and Betty's. At fifty-three, Jerry is not ready to diffuse his warmth into vicarious emotional relationships. He is thrilled with the chance to respond virilely to his tenderness and need for a woman. Had that woman been one of Evelyn's hopeful friends, Jerry would not know the keen joy of loving "like a schoolboy" with an ebullience that sends him walking forty blocks in the snow. Were Betty not so young and so dependent upon him, perhaps he would not be so painfully lucid about the chance he is taking, "I'm afraid of myself. At my age, you become afraid of things. . . . I don't know what I'll be like in five years, Betty. I don't want a five year marriage" (pp. 80–81). However, precisely because Jerry's Judaism has instilled in him a reverence for life and the drive to make the most of it, he decides, "Even a few years of happiness you don't throw away."

If Jerry Kingsley's decision invites criticism or ridicule, it also leaves him open to comparison with Arthur Miller's Gregory Solomon, another character from whose point of view life is worth taking big risks for, in the middle of the night, or any time at all. The courage to live according to that kind of wisdom constitutes a very special "otherness" indeed.

A final love story puts on stage an extraordinarily fully developed image of the Jew as other. As in *Middle of the Night*, the couple whose affair supplies the plot of William Gibson's *Two for the Seesaw* (1959) are drawn together by basic differences, one of which is their cultural backgrounds. In *Seesaw* too, the married member of the pair, here the man, is attracted to the very antithesis of his spouse. Jerry Ryan deliberately leaves behind in Nebraska a patrician wife named Tess who is divorcing him, a law practice, and a suburban home he owes largely to his influential father-in-law. After a month in New York, "drowning in cement," as he puts it, and in self-loathing as well, he meets Tess's opposite number.

She is an impulsive, uninhibited Bronxite who calls herself Gittel Mosca, a form of Moscowitz she hopes appropriate for a marquee. On her own since she was sixteen, Gittel has spent the last thirteen years trying to become a dancer, drifting, but mostly giving. Spontaneously, happily, Gittel gives herself away—in energy, in love, in presents, in empathy—to whoever appeals to her limitless need to give. In return, she has acquired a divorce, an ulcer which occasionally bleeds, and a lot of broken promises and I. O. U.'s she doesn't like to mention. Toughened but unrepentent, she offers Jerry the first laughs he's had in a month and a candor that opens his eyes to the first of several personal insights he will gain through knowing her.

On their first date, Gittel helps Jerry see he's always hinted for handouts—and gotten them. Indeed, Gittel's extraordinary generosity is what originally engages Jerry's interest in her. Seeing how vulnerable Gittel's liberality has made her appeals to Jerry's ego. Because he feels protective, he wants to teach this "crackpot, lovable waif" to stop disregarding her own feelings and stand up for her rights. But it is not just Gittel's refusal of the most ordinary posturing that catches Ryan off guard and delights him. She operates by a code of behavior all her own. Learning a lot about people has made her perceptive ("When it comes to men I expect the worst!"), but not prudent. She is resilient and immensely confident in her own imagination and energy. When Jerry cuts short her fantasies of careers on the stage and as a dance instructor and costume designer by observing, "None of this will ever happen," she promptly retorts, "So I'll think up something else!"[10]

Gittel's greatest and most self-destructive charm is being more honest and generous with other people than with herself. Though she never stops giving, she can't function when she is on the receiving end. Consequently, she is overwhelmed when Jerry devotes himself to nursing her back to health after her ulcer has hemorrhaged. "Nobody ever took care of me so good," she says, and who could doubt her? She never learns to take freely, however; after her recovery, at the moment when the affair is breaking up, she confesses, "Jerry, I haven't taken one happy breath since that hemorrhage. I want to get out of here and breathe" (p. 268).

Although Gittel cheerfully agrees she is a "born victim," she simply does not know how to make claims on people. That is perhaps the only lesson Jerry teaches her, even if he breaks her heart by refusing when she makes her very first claim, "Look Jerry, whyn't we just, sort of, get married and get the goddam thing over with, huh?" (p. 259). True to form, the rejected Gittel bounces back, thanks Jerry for helping her form a better opinion of herself, and resolves that she is going to find somebody "who'll take care of me who's all mine."

Jerry could never have been all Gittel's because, for reasons the play leaves open to conjecture, he cannot get free of Tess. If Jerry clings to Gittel, it is because she satisfies so many of his needs, not only for fun, sex, and warmth, but for what we have earlier called wisdom. Gittel sees Jerry's weaknesses and makes him see them as well. His propensity to ask for handouts is only the beginning. Jerry's campaign to train Gittel to make a claim on people is fired by his own desire to be needed, a desire Tess did not fulfill. Brought to the admission that she does need Jerry, Gittel, in a rare accusation, calls him to account for cultivating her dependence in order to prove something to himself and to Tess. "You shortchange people, Jerry," she charges, and he knows she is absolutely right, that he has been less than honest in his dealings with both women. That perception motivates Jerry to stand by Gittel through her recuperation. It gives him the honesty to answer her marriage proposal by confessing that he is ready to go back to Tess, who has decided she needs him. "She'll owe you more than she'll know," he says in gratitude to Gittel as they part.

Gittel is left with little more than the assurance that she has made a substantial contribution to a life from which she is excluded. That is one of several images that attaches her to the tradition of stage Jews. A *belle Juive* whose pity and compassion are demonstrated qualities, she is victimized, albeit with her own cheerful cooperation. In addition to these customary traits, Gittel incorporates the zest for life and the wisdom previously noted as frequent attributes of Jewish personae.

Gittel is an outsider in several senses: in her exclusion from Jerry's life, in her own freewheeling lifestyle, and, most important, in her lack of connections with any group or loyalty to any creed other than her own highly personalized one (her single Friday night visit to her mother for gefüllte fish notwithstanding). This last kind of "otherness" seems by far the most consequential in the characterization of Gittel and in her role in *Seesaw*. Is there a paradox in the figure of a Jew who is best defined by her freedom from affiliations? Why should Gittel Mosca be Jewish?

I addressed that question to William Gibson. His generous reply goes beyond the query, explaining one of the ways in which the Jew in our time has come to be viewed as the other by the non-Jew:

Gittel is Jewish first because she *was* Jewish—the girl the characterization began with, I mean [writes Mr. Gibson]. The character actually embodies much more than that girl, much of me, much of my mother, much of the working-class Irish girls on the maternal side of my family. All of that is hidden, the outer texture is Jewish . . . because my youth was that of a middle-class gentile boy surrounded by inhibited "correct" people who smothered me, and my emotional liberation lay with poor people and with Jews. . . . The "outcast" is a not untraditional character standing for freedom from all the social decorums of the petit bourgeoisie, see Grushenka in Karamazov, for instance, of whom Gittel is some kind of descendant. Seesaw is a play whose essential tension lies between a middle-class gent and a pseudo-lower-class girl, the one constrained and the other spontaneous, and it could not happen between two middle-class goyim; on another level, it is thus an internal dialogue between halves of myself. A generation behind my immediate family lurked a heritage of workers; . . . when in my adolescence I had to break out of our middle-class manners in order to live, it was that heritage I had to hark back to, and the Jewish revolutionaries of the thirties were the contemporaries I found it in. At the same time the image of the Jew on stage . . . was being created by the work of principally Clifford Odets, who combined Jewishness and revolution, and in his plays Jews for the first time became protagonists, even heroes.

William Gibson's perceptions bring full circle this survey of the Jew as other, and help turn the circle inside out. Like Poppa Brodsky and Jerry Kingsley, Gittel Mosca inspires others with the energetic versatility with which she greets life's challenges. As the keeper of sane perspective, Gittel's long view parallels Esther Peyrolle's and Barney Greenwald's, though her eclectic, endearing wisdom enriches other people's lives while making a muddle of her own. Along with Joe Feinson and Dr. Isaac Jacobson, she provides insights which open others' eyes to the potential within and outside themselves. In *Two for the Seesaw*, as in plays like *The Visit*, *The Boys in the Band*, and *The Old Jew*, "Jew" designates a part of the individual, with a critical difference. It is not a part he seeks to repress, isolate or repudiate. Quite the contrary. With Gittel Mosca, "Jew" becomes the name for an "otherness" within himself that a character consciously seeks to cultivate.

5

The Jew in a Jewish World

There is a certain place where dumb-waiters boom, doors slam, dishes crash; every window is a mother's mouth bidding the street shut up, go skate somewhere else, come home.

—Grace Paley

The theatre's durable repertory of Jewish roles is essentially the work of gentile cultures. Jewish images designed by and for Jews are relative newcomers. Except for some closet drama in Hebrew in the seventeenth century,[1] until the advent of the Yiddish theatre, Jewish dramatic activity was confined to merrymaking at weddings and joyful holidays and to Purim celebrations. The first modern Yiddish play was produced just a little over a hundred years ago. The Hebrew theatre came into being only with the twentieth century.

Jewish culture traditionally stigmatized theatrical activity. With the significant exception of the Purim plays, which evolved in the sixteenth century out of the revelries appropriate to the celebration of the holiday, "spectacles and plays were considered un-Jewish at other times of the year."[2] The stage provoked objections because of the idolatry and immoral acts associated with it, and because of Judaism's injunctions against a female voice being heard publicly and men impersonating women by donning their apparel. After the destruction of the Temple in 70 C. E., even music came to be considered unseemly, if not profane. Israel Abrahams points out that none of the Talmudic rabbis were proficient musicians, and it remained for talented rabbis and chazans to redeem much later the dramatic power of the human voice.[3] The spirit of Jewish religious bias—comparable to that of the Puritans who closed London playhouses in the mid-seventeenth century—animates this first-century prayer uttered by the orthodox at least until the end of the last century: "I thank Thee, my Lord, that I spend my time in the temples of prayer instead of in the theatres."[4]

These prejudices were assailed in the eighteenth century by the Haskalah, a movement toward enlightenment aimed at cosmopolitanizing Jews by promoting the study of the arts, sciences, foreign languages and literatures, and the revival of Hebrew literature. At first the Haskalites composed highly literate plays in Hebrew for a reading public. Then, at the end of the eighteenth century, Isaac Eichel, an associate of the Haskalah philosopher and pioneer, Moses Mendelssohn, wrote the first modern Yiddish comedy. It was entitled *Reb Henoch*, and its characters spoke Yiddish, German, French or English, according to their level of learning! While *Reb Henoch* was also meant to be read rather than staged, it represents the first Jewish play to deal with the everyday life of the people.[5]

The Haskalah challenged orthodox practices of every kind, particularly those by which education had been narrowed to the study of the Talmud. Like Hassidism, the contemporary religious and social movement which it opposed in so many other ways, the Haskalah promoted the ordinary man and his language. To reach the greatest number of their co-religionists, Haskalah authors adopted the mother tongue of the masses, Yiddish. It was in Yiddish that the pioneers of Jewish drama—Solomon Ettinger, Israel Aksenfeld, Abraham Ber Gottlober—wrote their plays, and in Yiddish that the wandering Broder singers acted out the songs that whetted appetites for staged productions. In a wine cellar in Jassy, Roumania, in 1876, Abraham Goldfaden and two Broder singers met the demand. Goldfaden produced the first staged Yiddish play by adding as continuity to the songs plot and dialogue improvised in the manner of *commedia dell'arte*. In light of subsequent extensive Jewish involvement in all areas of vaudeville and musical comedy, it seems entirely fitting that this first production should be recognizably an ancestor of those genres.

Fired by the enthusiasm of Goldfaden and his imitators, the Yiddish theatre thrived in East European cities and *shtetlach* (villages). When Jews were forced to migrate westward, major actors and writers figured among the emigrants. They brought with them to the West the aspirations of a new theatre, prepared and eager to plunge into the currents of theatrical innovations of the late nineteenth and early twentieth centuries.

The fascinating history of the Yiddish theatre has been detailed in a number of studies.[6] Since by the turn of the century, it was in New York with its dense Jewish population that the Yiddish theatre flourished (more than two million Jews came to the United States between 1881 and 1914, three-quarters of them living for a while at least on the lower East Side), a brief consideration of the New York scene may serve to indicate the purview of the Yiddish theatre and to suggest its place in modern drama.

The most prominent Jewish theatre in New York was Maurice Schwartz's Yiddish Art Theatre, founded in 1918 and disbanded in 1950. Its principles echoed the influence of Antoine, Reinhardt, Dublin's Abbey Theatre and the Moscow Art Theatre and aligned it with its American cousins, the Washington Square and Provincetown Players. Opposed to the star system, shoddy productions of cheap plays and the primacy of the box office, it set high standards for ensemble acting and established a repertory system and a studio to train young talent. It sought to incorporate the innovations of Craig and Meyerhold to counteract the "tawdry primitiveness" of the early Yiddish stage. In practice, the Yiddish Art Theatre apparently was not always able to meet its own criteria for literary or artistic success. In 1946, Brooks Atkinson characterized Schwartz's enterprise this way: "He is traditional theatre: story, costumes, beards, lots of scenery, music and acting. He is not afraid of theatre—animation and latitude, wide gestures and excitement—and you always know you are not in a library."[7]

Two noncommercial amateur theatres complemented the Yiddish Art Theatre and Jacob Ben-Ami's serious but short-lived Jewish Art Theatre (1919–1920). Artef, active from 1928 to 1937, served as the collective voice of workers, devoting itself to "spreading radical politics through expressionist productions."[8] One of Artef's directors was Benno Schneider, who brought the influence of Stanislavsky and Vahktangov from the Habimah (Moscow's Hebrew Theatre) to the New York players who, unfortunately, were not always equipped to benefit from it. Many states emerged from the myriad self-help and fraternal associations. By far the most successful was Die Freie Yiddishe Folksbiene (The Free Yiddish Folk Theatre). Established in 1915, it has earned the distinction of being "the only theatre in America with an uninterrupted record of production"[9] for over sixty years.

Three kinds of plays were produced by these dissimilar Yiddish theatres. The disclaimers of their spokesmen notwithstanding, their doors were not closed to a certain amount of *shund* (crude melodrama, or, as Nahma Sandrow describes it, theatre that "feeds the human appetites for amusement, excitement, escape, affirmation"[10]) which had great mass appeal. With an eye to the box office, Maurice Schwartz opened his Irving Place Theatre with a piece by popular playwright Solomon Libin. Libin's works were frequently realistic depictions of the sweatshop tenement existence of greenhorns in New York. They exemplify one kind of production that kept the customers coming.

By contrast, translations and adaptations of masterpieces of world drama catered to the tastes of more cultivated immigrants, particularly Russians who had frequented the Moscow Art Theatre. Jacob

Adler earned renown as Lear, Maurice Schwartz as Othello, and both of them as Shylock. Ben-Ami's literary Wednesdays and Boris Tomashevsky's literary Thursdays, among others, featured productions of the same plays that electrified audiences of the free theatres in European capitals, works by Ibsen, Strindberg, Gorki, Björnson, Brieux, Shaw, Wilde, Schiller and Tolstoy. *Uncle Vanya* was done by the Yiddish Art Theatre in 1922, a year before the touring Moscow Art Theatre "introduced" Chekhov to America. Gogol's *The Inspector General* and Andreyev's *Seven Who Were Hanged* likewise had their American premières on Schwartz's stage.[11]

However, the crowning glory of the Yiddish theatre was to attain a goal common to all the literary theatres of the late nineteenth and early twentieth centuries, the fostering of native talent. The stages of New York produced works whose considerable merit had already been recognized in Europe by prominent companies of the burgeoning Yiddish theatre, like the Kaminsky, the Hirshbein and the Vilna troupes and Vikt, the Warsaw Yiddish Art Theatre. Playwrights included Jacob Gordin, who was frequently inspired by classics of world literature; David Pinski, whose plays were also translated and produced by Reinhardt in Berlin, the Habimah in Moscow and the Theatre Guild in New York; Sholom Asch, whose *God of Vengeance* in any language provoked a *succès de scandale* and, of course, Peretz Hirshbein, Isaac Loeb Peretz, S. Anski, and Sholom Aleichem. American productions of plays by these men sparked both their creativity and that of younger dramatists like Fishel Bimko, H. Leivick and Gotesfeld. Moreover, the popular reception and critical acclaim that greeted these productions confirmed the natural affinity between the Yiddish theatre and plays that emphasize the daily life, draw on the legends, speak the language and sing the melodies of the Jewish people. Despite the Yiddish theatre's leanings toward the aims and innovations of the great contemporary European theorists, "neither Stanislavsky's realism nor Reinhardt's modernism supplied the complete answer" to Jewish search for identity in the theatre.[12] The Yiddish stage was most successful when it heeded J. M. Synge's dictum that "literature is essentially national and writers should draw from the spirit of their race."[13]

Perhaps it is just that spirit, which includes the characteristic ability of the Jewish people to survive, that revitalized interest in all things Yiddish after the second World War when, objectively speaking, the subject might have been considered extinct. In spite of the disappearance of the *shtetlach*, the annihilation of the ghettos, the shift of emphasis from Yiddish to Hebrew effected by the establishment of the State of Israel, and the widespread casualness towards things

Jewish on the part of so many Jews in the West, or maybe because of these factors, Yiddish has enjoyed renewed popularity since the 1960's. Discussing the renaissance in the preface to the 1972 edition of *The Great Jewish Plays*, editor and translator Joseph Landis observes that the current general ethnic revival coincides with the contemporary search for a simple, more genuine world and for "moral attitudes in a troubled time."[14] It is interesting to see that in America, *Yiddishkeit* (Jewish culture) holds forth the same strength and solace for the kin of those perhaps too integrated into the mainstream as it did for their forebears who, two or three generations ago, felt estranged from it.

Although the voice of the Yiddish theatre is still vigorous, it can be appreciated today only by theatregoers who grew up in Yiddish-speaking homes or who have taken the trouble to learn the language. Fortunately, the influence of Yiddish theatre leaps linguistic barriers. Examples of that influence are delightfully apparent on the post-1945 stage. Indeed, it is easier to recognize the imprints than to characterize the Yiddish theatre itself for it is a richly heterogeneous phenomenon, ill-served by generalizations. Yiddish theatre, like the language it speaks, is, to borrow Landa's term for the latter, "voraciously assimilative." Despite its late emergence on the world stage, it arrived in time to draw inspiration from the creative revolution that began to energize the theatre at the end of the last century. The Yiddish stage has made a distinguished contribution in return. In addition to the playwrights and actors it nourished and the new images of Jews it projected, its spirit and tone, its themes and subject, and the very special universe it portrayed have enriched the general domain of theatre.

The spirit of the Yiddish theatre is that creative vitality that bubbled out of London's East End and New York's lower East Side, to name only two of its headquarters, to animate whatever stage and stage personnel it touched. One could readily compile a catalogue of the eminent producers, directors, actors and writers those theatrical education and artistic standards were early shaped by the Yiddish stage. Let Harold Clurman's testimony stand as representative:

> Between the ages of six and twelve [Clurman was born in 1901] I had attended the theatres of the East Side where my father practiced medicine. In a way, this theatrical experience was fortunate, since the Yiddish Theatre, as Lincoln Steffens, Norman Hapgood, and other observers of the period pointed out, "was about the best in New York at that time both in stuff and in acting." The "stuff" was frequently Shakespeare, Tolstoy, Andreyev, or charming folk operettas and plays modeled after original works by Sudermann, Hauptmann and other contemporary Europeans. The actors were among the best I have ever seen in many years of playgoing all over the world.[15]

The unmistakable tone of the Yiddish theatre is also more easily and accurately recognized than described. It is a web of paradoxes: simultaneously sentimental and humorous, upright and sensational, naïve and proud, realistic and figurative. It tugs unashamed at the heartstrings while challenging the intellect to confirm its reflections on human experience. It has an astonishing plasticity that allows it to encompass and harmonize the most disparate elements into what can only be called a mixed tone. M. J. Landa recounts an anecdote illustrative of the Yiddish theatre's mixed tone. Recording how one of the many difficulties encountered by the Yiddish theatre in London was obtaining appropriate playhouses, properties and costumes, Landa writes:

> I remember a hall where evidently the sole outdoor scene was a back-cloth representing Windsor Castle. It was a much overworked edifice. I have seen that Castle, under a ruddy glare, shamelessly trying to pass itself off as the destroyed Temple of Jerusalem. It has made me regret its inhospitality to the Jews wandering in the wilderness who included it in their tortuous route, and its windows have gazed stonily on the Siberian exiles escorted by British guardsmen fluent in Russian oaths. Those exiles I remember with especial joy. One, of course, had fallen in the snow, unable to withstand any longer the miseries of the march. "I am dying of thirst," he cried; and the funny man, who had been staring at the audience and had noted its tear-bedimmed eyes, put all in a better humor by knocking at the gate of Windsor Castle and asking for water![16]

Yet another dimension of the mingling of elements that gives Yiddish theatre its characteristic tone appears in the blending of words, melody, and frequently, dance in a manner which reflects "the spirit of the race." Bernard Kops, one of the dramatists whose work will be considered presently, comments on the songs in *The Hamlet of Stepney Green:*

> There are songs in the play and these are an integral part of it; no character steps forward out of the action. When I wrote this play in 1956 I was told that I had written it in the form of traditional Yiddish Theatre. These songs came about because I remembered how my mother would suddenly burst out singing. How when words or emotions got too much for her she expressed herself in song. In quite a few of my plays, songs are placed throughout the action; underlining or summing up a certain point.[17]

Since the Yiddish theatre draws its subjects from an old, rich heritage, it is hardly surprising that it has furnished stories and themes to challenge the imagination of modern dramatists. Probably the most illustrious example is Anski's *The Dybbuk,* a near-perfect blend of legend, parable, mysticism and realism. *The Dybbuk*, whose own dramatic value remains unattenuated, has inspired in our day a number of original works from the Jerome Robbins-Leonard Bernstein ballet to Bruce Myers' ingenious adaptation, *A Dybbuk for Two People*, written in 1979 for the first Yiddish festival in Paris, to the germ of Michael Hastings' plot in *Yes and After*. The enormous debt Paddy Cheyefsky's *The Tenth Man* owes to *The Dybbuk* will be examined in the pages that follow. It is worth noting a special contribution of the Yiddish theatre to the Chayefsky work. The cast of its New York première in 1959 included veteran actor Jacob Ben-Ami and Risa Schwartz, daughter of the founder of the Yiddish Art Theatre.

Original works like *The Dybbuk* illustrate one way in which the Yiddish theatre has inspired the subject matter of more modern plays. It has exercised a second, very different kind of influence as well. The enthusiasm with which the Yiddish stage explored and emulated masterpieces of world literature has already been indicated. At its worst this practice resulted in the pirating practiced by Moses Hurwitch, a late nineteenth-century "theatrical architect" who, into the blueprints of his scripts, integrated appropriate scenes from masterworks, so that "it was not unusual, for example, in a scene involving a shoemaker who is jealous of his wife, to recognize the dialogue of Desdemona and Othello."[18] More often, Yiddish playwrights followed the lead of Jacob Gordin who sought to upgrade the artistic quality of Yiddish plays by drawing on classical themes, characters and plots as he went about creating distinctly Jewish milieux, situations and dramatis personae. One of Gordin's most successful works, *God, Man and Devil*, deals with the downfall of a poor Jewish scribe who succumbs to the temptation of the devil in the shape of a shrewd businessman. The play's borrowing from the stories of Faust and Job is apparent.

Three of the post-1945 plays to be discussed here follow in Gordin's wake. One need only glance at the title of *The Hamlet of Stepney Green* to see what Bernard Kops is up to. No less modeled on a classic protagonist is the eponym of *Enter Solly Gold*, a Jewish Tartuffe. Yet another example comes from Wolf Mankowitz, even though he is not the first to adopt Gogol's *The Overcoat* for the stage. Artef's penultimate production was, in fact, Chaver Paver's Yiddish reworking of the famous Russian short story. Mankowitz' version, *The Bespoke Overcoat*, synthesizes a trace of vaudeville with the Yiddish theatre's mixed tone and the moral imperative it often shares with authors like Gogol.

A final contribution made by the Yiddish theatre is the creation of a special universe. That sphere is exhibited in all the plays to be discussed here. It is a world where virtually everybody is Jewish.

The ethnic homogeneity reflected in these works results in anything but harmony, however. Jews are perhaps most contentious when no outside threat necessitates their closing ranks. *The Wesker Trilogy* offers an extended overview of such a universe. Its panorama is enhanced by the relief provided in the trilogy's middle play, *Roots*, whose entirely gentile world contrasts starkly with the thoroughly Jewish ambiance in the first play, *Chicken Soup with Barley*, and the last, *I'm Talking about Jerusalem*. In the largest sense, the Kahns and the Simmondses of the *The Wesker Trilogy* are representatives of the modern working class. Because they are also Jews, they are preoccupied with problems like supersensitive social consciousness and dissension among those closest to them in a way that unites them with their co-religionists in the Chayefsky, Kops and Mankowitz plays.

The traits these personae share often derive from what Joseph Landis calls the "the ethic of mentshlekhkayt," conduct issuing from a concept of mankind which the post-1945 plays share with their Yiddish antecedents. Man is envisioned as inherently good, capable of prevailing over the temptations of evil by self-discipline, good deeds and study, and by consciously demonstrating compassion, responsibility for others, and trust in the worth of humanity. When man violates this ethic, the common moral of these plays holds, he does so not because of original sin or innate depravity, but because he fails to marshal the necessary inner strength, or because he is the victim of superior outside forces. In either case, the burden of redemption is wholly on him. Explains Landis:

> Though justice may not triumph in the ordeal of tragedy, though the moral order of the universe may not be demonstrated in the action of its art, yet man's capacity for mentshlekhkayt is reaffirmed and the dignity and joy of man as mentsh towers above the suffering and the circumstance. In personal qualities the hero embodies the values of his world: the Jewish hero is the hero as mentsh.[19]

Although the characters in the plays we turn to now are hardly intended as heroes, a role conspicuously absent on the post-1945 stage, a reliable measure of the status and merit they embody is the degree to which they measure up as *menshen*.*

*In the interest of consistency, the spellings *mensh*, *menshen* are used here, following the model of Leo Rosten who writes, "To be a *mensh* has nothing to do with success, wealth, status. . . . The key to being 'a real *mensh*' is nothing less than—character: rectitude, dignity, a sense of what is right, responsible, decorous." *The Joys of Yiddish* (New York: McGraw-Hill, 1968), p. 234.[20]

The Tenth Man and Other Menshen

Paddy Chayefsky's *The Tenth Man* (1959) is constituted of many of the elements of Anski's *The Dybbuk* (1914) and makes at least one comparable affirmation about the power of faith. Paradoxically, what makes these plays most alike is their convincing reflection of two styles of Jewish life and of two concepts of theatre which could hardly be more dissimilar.

The Dybbuk is a tightly constructed work in which the resolution of the central problem, children's accountability for their fathers' deeds, is enlarged and illuminated by supernatural powers. Mysticism and reality intermingle everywhere in this often expressionistic play, reflecting the *shtetl* climate of superstitions, Hassidic ecstasy and harsh verities (e.g., the specter of the Chmelniecki massacres casts a black shadow across the work). Reb Sender fails to recognize the scholar Khonnon, to whom he has given hospitality in his house, as the son of his long-dead friend, Nissen. Long before their children were born, Sender and Nissen had betrothed the son and daughter they would someday have. Though Sender's daughter Leye and Khonnon fall deeply in love, Sender has promised Leye to a more prosperous bridegroom. Determined to prevent the marriage, Khonnon turns to mortifying cabbalistic rituals. The singing and dancing which celebrate Sender's announcement of Leye's forthcoming wedding prove fatal to the fevered Khonnon. It is his unfulfilled soul that takes possession of Leye. Exorcism succeeds in expelling the spirit of Khonnon, only to liberate it to join Leye's in the mystical union of light and shadow that ends the play.

The Tenth Man, which bears many imprints of the Anski piece, is also concerned with the working out of guilt and responsibility. It is likewise compounded of realism, mysticism and stage artifice, in proportions appropriate to the representation of a Mineola, Long Island neighborhood on the Broadway stage. The East European synagogue with its blackened walls and mysterious dark corners becomes a converted grocery store. One of its affiliates observes, "If it wasn't for the Holy Ark there, this place would look like the local headquarters of the American Labor Party. In Poland, where we were all one step from starvation, we had a synagogue whose shadow had more dignity than this place."[21] Yet for some of its members Congregation Atereth-Tifereth Yisroel, no less than its old world prototype, represents a source of strength, camaraderie and identity, or more properly, identities, since several persuasions of Jews belong here. The religious homogeneity of the Hassidic community in Anski's play with which Khonnon sets himself at conspicuous odds by cultivating proscribed powers contrasts sharply with the heterogeneity of the Long Island Jews in *The Tenth Man*. Even the hyphenated name of their synagogue (Crown of-Pride of Israel) indicates a composite.

Age provides the major division in the congregation. The old men are contemporary versions of Anski's *batlonim*.* There is Moyshe Alper, formerly a Yiddish journalist; David Foreman, a retired biology teacher; and Israel Hirschman, a cabbalist much less extreme in his practices than Khonnon, whose life has been devoted to earning his late father's forgiveness for rejecting the rabbinate sixty years before. There is Schlissel, a self-styled revolutionary, and Zitorsky, a veteran of the garment industry. These seventy-year-olds come daily to the synagogue as a refuge from every kind of cold and boredom. Except for Hirschman, the old men take their delight in "disputation," not over the holy texts, but matters more mundane. Are Reform Jews apostates? Is it better to be buried in Mount Hope, Mount Zion or Cedar Lawn? Whose daughter-in-law is the most insufferable? Chayefsky makes wonderful use of the wickedly ingenious Jewish blessing-curse, e.g., "My daughter-in-law, may she grow rich and buy a hotel with a thousand rooms and be found dead in every one of them."

Faced with the daily task of assembling for morning prayers the ten men required for the minyan, the sexton frequently has to call on the younger, less devoted congregants. Such are the Kessler brothers who come to commemorate the anniversary of their father's death, but recite the memorial prayer "painstakingly, with no idea what they are reading." Curiously, the congregation's young rabbi is relegated to the same group as the Kesslers by common agreement of the elders who resent his chiding them for not taking what he consideres an active role in synagogue life. Rabbi Bernard Marks's perspective, in turn, is revealed in a telephone conversation with a colleague:

> How in Heaven's name are you going to convey an awe of God to boys who will race out of your Hebrew classes to fly model rocket ships five hundred feet in the air exploding in three stages? To my boys, God is a retired mechanic . . . Well, I'm organizing a bazaar right now. When I hang up on you, I have to rush to the printer's to get some raffles printed, and from there I go to Town Hall for a permit to conduct bingo games. In fact, I was so busy this morning, I almost forget to come to the synagogue. (pp. 81–82)

*"*Batlon* (pl. *batlonim*): a man with no occupation who devotes all his time to religious study and synagogue service and lives on the charity of the community; therefore, also, an impractical man, an idler, a daydreamer." Joseph C. Landis, *The Dybbuk and Other Great Yiddish Plays*, p. 21.

A third dissimilar representative of the younger Jews is Arthur Landau, a total stranger whom the sexton has literally pulled off the street to complete the minyan. Hounded by personal problems, this tenth man has just sobered up from a three-day drunk; he is far less interested in prayer than in getting in touch with his analyst.

It is through the figure of Landau that the playwright succeeds in juxtaposing manifestations of not one, but several kinds of dybbuks. The most sensational is the migratory soul which has taken possession of David Foreman's granddaughter Evelyn, who has a history of mental illness. Foreman has kidnapped Evelyn from her parents' home and brought her to the synagogue partly because he cannot accept her psychiatrist's prognosis that she will probably spend much of her life institutionalized. There is a more dramatic reason Foreman has abducted Evelyn. To his shame he recognizes her dybbuk. She is Hannah Luchinsky and she calls herself the Whore of Kiev. Foreman admits his responsibility for her original debasement a half-century earlier.

While in the Anski play the Khonnon dybbuk is uniquely the consequence of Sender's reneging on his pledge, Chayefsky affiliates the Hannah dybbuk with the guilt of several personae. Immediately apparent is Foremen, whose grandchild is possessed by the restless soul of the woman he had abused. But the Hannah dybbuk's accusation, "There is one among you who has lain with whores many times and his wife died of the knowledge," shocks from Zitorsky the confession that his wife's discovery that he played by the garment industry's rules for entertaining out-of-town buyers had indeed led to her premature death, "cursing my name with her last breath." For Hirschman, who had heard a voice he now recognizes as Hannah's whimpering during his most recent three-day fast, the dybbuk appears a sign that his long penitence is almost over. For once there is immediate consensus: the dybbuk must be expelled.

Like all prayers in the synagogue, exorcism requires a minyan. That means that Arthur Landau is as necessary now as he had been earlier. Landau is still on the premises, deep in conversation with Evelyn whom he overheard proclaiming, "I am the Whore of Kiev." It is difficult to know how authentically Evelyn represents those diagnosed insane in their lucid moments, but she seems amazingly prescient. "I'm a little paranoid and hallucinate a great deal and have very little sense of realty, except for brief interludes like this, and I might slip off any minute in the middle of a sentence into some incoherency," she warns Arthur. "If that should happen, you must be very realistic with me" (p. 66). Within minutes, she thinks she is

Susan Hayward, and Arthur's appropriately "realistic" response earns him her gratitude and in short order, her love.

The Evelyn possessed alternately by the Hannah dybbuk and her own illness offers schizoid contrast to the vital young woman who has such interesting things to say for herself ("I have discovered through many unsuccessful years of psychiatric treatment that religion has a profound sexual connotation for me"). She is alert and sympathetic to Arthur's problems. Having tasted life's successes, he is disenchanted and weary. But Evelyn insists he is a mystic. "I never knew anyone who wanted to know the meaning of life as desperately as you do," she says, running to fetch him a cabbalistic text of Hirschman's. She suggests that he too is possessed by a dybbuk who locks up his emotions. Coming upon the couple engrossed in one another, Foreman and his cronies naturally propose a match. But Arthur protests that he no longer believes anybody really loves anyone else. Hirschman seizes that declaration to strike an aphorism central to the play's subsequent action: "Love is an act of faith and yours is a faithless generation. That is your dybbuk" (p. 132).

The exorcism in the Anski play is a solemn rite conducted with awesome majesty by the powerful Tsaddik of Miropolye. By contrast the ceremony in *The Tenth Man* is a weird pageant full of improvisation which seems exactly right for the time and place of Chayefsky's play. The requisites that are so easily met in the *shtetl* synagogue become formidable obstacles for the Jews in Mineola. Overcoming them demonstrates the determination of these old men and simultaneously supplies the play with its funniest moments. There is the chronic problem of assembing a minyan. In the middle of a weekday afternoon, most men are at work and the matter at hand is sensitive. They hesitate, for instance, to call their friend Harris ("You tell an eighty-two-year-old man to come down and make a tenth for an exorcism and he'll have a heart attack on the phone talking with you").

A far more serious problem is finding a rabbi of stature to conduct the ritual, Rabbi Marks being dismissed as too young. The old men totter on the brink of a disputation over who is the biggest rabbi in New York—the Korpotchniker of Williamsburg, the Bobolovitcher of Crown Heights or the Lubanower of Brownsville. When Hirschman quietly admits the Korpotchniker is his cousin, it is decided that they must go directly to Williamsburg to consult the great man. Foreman and Schlissel make two unsuccessful sorties on Brooklyn. Back at Atereth-Tifereth Yisroel hours later, their comic explanation is tinged with the frustration of resolute old men bewildered and demoralized by the big city:

Who saw the Korpotchniker? We've been riding in subways for four hours! Back and forth, in this train, in that train! I am convinced there is no such place as Williamsburg and there is no such person as the Korpotchniker Rabbi! I tell you, twice we got off at two different stations, just to see daylight, and, as God is my witness, both times we were in New Jersey! (p. 109)

It is Hirschman who finally conducts the ritual. The persistence of the little group is rewarded. They conjure forth a dybbuk. Unexpectedly, it is Arthur's rather than Evelyn's. The ceremony restores his "desire to wake in the morning, and a passion for the things of life, a pleasure in work, a purpose to sorrow." He resolves to care for Evelyn and to exorcize her dybbuk with his love.

There is little question that the resolution of *The Tenth Man* lacks the Anski play's emphatic assertions of God and of the inevitability of justice in the universe. That is not to say that the contemporary work does not make its own kind of affirmation. Through their experience with the dybbuks, believers and nonbelievers alike catch a fresh glimpse of lost or buried faith. Arthur's renewed conviction of the worth of life and the power of love is perhaps the most spectacular statement. His rediscovery has a variant in Schlissel's proclamation, "Praise be to the Lord, for His compassion is everywhere," a real about-face from this revolutionary's earlier skepticism. Zitorsky too marvels that, "If I didn't see this with my own eyes, I wouldn't believe it." Even the rabbi, who declined to take an active role in the exorcism admits, "It would please me a great deal to believe once again in a God of dybbuks." Alper entertains reservations about Arthur as proselyte, but makes a perceptive observation: "He still doesn't believe in God. He simply wants to love. And when you stop and think about it, gentlemen, is there any difference?" (p. 154).

Within the context of a play which accurately reflects a corner of the pluralistic American Jewish community at mid-century, Chayefsky portrays a rather credible affirmation of belief. The equating of religious faith with the healing and redemptive power of love in Alper's final speech echoes the indomitable love between Leye and Khonnon, a love capable of lifting their souls from the depths of sorrow and self-destruction to a divinely blessed union. The little poem with which Anski's play begins and ends celebrates just this saving strength of love and conviction:

Wherefore, wherefore
Did the soul
From its exalted height
Fall into abysmal depths?
Within the fall the power lies
To rise again.

Applied to *The Tenth Man*, Anski's poem fits Arthur Landau's renewed trust in life and love, and Evelyn's healthy delight in Judaism and humanity whenever she is lucid. Finally the verse's celebration of enduring spiritual strength applies to the little knot of Long Island Jews whose persistence in exploiting the real but inconspicuous resources of Congregation Atereth-Tifereth Yisroel offers a wonderful illustration of "man's capacity for mentshlekhkayt."

Dead-shmead, As Long As He Has His Coat

If Gogol's *The Overcoat* provides the skeleton of Wolf Mankowitz' *The Bespoke Overcoat* (1956), it is the Yiddish theatre that supplies its soul. The playwright pares away many of the details from the Russian story to develop the significance of the titular coat in the life and death of the play's protagonist, Fender. That hapless Jewish warehouse clerk has much in common with his prototype, Akaky Akakyevitch, Gogol's unlucky civil servant. Gogol's hard-drinking tailor becomes with very little transformation the simple and compassionate Morry, also a tippler, who makes a coat for Fender. The play's characters inhabit a world where hunger, cold and poverty make a warm overcoat a matter not only of creature comfort, but of security, personal dignity, and pride. The callousness of the ruling class, which Gogol embodied in the Person of Consequence, becomes in Mankowitz' play an exploitative boss named Ranting in whose clothing warehouse Fender toils away his life.

An important difference between story and play is implicit in Mankowitz' version of the title which announces that this "bespoke" coat represents a special arrangement between customer and supplier. An appreciable dissimilarity in tone results when the studied detachment with which Gogol presents his clerk's tale is replaced by the unabashed sentimentality, irrepressible humor and beguiling naïveté typical of the Yiddish theatre and marked in *The Bespoke Overcoat*. Mankowitz warns the reader, "The only stage, the only effects, the only theatre I had in mind were in the heart of the drunken tailor. There was no indication of time past or time present, because a twinge of conscience lasts a moment or a lifetime, and *The Bespoke Overcoat* is about the unreasonable conscience felt by the poor who love the poorer with a love that conquers nothing."[22]

The love and conscience the playwright refers to are immediately on view as the tailor Morry sadly reminisces about his friend Fender who had died of pneumonia before Morry had a chance to finish his fine new coat. It was to have replaced the threadbare one which finally became useless in the unheated warehouse where Fender had clerked. Maybe if Morry had patched the patches one more time? If he'd offered Fender his own coat? The tailor's regrets are scattered by a visit from Fender:

Morry: Fender, you ain't dead?

Fender: Sure, I'm dead. Would I sit up half the night if I wasn't dead? I can tell you I won't be sorry to get back. They got central heating, constant hot water, room service. And the food—as much as you like. Kosher, of course. (p. 258)

Fender has not come back to haunt Morry, even less to get the coat he was having made. By his own admission he doesn't need the garment at his new address. Yet however reliable the physical warmth at the "hotel," it does not satisfy Fender's needs. For the clerk had come to the tailor originally only after abandoning all hopes of achieving his heart's desire, one of the company's sheepskin-lined coats bought on time. A villain straight out of melodrama, Ranting had scoffed that Fender wouldn't live long enough to meet all the installments. As if Ranting's overdrawn self-interest weren't enough to guarantee an audience's hissing him, Mankowitz has him discharge Fender, who had worked all his life in the company, without a word of regret: "I used to give him a handkerchief he should wipe his nose. A little boy crying round the warehouse with his stockings down gives me the sack" (p. 268). Small wonder Fender dies cursing the boss.

If once dead, Fender no longer suffers physical cold, he can't get the injustice out of his mind. His sights are firmly set on a certain coat which he considers "bespoken," made-to-order for him. His obsession wins him permission to come back for it. Now he explains to Morry, whom he wants to help him pick out a factory coat, "I am not saying your coat isn't wonderful. It is. But I must have from Ranting a coat. I give him forty-three years nearly. He must give me a coat" (pp. 270–71).

That speech contains the whole point of the play. In a way, it also serves as the punch line, since it explodes our expectations by showing that the overcoat of the title, the one important enough to bring Fender back from the dead, was the one he'd promised himself, his custom-made way of evening up the score with Ranting. To refer to Fender's "He owes me" speech as a punch line does not seem inappropriate in view of the dramatist's published praise of Alec Clunes who, in producing the play, "understood that The Bespoke Overcoat was a sustained, typically over-long Jewish joke—than which there is no sadder and no funnier story" (p. 253).

Sorrow and humor co-exist with other extremes that are paired off throughout to achieve the mixed tone of the work: the coldness of Ranting and the warehouse with the warmth of Morry's friendship, the coat he is making, the brandy that the friends share; the complicated bookkeeping systems at the warehouse with the simple justice Fender asks of Ranting. Mankowitz has a deft touch with sentimental moments where, in the manner of David Pinski and Sholom Aleichem, he checks a lump in the throat with a giggle, as when Morry says he will finish the coat even though the jobless Fender can no longer pay for it.

Fender:	How?
Morry (puts an arm around Fender and pats him on the shoulder):	With a needle. How else? (p. 268)

Almost as important as what the play says is what it leaves unsaid. Mankowitz could have explored the values that lead Fender to prefer a factory-made coat to a literally custom-made one. He could have shown what, if anything, Ranting learns. Like the Jewish vaudevillian who relies on "private jokes," and like Gogol in his short story too, Mankowitz leaves the supplying of motives and moral to his audience. He appears confident that audiences will respond with appreciative understanding to Fender's and Morry's "unreasonable conscience felt by the poor for the poorer." The playwright's confidence is eminently well placed.

A Jewish Hamlet

In *The Hamlet of Stepney Green* (1959), Bernard Kops distills elements freely adapted from Shakespeare into "a sad comedy with songs." While the Kops play accepts the Shakespearean notion of the providential nature of existence, it explores no mysteries nor does it portray any noble conflicts. Instead it focuses on living life fully and in harmony with others, especially and most Judaically, with one's family. The point is made initially by the set, the Stepney Green house and garden of Sam and Bessie Levy, an oasis surrounded by a great area of bomb damage. Depressed by the imminence of death, Sam insists on spending his last hours in his garden where he can enjoy the sun and flowers and listen to the songs and dances of the neighborhood children.

Despite the Old Testament implications of their names, Sam, a fish merchant, is not much of a prophet, nor is his son David, the Hamlet of the play, a future monarch. David procrastinates like the Prince of Denmark; like him, he does not always "suit the word to the action," but expresses himself alternately in Yiddish-enriched vernacular and grandiloquence: "I'm consigning my father to you, oh mighty dead; he is a king if ever there was one, first because he is my father, and then he is a king of the herrings."[23]

Sam makes the mistake of confiding his disappointment in life to David in terms that seem to incriminate Bessie of having poisoned him. Though that is not literally true, administering poison does not seem beyond the capabilities of the generally insensitive Bessie who, like Queen Gertrude, demonstrates a limited capacity for looking unpleasantness in the face. Accusing her husband of malingering, she tells him, "You disgust me, you old fool, and if you're going to die, please do it before tea-time because I've got a sponge cake in the oven" (p. 29).

The poison Sam complains of is his dreadful realization that "life slipped through my fingers and as it was slipping, that was life." David doesn't understand that his father laments less his own approaching death than the demise of everything he had once valued— love in his marriage to Bessie, the sights and sounds of Whitechapel ("Where are all the old men with the long white beards, where all the women selling beigles?"), the standards of a way of life now antiquated. He seeks reparation not for the way he dies, but "for the way I lived—for the self-deception, the petty lies and the silly quarrels." Apparently, Sam hopes to find ultimate compensation in his son's life. But David at twenty-two is immature and irresolute. He aspires to fame and fortune as a pop singer. Craving adoration from the masses, he fails to notice it in the eyes of Hava, the girl next door. Convinced he would score instant success if given his big chance, he disdains taking his place in his father's smaltz herring business. From their respective vantage points, either Sam or David could proclaim, "How weary, stale, flat and unprofitable/ Seem to me all the uses of this world."

Death does not end Sam's determination to help David find the satisfactions he lost or missed. Unable to rest until David finds himself, Sam "comes back" after his funeral, visible only to his son. Suddenly, David's dramatic imagination puts all the pieces together: he is visited by a ghost, he is thought mad by those who observe his exchanges with the father only he can see, and he has reason to avenge his father's death. Striking a Hamlet pose, he proclaims that he will "become a crazy prince to the bitter end." Dressed as a hybird of the Danish prince and a Teddy boy, David startles the mourners by singing:

Yiddisher father
I bet he misses Matzo Bry,
Cheesecake and Smoked Salmon,
I hope he finds some in the sky,
Will you look at them here,
As they stand and pray,
When they're all very glad that he's out of the way.
Oh my wonderful yiddisher father—
Somebody will have to pay. (p. 59)

With the last line, he points at Bessie.

David's campaign of unspecific grievances against his mother gathers full force after the week of mourning. Bessie is confused and hurt. But David is enjoying his melancholy posturing too much to trouble to communicate with her: "To be or not to bloody well be, believe me, that is the question! Whether it is besser to be a bissel meshuga— [better to be a little crazy]" (p. 61). Watching David, Sam realizes that being *is* the question and that burdening David with his own regrets isn't helping his son to make anything of his life.

With the confirmation of his suspicions that his friend, widower Solly Segal, is interested in Bessie, Sam swallows his pride. Cunningly he maneuvers David into fostering the romance between Bessie and Solly. At their wedding eight months later Sam works a final ruse designed to teach David to value life and love. He tricks his son into serving everyone a love potion which David thinks is poison. Significantly, he forgets to serve Hava and himself. As he raises his own glass, David catches sight of Hava and is smitten. The wonder of love brings him to the rather basic awareness that he can sing and sell herring at the same time. "Why didn't I think of it sooner?" he asks, while Sam comically shrugs at the audience. Finally Sam convinces David that "Hamlet" must consider himself indemnified by Bessie's marrying Solly who is moody and stingy. They're made for each other, he chuckles. With David's perspectives and aspirations assured, Sam can rest, though not without a swan song in which he asserts his restored faith in life and counsels, "Make the most of your life— because life is a holiday from the dark."

The play ends as it begins, with the voices of children singing, in both cases jump rope jingles whose very familiarity underscores Kops's use of them. The commonplace rhymes accompany commonplace events—a death, a wedding—whose importance the dramatist stresses by having them open and close his play. In between, the most ordinary emotions move the characters to song: David's loneliness and confusion at Sam's death, Bessie's despair over her son's strange behavior, Segal and Bessie's delight at their second chance for marital bliss.

To be sure, one of *Hamlet*'s fundamental themes operates in the Kops work as well. Sam and David too are "sick at heart," and for essentially the same reason as Hamlet—they sense the corruption in the world about them. Here the Schopenhauerian distinction that life is a tragedy in its entirety and a comedy in its details offers a useful guide. Shakespeare develops the broadest and deepest implications of that soul-sickness through the eyes of the extraordinary man. Kops concentrates on the quotidian woes and joys that those of Levy stature experience. *The Hamlet of Stepney Green* depicts the poignancy with which unremarkable people perceive the major events in their lives, experiences no less significant because they happen to everyone, no less precious because they occasion tears as well as jubilation. The play argues the value of savoring every minute, aware that

> Life is a time of light, that's not forever,
> It happens only once, so while we have a chance,
> Come on, let's sing and dance. . . . (p. 84)

Stepney Green's references to *Hamlet*'s cups of poison are mischievous. With its kaleidoscope of songs and speeches, its mélange of drama and melodrama, its emphasis on the family and its affirmation of love and fulfillment, *The Hamlet of Stepney Green* proposes instead a toast, *l'chaim* (to life).

A Kosher-Style Tartuffe

In a rare moment of candor induced by the proximity of his second greatest weakness, a fat girl, Solly Gold confesses that he is a liar and "the best con man in the business."[24] He also calls himself a *gonif*,* an entirely appropriate designation. Inexplicably, unless all that trembling flesh nearby tempers his chutzpah, Solly does not lay claim to the title he most richly deserves: he is a consummate *schnorrer*.*

At the beginning of *Enter Solly Gold* (1964), Kops's man is homeless,

---

*Astonishingly, Solly exemplifies all the nuances of these Yiddish terms as defined by Leo Rosten in *The Joys of Yiddish*. *Gonif*: "thief, crook; a clever person; a shady, tricky character it would be wise (a) not to trust, (b) to watch every minute he's in the store; a mischievous, fun-loving prankster." *Schnorrer*: "beggar, panhandler, moocher; a cheapskate, a chiseler; a bum, a drifter, a compulsive bargain hunter and a bargainer; an impudent indigent."

penniless, hungry and cold. By the end of the first scene, he has mooched food, wine and fifteen pounds from a tailor (five of which he later uses to spend the night with a prostitute whose "last word" was seven pounds ten) and swindled an elderly widow of her flock of chickens. But by far the most valuable item in the day's take is the clothing the old lady gives Solly because she can't bear the reminders of her late husband, a rabbi.

Posing as a peripatetic rabbi, Solly insinuates himself into the Golders Green mansion of Shoe King Morry Swartz. He arrives just in time to offer either the "significant cabbalistic eternal marriage blessing" (£250) or the "simple blessing of the bedchamber" (£25) to Sarah Swartz and Alan Fink whose wedding reception is in progress. When, by lucky accident, Solly rids Morry of a chronic back ailment, his future is assured:

Morry (he kisses Solly resoundingly on the forehead):
For years I've suffered and now I'm well, thanks to you.

Solly: It's the work of God, I'm just his instrument.

Morry: It's a miracle. And to think I doubted. He sent you to me—
I can't believe it—how can I thank you? How can I repay you?

Solly: We'll find a way.

Morry: Stay here with me—stay here for a time—for a few days. Please by my guest. (p. 124)

Once firmly lodged in the affections and the household of Morry Swartz, Solly Gold's conduct increasingly recalls that of Tartuffe. Like Molière's quintessential hypocrite, Solly presumes on his host's innermost spiritual yearnings. When Morry complains that his prayers are empty and he can't "get through," "Rabbi" Gold promises him that he has a direct line. Before long, Morry exults, "For some reason I trust you with my life. I dreamed and dreamed last night—wonderful dreams—you may be a stranger but you're not so strange as my own family" (p. 130), his unnatural devotion is akin to Orgon's:

Under his [Tartuffe's] tutelage my soul's been freed
From earthly loves, and every human tie:
My mother, children, brother, and wife could die,
And I'd not feel a single moment's pain.[25]

The degree to which Solly captivates Morry is indicated by the latter's willingness to banish his wife and children (who, like Orgon's, are suspicious of their pious visitor) for two weeks, the better to concentrate on developing his future plan of action. For God has spoken to Solly and announced that Morry is the Messiah. Clearly there is much work to be done to get Morry ready for the world, and vice versa.

A good measure of reluctant self-discipline accompanies Solly's encouraging Swartz to send his daughter away. The imposter has lost little time apprising the dense Romaine of his feelings for her:

Solly: Thine eyes are as a dove's.

Romaine: You been listening to Housewives' Choice?

Solly: Thy hair is a flock of goats.

Romaine: Cheek! I shampooed it last night.

Solly: Thy mouth is comely and thy breasts are like two fawns—

Romaine: How dare you! You're a dirty old man.

Solly: I'm not, that's in the Bible—here read!

Romaine: Wait till I see my father, he'll throw you out—Man of God!

Solly: Wishful thinking, my daughter. I have not behaved improperly. I will admit though to being human. Under this habit is the same old habit—the desire for a beautiful girl like you. (p. 128)

The scene echoes Tartuffe's attempted seduction of Orgon's wife Elmire. Solly's defense of himself as a man of God, but a man nonetheless recalls Tartuffe's "I may be pious, but I'm human too."[26]

Solly's hankering for Romaine leads to yet another episode reminiscent of *Tartuffe*. Morry's family, exactly like Orgon's, plots to undo the charlatan by exposing his authentic character to his duped host. The Swartzes contrive a scenario which, if it worked, would replicate the celebrated scene in which Orgon, hiding under a table, witnesses Tartuffe's lust and cynicism. Romaine is supposed to lead Solly on by protesting that she couldn't possibly give herself to a rabbi, but could make love with a layman. When Gold confesses his imposture, Romaine is to switch on a tape recorder to collect the incriminating evidence. Like Elmire, Romaine arrays herself seductively for the encounter. Like Tartuffe, Solly, on entering, secures the doors. And there the similarity ends, for Romaine lets Solly kiss her, then promptly confesses the whole plot. The unregenerate Solly urges Romaine to run away with him, chortling that now he can have the fat girl *and* her father's fortune.

Like Tartuffe, Solly meets his downfall in a most unanticipated way. Where Molière saves the day for Orgon by making royal justice the *deus ex machina*, Kops devises a more comic comeuppance. Morry, forgiving all, offers to take Solly into his business, and Solly appears ecstatic about selling "Swartzes Everlasting Immortal Soles." Unexpectedly, Romaine turns Solly down flat. She declares she can't trust him unless he agrees "to go off into the world with nothing except our love." (Romaine's idealism rings echoes of a different Molière persona, Alceste in *The Misanthropist*.) The rejected Solly is crestfallen but unrepentant. He vows to think of "something really spectacular this time" in his determination to avoid work.

Though not reciprocal, Solly Gold's impact chez Swartz is certainly salutary. An important parallel between *Tartuffe* and *Enter Solly Gold* lies in their common demonstration that something is terribly wrong in a family that can be so completely disrupted by such an outrageous faker. The French play points its finger at the priority given to appearances rather than to the cultivation of genuine inner life and real communication among family members. While different, the values of the family in the English play are equally reprehensible. Here basic appetite is accentuated until it dominates all other needs. Kops makes an effective metaphor of the Swartzes' love of food. These people hardly stop eating; when they do, they talk about food. Their mental and emotional states find expression in terms of how hungry they are. Sarah Swartz Fink pinches her new husband's cheek throughout the play clucking, "Isn't he lovely? I could eat him." While Solly whispers hotly into Romaine's ear, she wonders what's in the fridge. Liberated from his back pain, Morry proposes going out for corned beef sandwiches. Only the revelation that he is the Messiah robs him of his appetite. "Rabbi" Gold's sure-fire device for persuading the rest of the family to leave their house in order to get Morry firmly under his control is to proclaim no meat can be eaten under the Messiah's roof.

Although eating, together or alone, is virtually the only common interest the Swartz family shares, this essentially solitary satisfaction has become a surrogate that makes contacts with the rest of the world unnecessary. Hence the elaborate wedding feast Solly interrupts when he first arrives at the Swartzes' is attended only by the immediate families of bride and groom. "Who do I need to impress?" Morry asks, by way of explaining the guestless wedding reception. "Anyway, I don't like anyone, not even myself. . . . I don't trust no one." Similarly, Morry's son Melvin confides in Solly that he would really like to substitute women for tennis in his life, but "How do I start?" It takes Solly, who demands so much of other people, to reorient the

Swartzes outward by convincing them there is something missing in their lives.

The entrance of Solly Gold ameliorates the lives of all but one of his hosts. At the end, Melvin has not only approached a girl, but plans to marry her and move to Israel to found a kibbutz devoted to English sportsmanship. Mrs. Swartz discovers that she really likes being a vegetarian; it makes her feel wonderful about herself. Oddly, Morry has profited the most from being hoodwinked. He was really happy trusting another human being and supporting a cause he believed in. The unmasking of "Rabbi" Gold does not alter the fact that Morry has rediscovered his zeal for life and learned an amused tolerance of the people (his wife, solicitor, accountant, doctors, son-in-law) whose real or imagined efforts to bamboozle him pale by comparison to Solly's. Only Romaine reverts to her original distrust of men. "What's for lunch?" she asks.

Both Solly Gold and Tartuffe end up with much less than they bargained for, having accomplished more good than they had intended. In portraying the redeeming value of the *schnorrer*, Kops once again aligns himself with Molière by illustrating the French master's dictum that on both sides of the footlights, comedy serves to correct men while amusing them.

The Wesker Trilogy

While the Chayefsky, Mankowitz and Kops plays adopt the Yiddish theatre's practice of reworking major drama from other languages, Arnold Wesker ambitiously draws on another part of the legacy. *The Trilogy* (1960) adapts the Yiddish theatre's tendency to dramatize the realities of Jewish life. However, Wesker betters the lesson, for the Jewish protagonists at the center of the trilogy's first and last plays represent a working class much more extensive than that of London's East End. Similarly, the gentile Norfolk families in the middle play, *Roots*, also typify a larger group. The Bealeses and the Bryants in *Roots* are country people everywhere, utterly caught up in the struggle for survival, their imagination satisfied by local gossip, family feuds and comic books. Wesker's delineation in the second play of the characters' mental and physical sluggishness, their deficient moral and aesthetic values and the scanty nourishment they draw from their world (in one sense, *Roots* is an ironic title) works as an effective device to enhance the observations he makes of the Jewish Kahns and Simmondses in the other two plays.

Although each work can stand alone, the characters' search, or refusal to search, for the attainment of ideals forms a major theme throughout the trilogy. The inactivity of the country folk in *Roots* is one of the foils which sets off the various endeavors of the East Enders in *Chicken Soup with Barley* and *I'm Talking about Jerusalem*. It is not the only contrast. The forward strivings of the Kahns are juxtaposed against the generally cyclical movement in the work. Specifications of the passage of time pepper the stage directions and dialogue. The characters grow older and wearier as the generations succeed one another. The physical deterioration of Harry Kahn provides the most dramatic but hardly the sole reminder of the fragility of human endeavor. The laws of heredity contribute yet another inexorable cycle. As firebrand Ronnie Kahn grows up, he manifests precisely those ineffectual characteristics he admires least in his father. Harry's resemblance to his own bed-ridden mother is established at the beginning of the work. There is circularity in the action as well. The first scene of *Chicken Soup* takes place in the Kahns' East End basement in 1936. Twenty-three years later, in the last episode of *Jerusalem*, Ada and Dave Simmonds move the remains of their faith and aspirations from Norfolk to a London basement.

The trilogy is full of characterizations which shade or comment upon one another. Ronnie Kahn, the only Londoner to have a role, albeit an unseen one, in *Roots*, is instrumental in showing that play's heroine, Beatie Bryant, how to take a stand and grow (a more literal application of the play's title), an ironic lesson, since Ronnie is incapable of doing these things with his own life. Harry Kahn in the East End, like Stan Mann in *Roots*, has suffered two strokes and becomes incontinent. In comparison, Stan's death from pneumonia after a well-intentioned friend has hosed down his soiled trousers seems much less cruel than Harry's, surrounded by the family he knows he has consistently disappointed. The rural site that ultimately defeats Dave and Ada Kahn Simmonds' plans for an Arcadia is only twenty miles from where the Bealeses and Bryants do manage to scratch out a living. Indeed, one of the most sobering lessons the failed experiment in William Morris socialism teaches the Simmondses is that their ideals are more susceptible of modification than their constitutions. As Colonel Dewhurst observes when he fires Dave, "It's a different way of life here, y'know. They're a slow people, the country people—slow, but sound. I know where I am with them, and they know their place with me. But with you, I could never—."[27]

In counterpoint to the mostly dispiriting downward spirals, and accentuated by their implacability, stands the dedication of the protagonists to their ideals—or, when these ideals turn to dust, to the very notion that faith in ideals is inherently worthwhile. One of the most Jewish traits of the trilogy is that it is concerned less with the achieving of objectives (indeed, the gentile Beatie Bryant's discovery of self-confidence is the nearest any character in this work comes to fulfillment) than with dedication to the values that inspire goals.

The citadel of unshakable, unrealizable idealism is a woman named Sarah Kahn. Hungarian-born, doubtless early imbued with the spirit of the General Union of Jewish Workers, she is devoted to communism with a conviction that the hostile criticism of those around her cannot shake. Endowed with enormous vitality, armed with a rolling pin, Sarah is in her element in the very midst of the street demonstration supporting the Spanish Civil War in the first scene of *Chicken Soup*. Like many zealots, she is prone to underestimate the painful costs of her cause and to blur distinctions. A former party comrade observes of her:

> She can't see people in the round. "They" are all the same bunch. The authorities, the governments, the police, the Post Office—even the shopkeepers. She's never trusted any of them, always fighting them. It was all so simple. The only thing that mattered was to be happy and eat. Anything that made you unhappy or stopped you from eating was the fault of capitalism. Do you think she ever read a book on political economy in her life? (*Chicken Soup*, p. 62)

However idiosyncratic Sarah's understanding of socialism, it remains compelling enough for her to defend it staunchly long after her family and friends have abandoned the cause. When her disenchanted youngest, Ronnie, flings "communist" at her as an epithet, Sarah retorts that being a communist means thinking and fighting for oneself and for others:

> All my life I worked with a party that meant glory and freedom and brotherhood. You want me to give it up now? . . . If the electrician who comes to mend my fuse blows it instead, so I should stop having electricity? I should cut off my light? Socialism is my light, can you understand that? A way of life. (*Chicken Soup*, pp. 73–74)

Sarah is married to a man who seems her opposite number in every respect. A reader, a dreamer, Harry Kahn supposes socialism might be instilled by exposing young people to it gradually so they will "recognize life." He explains to his son, "You can't alter people, Ronnie. You can only give them some love and hope they'll take it" (*Chicken Soup*, p. 56). If Harry is less enthusiastic in his beliefs than his wife and some of their friends, it is simply that he isn't as committed or as energetic. In the *Chicken Soup* opening scene street demonstration, Harry obediently carries a red banner, but when he provokes the police with it, he seeks refuge at his mother's house in a cup of tea and a book. It is not just political causes that fail to engage Harry's allegiance. He has never been able to keep a job for any length of time. He could not even make money during the war. He has a penchant for dropping out of difficult situations, not just street demonstrations, but more memorably, years earlier when Ada had diphtheria, Sarah was pregnant with Ronnie and there was no money in the house.

Sarah stands by a husband like Harry partly because his apparent indifference and nonresistance intrigue her. Harry's sister Cissie forces Sarah to admit her determination to change Harry when she married him. Twenty-five years later, she is still pleading with him to let her help him find out what makes him the way he is. After Harry's first stroke, Sarah persists in trying to get him to join her at branch meetings. After his second stroke, which leaves him partially paralyzed, his wife uncomprehendingly observes, "He didn't want to die but doesn't seem to care about living." Harry is a challenge to Sarah in the same sense as the capitalist world. She can't accept him as he is. She wants to save him from himself. She is convinced that he is worth saving because she thinks him a basically good man, because she needs his dependence upon her, and for all the gnarled reasons that create mutual attraction between scrappers and nonresisters.

Ronnie Kahn is one result of this attraction. He has much of Sarah's personal warmth and élan and much of Harry's need to have other people succeed for him. Like his mother, he loves to talk. He sets out to be a socialist poet, but is ultimately disillusioned by the fate of the Hungarian uprising of 1956 and by the assassination of the Jewish Anti-Fascist Committee in the Soviet Union. His beliefs were obviously learned at Sarah's knee, and it is amusing to hear them come out of the mouth of his girl friend Beatie Bryant in Roots: "'Christ,' he say, 'Socialism isn't talking all the time, it's living, it's singing, it's dancing, it's being interested in what goes on around you, it's being concerned about people and the world'" (Roots, p. 129). Ronnie's abrupt forsaking of Beatie after a three-year romance and his wandering from one dead-end job to another are manifestations of the fecklessness inherited from Harry. Yet he is appalled to recognize his resemblance to his father in his own loss of faith and ambition. At the same time, his growing likeness to Harry causes Ronnie to feel sorry that he hadn't always been patient with his parent, a regret not altogether warranted. Long ago he had intuited his father's heavy conscience. "No one knows more than he does how he's failed," the sixteen-year-old Ronnie told his Aunt Cissie. "Now that's tragedy for you: having the ability to see what's happening to yourself and not being able to do anything about it" (*Chicken Soup*, p. 47).

Although the Kahns do a lot of talking about love, Ronnie is the only one who demonstrates much affection. His playful adolescent hoisting of Harry over his shoulder, fireman-style, foreshadows his later carrying the paralyzed old man about in his arms. But Ronnie can't connect, can't find mutually supportive relationships, and in this he becomes a broadly representative contemporary figure. The first time we see him (*Chicken Soup* I, 1), he is five years old, a bewildered witness to a battle between his parents. He delivers the curtain line in the last scene of the trilogy's last play; here he is twenty-eight and weeping because his sister and brother-in-law have come "home" to London. "We—must—be—bloody—mad—to—cry." Ronnie yells to the sky, incapable of expressing in any other way his crushing disappointment that the two people he believed in most have abandoned their goals and thereby, his:

> There isn't anything I've seen through to the end—maybe that's why you two were so important to me. Isn't that curious? I say all the right things, I think all the right things, but somewhere, some bloody where I fail as a human being, like my father—just like poor old Harry. (*Jerusalem*, pp. 216–17)

Ronnie's dashed hopes, however touching, come through vicarious defeats—his father's, the Simmondses'. By contrast, Dave and Ada Kahn Simmonds are beaten in the pursuit of their socialist ideals only after doing battle for ten years. Dave had been searching to make sense of his life when he went off to Spain with the International Brigade in 1936. By the time he came back from the second World War, he and Ada had a common, clear-sighted understanding of what they meant by socialism. To Sarah's chagrin, it had nothing to do with political activism. The Simmondses rejected the values of an industrial society as well as the communist ambition to "harbor a billion people in a theory." They believed their first goal was to find themselves before they could offer any solutions to society. From the natives in Ceylon during the war, Dave learned that when a man works, "he's giving away something of himself, something very precious." In order to combine work and family life into a seamless existence, the Simmondses move to the wilds of Norfolk. There Dave is to do carpentry for Colonel Dewhurst until he has established himself as a craftsman.

Although their rustic life brings them great personal satisfaction, their utopia is vulnerable to attack and reversals. While she helps them move, Sarah is openly disapproving. As indicated earlier, Colonel Dewhurst and Dave have a falling-out, forcing Dave to start his own shop before he is ready. Custom-made orders are cancelled after the furniture has been built. Dave's carefully trained apprentice leaves for a factory job. The most damaging blow comes in the person of a cherished buddy who had shared Dave's ambitions in their army days, but who since has grown cynical, "dirtied up" by the failure of his own schemes. Invited by Dave eager to show off his Norfolk life-style, the friend bluntly counsels the Simmondses to go home. In relinquishing their Norfolk experiment after a decade, Ada and Dave also abandon much of their conviction that they could live their Jeru-salem instead of only talking about it. For different reasons, they come to the same conclusion as a friend who left the Party to become a greengrocer, complaining, "There's nothing I can do anymore. I'm too small; who can I trust?" (*Chicken Soup*, p. 62). In his turn, Dave laments, "Face it—as an essential member of society I don't really count" (*Jerusalem*, p. 216).

Dave and Ada's return to London doesn't solve or change any-thing. Unlike the plays of the Yiddish theatre which, whatever their aspirations to realism, managed to end happily, Wesker's trilogy ter-minates without resolution or even explicit message. Yet in an intri-guing Author's Note the dramatist confesses, "I am at one with these people; it is only that I am annoyed with them and myself." It is apparent that Wesker as playwright is devoted to the authenticity of his characters. His irritation is not likely to be aroused by their inabil-ity to strike a compromise between setting goals and attaining them. More probably, he deplores their failed communications and the iso-lation that their commitment to ideals effects. His target may well be the alienation his personae tolerate and even foster by not getting in touch with one another in spite of all the talking they do.

The biggest offender would be Sarah who claims "You have to start with love" and who has dedicated her whole life to brotherhood. Yet in *Chicken Soup*, when Ronnie tries to ward off another squabble be-tween his parents by reassuring his father, "She wasn't talking to you," Harry retorts, "Your mother never talks *to* me." Sarah begs Harry to "talk, talk," only to deride his ideas when he does. Ada gives up trying to explain to her mother why she and Dave are set-tling in Norfolk: "Because language isn't any use! Because we talk about one thing and you hear another, that's why."

But Sarah is not the only one who doesn't make contact. Shaken by her father's last words to her, "You hate me and you've always hated me," Ada admits to Dave, "But perhaps I didn't tell him I loved him." Ronnie's eleventh-hour letter to break off with Beatie (characteristi-cally, he can't bring himself to tell her in person) acknowledges his inability to maintain a lasting relationship with her. He accurately assesses all his own efforts to establish rapport with others: *"That's all I ever get away with—gestures."* The broadest indictment comes from Dave near the end of the trilogy:

> Everyone was choking with their experience of life and wanted to hand it on. Who came forward with a word of encouragement? Who said we maybe had a little guts? Who offered one tiny word of praise? (*Jerusalem,* p. 207).

Wesker's annoyance seems to acknowledge a violation of "the ethic of mentshlekhkayt." The trilogy stresses the human tendency not to listen or to share the aspirations and disappointments of the people closest by, a fault scarcely confined to the Wesker universe. The deceptively homey title of the first play refers to that hearthside indifference, for the chicken soup with barley which saved little Ada's life was supplied not by a member of the family, but by a neighbor who plays no other role in the work. Detachment is dramatized again in *Roots,* where Ronnie is infinitely more successful as a teacher than a practitioner of finding sustenance in "the things you come from." Lack of human contact is stated resoundingly in the title of the last play in which talking, a quintessentially Jewish activity, goes largely unheeded, and Jerusalem, the ultimate goal for all Jews in one sense or another, is unattainable. How pointed, particularly in reference to an articulate family accustomed to thinking as socialists, the first person singular pronoun in *I'm Talking about Jerusalem!*

These post-1945 works incorporate many of the typifying elements of the Yiddish theatre. They portray an essentially Jewish world. Ghosts—manifestations of the unvanquishable human spirit—figure in three of the plays. The characteristic mixed tone is everywhere evident. Except for *The Bespoke Overcoat,* singing, chanting and dancing are widely integrated into the action; in all of the plays, life's aches and pains are palliated by judicious applications of humor. Of the animating spirit of the works and their special image of the Jew, more presently.

The plays exhibit some of the difficulties inherent in presenting a Jewish universe to general audiences, a consideration the Yiddish theatre never had to worry about. Language itself presents knotty problems. For example, while it is probable that the words are meaningless even to many Jewish theatregoers, Kops in *The Hamlet of Stepney Green* and Wesker in *I'm Talking about Jerusalem* have their elderly protagonists express their dying thoughts in Yiddish. Authenticity is reasonably given priority over serving the audience's complete comprehension. The language of the stage creates a predicament for Chayefsky in *The Tenth Man* where synagogue ritual plays such a prominent role. The dramatist made a hard choice when he translated prayers into English, rendering them intelligible to spectators, but utterly inauthentic. Even granting the theatrical necessity of the resultant caricature, when the cabbalist responds to the fulfillment of a sixty-year quest by exclaiming, "It is good to sing praises unto God; for it is pleasant and praise is seemly," he risks appearing ridiculous.

Like modern life, the modern stage sometimes makes troublesome the strict observance of the practices of Judaism. Here Bernard Kops gets himself into a jam. "No, no—don't go. We need you for prayers," Solly Segal begs the tombstone salesmen in *Stepney Green*, thereby inviting the audience to count the men assembled to recite Kaddish. There are six. Later in the play, Kops addresses audience curiosity about Jewish ritual, simultaneously commenting on it:

Sam: When I came in just now I went to look at myself, and when I saw the mirror was covered I knew definitely that I was dead.

David: Why do we cover mirrors?

Sam: So that we shouldn't see our own grief.

David: Why shouldn't we see our own grief?

Sam: How should I know? (pp. 46–47)

Earlier it was asserted that a capital achievement of the Yiddish theatre was the fostering of native playwrights. The plays discussed here, all the work of Jewish authors, demonstrate the continued vitality of that influence. Nor are these isolated examples. When the newly founded Jewish Theatre Association held its first conference in New York in June 1980, it took five days of morning-through-night, three-ring programming to include all the performances by theatre artists and scholars "investigating expression of Jewish identity and culture."[28]

One of the liveliest debates at the Jewish Theatre Conference centered on the question "Jewish theatre for whom?" The question is largely rhetorical. As both the experiences of the conference participants and the concessions to noninitiates made in the plays discussed above testify, Jewish theatre today attracts general audiences as never before.

Two reasons for the appeal are immediately evident. The first is a common principle manifest in Jewish plays including those examined here. It appears as the source of satisfaction felt by the old men who watch Evelyn and Arthur go off together at the end of *The Tenth Man*, and by Sam Levy as first Bessie and Solly, then Hava and David find one another in *Stepney Green*. It is the reason Morry Swartz is willing to reckon Solly Gold's mischief a reasonable price to pay for learning to tolerate and even enjoy other people again. It probably explains why Wesker expresses annoyance with characters who first insist, "If you don't care, you'll die," and then don't show that they do care. The shared affirmation is reverence for life and for the living.

That these modern Jewish plays are faithful to the spirit of the people is indicated by the worth each of them attaches to savoring life and respecting the living. *L'chaim* is a tribute that comes readily from the Jewish throat because it reflects a concept integral to the Jewish psyche, but one hardly unique to it. Consequently, it is not difficult to understand the broader relevance and appeal of life-affirming Jewish plays, witness the extraordinary international success of *Fiddler on the Roof*.

A second reason for the wider attraction of the contemporary Jewish theatre is that it puts on stage Jews who frequently have another level of authenticity. The characters in the works discussed in depth here are typically simple, plainspoken and very much a part of their societies. As Jews, they often embody the sensitivity and responsibility of *menshen*. Foreman kidnaps his granddaughter out of compassion and the need to expiate his own sins. Mankowitz' Fender and Kops's Sam Levy cannot rest in their graves until they have cleared the moral scoreboard. Wesker's Sarah Kahn persists in trying to shape her world to the image of it she sees as right. Dave Simmonds, who devotes much of his life to actualizing a humanistic order, comes as close as anyone in these plays to incarnating all the qualities of the *mensh*. At the other extreme, Solly Gold becomes a scoundrel precisely because he breaks every tenet of the ethic.

But *menshen* are, after all, human beings; while these personae are authentically and unmistakably Jews, they incorporate a broader applicability new to the stage Jew. The dimension is illustrated nicely by the title of the third part of *The Wesker Trilogy*. *I'm Talking about Jerusalem* restates two dominant motifs: the first word refers to the search for self, the last, the quest for elusive goals. Viewed generally as well as specifically, the Jews in the trilogy represent all men and women hobbled by solipsism and thwarted in the pursuit of unrealizable dreams. A number of the personae who have figured in this chapter, in common with those in play after play which deal with Jewish life today,[29] speak out of experiences of life which are not all that different from certain of their gentile neighbors'. That function is a major development, simultaneously exciting and dismaying, which needs to be explored in drama that draws variously on the Jew as a representative figure.

PART TWO

The New Jew

The unprecedented congregation of Jews on the post-1945 stage is not constituted entirely of updated traditional characters. The revised images mingle with the newcomers who emerge after the first half of the century with its cataclysms and rebirth.

In a sense, the intensified vitality of stage Jews is an anomaly. Social and artistic influences operating on post-World War II dramatic literature ought to have vitiated the usefulness of any kind of Jewish images. For one thing, as we have seen, the fundamental source of the Jew's dramatic value is that he is considered different from everybody else. However, he grows ever less likely to be viewed predominantly as an outsider in countries with sizeable integrated Jewish populations. And when other minority groups appear in these same societies, they make outsiderness less than ever an exclusively Jewish attribute.

Then too, otherness has become a universal mode in the theatre. Post-1945 playwrights are likely to disregard the Jew as other for different ethnic or behavioral specifications (e.g., the black in Baraka's *Dutchman*, the white in Genet's *The Blacks*, the drug addict in Gelber's *The Connection*, the homosexual in Delaney's *A Taste of Honey*). A significant group of dramatists are even more likely to express their sense that anonymity and alienation are the essence of the human condition by stripping away all but the most basic definitions of identity (e.g., Albee's Mommy, Daddy, and Grandma in *The American Dream*, Ionesco's Old Man and Old Woman in *The Chairs*, Beckett's M, W_1 and W_2 in *Play*).

Curiously, the very factors that might have diminished the pertinence of the Jew on stage have instead enhanced his role there. Particularly in the United States, the increased visibility of other minority groups in society and in the theatre has energized the creation of new Jewish roles. The Jewish experience frequently serves as pro-

149

totypical in plays that deal with the acceptance and participation of cultural groups in society. The chapter that follows explores the impressive range of apposite parallels between ethnics which have inspired authors writing about outsiderness.

Paradoxically, the Jew's fuller integration into modern life also contributes a new role on the stage which obviously has not given up altogether its penchant for characters endowed with a readily recognized prior history. If, on the one hand, the Jew seems less conspicuous because he is more widely admitted and matter-of-factly received, his very presence serves as a subtle reminder that acceptance, a low profile and even assimilation did not save the six million. The harrowing trials endured by the Jewish people in the last century have inspired a good deal of drama. Since the theatre reflects attitudes more accurately than facts, plays about the Dreyfus Affair, the Holocaust and the plight of Soviet Jewry are examined here for the impact of these crises on Jewish identity in a pluralistic society where more than one allegiance often defines Jews. It would be injudicious to exaggerate the perceptions of selected dramatic literature by insisting that they pertain in the world outside the theatre. Nevertheless, the plays in Chapter Seven make a compelling case for a dominant contemporary image of the Jew as stunned seeker in a world from which all the accustomed values have vanished. It is an image of major consequence, for with it the Jew becomes a generally representative figure. He is seen to be like everybody else, only more so— more so in the sense that he has been more vulnerable to the elemental forces shaping the human condition in the twentieth century: the menace of the unknown, fear, helplessness, reduction to cipherdom.

The affinity between Jews and the rest of mankind is demonstrated by a last group of plays which treat Jewish characters or Jewish experience as metaphors. With works like these, the stage projects attitudes toward the Jews which contrast sharply with those that prevailed for so many centuries. The new drama reveals an appreciation of the Jews' suffering, resilience, social commitment, longevity and, of course, their life-sustaining sense of humor. Collectively, these works depict a varied group of characters who have only two things in common: they represent some response to life that has broad if not universal relevance, and they could not have appeared on stage much before mid-century.

It is more feasible to demonstrate that the role and image of the Jew in the theatre have evolved tremendously since World War II than to pinpoint the workings of cause and effect. There can be little question that the Holocaust and Israeli statehood have indelibly stamped the history of Judaism and with it, the way Jews are perceived. It was inevitable that the revised perceptions work their way into dramatic literature, especially in societies like the ones under consideration here where Jews are active in the entertainment arts. Radio, film and television have contributed to the proliferation of Jewish types. The media are certainly responsible for vulgarizing some of the less esoteric aspects of Jewish life. Yiddishisms, for instance, have earned general currency. No one has trouble understanding the humor of the overzealous police in *Don't Drink the Water* who mistake the caterer's estimate for the Levine-Wasserman wedding dinner for information about military troop provisions. Finally, the iconoclastic sixties prepared the way first for wider acceptance, then for the celebration of ethnicity.

While the modern stage has abandoned some stock characters and renovated many others, it has also created new stereotypes. Appropriately, many of them grow out of the conventional notion of Jews as a family-oriented people. Like the formulaic usurers who follow in Shylock's wake, almost all the new stock types begin as fully-dimensional characters in early plays, notably by Jewish dramatists. Odets' *Awake and Sing!* and *Paradise Lost*, for instance, offer superb prototypes of the dynamic Jewish mother, her bewildered husband, the discontented *belle Juive* daughter, the sensitive, restless son, and the family's devotees of hedonism.

The Jewish mother bursts onto the stage with an energy she must have been storing up during the seven centuries during which she was a nonentity. It is hardly necessary to document her career as unfailing source of seltzer, pocket money, and solutions that work. A woman whose managerial skills are almost as inexhaustible as her litany of complaints, she is not always married to an ineffectual dreamer. Sometimes her husband is a contemporary version of the moneyman, preoccupied with a business that is typically slightly ridiculous (e.g., the manufacture of waxed fruit in Neil Simon's *Come Blow Your Horn*), or, in more realistic variations, not conspicuously successful (e.g., a little tobacco shop in Dannie Abse's *Eccentric*, a frequently-robbed liquor store in Howard Sackler's *Skippy*).

Given her choice, the *yiddishe momma* would brag about her son the doctor. She is, more often than not, denied her choice. Her son is a *schlemiel*, neurotic, compulsive, plagued by insatiable libido and premature balding, and distinguished by a marvelous sense of humor. Because of the roles he writes and the on-and-off-stage persona he projects, Woody Allen has become the consummate exemplar of the latter-day *schlemiel*—confused, frightened, wearily innocent and supremely funny about his outrageously bad luck. It is worth noting that even as a stereotype, the figure of the *schlemiel* has acquired a very special relevance in our age whose finer opportunities are apparent (if denied) only to the Chaplinesque anti-hero. There is a discernible resemblance between, say, Ionesco's Berenger in *The Killer* and Kleinman in Woody Allen's *Death*.

If the Jewish mother *kvetches* about her son, her *belle Juive* daughter (who in this country is sometimes styled as the Jewish-American Princess) gives her even less cause for rejoicing. Whatever her other attributes, it is her body which is typically the *sine qua non* for the young Jewish woman on today's stage. Occasionally, she has no other attributes. With astonishing regularity, "Jewess" becomes a synonym for overt sexuality. The examples are numerous: Holly Kaplan is preoccupied with the physical relationships that repel her in Wendy Wasserstein's *Uncommon Women and Others*; Deborah has all the adventures in David Mamet's *Sexual Perversity in Chicago*; and Doris Klein, in Woody Allen's *God*, propositions everyone in the cast and the entire audience as well.

Like their repugnant precursors who dominated the theatre for centuries, the new stereotypes have Jewish names and speech patterns, but little specifically Jewish substance. Clearly they are much more appealing than the malign or ridiculous figures who skulked through earlier drama. That the portrayals are very often the work of Jewish playwrights only partially accounts for their new-found palatability. Not only do Jewish authors vary in their philo-Semitism, whatever their own predilections, they must respect audience tastes just as playwrights have always done. The big difference is the human substance implicit in the recently coined clichés. Where the profaners, villains and usurers of old embodied what man rejected about himself, the contemporary types reflect the faults, follies and fancies he wryly admits. Jewish stereotypes tend to become generic references. The Jewish mother thrives in many national and cultural groups; the voluptuousness of the *belle Juive* is often no more ethnic than Marilyn Monroe's; the Jewish shopkeeper is robbed along with all the other merchants who do business in a high crime district. Society, it has already been noted, has come closer to the Jew.

The actual proximity was revealed rather startlingly to the present writer in a drama bookshop in Paris. Prominently displayed by itself in a niche surrounded by thousands and thousands of paperback copies of Molière, Shakespeare and O'Neill there was a single leather-bound book. It was *The Collected Works of Woody Allen*. Its place of honor seemed a fanciful confirmation of Fiedler's prophecy about the Jew's coming to seem a central symbol and an essential myth of the whole Western world.

6

The Jew and Other Outsiders

In Sholom Aleichem, a Russian student changes places with a Jewish schoolmate to discover for himself that, as the play's title states, it's *Hard To Be a Jew*.[1] Such a noble experiment is rarely necessary. More typically, the credentials compiled by the Jew over the centuries earn him unquestioned recognition as the quintessential outsider. Indeed the role of the Jew as a "central symbol" rests primarily on his reputation as marginal man.

The Jew as outsider becomes a workable symbol when the misfortunes that befall him by sole reason of his ethnicity have their parallels in the adversities endured by other minority groups. Nowhere is the representative value of the Jew as alien more vividly delineated than on the American stage which reflects the destinies of many and various aliens in the modern-day Promised Land. In plays about outsiders in American society, the Jew appears both as a symbol and, with more frequency, as comrade in the trenches.

An early example comes from Elmer Rice, one of America's first successful Jewish playwrights. In *Counsellor-at-Law* (1931), the career of an eminent Jewish attorney, George Simon, is threatened by an upperclass Yankee colleague. Simon is alerted to impending trouble by his Irish friend, politician Pete Malone, who remarks: "These guys that came over on the *Mayflower* don't like to see the boys from Second Avenue sittin' in the high places. We're just a lot of riffraff to them. They've had their knives out for me for a long time too, but, hell, it's me that has the laugh when the votes are counted."[2] And when Simon confides his difficulties to his Italian law partner, Tedesco responds, "He's out after our scalps, isn't he? And why? Because we came from the streets and our parents talk with an accent."[3]

It is not surprising that the significant body of dramatic literature which treats the Jew as outsider is largely the work of minority playwrights. What is striking, however, is that the preponderance of ethnic dramatists who write about Jews are black. Correspondingly, there is a marked interest among Jewish playwrights in black characters. The figure of the outsider is brought to life so often and so perceptively by these two minorities observing themselves and one another that a consideration of their plays demonstrates a full range of dramatic images of Jews and other outsiders. For that reason, with just two exceptions, this chapter focuses on works written either by blacks or Jews.

The affinities between the two groups are apparent even to foreign observers of the United States. For instance, from France the lawyer and littérateur Rabi, discussing Richard Wright's *Black Boy*, wrote:

> The black problem is historically linked to the Jewish problem with a certain constancy. . . . We have no choice but to observe that wherever the problem of blacks appears, the problem of Jews is not far off. When Jews are liberated, blacks too are set free. Actually the black problem appears to me a heightened manifestation of the Jewish problem.[4]

Rabi adds that "our destiny as Jews is irrevocably linked to the destiny of all the poor, all the oppressed, all outcasts. In the struggle between blacks and whites in the U.S.A., I think our place can only be beside the blacks."[5]

Rabi's sympathies were obviously shared by his compatriot Gabriel Cousin, who in 1960 wrote *Black Opera* (*Opéra noir*) because of "the problem of white racism against blacks which distressed me to the point where it became almost intolerable. I had to do something."[6] In Cousin's play the improvisations of musicians in rhythm within their mixed Chicago jazz group serves as a microcosm of the harmony blacks and whites can create together. The doomed hero and heroine, a Jewish trumpeter and a black singer, manage to trigger every conceivable bigotry in their passion not only to join their lives, but to meld into one another's ethnic identities. Cousin's intentions are more convincing than his play which, unfortunately, betrays the lack of first-hand acquaintance with its subject.

Far more authentic are images devised by artists living close to the ethnics they put on stage. Still the dramatic representations Negroes and Jews make of themselves and of one another are not completely devoid of stereotypes. In Imamu Amiri Baraka's *Junkies are Full of (SHHH. . . .)*, for example, the accountants who keep score for an Italian dope ring are Izzy and Irving. The Halpern family in Lillian Hellman's *My Mother, My Father and Me* has a black maid. Stereotyping itself becomes a concern in Loften Mitchell's *Star of the Morning* where black performers just before the turn of the century wonder what their future will be when "In this growing country every town and hamlet will have a theatre by the year 1900."

George: Yeah, but will we play in them?

Lottie: *How* will we play in them is the question. The Irish will be the drunks, the Jews the money lenders, the Italians the fools. You know what that means for us: (In dialect.) "Poor black me is just old Black Joe— The white man is boss, the whole show!"[7]

Black and Jewish stereotypes have served American drama since the eighteenth century. One may not expect to find the convention preserved in the post-1945 work of black and Jewish playwrights, particularly in light of the fact that contemporary dramatists, as we have noted, tap the "outsiderness" of many minorities or eschew ethnicity altogether in portraying the marginal man. That Jewish and Negro authors have perpetuated the tradition of depicting their people as outcasts may be a way of righting the record, for often they take broad liberties with the simplistic dimensions of established formulas in characterizing the ethnic outsider. Hallowed literary truisms are deliberately inverted or dislocated. Lorraine Hansberry introduces a Jew who is neither wicked, nor crafty, nor even a good businessman. Louis Peterson creates a college-bound black youth whose vision and compassion guide his less perceptive Jewish buddy. Their portrayals, among others to be discussed here, suggest that ethnic dramatists have found rich material for characterization in challenging stereotypes and, more importantly, by asserting the value which lies inside the figure of the outsider. For it is from this vantage point that blacks and Jews tend to describe themselves and one another.

Their plays fall into three large categories: those in which the Jewish past is seen as prototypical of the minority experience, those in which Jewish personae share events which belong essentially to the blacks, and those in which Negroes and Jews are caught up in circumstances which affect both of them.

Plays which focus on the Jew as paradigm have the longest history. Even before the black theatre came of age, Negro playwrights were equating the situation of blacks and Jews and demonstrating that traits heretofore considered peculiar to the latter represented blacks as well. In Frank Wilson's *Brother Mose* (1934), a mildly skeptical black woman challenges her docile husband to name anyone "who, outside the Bible, has inherited the earth by being meek." The husband responds, "Who's any mo meek and humble den de Jews; dey never fight and dey got ebery thing."[8] Both black and Jewish dramatists explore the manifold parallels between their people's histories. This motif becomes a grisly simile in Kingsley Bass, Jr.'s *We Righteous Bombers* (1938), where blacks, discussing how the power structure has systematically tracked them down and exterminated their leaders, observe that they were "killed like Jews." By contrast, the theme of history repeated is given comically brainless expression in Lillian Hellman's *My Mother, My Father and Me* (1963) by Berney Halpern, a twenty-six-year-old who can't find himself and envies the opportunities he sees open to Styron, boyfriend of the Halperns' maid:

> Berney [to Styron]: I wish I'd been born a black man. I wish I had a chance to raise up a downtrodden people.
>
> Styron: Ain't you a Jew, Mr. Berney?
>
> Berney: Yes, but nobody does anything to us anymore.[9]

A notably sensitive concept of the Jewish experience as archetypal furnishes the subtext of Lorraine Hansberry's *The Sign in Sidney Brustein's Window* (1965), at the same time illuminating one of the most successful characterizations of the Jew on the post-1945 stage. Brustein is the literary heir to the lineage established by Galsworthy's Ferdinand de Levis (*Loyalties*, 1922). He is the Jew who has found his niche in society and occupies it with the same aplomb with which he wears his identity.

In making Brustein the axis of her play and the magnet that attracts its other outsiders, Hansberry draws on the historical experience of the Jew. Her protagonist personifies an alien factor that has earned a degree of acceptance in society. Having accomplished that, he tends to regard race, creed and previous conditions of servitude largely as bothersome clichés and to devote himself to other pressing concerns. Hence Sidney, not unkindly, dismisses his black friend Alton's preoccupation with making a cause of his blackness: "Be a Martian if you wanna." He admonishes the homosexual David:

> If somebody insults you—sock 'em in the jaw. If you don't like the sex laws, attack 'em. I think they're silly. You wanna get up a petition? I'll sign one. Love little fishes if you want. *But,* David, please get over the notion that your particular sexuality is something that only the deepest, saddest, the most nobly tortured can know about. It ain't . . . it's just one kind of sex—that's all. And, in my opinion . . . the universe turns regardless.[10]

There is no question of Sidney Brustein's *becoming* assimilated. Married to "the only Greco-Gaelic-Indian hillbilly in captivity," preferring

Sidney Brustein enthuses about life as Alton Scales looks on. A musical version of Lorraine Hansberry's *The Sign in Sidney Brustein's Window*. New York 1972. Photograph by Martha Swope, New York.

his bohemian life in Greenwich Village to the conventional security of his brother Manny's uptown office, removed enough to laugh with genuine amusement at his mother's carping, "*Not* that I have anything against the goyim, Sidney, she's a nice girl, but . . . ," he justifiably feels entitled to his past participle: "I'm assimilated," he declares.

Although he attributes his need for periodic retreats to an imaginary mountain top to a Jewish psyche "less discriminating than most," Brustein manifests distinctly Jewish traits. He loves life with the love of an idealist who prides himself on being true to his moral principles. An incurable optimist, at thirty-seven he refuses to be daunted by bad luck. For instance, the failure of his cabaret and his consequent indebtedness do not discourage him from investing in a small weekly newspaper. Even though he has sworn to put an end to his long career in the service of "every committee To Save, To Abolish, Prohibit, Preserve, Reserve and Conserve that ever was," Sidney is easily persuaded to support ward politician Wally O'Hara's campaign to clean up city government. Sidney is an incorrigible insurgent. "I *care!*" he explains to his gay friend David who writes plays about meaninglessness and alienation, "I care about it all. It takes too much energy *not* to care" (p. 66).

Brustein's spirited concern for other people manifests itself in ways reminiscent of other Jewish characters we have observed in these pages. Like Joe Feinson of *Detective Story*, Brustein affirms the relativity of moral rightness and the importance of tolerance and forgiveness. He refuses to take part in the running quarrel between his wife Iris and her sister Mavis, the ostensible guardian of rectitude, over the attitude they ought to take toward Gloria, a third sister who is a high-priced call girl. Sidney sees Gloria as a worthwhile human being of whom he is genuinely fond. He is cautious but hopeful about the budding romance between her and Alton, the Brusteins' Negro friend, who thinks Gloria is a fashion model. When Alton discovers the truth about her, he is repelled. As an assertive black man, Alton protests he couldn't marry "white man's leavings." "*Would you marry her?*" he challenges Sidney, who responds promptly, "If I loved her." Unlike Sidney, Alton is afraid to think with his heart. He leaves a farewell note for Gloria and runs off, probably proving the accuracy of Sidney's prediction that Alton would forgive Gloria were he to see her again.

A subsequent scene in which Sidney, in the midst of an ulcer attack, cushions for Gloria the blow of Alton's rejection is one of many in which Brustein's behavior recalls Gittel Mosca's. In common with the heroine of *Two for the Seesaw*, Sidney's awareness that people are

often ungrateful and insensitive does not stop him from giving himself away. It is especially in his manner of caring for his beloved that
Sidney invites comparison with Gittel. Like *Seesaw*'s Jerry Ryan, Iris
Brustein has problems ordering her priorities and learning to cope
with her limitations. While this dimension of her life remains closed
to her husband, he finds ways to sustain her emotionally. Sidney's
fantasy world is more elaborate than Gittel's, a magic place where he
can feel that he and the earth are just starting out. He eagerly shares
this precious spot with his wife. Although Iris reproaches her husband for his naïveté that the Wally O'Haras of society exploit, she
clings gratefully to Sidney's resolute belief in himself as

> a fool who believes that death is waste and love is sweet and that the
> earth turns and men change every day and that rivers run and that
> people wanna be better than they are and that flowers smell good and
> that I hurt terribly today, and that hurt is desperation and desperation
> is—energy and energy can *move* things. . . . (p. 142)

Iris is not the only character who is drawn to Sidney's outlook.
A frequent, if not always welcome visitor to bohemia is her sister
Mavis. Mavis' conventional prejudices (e.g., her censure of Gloria,
her initial objection when Iris married a ᴶew and, worse, a Jew who
turned down a job in the business world) prove to be part of the
defenses that disguise the shattered life of a sensitive and gritty woman. Gradually it becomes clear that Mavis looks to Sidney for insight
and strength, very much as Pascal Laumière relies on his sister-in-law
Esther in *Rome Is No Longer in Rome*. Mavis ultimately confides in
Sidney (but not in Iris) the deception that masquerades as her respectable marriage. She concludes, "I knew I was going to tell you about it
though, Sid . . . Since I first saw you I knew those eyes could find a
place for anybody's tale" (pp. 110–11).

Sidney Brustein "finds a place for anybody's tale" because he is
perceived by all those who have known rejection as a veteran of the
battle against the quota, the raised eyebrow and the pointed forefin-
ger, skirmishes which qualify him to fight the real Philistines. In an
unforgettable curtain scene Sidney, felled by an ulcer attack, agonizes:

> In the ancient times, the good men among my ancestors, when they
> heard of evil, strapped a sword to their loins and strode into the desert;
> and when they found it, they cut it down—or were cut down and blood-
> ied the earth with purifying death. But how does one confront these
> thousand nameless faceless vapors that are the evil of time? . . . One
> does not *smite* evil any more: one holds one's gut, thus—and takes a pill.
> . . . Oh, but to take up the sword of the Maccabeans again! (He closes
> down from the mighty gesture and sets down the "sword" [a yardstick],
> then turns and lamely takes his pill and water) *L'chaim!* (p. 96)

Hansberry's play affirms faith in the creative energy of the individual whose ultimate loyalty transcends all particular ethnic and ideological designations to reside in *"Man! The human race!* Yesterday he made a wheel, and fire, so today we're all demanding to know why he hasn't made universal beauty and wisdom and truth too! . . . All he needs is a little more time. . . ." (p. 99). Sidney Brustein emerges not just as the Jew making his way in a frequently hostile society and helping others as he moves along, but as unaccommodated man, determined to shape his world to more human proportions.

But the Jewish persona does not always stand first in the throng seeking admission to the Promised Land. Jewish companions lend perspective and sometimes support in a number of plays whose central protagonists are blacks. In Louis Peterson's *Take a Giant Step* (1953), a Negro youth growing up in an almost completely white neighborhood summons the courage to face the problem created by his reaching dating age. Determined to "say it to them before they said it to me," he rejects all his friends except the Jew Iggie, whose comparable imminent exclusion from the old gang the black sees and responds to before the Jew does so himself. In Peter DeAnda's *Ladies in Waiting* (1968), a white liberal named Lana Kaufmann is sentenced to the very jail whose corruption she had been picketing by a judge who recognized and sought to punish her as the daughter of a man repeatedly brought before him during the McCarthy hearings. Locked up with a lesbian murderess, a mentally disturbed assailant and an unrepentant prostitute, all black, guarded by a sapphic, sadistic white matron, Lana proves her genuine concern for her cellmates by insisting, at considerable personal risk, that their fundamental human rights be respected. Her persistence in caring about others who have stopped caring about themselves restores some sense of human worth to the prison life they share. In William Branch's *A Medal for Willy* (1951), the lone voice of reason among military personnel and southern white civic leaders who aspire to pay homage to a fallen black war hero without encouraging "the Negras too much" belongs to a Jewish captain:

> If you don't mind, General, sir, I'd like to say a word here! (To the Mayor, who is astonished.) I'm from the Bronx in New York and I went to school with plenty of colored fellows, and they were all right! Well— good, bad, indifferent, like anybody! And when I hear somebody like you talk like that about a whole race of human beings, it just—
>
> General (interrupts): All right, that will do. . . . I'll handle this. (Pause. The General turns to the Mayor as if to speak, then imposingly turns back to the Captain with weighted words.) What did you say your name was, Captain?

Captain (his face flushes as he realizes what the General has in mind.
Then defiantly): Berger, sir! Captain Alvin M. Berger.[11]

A sustained portrait of a symbiotic relationship between black and
Jew appears in Howard Sackler's *The Great White Hope* (1968), a work
based on the career of Jack Johnson, the first black to win the world
heavyweight title. Prizefighting functions both literally as the subject
of the play, and figuratively as a metaphor for other brutal contests.
Sackler incorporates into the work three discrete arenas of antagonism: vigorous white bigotry, black discord over black aspirations,
and the conflict of a talented, strong-minded individual with his own
ethnic group and with society at large. While Jack Jefferson is the
focal point of each set of tensions, he is not alone. He is supported
and succored at virtually every encounter by his manager, a Jew
named Goldie.

Forced to agree to all the lopsided financial arrangements and psychological disadvantages under which Jack must meet the reigning
White Hope, Goldie snaps, "He don't have to fight with his feet tied
together?" The manager's loyalty to the boxer springs as much from
friendship as from sound business sense. When the inopportune ir-
ruption of Clara, the black woman ferociously jealous of Jack's white
mistress, threatens to give newsmen yet another angle for scandal,
Goldie prevails upon them to print nothing about the fighter's love
life. He personally posts a substantial bond for Jack after the latter's
arrest for violating the Mann Act. When Jack jumps bail and wanders
through Europe, looking in vain to continue his career, Goldie goes
along, returning to the States only long enough to serve as pallbearer
at Jack's mother's funeral. There the Jew runs into a barrage of abuse
levelled at him as the symbol of all that has lured Jefferson away from
Clara, from his mother and from service to his people.

In representing Jack both in his career and in coping with racial
animosity and with the tensions of a black world unsure of how
"white" it wants to be, Goldie often seems to speak out of the historical experience of the Jew whose life on the edges of society has taught
that sheer existence—never mind the assertion of one's uniqueness—
frequently necessitates tolerating humiliation. Hence Goldie persists
in trying to spare Jack the pain of accepting the American government's degrading conditions for repatriation and a reduced prison
sentence, the ultimate requirement being a rigged fight.

Jack's last desperate yearning for individualism is reduced to ani-
malistic expression in the vicious pummeling he administers to the
new White Hope. Fearful that his man is not going to keep his word
to dive, Goldie collapses and has to be carried from ringside. A spec-

tator jeers at Jefferson, "How you gonna fight without your Jew, spook?" The jibe rather accurately describes the relationship between Jack and Goldie. At the play's end, they stand together in the shadow of the new champion's victory procession. "Let 'em pass by," counsels Goldie. That weary advice responds to several larger questions posed by the play. What other reaction is possible to a value system that rejects the individual who, wanting only to "live like Ah got to," refuses to exercise his talent in the name of a larger cause to which he is not sympathetic? What other course of action is open to outsiders menaced by the boiling passions of a society which finds assurance of its supremacy in the prize ring?

While Sackler's play offers no solution to the outrageous prejudices it exposes, it does break new ground in its delineation of black and Jewish personae. Much of the dramatic power of The Great White Hope is fueled by its deliberate explosion of clichés. Jefferson confounds white suspicions and thwarts black expectations by disdaining any role as savior. "Ah ain't fightin for no race, ain't redeemin nobody," he declares to newsmen before his first championship fight. He chides a contingent of black well-wishers who pray for a victory that will enhance Negro self-respect: "if you ain't there already, /all the boxin and nigger-prayin in the world/ ain't gonna get you there."[12] A second commonplace interestingly twisted by the play lies in its apparent inversion of the master-servant relationship. Yet it is problematic—in Jefferson's era as in our own—to what degree the champion really is the employer of the manager he hires to manipulate and exploit his talents. The relationship between Jefferson and Goldie is more accurately an interdependency which acquires dimension by drawing on yet another displaced convention—the legendary wisdom of the Jew. Put entirely at the service of the black in his fight for the freedom to assert himself, that wisdom supplies just about the same kind of solace, direction—and defenselessness—it has more traditionally provided to the Jews' struggle with the strangleholds of bias and persecution.

By contrast with plays which depict Jews as pacesetters or friends to a fellow alien, a third focus on outsiders shows members of the two minorities as they experience life shoulder to shoulder, if not always eye to eye. There is a great variety of responses to shared plights, from mutual antagonism to mutual growing and adjustment. If The Great White Hope leaves the black and the Jew on the sidelines, William Styron's In the Clap Shack and Phillip Hayes Dean's Thunder in the Index move them even further from the mainstream. Both plays are set in hospitals where the two ethnics are literally segregated from society, a situation which exposes their similarities and rouses the irreconcilable differences between them.

Both works at first represent the Jew as the older and ostensibly more civilized by endowing him with a studied, fragile self-control that contrasts sharply with the Negro's unrestrained hostility. So *Thunder*'s composed Samuel Goldberg rejects hippy black Joshua Noon's suggestion that Goldberg might like to call him "Coon," "Spade," or "Boogie," with a careful, "I don't use that kind of language." Similarly, in *Clap Shack*, Schwartz checks himself as he points out Lorenzo Clark to a newly arrived patient, "He's a mean one, that ni—, oh, I almost said *nigger*. I never like to use that word. You know, I'm an oppressed minority myself." In both plays, deep-rooted enmity frequently bubbles up in mordant humor as Styron and Dean probe some of the reasons for animus between outsiders.

As the title suggests, *In the Clap Shack* (1972) takes place in a urological and venereal ward, this one in a naval hospital at a southern Marine Corps base. Even here the Jew and black stand apart from the other patients because neither has gonorrhea. Lorenzo Clark is dying from granuloma inguinale, a particularly loathsome and fatal disease contracted almost exclusively by blacks. Schwartz has renal tuberculosis; he is thus denied both the comaraderie and the "normal" status of having a social disease.

The prevailing attitude toward Jews as pariahs is expressed only slightly more subtly than the overt prejudice against blacks. When, for example, Magruder, a suspected syphilitic is brought into the ward, he is assigned a separate toilet and sink and issued a special bathrobe, all identified with a yellow S, "so you'll get used to your new status."

Magruder
(Looking at the
letter on the robe):   "S." It's yellow. A particularly repulsive shade of
                        yellow. (Turns to Schwartz) Why yellow? It makes
                        me feel like—(He halts)

Schwartz: Yes Wally? (He exchanges a significant look with
                        Magruder.)[13]

Schwartz, obviously well acquainted with bias, has nonetheless remained a stubborn idealist. He is given to meditating with a book by Rabbi Max Weinberg entitled *Tolerance for Others, or How to Develop Human Compassion*. He goes out of his way to improvise reasons for optimism to counter Magruder's growing alarm about the gravity of his illness. He finds alibis for their urologist's insensitivity. And he tries stout-heartedly to explain away Lorenzo Clark's anti-Semitic jibes and mean tricks by pretending that the black is half-crazed by his terminal malady. Even so, Schwartz cannot always cope with Clark's animosity. He is dismayed and eventually infuriated by the extent to which the Negro is ruled by malevolence and loathing.

As a more dispassionate and intelligent observer, Magruder too is struck by the virulence of Clark's anti-Semitism and asks him to account for it: "Why do you hate Jews like you do? Because they crucified Christ?"

> Clark: No, man, because dey crucified de niggers. Ever hear tell of Ole Man Klein in my hometown of Bolivar, Tennessee? Mr. Samuel Klein who owned de Shoprite Department Sto'? My *daddy* owed Mr. Samuel Klein for ev'y blessed thing he had—owed fo' de raddio, 'frigerator, ten-piece suit of furniture in de front room, an' a fo'-foot picture of de Last Supper dat shined like de rainbow. Den dat year de cotton crop failed, and Daddy couldn't pay de 'stallments, and Mr. Samuel Klein he done *reclaim* ev'y stick, an' lef' dat house picked clean as a bone. (Pauses) Dat is de *Jew* way! Dat is de Jew way of skinnin' de black man's hide. (p. 50)

Magruder's retort that *everybody* has defrauded and victimized the blacks falls on deaf ears. So do his observations that Schwartz has never harmed Lorenzo and, finally, that Clark's unreasonable abhorrence of the Jew won't help any of them in their present situation. Clark's enfeebled response burns with an extravagant contempt beyond the reach of reason.

For all its irrationality, Clark's abhorrence of Schwartz is understandable. The black knows that Schwartz is also seriously ill and that death is the ultimate leveller. He scorns the Jew's tireless efforts to relate to the world of the "clap shack" and beyond as posturing to deceive himself and other people. Schwartz's behavior typifies the pretensions Clark associates with Jews. Even in dying, the Jew, in the eyes of the more realistic black, lays claims to distinctions he does not deserve. "I *do* stink and I *is* black, and I is po' as Job's turkey, and I isn't got kinfolk to mou'n me to my grave," he declares. "But one thing I does know is dat dere ain't no difference between a dead nigger and a dead Jew-boy when dey is both food for de worms. *Equal!*" (p. 34).

Although Magruder can see that Lorenzo makes the Jew a scapegoat for his own miseries, Schwartz does not know how to keep from interpreting Clark's contempt as a direct attack, all the more unnerving because impersonalized:

> Schwartz (At white heat): Hey, listen, Clark, why can't you call me by my real name? I mean, that's not so much to ask, is it? I call you by *your* real name. I don't call you nigger. I call you *Clark*, you nigger! . . .
>
> Clark: Jew-boy don' like to be call a Jew-boy, 'cause de Jew-boy *is* a Jew-boy, and who wants to be a Jew-boy? (p. 79)

Though by pure chance Schwartz is with Clark at the end, not even the approach of death reconciles these two. Afterwards, Schwartz tells Magruder that the Negro's final agony was so great, his helplessness and loneliness so overwhelming that the Jew attempted to console the black with the naturalness of dying. Clark summoned the strength to respond, very softly, in well-chosen obscenities. Undaunted, Schwartz swallowed his pride and begged Lorenzo to forgive him and the whole white race for all they'd done to him. Lorenzo remained intransigent to the last, despite Schwartz's pleading:

"Lorenzo, we mustn't live and die with this awful hate inside us. We must be brothers and love one another." Then at last I said, "I love you, Lorenzo. I love you as a brother. Please allow yourself to love me in return." (Pauses) And finally he spoke—so faint and weak—they must have been almost the last words he said. And you know what they were? (Pauses) He said, "Yes, I'll love you." (Pauses) "*Yes*, I'll love you. I will love you, Jew-boy. I will love you when the Lord makes roses bloom in a pig's asshole." (p. 84)

In the Clap Shack revises several images of erstwhile antagonists. Magruder, a young Southerner drafted out of college, sees the older, less bright Schwartz simply as a white man whose Jewish compassion seems to check masculine assertiveness. Even when Clark tricks Magruder into thinking Schwartz has stolen his wallet, Magruder does not take advantage of an obvious opportunity to voice anti-Semitic sentiments. As an embittered black, Clark makes a careful distinction between Schwartz and Magruder as whites. He responds positively only to Magruder in accordance with a rationale that has not operated very long in race relationships below the Mason-Dixon line: "Us Southern boys got to stick together. Born together. Die together. Dat's equality" (p. 50). Schwartz's acting as spokesman for the white race when he appeals to the dying black for forgiveness is an emphatically contemporary image of the Jew. Such a concept counterbalances the black's regarding the Jew as somehow responsible for his earthly ills and mortal fears, a view which perpetuates a venerable tradition of the the Jew as outsider.

Lorenzo Clark is especially annoyed by his suspicions that Schwartz dissembles (e.g., his fear of death), a charge against Jews levelled much more eloquently by Joshua Noon, the black in *Thunder in the Index* (1972). Much of the pungent humor of the plot issues from hipster Joshua Noon's malicious and finally successful attempts to unmask Samuel Goldberg, a contemporary version of my-son-the-doctor, who protests, "I'm not really [Jewish]. I mean my mother and father were, but I'm not religious."[14]

As *Thunder in the Index* opens, Joshua wakes up in a strait-jacket, in a room with steel bars on its door, remembering an incident during which he urinated on the floor of an office where he'd gone to apply for a job. He recalls vividly that in that room filled with women, "all th' chicks on th' left side . . . had Jewish noses an' all th' chicks on th' right side . . . had Christian noses. An' amongst the Christian noses I spied some castrated noses" (p. 20). Noon's rancor against the Jew who tries to pass for what he isn't is also directed at his sister-in-law, who has created a rift between Joshua and his brother. "Told me she wasn't Jewish 'cause she didn't believe in religion. . . . I told that chick that if the Gestapo knocked on her door, they wouldn't be askin' her if she believed in religion" (p. 13). That animus, added to Noon's awareness of the popularity of rhinoplasty among Jews, makes him immediately suspicious of the doctor who attends him in the psychiatric ward. "Who you supposed to be, Baby?" he inquires:

Goldberg: My name is Doctor Goldberg.

Joshua: Had your nose fixed, huh?

So convinced is Noon that Dr. Goldberg's cool superciliousness must be part of a false face worn over bubbling prejudices that he launches immediately into a campaign to provoke the doctor into betraying himself. Although Goldberg holds his ground and his temper, refusing to take Joshua's bait, his tenacious grip on the self-assurance prescribed by regulations comes off as wishy-washy compared with Joshua's angry, imaginative attacks on the system and on the deceptions that glue it together.

Joshua Noon's original perceptions and his colorful expression of them may well be the products of whatever unspecified disorder has hospitalized him. Nonetheless, he argues convincingly that he really doesn't know his name because he has answered to the inaccurate and unjust names given to him for so long that he's gotten separated from himself. There is no questioning the lucidity of his rage against the office personnel mentality that designed a pink card exactly seven and one-half inches by seven and one-half inches, sectioned into boxes intended to hold the entire, chronological history of Joshua Noon, who is applying for a job cleaning toilets.

The black's alertness and his war on hypocrisy effect the play's peripeteia. Having accused Goldberg of every other kind of posturing, Joshua, who has overheard Nurse Towers confide in the doctor that the patient in 2A is missing from his room, abruptly asks Goldberg how he got out. "You may be foxy enough to pull th' wool over ev'ry-body's eyes, but I done dug you, my man. I see right through your act." Goldberg's nervousness in urging Nurse Towers to leave the room confirms Noon's suspicions. The black continues his attack on both aspects of the Jew's masquerade by going through the motions of "sitting shivver" (formal mourning) for "Dr." Goldberg. Although Goldberg retains enough control to have Joshua sedated into unconsciousness, the success of the unmasking is already assured. Goldberg's protests, "Do you know who I am?" are muffled efficiently as he is bundled into a strait-jacket and given a knockout injection.

Thunder in the Index leaves unanswered the question it raises about who, if anybody, in our society is sane, while making two significant observations about its ethnics. The first is the black's perception and resentment of the Jew as a *poseur,* occupying a precarious, fabricated position wherein he concedes to a certain degree of otherness while earning his niche on the inside by paying obeisance to establishment values. This assessment occurs in the context of the play's second comment, its setting, which depicts black and Jew at the mercy of institutions that reserve the right to single them out and further isolate them, and back up that right with hypodermic syringes, strait-jackets and husky, blond attendants.

The hostility between established institutions and ethnic outsiders becomes the background for tensions between the outsiders themselves in plays that treat the cultural revolution of the sixties. In these plays, the focus is frequently on individuals richer in the determination to grow than in the requisite insight and direction. The manner in which blacks and Jews perceive one another tends to reflect the ethnic personae's own quests for self and status.

In Leonard Berkman's *A Shock of Hair and Burning Eyes,*[15] a Jew named Kitty earnestly seeks outlets for the profound commitment her personal ethics demand she make to serving others. Although Kitty is unable to bridge her estrangement from formal Judaism, her actions are frequently informed by the spirit of *tsedakah.** She thinks she has finally found the opportunity for the total involvement she seeks when her lover Paul, a Jew even more removed from the tradition than Kitty, brings home an indigent black named Isaiah B. Franklin. Paul's insistence on treating Isaiah like dirt and his refusal to cooperate with Kitty's plan to take the Negro in until she's helped him become self-supporting leads to Paul's moving out of the apartment.

But Kitty's act of kindness fails miserably. Isaiah is averse to holding a steady job or even helping around the apartment. Kitty's attempts to change his ways just don't work. In a painful scene in which they try to figure out what has gone wrong, Kitty urges Isaiah to understand that she still believes in what she is trying to do. For

*Tsedakah is a biblical term applied specifically to the relief of other people's poverty as "an act of justice and moral behavior."[16]

his part, Isaiah is all too aware of her efforts in his behalf. He complains of the humiliation of accepting a month's hospitality, "That's a lot to be owing a white woman!" Isaiah does not say "Jewess"; indeed, nowhere does he acknowledge any awareness of Paul or Kitty as Jews.

By contrast with Kitty, Paul sized the black up correctly at first encounter. He recognized that accepting Isaiah at all meant accepting Isaiah as he saw himself. Consequently even in bullying and ridiculing him, Paul earns the black's respect and friendship. "Paul accepts me as I come," Isaiah says, meaning that Paul sees all of his limitations and neither tries to improve Isaiah's situation nor expects Isaiah to help improve it.

Much of the frustration that overwhelms Kitty at the end of the Berkman play stems from her realization that her assessment of another human being's worth and lifestyle, however magnanimous, simply failed to jibe with his view of himself. It is likely that a similar projection of self-concept into what one individual takes to be the image of another lies behind Joshua Noon's disdain for the Jew who pays his admission into the establishment by compromising his identity. Like Kitty's desire to upgrade Isaiah, Noon's disdain for Goldberg and his own sister-in-law reflect one ethnic outsider's unwillingness to admit the validity of the other's attitudes, manners or self-image.

That kind of repudiation is especially patent in plays where assimilated Jews come under the scrutiny of nationalistic blacks. So for instance, in Ed Bullins' *The Taking of Miss Janie* (1975), a black student activist protests the socializing of blacks and whites, including Jews and German-Americans, at a campus party: "The so-called negroes in America is in love with his slave master. . . . Jews are fraternizing and lying down with their executioners and exterminators. Woe woe woe . . . the last days of civilization are at hand."[17]

The Bullins play, a retrospective of the aspirations and anguish of the sixties, includes three Jews whose achievements in the pursuit of role and identity are judged pretty much by how appropriate these accomplishments seem in terms of black ideals. There is Lonnie, a jazz musician, who has escaped from the fanaticism of his Zionist upbringing to the Baha'i World Faith. While Lonnie is no hero, his stance that "all mankind are my family" and his livelihood earned in the integrated domain of popular music give him more room to grow than, say, the play's single-minded black activist, quoted above, who categorically rejects everything white.

A more complicated mode of response to the upheaval of the sixties is portrayed in the marriage of Sharon, a nymphomaniac from a middle-class Jewish family, and Len, a black who prides himself on his intellectualism. The most impressive fact about this marriage, whose unpromising early years Bullins dramatizes in a play entitled *The Pig Pen*, is that it finally works. It furnishes Len the stability and the motivation to go into his own business, and Sharon the mature perspective to respond with spirit to a co-religionist who accuses her of betraying their heritage, "Leave me alone, will ya? I have a baby who is half-black. That's the only reality I can deal with now."

Sharon's accuser is named Mort Silberstein. He is a curious figure, constructed somewhat in the manner of Peer Gynt's onion. As a whining, importunate drug pusher, he updates the stereotyped Jewish moneyman. In his dark glasses and outlandish clothes, boasting of his radical poetry and his participation in civil rights rallies, he embodies the self-styled Jewish beats of the fifties and liberals of the sixties. His complaint that his mother tried to drown him in chicken soup and bury him under lox and bagels exploits yet another cliché to explain how he got that way. But finally, Mort is a rebel not merely without a cause, but without a core. He has neither the seriousness of purpose to remember which values he has supposedly traded off, nor the depth and sincerity to sustain allegiances. Indifferent to his own apostasy, he upbraids Sharon for a betrayal of Judaism of which he is at least as guilty as she. He relies heavily on drugs, both as an escape and as a source of income, and when his black customers no longer pay for his habit, his taunts reveal how expedient his support of black causes has been.

Mort Silberstein stands apart from all the outsiders, black and white, in the plays discussed here. Called by Bullins a "mythic figure," Silberstein might be viewed as a puny vestige of the Jew villain. However, his mythic quality here bears special pertinence to the previously discussed image popular among outsiders of the Jew as initiate to be emulated by other aspirants. The explosion of this myth provides the turning point of the play. Mort's mocking inauthenticity and his lack of real substance galvanize Bullins' black protagonist Monty. Recognizing at last the barrenness that Mort represents, the upward-bound Monty beats him into unconsciousness. Even the connotations of the adversaries' names underscore the significance of the act. That the violent rejection of the Jew as symbol delivers Monty to his moment of truth is patent in his exultant, "I don't want to be a whiteman, do you hear me, Mort Silberstein? I don't want to be a token Jew even. I'm me. You understand?" (pp. 232–33). Having discovered his own identity, Monty shortly asserts it by toppling another icon with the taking of Miss Janie, the "untouchable" white woman.

The Bullins' play presents uncommonly diversified images of the

Jew incorporating as it does the effectively reworked legendary figure with its two unmistakably human but dissimilar contemporary types. While Lonnie and Sharon are certainly outsiders, their Jewishness does not account completely for their marginality. Both find themselves the targets of anti-Semitic derision to which they respond by disassociating themselves from Jewish causes or traditions, though not from their Jewish identity. Tellingly, in answering his taunter, each Jew points to his most compelling concern, as if the calling into question of his cultural identity provoked him to supply a more authentic reason he should be considered an outsider. For Sharon it is her marriage to a black and their biracial child. Lonnie's self-defense is based on overcoming his scepticism about people so he can form enduring personal relationships. In reaching behind surfaces, the play insists on the inside of its outsiders and continues the unmasking we saw at work in *Thunder in the Index* and *In the Clap Shack*. *The Taking of Miss Janie* carries the process one step further, revealing something of the substance that distinguishes one marginal man from his neighbor.

The human dimension of the outsider becomes the center of interest in Lewis John Carlino's *Sarah and the Sax* (1964). Here a dramatist who is neither black nor Jewish explores the possibility that the interaction of Negro and Jew can bring each to a clearer understanding of himself. The play is built on the chance meeting of two ostensibly dissimilar people. Sarah Nodelman, plump and middle-aged, only seems to be concentrating on her crocheting as she occupies a New York park bench. Actually Sarah is very much attuned to what is going on around her, like the arrival of the Sax. He is a thirty-year-old black, filthy and barefoot, sporting sunglasses, a sparse beard and a battered saxophone. If Sarah is something of a *yenta*, the Sax is "away, gone, floating in a world of his own making." Out of their encounter, Carlino creates a brief but satisfying view of human nature.

As Sarah wears down the Sax's resistance to sociability, their comically juxtaposed idioms reveal the disparate experiences that have shaped them. Sarah, who fondly recalls family outings when her husband was alive and their son Herbie was a little boy, believes that every age has its season. The Sax flatly denies the concept of age: "I am the embryo of the universe. I am the fetus shrinking into pre-natal reality . . ." His glib sarcasm betrays his intelligence and sensitivity. Sarah's well-meant but tactless intrusions get under a skin that is thinner than the Sax would like to admit. When she offers him money for a new pair of sneakers, putting the bills into the bell of his saxophone, he removes them and wipes out the sax. Sarah apologizes, "What a world. You think you know how to do things, you don't. Everything is changing. Just now I don't know if I offered you the three dollars for your good or mine. You got a right to be insulted."[18]

The Sax prides himself on not needing anybody. His family, he says, are all over town—in orphanages, jails, hospitals and subways. He caresses his saxophone, "I got my man here and we wail." Sarah objects, "So what's the matter with people?" That is the wrong question. The Sax retorts that unlike his horn which is "straight and true and enough," people are hypocritical and unreliable. In an angry flash of inspiration, he feigns a phone order to "Frankenstein Laboratories" to produce just one human devoid of greed, deceit, hate, paranoia, violence and ignorance. Sarah understands, but still objects. Does the Negro really need people to be saintly before he can respond to them? But the Sax doesn't want to respond. "I just want them to leave me alone. I want *you* to leave me alone!" The determined widow is not to be dissuaded. She is too lonely and ingenuous to be offended by the black's calculated aloofness.

The act that finally breaks the ice between them occurs when the Sax brings out a sun reflector which Sarah finds terribly funny. Her infectious laughter gets through to him and he knows she's on to his need for pretense. The reflector is the black's way of demonstrating that he's as good, i.e., as pale, as "them office cats in Rockefeller Center." Their rapport is shattered by Sarah's impetuous but gracious invitation. Would the Sax like to come Friday night for chicken paprikash, her son Herbie's favorite? The Sax is insulted by what he regards as charity, and his disposition is not sweetened by Sarah's accurate observation that he is too afraid of the world and of people to know how to relate to the simplest kindness. A real argument mounts in which the black's nihilism is pitted against the Jewess's homely values. He furiously denounces clean shirts, cars, bungalows by the shore and "the cats that got 'em." He warns, "We gonna break, break it all up and it don't matter who's got what and who's got who. We gonna have a helluva time when it goes, mamala! An' that's why I hate it. . . . I want to start breakin' it up right now!" (p. 82). Meantime, if Sarah is avid for philanthropy, she should buy sneakers for Herbie and invite him for chicken paprikash. Pushed to the limits of his considerable verbal powers, the black finishes his denunciation with a menacing, cacaphonic saxophone solo that brings frightened tears to Sarah's eyes.

Sarah gets up to leave, then reconsiders. First she has a confession to make: perhaps she doesn't believe life is all that wonderful. The story she told the Sax about Herbie's living on Long Island surrounded by life's good things is pure fabrication. It might have been true if Herbie hadn't been killed in Korea in 1951:

It's funny how things happen. One second, there's a Herbie in the world, the next, there's not. It's a gyp, that's what it is. A buddy came to see me. It happened in a place by the name of K-Eleven. What kind of place is that for a nice bar-mitzvahed Jewish boy to die in? What kind of country is that with places with names such as that? So I'm making up a big story. And I'm a phony. (p. 84)

For once, the Sax has no words. Instead he improvises an extended jazz solo interwoven with Yiddish melodies which acknowledges his new awareness that he is not the only one who finds life baffling, painful and "a gyp." The tenderness and spontaneity of it express a compassionate reaching out from one point of view to another, from one human being to another. They are both embarrassed when it is over:

The Sax:	Well . . . like . . . er. I'll see you, baby. I gotta . . . Well, I gotta go meet the Wolf Man, dig?
Sarah (Quietly):	I dig.
The Sax:	OK?
Sarah:	OK.
The Sax:	Take care, hear!
Sarah:	You too. (p. 85)

Sarah's therapeutic effect on the Sax is indicated by the bouncy tune he plays as he goes off. As for Sarah, she goes back to her crocheting. "And," she chuckles to herself, still marvelling at the Sax's vocabulary, "he calls me *baby*. At my age!"

This excellent little play achieves remarkable effects in characterization. Its personae function as exponents of distinct value systems for which the labels "black" and "Jew" are hopelessly inadequate. Conscious of themselves and of one another as outsiders, the Jew and the black are concerned with more pertinent issues. Their unusual encounter proves a learning experience for both of them. Sarah finds she can admit her misgivings about life and still cherish it with all its sadness and injustice. The Sax discovers that it is all right to give himself to "the enemy," that instead of compromising his zealously guarded individuality, relating to others makes him feel good about himself. In short, Sarah and the Sax come alive in Carlino's play, and as they do, they come across not as ethnic outsiders, but as individuals.

In concentrating on the human nature of the outsider, *Sarah and the Sax* aligns itself with the other plays examined here. In all these works, the human dimension prevails as a principal concern irrespective of the degree of friendship or antipathy among ethnic personae. If such insistence on the whole person does not accurately mirror the stereotyped thinking still widespread in society, it certainly reveals the point of view of the playwrights, most of whom are themselves blacks and Jews. The emphasis on the inside of the outsider apparent in these works reflects an enlightened attitude toward ethnic groups which characterizes the theatre of our day.

From a broader perspective, plays about ethnic outsiders offer another observation. On today's stage generally the center of action is very likely to be at the edges. Barren landscapes (typically less inviting than the park in *Sarah and the Sax*), cluttered rooms that offer frail protection from the woes and menaces outside (not unlike Sidney Brustein's apartment and dream house), and hospital wards (like those in the Dean and Styron works) appear again and again. This is a theatrical universe where man is described by his nightmares and neuroses and defined by his marginality or exile. Alienation represents the human condition.

The horde of aliens that populate the contemporary theatre join the more traditional outsider figures of the Jew and the black, obscuring the universally understood image of marginality the latter once projected by their very appearance on stage. Hence the character in a post-1945 stage who identifies himself only as an ethnic tells us very little about why he is there. His role and his identity come through his individual behavior which, as we have seen here, varies from outsider to outsider, and from one notion of "otherness" to another.

Notwithstanding the expanded relevance of alienation, the image of the Jew in today's theatre regularly evokes the specter of specific events which mark him out among the citizens of an inhospitable world inhabited by so many haunted, crippled and displaced persons. Those events merit close examination.

7

Crises of Conscience
and of Consciousness

Though the business of defining the Jew posed a preliminary challenge in writing this book and elicited the working formula set out in
the Preface, the questions "Who is a Jew?" and "What is a Jew?" are
not easily resolved or exclusively academic. The personae who have
already figured in these pages show that even a simple identifying
principle—a character says he is Jewish and those around him acknowledge the fact—can yield a virtual society of individuals. In life
as in the theatre, the big questions about identity arise less from
recognizing who is Jewish than from the disparity between that determination and what it represents for the person identified. The
elusive question "What is a Jew?" prompts myriad contradictory answers because everybody—and Jews first of all—exercises the authority to say what being Jewish means.

During halcyon days Jews may claim the right to determine "how
Jewish" they are and to decide "not especially." Stimulated by some
social, political or historical circumstance to regard alternate loyalties
as less desirable, attainable or authentic, the Jew begins to reckon
with his Jewishness, to establish how it shapes the person he is. In
the early sixties a scholar who had been observing modern western
European Jewish intellectuals drew up a composite profile of them
which illustrates the phenomenon:

> Absorbed as he was by the culture around him, rejecting all religious,
> national or spiritual attachment to Judaism, he remained at the most
> Jewish by loyalty or dignity, without knowing at all what his "Jewish-
> ness" consisted of. His Jewish existence no longer had any content, except
> sometimes in a thoroughly negative way, as a reminder of social or
> professional difficulties. Persecutions, then the war, finally the establish-
> ment of the state of Israel provoked a series of reactions whose effect was
> to recall the Jewish intellectual's identity to him in one form or another.
> There was a kind of return to the Jewish condition, with all the variations
> that that term implies.[1]

The "return to the Jewish condition, with all the variations that that term implies" is of central interest here, specifically as the return manifests itself in modern plays. The recent past has been exceptionally prolific in stimuli that prick the Jewish conscience and arouse Jewish consciousness. Ushered in by the Dreyfus Affair, our century nurtured from its inception the germs of the pestilence that ultimately marked it as the blackest in Jewish history. At century's start, hordes of Jews were migrating westward to escape pogroms and forced conscription at the hands of the Russians whom revolution, world wars and political expansionism have still not diverted from active anti-Semitism. On the other side of the ledger, the era fostered the seeds of Zionism which put down roots at last in a Jewish state.

All of these events constitute crises of conscience and of consciousness. They have made a difference in the way the world sees its Jews and the way Jews see themselves. They have stimulated a chorus of answers to "What is a Jew?" As turning points, these events have worked their way into literature in differing ways, for art can be quirky as it imitates life. As an example, while the Dreyfus Affair—a series of intrinsically dramatic scenarios if ever there was one—early engaged the passions and creativity of novelists like Emile Zola, Anatole France, Roger Martin du Gard and Marcel Proust, it has inspired little drama. The Dreyfus plays we look at here may offer at least a partial explanation by showing the difficulties Jews have had in identifying with the man at the center of the *cause*.

By contrast with the Affair and despite the intractability of its subject, the Holocaust has stimulated an enormous literature of its own. Moreover, since it so radically revises the way all men, not just Jews, think about themselves, it has very likely altered the future of literature. All Holocaust art exists to bear witness, perhaps nowhere more overtly than in the communal act of live theatre. The Holocaust plays included here were selected because they are especially effective in making us understand something of what it means for a Jew to seek identity in a world where traditional values have been nullified.

Like the Dreyfus Affair, the persecution of Jews in Russia has been treated in the novel and the short story more often than in the theatre. A notable exception is Elie Wiesel's *Zalmen, or The Madness of God*, which delineates a variety of responses to the question of what a Jew can be when he lives with institutionalized repression.

Israeli statehood has made a great difference in the way Jews conceptualize themselves, yet the consciousness of a people that has regained its homeland after almost two thousand years seems to have only begun to permeate contemporary literature. In the theatre, the new spirit resides chiefly on the lively Hebrew stages of Israel which

lie, unfortunately, outside this writer's linguistic competence.[2] However, in this context it is appropriate to recall René Kalisky's *Dave at
the Sea,* discussed in Chapter Two, because its dramatic tension grows
out of divergent views of what constitutes the responsible Israeli citizen. The question of identity is also fundamental to Leon Bernstein's
Dark and Bright, which dramatizes the rancor between well-established
European Jews in Israel and newcomer Yemenites. In portraying conflicts between orthodox and vanguard, powerful and aspiring, and
white and black, Bernstein's play shows the modern-day children of
Zion thwarted in building their country because they are as quarrel-
some as their biblical forebears. Although the ambitious scope of *Dark
and Bright* is not well served by its heavy-handed plot, it does make
the point that Israelis of good will recognize that patience and sacrifice are essential to forging a nation of people "living together for the
same purpose, bound together by the same fate."[3]

One of the most curious aspects of the Dreyfus Affair is that the
figure in its center appears so enigmatic. Over the years an outpour-
ing of rejoinders, both fiery and dispassionate, has attested the general public's identification with one side or another of the *cause.* The
man himself has inspired a far skimpier, less sympathetic reception.
Although Alfred Dreyfus may be a perplexity from any point of view,
an upper-class Jew who pursues a career in the military, the most
gentile branch of the establishment, is nearly incomprehensible to
many other Jews. The point is scored with comic clarity by Sholom
Aleichem in "Dreyfus in Kasrilevke." Upon learning of the French
captain's imprisonment, one of the villagers opines, "A Jew has no
business climbing so high, interfering with kings and their affairs."[4]

However, Jews could not ignore Dreyfus, and they identified with
him if only by regarding him as an unwelcome scapegoat. There is
evidence of that in the uneasiness he stirred up among his French
co-religionists, especially after the disclosure that Dreyfus had been
incriminated by fabricated evidence led to widespread demands for
reconsideration of the injustice done him. The eminent statesman
Léon Blum wrote:

> The Jewish masses even greeted the beginning of the campaign for revi-
> sion with wariness and distrust. The dominant sentiment was expressed
> by a statement like "It's something Jews shouldn't get mixed up in . . ."
> Jews didn't want people to be able to think that they were defending
> Dreyfus because he was Jewish. . . . Jews of Dreyfus' generation who
> belonged to the same social stratum . . . were annoyed by the idea that a
> hostile prejudice might be aroused which would limit their impeccable
> careers.[5]

Possibly the misgivings that Dreyfus aroused among Jews in his
own country served to spice the melodrama that appeared in the

United States. As early as 1898, a play called *Devil's Island* went up at the Fourteenth Street theatre in New York, followed by two related productions in the next two years.[6] In 1917, Jacob Gordin wrote a one-act in Yiddish called *Captain Dreyfus*. The earliest evidence we find of the subject's receiving full treatment rather than casual reference on the French stage is Rabi's mentioning that Jacques Richepin had presented in Paris in 1931 "a bad play on the Dreyfus Affair."[7] Perhaps one would not expect that both recent plays about the Affair would be the work of French Jews. What is more predictable is that each, the first unintentionally, the second quite purposely, draws upon the inability of Jews to walk in Captain Dreyfus' boots.

In Emmanuel Eydoux's five-act *Captain Alfred Dreyfus* (*Capitaine Alfred Dreyfus*, 1967), the Jewish playwright seems convinced his title character can take care of himself. The play, part of a projected tetralogy entitled *The Birth of Zionism*, aims at portraying the prejudice which fostered the Affair and gave the impetus to Zionism. Theodore Herzl, in a cameo role as correspondent for the Viennese *Neue Freie Presse* is stunned by the virulence of the anti-Semitism in Paris. The case is recreated from the delivery to the authorities of the *bordereau* (schedule) that will convict Dreyfus, to his military degradation three and a half months later. Eydoux chooses incidents judiciously, staging them almost exactly as they are recorded by authoritative chroniclers of the Affair, especially Joseph Reinach who in fact plays a small role.

More exceptional examples of minor roles are those assigned the Captain's wife and his brother Mathieu and, most puzzling of all, the shadowy, wooden portrayal of Dreyfus himself. Colorless beside his vividly delineated government and military adversaries, he appears infrequently to protest his innocence or the dishonesty of the investigation. Only one scene allows a glimpse into the man. On the eve of his final hearing, encouraged by his defense attorney to hope for acquittal, Dreyfus permits himself a moment of joy looking forward to a family reunion. But almost immediately, his attention veers to what must pass for his unique passion: he savors the renewed opportunity to pursue the major goal of his life. He recalls how ten years before, hearing the German music that celebrated the anniversary of Sedan, "I wept with rage and despair, I bit my sheets in anger, I swore to devote my life to Alsace and to France . . ."[8] While historical accounts of the Affair invariably report Dreyfus' "military correctness bordering on stiffness,"[9] it is rare to find drama since Corneille which asks audiences to empathize with a character who declaims, "Your homeland has the right to ask your life, but not to ask your honor, for your honor is your patrimony, your honor is the patrimony of your family, your honor is the patrimony of your children" (p. 89). In short, *Cap-*

Maurice rehearses his Vilna players. Jean-Claude Grumberg's *Dreyfus*. Paris 1974. Photograph by Bernand, Paris.

tain Alfred Dreyfus depicts the Captain far more convincingly than it does a man named Alfred Dreyfus. Given its date of composition, 1967, the play can only leave audiences wondering what relationship the Jewish playwright saw between this classical model of a European soldier and the birth of Zionism.

The remoteness of the man Alfred Dreyfus to the generations which followed him is given fuller and more artful treatment by Jean-Claude Grumberg in his *Dreyfus* (1974). The focus here, as in several of the plays included in this chapter, is not on the historical event itself, but rather on a re-enactment of it. In Grumberg's work, a Yiddish theatrical group in a Polish *shtetl* (village) in 1930 is struggling to rehearse a play their director Maurice has written about the *cause célèbre*.

The amateur actors find Maurice's work all but unplayable. Michel, the young man cast as Dreyfus, cannot speak the Captain's lines convincingly. The high drama of the scene where the adjutant tears off the convicted officer's stripes and breaks his sword, repeated over and over again by the uncomprehending players, would have delighted Bergson as an example of the comic effect of mechanizing the human. Michel's mother, a supernumerary in the play, pesters Maurice to write a larger role for her. Surely Alfred Dreyfus' mother must have told her son that the military was no place for a nice, rich Jewish boy. Similarly Arnold, who is generally the leading actor in the troupe's productions, protests that there must be more he can say in this one than "I accuse," although he cannot imagine what.

To little avail Maurice chides his players for failing to respect authenticity. But verisimilitude is exactly the problem. The conviction prevalent in hostile French circles that only a Jew could betray finds its correlative here in the certitude of these Polish Jews that a Jew's being an officer in the French Army is utterly improbable. To the amateur actors, there is nothing real, and certainly nothing Jewish, about Alfred Dreyfus. They continually break into the rehearsal to discuss matters that *are* relevant to them: troubles with the authorities, their love affairs, the plans of Michel and his fiancée to move after their marriage somewhere more tolerant and cultured than Poland. The Dreyfus rehearsal is interrupted by what threatens to be the vanguard of a pogrom. But the brutal hoodlums are routed by Michel who, for the first and only time in the play, finds it appropriate to be wearing a dress uniform and an officer's sword.

In the final scene of Grumberg's play, the actors who have remained in the village eagerly share letters from those who have moved away during the last months of 1930. The young couple who had flirted with the idea of living in England after their marriage have chosen Berlin instead. They write delightedly of the opportunities open to them in a "civilized country where everybody is educated." Equally appalling is the irony of Maurice's apology to the *shtetl* players for having faced them in the wrong direction by trying to stage the Dreyfus Affair. He writes:

> Man today be he artist or worker ought not look back, he ought to look ahead and build the future. Here in Warsaw I'm working in a big factory, I no longer live in an exclusively Jewish world, I am a man among other men, a worker among other workers. . . .[10]

Maurice, now as committed to communism as he once was to his Dreyfus play, ends his letter, "Long live the Polish Communist Party, long live the Soviet Union and—why not also, of course—long live the eternal and international Jewish people" (p. 36).

There are other ironies. An obvious one concerns these warm-hearted Jews in the Poland of the thirties who refuse to believe that in France they put a man in jail "simply because he was a Jew," and who naïvely add, "Here yes, in France no. That doesn't happen." But there would seem to be another irony in the way the play itself has been perceived. Grumberg's use of the Dreyfus case to dramatize the perennial threat of anti-Semitism and the equally eternal idealism of Jews was not lost on theatregoers in Paris where *Dreyfus* ran successfully in 1974. Brought to the United States that same year, even the more obvious title *Dreyfus in Rehearsal* did not get the play across the footlights. All sorts of capricious factors can doom a production, of course, but the present writer, seeing *Dreyfus in Rehearsal* in Boston, was struck by the unresponsiveness in the auditorium. The reception in New York was similarly passive. For American audiences too the Affair is essentially an entry in history books. It is curious, however, that they found equally far-fetched a troupe of Polish Jews as oblivious to Dreyfus as to the storm about to break over their heads.

That storm has already been made the subject of a vast number of plays. They run the gamut from amateur scripts to Goodrich and Hackett's *The Diary of Anne Frank*, probably the best-known play about the Holocaust despite its shortcomings. Holocaust literature presents unique problems for everyone connected with it. The most crucial matter is that art must represent reality as nearly as the artist and his audiences can grasp it, while the reality of the unique subject eludes the grasp. Nowhere is the dilemma more troublesome than on the stage where people and scenes from the unfathomable past are revivified and—if the play uses the theatre effectively—playgoers are drawn irresistibly into the action so that they emerge with a more intimate sense of what they have just experienced. Drama about the Holocaust has demonstrated its potential to sharpen people's awareness of who they are. It easily gets under the skin. It is especially apt to provoke bitter controversies such as Meyer Levin's unsuccessful campaign to get mounted what he considered a more Jewishly authentic dramatization of the Anne Frank *Diary*, the contention raised by Martin Sherman's *Bent* which opens the question of whether homosexuals or Jews were more relentlessly hounded by the Nazis, and the enormous brouhaha that greeted Rolf Hochhuth's *The Deputy*, which accuses Pius XII of failing to intervene on behalf of the Jews.

The Holocaust plays presented here may also be shocking, particularly to those unfamiliar with the genre. They were not selected for that purpose, but rather because they illustrate cogently in five distinct modes the quest for identity initiated by unparalled catastrophe. The first play shows a Jew who adopts fundamental Christian attitudes; the second, a Jew who embodies both tormented and tormentors. A third play puts forth a Jew who persecutes his own people, and the fourth, a Jew who identifies with Nazism. Finally we come to plays about survivors, undaunted butterflies pinned to an inscrutable background.

Gabriel Marcel's *The Sign of the Cross* (*Le Signe de la Croix*, 1953)[11] follows the destinies of a family of French Jews from 1938 to 1948. The play's title is rich in connotations. One of the most important refers to the decision of Jean-Paul, the second oldest son of the Bernauer family, to be baptized. Jean-Paul craves solidarity with Protestanism, wholly subscribing to its tenets. His spiritual quest is sincere; there is no suggestion that he thinks it preferable not to be Jewish in the France of 1938. In their reactions to his conversion, his parents reveal their own attitudes toward the Judaism they retain nominally at best. Simon and Pauline Bernauer's dissimilar attitudes toward conversion and assimilation contribute to making the crisis of Jewish identity a central concern of Marcel's play.

As anti-Semitism grows more vehement, Simon Bernauer's awareness of his own ambivalence toward Judaism sharpens. Simon is fascinated by the racism he deplores. Although he cannot bring himself to subscribe to the sensationally bigoted newspaper *L'Action française*, he reads it daily because he is convinced that Jews themselves have sown the seeds of French anti-Semitism. He refuses to acknowledge fellowship with Jews whose behavior, in his opinion, brings opprobrium on his people, or merely draws attention to them. In short, Bernauer is a snob intolerant of any Jew who is conspicuously Jewish. When a German-Jewish refugee comes to him looking for help re-establishing himself, Simon has him thrown out. He will not contaminate "his" France by encouraging importunate Jews to settle there. The fugitive understands the folly of the Frenchman's illusions all too well. He taunts him with the uselessness of thinking that anyone named Bernauer is a "pure" Frenchman who doesn't have to get involved.

The refugee strikes an exposed nerve. Simon is sensitive even to nominal references to Judaism. He named his firstborn David for an adored brother killed two days before the 1918 armistice serving the France he too loved. However gratifying it is for Simon to have honored the brother whose patriotic principle he shared, he confesses he would have preferred to give his son a less Jewish name. His subsequent children are Jean-Paul, Henri and Lucette.

It is David, a youth with a penchant for demanding logical answers, who makes his father articulate the reason he resists being "condemned to think and feel as a Jew." Simon loves France more than he does Judaism. For him, the loyalties are incompatible. He faults Jews for stubbornly maintaining a phony exclusivity, thereby antagonizing the first nation to grant them full equality. For Simon, the obvious solution is assimilation. He fully understands that Jean-Paul is converting because he needs to really belong and confides that he shares his second son's alienation from the "tribe." Wistfully, he confesses that his own generation is too inhibited to make the same leap.

Ironically, the destiny of this reluctant Jew is shaped by his wife's aunt, Lena Lilienthal. She is an impressively sane and cultured old lady who escapes to the Bernauers' home from Vienna. In 1938, she has no illusions about the future of European Jewry. She admits that her need to keep faith with those who are oppressed caused her to abandon thoughts of conversion she too once entertained. Her faith in Judaism is quiet and firm; it endows her with a depth of character which Simon finds irresistible. Except for their experiences of Judaism, they are kindred souls whose personal sensitivities and conspicuously French aesthetic tastes are exactly alike. Theirs is the most poignant and influential relationship in Marcel's play.

After the fall of France when most of the family has taken flight to the South, Aunt Lena salves Simon's guilt about the effect of Jewish acquisitiveness on black market prices. Pauline's greed in trafficking for meat and butter exemplifies the very behavior Simon deplores. Aunt Lena sustains her nephew when Jean-Paul arrives from occupied Paris with the horrifying news that David has been arrested and sent to Drancy. Finally faced with the cruel choice of escaping to America with Pauline and the other children or remaining with Aunt Lena, who can't leave France or find asylum there, Simon undergoes a remarkable transformation. To his own amazement, he finds himself drawn to share the fate of the very Jews he would once have gone out of his way to avoid.

The doomed whom Simon and Aunt Lena join are not the only endangered Jews depicted in *The Sign of the Cross*. Simon's wife Pauline is an opportunist whose religion serves her as proof of a superiority she has never doubted. Her life is based on a single principle: her family is worthy because it is her family; her people are exclusive because they are her people. Unable to see herself as a member of an ethnic minority ("A tribe!" she expostulates to her husband, "Are we niggers?"), she prefers to think of French Jews as a community which, when threatened, will close ranks. Far from sharing Simon's guilt over the alarming growth of racism, Pauline simply renounces both responsibility and loyalty: "If France rejects us, it's no longer our homeland," she declares.

Simon describes his wife accurately as a hypocrite who loves "power and privileges because you cherish the need to feel yourself chosen all the while long ago having stopped believing in a God who might have chosen you" (p. 497). Significantly, Pauline finds Jean-Paul's conversion to Protestantism ridiculous and never loses an opportunity to shame her son for his decision. When, for instance, Jean-Paul makes his way back to the unoccupied zone to report his brother David's arrest, Pauline wonders aloud why he too was not captured: "Where was he? Out singing hymns with the Scouts?" Reminded by her husband that Jean-Paul too is grief-stricken, Pauline snaps, "He has his Jesus to console him, but I haven't got anybody" (p. 527). A similar display of callous intolerance marks her reaction to the rupture between her brother Leon and his non-Jewish wife Odette. In their divorce she finds triumphant proof of her long-standing opinion of mixed marriages.

Pauline's egocentricity and insensitivity appear to be family traits. Her brother Leon, having decided to escape the intensified prejudice against Jewish doctors by accepting a medical post in America, treats Simon's scruples high-handedly:

Simon: It seems to me that in your place I'd ask myself a simple question: Don't I have a responsibility? Aren't I contributing to having us Jews judged as people attached to France by bonds that are not only flimsy but even a little contemptible, bonds of self-interest and not affection?
Leon: Other people's interpretation of my actions or thoughts do not interest me in the slightest. I have to debate only with myself the only problem which counts: how can I avoid wasting my life? (p. 500)

When Leon goes off to America with his son, he leaves behind his former wife, Odette, who had always been scorned by Pauline. Remarried to a Nazi sympathizer named Reveillac, Odette generously persuades him to come to the aid of the remaining members of the Bernauer family. It is too late to save David, Simon and Aunt Lena, but Reveillac gets the others out of France. Odette's magnanimity must only have confirmed Simon's impression of the true Gallic nature.

The epilogue that Marcel added four years after the play was written, which he claims gives the work all its meaning, supplies details of Simon's last days in a camp. His thoughts bespoke the mingling of Christian and Jewish inspiration. Befriended by a Protestant minister, he read the Psalms and spoke longingly of joining Aunt Lena, who died almost immediately after deportation. Simon wanted Odette to be shown appreciation, and Reveillac, mercy, for whatever his activities as a collaborator, he had redeemed himself by saving the rest of the family. Simon explained that his own decision to remain in France was motivated by his sudden understanding of the term "oblation." David's death and the persecution of French Jews struck him as a sacrament he had to share. He told his clergyman companion in the camp that the only way he could do so was to make himself "part of the suffering of the most Jewish among Jews, the ones who have been mercilessly delivered up to the horror" (p. 536).

These sentiments and Simon's un-Judaistic turning the other cheek to Reveillac indicate that the allegiance he finally pays his Jewishness is largely tinged by the sign of the cross. For Bernauer, "French" is unalienably allied with "Christian." He dies as a Frenchman who ultimately accepts the consequences of his Jewishness without fully reconciling the two identities. His conduct illustrates a phenomenon recorded by several survivors of the camps and expressed by one of them this way:

> Very few [prisoners] had a clear consciousness of being Jewish. The immense majority felt themselves to be French, Russian, or German, capitalists or proletarians, almost always Gaullist, very rarely Pétainists, always ferociously anti-Nazi. For the largest number, things went no further than that. There was a minority—especially among the aged— who manifested the feeling of being Jewish. But even when this feeling existed, it often remained muddled and was poorly expressed.[12]

Readers of Holocaust documents will recognize the reactions in this testimony as a prelude to the state of mind in which countless victims first acknowledged a Jewish identity that, like Simon Bernauer's, often intermingled with various non-Jewish inclinations and allegiances.

While Gabriel Marcel's play shows that truth is complex and rela-

tive, it observes a careful verisimilitude. Reveillac is judged and executed, and although Pauline and Leon see no reason to stand by
Odette, Jean-Paul does. Inevitably, one is tempted to perceive in
the resolution the viewpoint of a Christian playwright. Yet Marcel is
not Racine and he is certainly not Claudel. Rather, he maintains the
primacy of commitment to person-to-person relationships in which
the participants come to self-realization, a position he dramatizes also
in *Rome Is No Longer in Rome* discussed in Chapter Four of this volume. Marcel's play pays tribute to the Simon Bernauers who resolved
doubts about their Jewish identities when they died as Jews by revering that act as equally sacred as if it had been inspired by the sign of
the cross. But it is surely a cross rooted in the Old Testament, specifically in one of its noblest precepts: "Thy shalt love thy neighbor as
thyself." As noteworthy as the play's value judgment is its paradox-
ical resolution of the identity crisis at its core: the Jew who yearns for
a more authentically French identity achieves it not by converting to
Christianity, but by embracing Judaism in the jaws of peril.

If in the shadow of the Holocaust Gabriel Marcel's protagonist is
torn between being French and being Jewish, the survivor in the
center of Robert Shaw's *The Man in the Glass Booth* (1968) is uncertain
whether he is victim or victimizer. He is Arthur Goldman, German-
born and now a naturalized American. At the beginning of the play,
he appears to be a fabulously wealthy eccentric. From his Manhattan
penthouse, he exercises important influence in real estate, banking
and political circles. Many of his actions can be understood as the
self-indulgence of the *nouveau riche* who derives enormous pleasure
from making rituals out of the luxuries and obligations of a lifestyle
he hasn't learned to take for granted. Goldman prides himself on
bizarre demonstrations of his philanthropy, mental acuity and healthy
libido.

Not all of Goldman's behavior seems merely idiosyncratic. Two
consecutive events inspire manic reactions. The first comes when Goldman reads in the morning papers that the Pope has absolved the Jews
of deicide. Sardonically, Goldman watches the televised ceremony
from Rome, improvising his own sound track. He invents a conversation where Hitler tells the Pope that Jews repudiate their true nature
the better to feed on other peoples. "The more intelligent the individual Jew is, the more . . . the more he will succeed in this deception,"[13]
mimics Goldman, evidently preoccupied with the idea of imposture.

Then a delivery man from the florist arrives via the apartment's
glass elevator. He is Goldman's age and size, and the wealthy New
Yorker is alarmed by their resemblance and by his sense that he
knows him. Goldman abruptly manifests paranoia. He cancels all

his appointments and locks himself in his secret room. When he emerges, he is carrying a gun. He identifies the delivery man as "cousin Adolph Dorff." Goldman launches into erratic behavior to "inspire and distract" himself from whatever is bedeviling him. He recites sports records (the hallmark of the quintessential American), orders expensive clothes from his tailor (a silk suit and a vicuña are, he says, "the secret of America"), and does imitations of Hitler, recalling that one of the last times he saw cousin Dorff, he was tapping on skulls with the barrel of his gun. Admitting finally that it doesn't really matter whether the delivery man was Dorff, and thus implying that people are easily mistaken for one another, perhaps even interchangeable, he asks to be left alone, lights a cigar and inflicts a burn in his armpit.

Shortly afterwards, Goldman journeys to Buenos Aires. Upon his return, he instructs his secretary to call him Colonel henceforth. Shortly, three armed Israeli government agents burst in. One of them, Brooklyn-born Rosy Rosen, embodies the intransigence of the eternal feminine with a half-realized caricature of Golda Meir. The inspectors search the secret room, finding boxes of chocolate bars and a copy of *Mein Kampf.* Examining Goldman, they discover the scar under his arm. They have all the proof they need to accuse him of being Colonel Adolph Karl Dorff of the SS mobile killing unit. One assumes that the purpose of Goldman's trip to Argentina was to plant the evidence that helped incriminate him.

Brought to Israel for trial, Goldman-Dorff makes an issue of his rights as an American citizen, but only to negotiate a demand: he will agree to face trial voluntarily and exonerate Israel of kidnapping as long as he can defend himself. He plans to "present such a case as will interest the new generation." He requests a Nazi uniform in parade condition.

Goldman-Dorff stands trial in a glass booth reminiscent not only of Adolph Eichmann's, but of the glass elevator that had carried the Dorff-like delivery man into his Manhattan apartment months before, perhaps suggesting the whole scenario to Goldman. This time it matters terribly who the real Dorff is, and Goldman is determined to prove it is he. He encourages witnesses who testify against him. He jostles the memories of those whose testimony is not sufficiently damaging by reminding them of ghastly details of how prisoners could be made to co-operate in their own ruin. He claims to have ferreted out those who were "still human. . . . They smelled of freedom. And I sought 'em out and I shot them because I could not let them live" (p. 65). Goldman-Dorff exploits his position in the Israeli courtroom to raise a plaguing question. "Why," he demands, "did all those people keep gettin' on cattle trains and goin' to quarries and such like?" (p. 62). In a rhapsodic account, he extols Hitler's charisma and achievements, chillingly indicting all humanity for its vulnerability to delusions of grandeur which derive from standing on the corpses of men and the ruins of civilization. "People of Israel," he charges boldly, "if he had chosen *you . . . you* also would have followed where he led" (p. 68).

Abruptly, the defendant is unmasked by a woman who recognizes him because they were in the same camp. The prisoner is enjoying himself too much to be Dorff, she says, identifying him as Arthur Goldman, a German Jew who saw his wife and three children perish. The real Dorff looked something like Goldman. Perhaps he had Jewish blood; maybe they were indeed cousins. The woman recalls how the SS man visited Goldman in the camp on the Holy Days, bringing him chocolate bars which the prisoner always gave away. But those who ate the candy died from the unaccustomed rich food. Goldman surely feels responsible for their deaths. Moreover, there is an accusation of complicity in the witness's remembering Dorff's "sniffing in the sweet brown smoke from the chimneys and laughing at Mr. Goldman and calling him Cousin Arthur" (p. 69). After the liberation, Dorff came back, shooting prisoners in the nape of the neck. The woman's story corroborates Goldman's earlier memory of Dorff tapping on skulls. When the Russians arrived, Dorff was torn to pieces by the survivors, but Goldman took no part in the mutilation.

The Israeli court pieces together the methods by which the accused man accomplished his stratagem without uncovering any satisfactory explanation for it. The presiding judge suggests that Goldman was driven by his guilt as survivor and as nonparticipant in Dorff's murder, by the desire for justice, and by the need to put on display "a German who would say what no German has said in the dock." Mrs. Rosen demurs. She accuses Goldman of anti-Semitism and of the masochistic desire to be scourged and crucified, a charge reinforced by Goldman's bitterness when he learned of the Papal Council's exculpating the Jews of deicide. As for the man in the glass booth himself, he enigmatically explains he wanted to do something for "them—something they'd understand," but it is not clear who the beneficiaries of his sacrifice were to have been. At the last, Goldman comes apart. In a frenzied confession, he muddles being chosen for the Final Solution with participating in a fantastic rampage. He boasts that "we who were German and Jewish" ravaged the countryside and annihilated blond soldiers. Then, as if to reject this image and all the others he has created for himself, Arthur Goldman strips himself to the skin, steps back inside the glass booth and locks the door.

Shaw's play raises more questions than it answers. It is not plain whether Goldman's elaborate artifice is intended to exorcize the past or give it meaning, to satisfy the Hebrew passion for justice or the human craving for logical answers, or to do penance for any one of various kinds of guilt. Like many creative works about the Holocaust, this one demonstrates that the zeal to probe even a corner of what happened sheds pathetically little light on the impenetrable. However, *The Man in the Glass Booth* poses two unanswerable questions with notable effectiveness. The first of these is the deceptively simple "What is a Jew?" Goldman-Dorff complains to one of his guards, "They keep askin' me if I'm Jewish. I don't know what that word means" (p. 47). At the beginning of the play, he remarks jokingly but accurately that even in Israel, councils are deliberating the question. Goldman's scornful reception of the Papal exoneration is not untinged by ambivalence at the loss of one of the traditional marks of Jewish identification: a Jew is he who is made a scapegoat with the approval of the Church. Just before he assumes his Nazi masquerade, Goldman sarcastically confides in his secretary Charlie that a "couple hundred years and my . . . effort might be in vain. Only Israel left."

Charlie: How'd you mean, Colonel?

Goldman: The final assimilation. What the council said . . . was: "The Jewish people should never be presented as one rejected, cursed or guilty of deicide, and the council deplores and condemns hatred and persecution of Jews whether they arose in former or in our own days." Overwhelming majority! Ain't that ironic? (p. 29).

What may strike Goldman as ironic is the anachronism of the Vatican Council's solicitude for the Jewish people. The apparent paradox in a Jew's reluctance to be forgiven or accepted can be explained if the Jew feels unworthy of pardon because he believes himself guilty, though it is not Christ's death but his own brethren's Goldman feels responsible for.

Out of that paradox grows the second, more troublesome question posed by Shaw's play. It is embodied in the very image of Goldman-Dorff and reiterated in much of the testimony he gives in the Israeli courtroom: to what extent are the persecuted and the persecutor inseparable? How answerable are Jews for their own destruction? Arthur Goldman never stops emphasizing that he is German *and* Jewish. Neither garbing himself in a Nazi uniform or a vicuña coat nor stripping himself naked resolves the conflict that tears the man apart.

The blurring of distinctions between oppressor and oppressed is explored even more intensively in a play whose startling subject is a

Jew who supervised the annihilation of his own ghetto. Such an improbable topic might be easier to believe if it were fiction. It is not. Harold and Edith Lieberman's *Throne of Straw* (1974) rests firmly on meticulous research in the archives of the extraordinary career of Mordechai Chaim Rumkowski, the Chairman of the Lodz ghetto. The Liebermans were initially intrigued by Solomon F. Bloom's "Dictator of the Lodz Ghetto" (*Commentary*, February 1949), which sets out Rumkowski's modus operandi and the circumstances under which he exercised authority from 1939 to 1944. The Germans established in Lodz, as in other conquered cities, a Jewish Council designed to beguile Jews into thinking that they could control their destiny by co-operating with the Nazi command. In a manner that has not been definitively explained, Rumkowski, an unremarkable citizen, got himself named Chief Elder of the Jewish Council. Bloom comments cynically, "He alone was to maintain relations with German officials, and through them with the planet."

If, as the title of the Liebermans' play suggest, the Chairman's position was largely illusory, his power was most definitely not. Under his leadership, the Jews in the Polish city were made to implement their own ghettoization, organize slave labor in the textile mills and maintain a mercilessly efficient Jewish police force. The Chief Elder's gravest responsibility lay in presiding over selections for the transports. Insatiable deportation quotas and the arduousness of existence in the ghetto ultimately claimed all but about a thousand of the city's quarter-million Jews.

In making a dramatis persona of Rumkowski, the playwrights take full advantage of the extravagant behavior educed by his rising star. He is shown in white cape and flowing locks, sitting for a portrait that will appear on the ghetto's postage stamps and currency. The Chairman's careful grooming and his travelling about by horse-drawn cart appear insensitive denials of the squalor in Lodz, just as his drive to make the city's textile mills indispensable to the Germans seems to ignore the fact that ever-diminishing ranks of workers in them are starving and ill. Yet Rumkowski's megalomania grows out of an extraordinary vision which *Throne of Straw* emphasizes above all else.

Chairman Rumkowski believed he had a mission. He envisioned himself as one in the long line of Jewish leaders who have had to sacrifice many to save a few. So compelling is his vocation that when an idealist chides him for not ransoming the entire Council which had been arbitrarily rounded up by the Nazis, the Chief Elder replies, "Even God doesn't save all." *Throne of Straw* focuses on a Jew who operates less out of his own psyche than out of a personal, fanatic dedication to the biblical forecast (Isaiah 10:21) and the folk-

loric command that a remnant of the Jewish people must be preserved. The principle renders him enterprising, for example, in dealing with Commandant Hans Biebow who would make of Lodz a Polish
Manchester. The Chairman guarantees the German an endless supply
of workers and a substantial bribe to route textile orders to Lodz.
His monomaniacal determination to save Jews at any price leads him
to support ghettoization as the most effective means of protecting
against hooliganism and of delimiting Jewish jurisdiction. When Rumkowski is challenged by his own people to defend his arrogance and
his ruthlessness in suppressing even a hint of insurrection, he replies,
"We work or we starve. There is nothing in between. . . . And why?
Because the price of survival is always right."[14]

The price of survival can be gauged in the disintegration of one of
the families in the Lodz ghetto, the Wolfs. To galvanize her household into appropriate action, Ada Wolf, a vigorous widow, forces her
daughters to abandon their rebellious activities to hawk armbands in
the streets and work in the factories. The family patriarch, Israel, a
perceptive diarist, is treated like a harmless madman, while the orphans the Wolfs have taken in are dispatched into the streets to
smuggle and steal. The son, Gabriel Wolf, is coerced into accepting
the "privilege" his mother has obtained for him, membership in the
hated Jewish police force. And Ada is not above currying favor for
herself and her family by indulging Rumkowski's philandering. Her
opportunism is most chillingly demonstrated when her distraught
sister-in-law Hannah, a lawyer resettled to Lodz from Berlin, arrives
seeking refuge. Ada takes her in reluctantly only after Hannah produces a large sum of money. Once Hannah's funds are depleted and
she herself is too broken to work efficiently, Ada cooly hands her
over for deportation. But even Ada's efficiency is checked by the
Nazis' crushing demand for the aged and for children under ten, an
order that reduces the Wolf family to deciding who among them will
be sent to die. In the end, of course, they all go. It falls to Gabriel to
arrest his own family and, through a grim stroke of prosaic justice, to
be betrayed himself into joining them in the cattle car.

Despite the trappings of his office and the adulation he encourages,
Rumkowski is fully aware of the misery and discord among his people. Still he quells uprisings, maintaining that the severest Jewish justice is preferable to Nazi cruelty. Although he knows the fate await-
ing those who board the trains, he promises them they are going to
work in Germany. Victims, he holds, are better left with their illusions. His resolution is shaken only when the Nazis insist on deport-
ing children. Himself childless, Rumkowski had directed an orphan-
age for years and was genuinely devoted to youth. One can guess at

the internal struggle that preceded his coming to plead with the Jews of the ghetto, "Give me your children. I must have your children. If not, God save us, they'll take everybody."

Ever worsening conditions and a strike in the factories fail to dissuade him. Rebuked by his disabused and insubordinate wife and by Israel Wolf, often the voice of the chorus, Rumkowski remains adamant in his mission. He argues that neither Jew nor German has the right to judge him, that is for God alone:

> I'll go willingly—with pleasure, before any court of Jews—here or in the next world and state my case. And if they dare to put me on trial, they'll have to try God, too. If you ask Him, He can tell you that we had an agreement, and that I upheld my part of the bargain. . . . I won't deny that I had to do terrible things, to give away women and children—but for every thousand, I saved two hundred! I stood as a watchman before the door of death and snatched them from the furnace one by one and I am not ashamed.

As Russian guns are heard in the background, the last of the Lodz Jews are bundled into boxcars. With dignity, Rumkowski joins them. At the end of the play, the fading clanging of the trains and the darkness are punctuated by the voice of Yankele, a Hasid whose songs and commentary hyphenate the episodes of *Throne of Straw*. Rumkowski, Yankele assures the audience, perished at Auschwitz. But Yankele is not quite through. Himself a survivor of Lodz, he is now the impressario of this play. In that role he bids the audience, "Please don't feed me your dinner table morals/About how they should have behaved./ Only say what you would have done."

Yankele's question is not answered easily. Certainly *Throne of Straw* depicts an ambitious, calculating individual who inspires no more compassion than he demonstrated. However, by insisting on the mythic role to which Rumkowski clung, the play allows us to perceive him as a stubborn seer if not a tragic visionary. The Chief Elder of Lodz was an ordinary Jew thrust into an extraordinary position. His daily lot was to do battle with antagonists almost too overwhelming to endure: pure evil and its concomitant, unmerited suffering. Mordechai Chaim Rumkowski acted where most men would have been immobilized. He appropriated freedom where there was none. It is as impossible to condemn him as it is to praise him, and the special achievement of *Throne of Straw* is the insight it permits into an all but unimaginable crisis of conscience in an all but inconceivable situation.

The image of a Jew whom Nazism turns into an authoritative collaborator is uncommon. The figure of a Jew who sees his own people as his oppressors and is enthralled by Hitlerism must be unparalleled.

This unique persona is the eponym of a play René Kalisky aptly entitled *Jim the Temerarious* (1972). The work is supported by aesthetic as well as historical underpinnings.

In an article entitled "The Air-Conditioned Theatre" which appeared in 1971, Kalisky censured the contemporary stage for abandoning its traditional sacerdotal function. He charged that modern drama short-changes society by depicting the sacrifice of "ambiguous man" in today's "ambiguous civilization" as if the tragic dimensions of his existence could be understood rationally. The erroneous premise that the present moment represents the zenith of human progress leads the theatre to facile interpretations and hypocritical catharses which, says Kalisky, ignore the essential causes of contemporary crises. As a prime example, he criticizes the presentation of Hitlerism as a "mili-tary-sado-masochistic hiatus." This reductive approach, argues Kali-sky, passes over those facets of the Nazi apocalypse which have no ready referent in the culture, psychology or metaphysics of our age, or perhaps of any other. He is pessimistic about art's failure to seize

the underlying causes of the fascist victory—the only ones which are likely to enlighten us legitimately about the power of the fascination exerted by such an ideology on men whose agonizing availability [*dispon-ibilité*] constitutes, moreover, the real problem of civilization in crisis. The very problem which still awaits elucidation.[15]

The play about Nazism which Kalisky published a year later begs to be considered his artistic explanation of the "availability" he saw as the real problem of our crisis-bound civilization. Availability is very much the status of the Jew in the center of the play.

Jim the Temerarious (*Jim le Téméraire*) has a simple but suggestive set, a room dominated by the immense red swastika on the floor, a bed its only furniture. The play gets at the question of "availability" by sub-verting a number of conventional notions. One is time. The work establishes its own chronology so as to put forth contrasting views of the Third Reich before, during and after the fact. On the simplest level, the distorted chronology comes through the depiction of the personages who fostered or incarnated the ideology of National So-cialism. In a near-parody of Nazism as a "military-sado-masochistic hiatus," prophets and chieftains appear and meld into one another. Hence the high priest of the New Order, Lanz von Lisbenfels, be-comes Dietrich Eckart, launcher of Hitler's political career who, in a subsequent transformation, turns into Heinrich Himmler. The fanat-ical founder of the secret Thule Society, Karl Haushofer, fades into Reinhart Heydrich, Eichmann's collaborator in the Final Solution, who ultimately is replaced by the brilliant Nazi apologist Ohlendorf. All these principals claim responsibility of various kinds for making Hitler the messiah of the Thousand Year Reign. Otherwise there is little consensus among them. The conflicting viewpoints of the initiates are given a powerful rival, however.

The infighting among strong men which constitutes one focus through which the changing fortunes of the Third Reich are seen in Kalisky's play is always countered by another—Hitler's egomania. The Führer devalues the lure of Lanz's mysticism and shrugs off Eckart's threats, proclaiming himself a latter-day Sun King: "The Party," he says, "is me." His supreme arrogance notwithstanding, Hitler cannot ignore entirely the influences of the shifting alliances among those who seek to control him and so leave their own imprint on history. Hence he feels compelled to remind his associates that they are hangers-on. "I carry the Party on my shoulders," he declares, "if I were to stop carrying it, it would fall on its face for eternity."[16]

Contrary to any expectations, Hitler's perspective is shared enthusiastically by the title character. Jim (the Anglo-Saxon overtone is misleading, it is a nickname for Chajim) is not alone in being rash. Kalisky has had the temerity to reject another conventional given—that Hitler is necessarily anathema to a Jew. Jim, at whose bedside the action of the entire play is laid, seems the very antithesis of a Jew. "I didn't want to be named Chajim or to be circumcised," he tells Hitler, explaining his alienation from his people. "I am not a man in accordance with their concepts. . . . The Jews have not accepted my suffering, although I suffered with them. But they laughed because I suffer all the time" (p. 44).

The physical effects of Jim's suffering are apparent. Deathly pale, emaciated, filthy, hardly able to stand, a stutterer, he evokes the image of a concentration camp survivor, which he is not, or one of Beckett's human wrecks. While sharing some of the afflictions of both, Jim endures highly singular woes. Twenty years after the war, he still trembles from fear of persecution which comes from several quarters. Pitied and mocked by his co-religionists who refuse to take seriously his incessant terrors, Jim feels exploited by Jews who persist in finding jobs for him so he can lead a "normal" life. In addition, he is thwarted by the German government which will pay only a pittance of reparations due him because Jim cannot prove that his stuttering is related to the war. He prefers to stay in bed and conjure up through his voracious reading phantasms of the Nazi era which was the most exciting in his life. "When others lose their humanity, I regain mine . . . I feel so well in extreme situations," he recalls gratefully to Hitler (p. 118).

That Jim must not be dismissed as malingerer, paranoiac or masochist is assured by the role he plays with Hitler and his henchmen. Here Jim earns his epithet "temerarious" and here Kalisky's play clarifies the dangerous appeal of fascism to the contemporary "ambiguous" man whom his protagonist represents. Jim accepts without question that he is "nothing at all." He resents the world which refuses to let him develop no other aptitude. "The Jews refuse to let you be yourself and nothing more," he complains. By contrast, National Socialism's New Order relies precisely on types, not individuals, on new men who are, in Hitler's words, "multiple products, standardized, insignificant and totally empty." No wonder that despite his fears, Jim spontaneously thrilled to the overwhelming sight of thousands of marching SS men. He is spellbound by Hitler because he recognizes in him a genuine superman in touch with cosmic energies, the actualization of a two-thousand-year-old myth destined to replace Judeo-Christian messianism. Attuned to a kind of cyclical time, Jim understands that the destruction of the present humanistic order is a prerequisite for the New Order in which the individual has no importance. He addresses Hitler exaltedly, "You are the soul of the world at work. You pass . . . and with your passage the century freezes. Human suffering counts for zero on our planet" (p. 96). His nihilism leads Jim to believe that only Hitler can give a sense to the world and to anguish like his.

Jim's estimation of Hitler is as informed as it is instinctive. Learned in the historical, legendary and mythological roots of Nazism, he perceives the differences between Hitler and the acolytes surrounding him and exposes the dangers the latter represent. Here Jim's audacity and awesome knowledge serve him well. He is able to detail the power structure's self-serving maneuvers, the source of its anti-Semitic fixations, underhanded methods and personal shortcomings. Jim's animus against the figures in the Nazi high command is fed by his resentment of how greatly they have falsified the great Germanic myths which he has studied with fascination, myths which should illuminate and inspire the New Order only in their purest form.

Predictably, Hitler is charmed by Jim's enlightened support and adoration. Unrelenting in his anti-Semitism, the Führer nonetheless appreciates that "This Jew is a marvel; he lets himself be rocked by the natural rhythms which govern the world" (p. 87). While Heydrich fiddles an Albinoni adagio, Jim, who ordinarily can barely get out of bed, expresses his joyous anticipation of the new age in a Hassidic dance. Watching him jump and twirl, Hitler makes one of the play's most intriguing observations about Jim as a Jew:

He dances with his brain. His body is a prisoner of its origins. But he lifts it despite its weightlessness; if he weren't a Jew to the marrow you'd say watching him that he was the new man, the master of space who will go through the universe determining the useful and the superfluous. (p. 88)

Jim the Temerarious bids us consider Jim as representative of the new man. His negation of individual worth, his alienation from the most basic values of Judaism, his inability to function in a nontotalitarian society, his turning his back on life to lead an intrauterine existence stimulated only by war all are aspects of the "anguishing availability" Kalisky cited in his 1971 essay. Of course Jim's Jewishness renders all the more shocking his lucid and eager offering of the abnegation essential to the triumph of a self-styled master race. It is hard to accept the terrible irony of a Jew's saying emotionally to Hitler, "You have absolute right of life and death over me." Still, there is no need to document the bewitchment exercised by the Third Reich on multitudes of disaffected, disenchanted human beings. Kalisky's play posits that the appeal of such identity-conferring ideologies is far from attenuated. It suggests that Jim, impossible to ignore whether he represents a grotesquely mutant Jew or "ambiguous man" generally, still lies abed, regretting the defeat of Hitler, thirsting for the days when he "vibrated in unison with so many, many people."

In shaking us loose from received ideas and inducing us to ponder its disturbing mysteries, Kalisky's play succeeds in reviving the theatre's hieratic role. *Jim the Temerarious* prevails upon us to consider the Hitlerian cataclysm not as a hiatus, but as a volcano, still largely unexplored despite all the accounts it has inspired, far less dormant or unique than we would like to believe.

While *Jim* constrains us to contemplate past and future from an unfamiliar focus, other Holocaust plays use the stage to penetrate different vistas ordinarily shielded from view. The theatre provides a specially effective medium for expressing some of the most perplexing aspects of the Holocaust—the unreliability of facts, the unfixability of time, and the confusion of identity. Unlike the printed page, performance can represent the simultaneity of conflicting truths. Characters on stage are de facto other than what they appear to be, an eminently suitable attribute for the personae of plays about the Nazi era when people underwent so many kinds of transformations. An intriguing observation about the theatre as an arena for relative verities came from Gustaf Gruendgens, an actor accused of scrambling to fame on the backs of Jews banned from performing in Hitler's Europe.[17] Gruendgens recalled that in the bewilderment of those times, "the stage was the only certainty: When the stage door opened, I knew out would come the lady in the green dress and not an SS man."

The premise that the stage represents a certainty renders communicable the situation of people suspended in a limbo where it is inconceivable to forget, impossible to remember and essential to do both. No crisis of conscience and consciousness ever wrought more torturous questions of identity, for who and what these Jews are depends on facts undertermined and undeterminable.

A particularly moving example comes from Jean-Claude Grumberg. In his autobiographical *The Workshop* (*L'Atelier*, 1979), he dramatizes the plight of his mother in the years following his father's deportation. Despite her obvious talent for living, Simone cannot form new bonds because she has no sure reason to abandon the old ones definitively. She lives in a kaleidoscope of resignation, hope and the blank stare of reality. She explains to a co-worker:

> The hardest thing is not to know, to think that perhaps he is lost somewhere, not even knowing his name any more, not remembering me or the kids, that happens, but I tell myself time will take care of it . . . The other day as I came out of the market I saw a man from the back with a shopping bag in his hand. I don't know why, but I said to myself, just for a second I thought, "It's him! With a shopping bag!" That's funny because he wouldn't even go buy bread, he hated doing the shopping. . . . Even though the authorities won't issue a death certificate, it's not that they still have any hope, it's that they aren't sure of anything, otherwise they'd be only too happy to do the paperwork and file all the documents so that everybody would be completely accounted for and nobody would talk about them anymore.[18]

The poignancy of Simone's predicament is redoubled for she is talking here to a man for whom she feels a palpable but unmentionable mutual attraction. He is himself a survivor. His knowledge of the camps and Simone's description of her husband leave him no doubts about the latter's fate. Yet he has no proof, only the wisdom of experience. His abrupt departure from the shop where he worked with Simone wordlessly acknowledges the perfidy of truth, particularly as a basis for hope.

The unconfirmability of the past is dramatized quite differently by Serge Ganzl in *Fragments* (*Fragments*, 1978). Here a group of homeless Jews, wanderers since their liberation from the camps, find themselves together on Passover. Incapable of sustaining a discussion of their recent past, vague about their immediate future, they recall bits and pieces of tradition, trying to find something of present relevance in them. The holiday reminds them of lines from the Hagaddah, the home service for Passover, which acquires a grim new pertinence to Jewish identity:

Samuel: There are thirteen attributes of God, Myriam . . . There are eleven stars in Joseph's dream.

Myriam: . . . I spent six days and six nights in a boxcar. I stood up for thirty-six hours and the dogs were polishing their teeth . . .[19]

Still another kind of endeavor to apprehend the past and make it contribute to the present is Leeny Sack's *The Survivor and the Translator* (1980). Sack characterizes the piece as "a solo theatrical work about not having experienced the Holocaust by a daughter of concentration camp survivors." The author's performance of her own work conveys vividly the anguish of the need to tell betrayed by the inadequacy of human language. The thread which unifies anecdotes, quotation, exposition, ominous sound effects, and even more menacing silences in *The Survivor and the Translator* is Leeny Sack's determination to make the experiences of the millions who did not survive, as well as those of her parents who did, reach into her life and give it shape and meaning.

One of the best-realized dramatizations of the fluidity of Holocaust time and fact is Armand Gatti's *The Second Existence of Tatenberg Camp* (*La Deuxième Existence du camp de Tatenberg*, 1962). Memory is the axis, mainspring and subject of this play about the ability of the past to wreak chaos in the present. Gatti does not try to duplicate external reality. He substitutes the reality of memory because memory accommodates the simultaneous existence of the living and the dead, the juxtaposition of different time frames, and abrupt shifts from one site of illusions to another. Uncertainty penetrates even the language in the printed script which is full of parentheses where characters reconsider their own remarks. Subjective perceptions are orchestrated with extravagant lighting and sound effects—barking rifles, blaring music, truck horns and turning wheels—appropriate to the grotesqueries both of a fairground and of a concentration camp.

The second, or remembered existence of Tatenberg Camp is in some respects as cruel as the first. Ambiguity renders nearly intolerable the post-war retrospect of the insane epoch of Tatenberg, which Gatti intends to stand for all of the camps.[20] The personae in the play are tormented by unanswerable questions about the impenetrable past.

One of the principal characters is not a survivor of Tatenberg. She is Hildegarde Frölick, the young widow of a Wehrmacht corporal. He and two companions on duty at a Russian outpost were shot for abandoning their post after two days without food had driven them to the pursuit of a snow hare. Alone, Hildegarde continues the puppet show she and Frölick ran before the war. At each performance, three soldier marionettes are executed against the Tatar wall and describe their burial in the steppe. That is the widow's way of taking part in the past which she did not share.

Hildegarde does share the professional life of Ilya Moïssevitch, a forty-five-year-old Baltic Jew. He survived camp after camp, only to end up at Tatenberg. Now he also makes his living in the deliberately artificial world of the carnival where one can master his life, at least for the duration of his act. Like Mrs. Frölick, Moïssevitch is obsessed by memories, in his case of experiences lived rather than imagined. He remembers convoys of trains which snaked across Europe after the first World War, dumping what remained of the men who had fought. Then too reality was insufferable, and both victors and vanquished felt the need to revise it. "The war left behind an immense dream-making machine which none of the survivors could (or wanted to) do without," Ilya recalls.[21] Twenty years later what he sees as the same war broke out again. At its end it left a new generation of dazed, wandering survivors and ghosts, Moïssevitch among them, making up their lives from day to day.

The possibility that Hildegarde and Ilya might console one another is effectively checked not by adversary nationalistic loyalties, but by the opposite directions in which their memories operate. As the playwright himself explains, "With Moïssevitch, the past creates the present; with Mrs. Frölick, the present reconstructs the past" (p. 244). At the beginning of the play they introduce themselves in the "Ballad of the Man and the Woman Who Were Searching for One Another (or Searching for Their Identity) Along the Danube." Unfortunately the Danube persists in overflowing its banks, throwing up people from the past who control the possibilities of the present. That is because the horrors they experienced together have fused them so that, as Richard Coe puts it, "The actual *identity* of each is compounded out of the identities of those who were once with him. . . ."[22]

Some of the deportees liberated at Tatenberg no longer had a country to which to return. A flashback shows them suspended in a protracted wait in front of the barbed wire, simulating a "normal" life. For four years after Tatenberg was freed, Moïssevitch and some of the others found refuge in its railroad station, a movie-set structure fitted out with false ticket windows, waiting room and motionless clock which had been designed to reassure the incoming prisoners. Here Ilya's companions are Abel Antokokoletz, a sixty-year-old Jew from Cracow, Gregor Kravchenko, a Ukranian boxer, and Manuel Rodriguez, a Spaniard who has spent a quarter of his fifty-two years in prisons and camps. Like Mrs. Frölick's marionettes, who are "really dead," Moïssevitch's comrades, some of whom may not have "really" survived Tatenberg, relive their past every day. Their recollections are troubled by inconsistent self-images and contradictory accusations. If the survivors' perceptions of themselves and their reality depend upon the presence of the others, that presence does nothing to assuage their solitude.

Alienation pervades the stories told by the displaced men. Usually it takes the form of a general mistrust of people or the human need to believe that each was somehow different from all the rest. Moïssevitch bitterly reminds Rodriguez of the barriers the non-Jewish inmates threw up against the Jews in the camps. The Jewish prisoners were excluded from plans for an uprising, which did not prevent their suffering the severest reprisals for it. Rodriguez counters that Jews had lacked the cohesion to participate in a mass action, that the only thing they had in common was the determination to betray one another.

Rodriguez' charge that Jews in the camps were disunited and disloyal is substantiated in the hatred Moïssevitch bears Abel Antokokoletz. Abel is a mysterious character given to tasteless expressions of the most superficial sense of his Jewishness. He cites Scripture for his own purposes, which include soliciting sympathy for his being chosen to be cast overboard like Jonah, or sent into the wilderness to expiate the sins of his people. The veneer of Abel's piety wears thin when the stateless Rodriguez remarks that were he in Abel's place, he would long ago have gone to Palestine. Antokokoletz retorts disdainfully that Eretz Israel is nothing but a camp to which Jews go only to fulfill the Scriptures.

Antokokoletz' sanctimony and abrasiveness are not the major reason for the contempt he has earned from Ilya and many other exprisoners. As kapo (a prisoner in charge of other prisoners) in several concentration camps, including Auschwitz and a camp Gatti calls the Goldpilz, Abel became legendary. He was in some way responsible for feeding Jews into a dreadful process referred to as the Buna. The horrible image of the kapo recalled by Ilya reminds us of the obsession of Lodz's Rumkowski. The Cracovian would strike Jews down, praying all the while, "I make one suffer in order to save a thousand. . . . God made me accountable for Jewish blood. You hate me today, but those who survive will thank me eternally" (p. 265). When Abel accompanied boatloads of prisoners set afloat on the Baltic, he froze their frenzied singing into despair by ecstatically quoting passages from Exodus. Those that endured the voyage were relieved just to find land again, surely a relative state of mind since they disembarked at yet another camp. But at least the kapo had somehow disappeared. However, when Moïssevitch was sent to Tatenberg, there was Antokokoletz once more.

After the liberation, Baltic and Polish survivors argued hotly about what Abel's activities had actually been. They were unable to determine whether he was a traitor or a hero. Ultimately the Balts, including Ilya, had stoned Antokokoletz to death. Yet here he—or his double, or his angel—is at the Tatenberg station, perhaps to claim the gratitude he vowed he would merit. How, Moïssevitch anguishes, can he pay him that recognition? How can he refuse it? He is tortured by the impossibility of identifying Abel positively and of defining precisely the relationship he and the other inmates had with him. He confronts Antokokoletz, beseeching confirmation of his memories, "You were the kapo at the Goldpilz, Abel? It was you, wasn't it?" But Antokokoletz' answers are maddeningly enigmatic and obliquely indict Ilya:

Antokokoletz: Can we return to the places where fire is burning?

Moïssevitch: So it wasn't you?

Antokokoletz: I'll become him [the kapo] Ilya. I'll become him in order to open your eyes.

Moïssevitch: Is that an admission?

Antokokoletz: Now you want to be a judge.—You already judged the kapo you liquidated. If you're so eager to resume his trial through me it's because you feel yourself basically guilty.

Moïssevitch: One is always guilty of something.—Is that why you've come back?

Antokokoletz: (The tenth day of the seventh month exists only for us.— Aaron set out two goats in front of the Tent of Meeting and cast lots upon them, one for Adonai, the other for Azazel. Only the one on whom the lot fell for Azazel became expiatory.)

Moïssevitch: Then the kapo of the Goldpitz was you?—Speak frankly, what do you want of me?

Antokokoletz: Will you ever know, Ilya?—Will I ever know? (pp. 272–73)

Whatever their past relationships, the four ex-inmates of Tatenberg cannot escape one another. Together they join the travelling carnival. Antokokoletz agrees to manage Kravchenko's boxing career, Rodriguez disguises himself as a bear, a more redoubtable antagonist for Kravchenko in the ring, and Moïssevitch has a musical robot. In Vienna, the city of illusions, Hildegarde Frölick's marionettes perform a fierce satire in which military cemeteries become a refrigerator for the bloom of a nation's youth, and war, an international act of love. Although her soldier puppets die regularly at each performance, this time shots ring out prematurely. Mrs. Frölick faints, understanding that they have been shot for good. The marksman is Moïssevitch, determined to annihilate the past and its persistent inhabitants. He kills Kravchenko, perhaps not for the first time, because the Ukranian had dispatched newly arrived deportees at Tatenberg to the gas chambers. Proclaiming himself the avenging heir of the Jewish inmates whose treachery Rodriguez censured, Ilya kills him too. Finally, he shoots Antokokoletz, even though the older Jew warns him of the futility of his act. "As long as you are here," predicts Abel, "I'll be here."

Declaring an end to the past, Ilya resolves to live in the future where he and Mrs. Frölick will have the largest mechanized circus in Europe. But Hildegarde demurs. Without her marionettes she has lost everything that gave her the impression she was alive. She must rebuild the world of the Tatar wall where her husband was shot. When Moïssevitch protests that *he* has no place in the steppe, Hildegarde wonders, not unkindly, if he will ever find a place on earth. She means a different place, of course, and she is right. Ilya will never be liberated from the world of Tatenberg or from the company of those with whom he endured the Holocaust.

The harrowing final scene dramatizes Moïssevitch's fate. Survivors of both existences of Tatenberg—those we recognize, others known only to Ilya—fill the stage. Mutely, the past challenges him to answer to it, to answer for it. But how can Ilya explain to former neighbors why he had been spared the choice of sacrificing wife or mother, since he had neither, or why he had recovered from the blood poison fatal to some of them? How to explain to a fellow inmate who had saved his life why he, Ilya, was plucked from a selection by a sharp-eyed SS doctor who recognized that he was still strong enough to work? In the eyes of the Holocaust victims around him, Moïssevitch sees reflected not only the immediate past, but centuries of Jewish persecution.

The ghostly crowd encircles Moïssevitch, moving him along with it. Desperately, he reaches into Hildegarde's puppet theatre for a German helmet to frighten away the specters. It is futile. Ceding to the overwhelming force which claims him, Ilya bids Hildegarde Frölick adieu. He probably never hears her promise to wait for him among the living. Just before shooting Abel Antokokoletz, Ilya had observed, "The past has burned behind us. It has also burned in front." For Ilya Moïssevitch, to be a Jew means to suffer guilt and solitude entrapped by memories as incomprehensible as they are faithful. For this son of Moses, to be a Jew is to be chosen to relive the eternal yesterday of the Jewish people, denied any knowledge of how—or if—he is responsible for it.

The strong characterizations developed in these plays present a range of highly individualized reactions to the influence of the Holocaust in crystallizing Jewish identity. For two characters, Nazi persecution effects a crisis of conscience and of consciousness which makes them reckon with the non-Jewish dimension of their Jewish selves. Simon Bernauer mollifies his ambivalence about his own people by uniting himself in a fellowship with them, imbued with the essentially Christian precepts of the nation he cherishes as his own. Arthur Goldman, a survivor riven by the suspicion that Jews were responsible for their fate either because they actually merited the supreme penalty or did not resist it actively, placates his doubts by absorbing the guilt of both the criminal and the victimized. Nazism drives two other protagonists to opposite extremes. Rumkowski's despair (or megalomania) causes him to sacrifice his terrestrial world in the name of an orthodox injunction. Jim's nihilism, perversely fed by the essentially Judaistic devotion to the study of history and legend, leads him to so radical a repudiation of Judaism that he offers himself gladly to its most relentless enemy. The central figures in the Grumberg, Sack and Ganzl works, Jews who survived the Holocaust and their children, are fettered in the search for who and what they are today by the impossibility of establishing certain, relevant connections between the past—both traditional and immediate—and the present. Ilya Moïssevitch has the least freedom to find himself. He is liberated from the camps only to be held prisoner by the past, unable to transcend the clutch of memory or build a new life impervious to the still smoldering embers of the old.

That interpretations of Jewish responses to the Holocaust as perceptive as these already exist appears all the more remarkable in light of man's continuing endeavor to determine what the event demonstrates about human nature in general. It is quite improbable that our understanding of the Nazi genocide will ever permit a definitive catalogue of all its implications for the image of the Jew alone. No doubt the Holocaust will continue to inspire the quest for identity of Jewish characters in literature. Meantime, reliably, there are new crises of conscience and of consciousness. An important example is the suppression of Jewish life in the U.S.S.R. which has inspired the creative imagination of one of the most expert observers of contemporary Jewish consciousness, Elie Wiesel.

In its largest sense, Wiesel's *Zalmen, or the Madness of God* (*Zalman ou La Folie de Dieu*, 1968) is a forum for arguing what it means to be a Jew after Auschwitz, to ponder why one was spared and how—and if—he can make his life as a Jew count. The diverse opinions on these questions within the play have to be considered in the context of its time, the "thaw" which followed Stalin's death in 1953, and its place, a small town in the Soviet Union. The continued ubiquity of governmental surveillance casts a special light on the play's various Jewish images. Its threatening climate prompts our understanding the postures of members of its Jewish community as reflections of their awareness that "forty years after the Revolution the Jewish question remains unsolved and burning."[23]

The perspective explicit in such an observation befits a congregation made up almost entirely of the old. Indeed, in the original French script of the play, the community's Chairman admits that he keeps young people away from the synagogue in what he believes to be everybody's best interests. By contrast, say, to the freedom with which the Long Island congregants in Chayefsky's *The Tenth Man* gather a minyan on an ordinary weekday afternoon, even drafting a Jewish policeman, the Russian Jews are regimented and policed during services on Yom Kippur, Judaism's holiest day.

Fear prevails in the town, reinforcing its Jews' sense of isolation. The extraordinary news that a group of Jews from abroad is stranded in their area and wants to attend Day of Atonement services provokes their incredulity and delight. They cannot recall having seen Jews from the outside for twenty or thirty years; at times, they have had the impression of being the last Jews in the world. The unwonted visit necessitates an emergency meeting of the Synagogue Council. When it is over, the joy of hosting foreign co-religionists has been trained to the bridle of official guidelines. The Rabbi and the councillors swallow their disappointment and agree to follow their pragmatic Chairman's plan to isolate the visitors, discouraging all contact between them and the congregants. These measures are approved by the Inspector from the Ministry of Religious Affairs who comes by to announce that the Ministry will help implement them by stationing its men throughout the sanctuary.

The spiritual leader of the congregation is a man in his seventies, now reconciled to entrusting to God many of the tasks he would have liked to perform himself. Challenged by the Inspector to say whether he is a partisan of those who ask or those who answer, the Rabbi

204 · THE NEW JEW

declares that he is on the side of prayer, which is both question and answer. However, the Rabbi cannot disregard harsh cultural realities or the urgent appeal of pure religious fervor. The first haunts him through his heartbreaking family life, the second, through the figure of Zalmen.

In the hours between the Council meeting and Kol Nidre, the call to prayer which heralds Yom Kippur, the Rabbi is visited by his daughter Nina. She brings her son Misha, the Rabbi's sole male heir. A bright, appealing twelve-year-old, he answers his grandfather's questions as well as a boy from a wholly secular upbringing can, defining Yom Kippur as an important holiday when old men gather to pray and to cry, perhaps because they are old. He does not know what to say when his grandfather asks him if he too will come to the synagogue when he is old. Nina reminds her father that it is difficult for a modern child to measure up to the Rabbi's image, especially when his father is not an observant Jew. Shortly, Nina's husband bursts in, furious that his family has made this New Year's visit. The assimilated Alexey resents his father-in-law's interfering in his determination to free Misha of the burden of Judaism and to equip him to live as a man undistinguishable from any other. "You want to preserve his past," accuses Alexey, "I want to save his future" (p. 75). In modern Russia, the goals are patently irreconcilable.

Misha's farewell promise that he will come back echoes in the Rabbi's ear as he collects his thoughts for Kol Nidre. His meditations are interrupted by the second troubler of his conscience, Zalmen the beadle. Zalmen represents unvanquished Jewish faith, pride and strength corporealized in the figure of a half-mad synagogue caretaker. Habitually pressing the Rabbi to be more assertive, the sexton now exhorts him to take advantage of the presence of the foreign visitors to publicize the desperate straits of Judaism in Russia. This time Zalmen will not yield to the Rabbi's objections. He must summon the vision and the courage to speak out, "For we are the imagination and madness of the world—we are imagination gone mad," argues Zalmen. "One has to be mad today to believe in God and man—one has to be mad to believe" (p. 79). Suddenly, amidst his own protestations, the Rabbi finds himself in the pulpit roundly declaring that Jewish life in Russia is doomed, that abandoned by the rest of the world, he and his congregants "will be the last of the Jews who in silence bury the Jew within them" (p. 83).

Zalmen's fugitive triumph becomes the focus of the rest of the play. An official investigation of the Rabbi's moment of madness calls forth a number of assessments from his congregants. The dialectics in the second act of Wiesel's play compels any diasporic Jew who has ever wondered about the consequences of trying to be inconspicuously Jewish in the modern world to put himself in the witness box along with the personae who actually testify.

There is of course a silent majority. Some Jews disappeared from the synagogue immediately after the Rabbi's tirade. Those who remained, given a nod by the Chairman, resumed the service as if nothing untoward had happened. Their spokesman assures the Inspector conducting the investigation that muzzled by fear, people did not discuss the outburst. Most worshippers, including those who transmitted the news to Nina and Alexey who were not present, disclaim any knowledge of what the Rabbi actually said.

A far different silence surrounds the Rabbi himself. The Inspector's efforts to uncover an insurgent plot net only a weary confession. The responsibility is the Rabbi's alone and he will accept any punishment. Earlier the Rabbi had said that to be a Jew is to demonstrate oneself capable of the miracle of turning suffering into a song, to opt for life regardless of the outcome of that choice. Now having attached himself to the impossible, he retreats to an inner reality where "He is with Zalmen. He *is* Zalmen."

The Chairman of the Synagogue Council is called to account. Because he is the only one who has grappled with the practical realities of Jewish existence and has adopted an active response, he serves effectively if not happily as liaison between the community and the Ministry of Religious Affairs. A man who lost his illusions when he lost his family during the war, he believes, "We have only one mission: to survive. To survive at any cost!" (p. 105). However, the Chairman is far more sensitive than Chief Elder Rumkowski of Lodz whose view of survival he shares. Although he concedes that the Rabbi's sermon was naïvely provocative, he refuses to condemn him. The Chairman delineates two distinct levels of Jewish existence. His own concern is to keep the maximum number of Jews alive, even those who accuse him of being an instrument of the enemy. But the President understands that the Rabbi can scarcely be satisfied with mere physical survival; his responsibility is for his people's spiritual life. The Chairman sees his own cause as less threatened than the Rabbi's. Because the Inspector has demonstrated his enlightenment, the Chairman pleads with him to understand what it must be like for the Rabbi to see Jewish learning and culture being processed away, "to witness silently . . . the disappearance—worse, the distortion—of one's faith, one's image, one's past in front of one's very eyes" (p. 108).

The vestigiality of Judaism is forcefully illustrated when Alexey, the Rabbi's son-in-law, takes the stand. He wants not only survival but success in a society that makes no allowances for religious deviations.

And he is even more ambitious for his son whom he hopes to be freer still of the ties binding him to the dead weight of the Jewish past. Pushed by the Inspector to declare whether he is prepared to denounce his father-in-law as a provocateur, Alexey concedes he would do his duty as a citizen, as he always has. His guilt in betraying family and heritage is implicit in his argument that the Inspector ought not to regard the Rabbi's outburst as a political act, but rather the desperate ploy of an old man who senses that the past is dying with him. Alexey claims that the sermon was directed against him personally. The Rabbi wanted to vent his anger that Nina and Misha had been stolen from him and, more importantly, he wanted to embarass Alexey into realizing that he will always be regarded as a Jew, irrespective of his wishes.

However exposed and implicated Alexey may feel, it is apparent that he is not going to abandon his own goals. Even Nina, deeply moved by her father's solitude, cannot bring herself to risk humiliating her husband by asking her father's forgiveness. Misha, who has insisted on being allowed to stay throughout the investigation, demonstrates obvious sympathy with his grandfather, stirred by his courage without understanding it. The youth wants to run to his grandfather, but his father holds him back. However, the impulse is not lost on the Rabbi. Only the signs that he has won Misha's attention succeed in rousing the old man from his lassitude.

One feels that Misha will not grow up to be as confused and irresolute as the idealistic Dr. Malkin, who stands apart from the other Jews because he has neither resigned himself to live in fear, nor has he devised an alternative. He vacillates among all the conflicting directions he can follow without finding himself. He is a member of the Party, but feels no fervor for it, a citizen of a country suspicious of his allegiance, a Jew from an assimilated background who, understanding nothing about Judaism, comes regularly to the synagogue and serves on its Council. Having lived through the wartime suffering he considers the common experience of his age, he is plagued by the shame of being a survivor without understanding what the implications may be for him.

Like Alexey, Dr. Malkin feels personally incriminated by the Rabbi's speech, with one big difference: the Doctor regrets that he was not in league with him. Belatedly, he tried to join the rebellion. Worried that the visiting Jews might have dismissed what they heard from the pulpit as senile raving, the Doctor sought the tourists out at their hotel, only to discover they had already left town. However, Dr. Malkin does not refute the President's accusation that he had not allied himself with the Rabbi until he was certain the gesture was useless. Malkin admits remorsefully that he was motivated more by personal need than by the welfare of his people.

Not surprisingly, of all the people in the synagogue Yom Kippur Eve, the only one whose testimony reveals a true appreciation of the Rabbi's motives and his message is Zalmen. Having already demonstrated the mercurial nature of the wise fool, he comes to bear witness reeling from drink. The beadle relives the Rabbi's flight into spiritual heights and his own joy and anguish at being unable to follow him. The Inspector, eager to pursue any evidence of a plot, gives Zalmen a chance to indict himself. However, the Russian official is unable to grasp the truth of the caretaker's confession that the maddened voice that had pleaded for Judaism was not the Rabbi's at all, but Zalmen's.

While dismissing the frenzied sexton's testimony, the Inspector does not fail to exploit the fact that even Zalmen denies the Rabbi his act. Nobody accepts the sacrifice. The Rabbi himself is willing to deny its existence, for it already seems a dream to him. The Russian official closes the investigation, declaring that to punish the old man would be to promote to martyrdom a dreamer whose cry in the wilderness was never even uttered, since it went unheard. The Inspector's trenchant closing remarks are obviously intended for those who see or read *Zalmen*, as well as for the Rabbi.

He wonders how the elderly Jew could possibly have believed that his act would matter to anyone, that his plea would be taken up by others. Everyone knows that people are preoccupied by their own concerns, including world Jewry which has proven its lack of solidarity:

> When, all over Europe, your people were being exterminated, how many Jews took part in how many demonstrations in how many communities to protest, to shout, to weep—yes, simply to weep? Day after day, night after night, hundreds and thousands were disappearing into mass graves or burning into cinders. All of this was known to the free world, and yet . . . holidays were celebrated; charity balls and dinners were organized; people went to concerts, to the theatre. . . . Everything went on as if nothing were happening. And today? Life goes on. And those who don't suffer refuse to hear about suffering—and particularly about Jewish suffering. (p. 169)

The most damning aspect of the indictment is that it comes from the mouth of a Russian Commissar of Jewish Affairs.

The rawness of his cynicism is quickly clad in art. Zalmen appears to laugh at the audience's discomfort. He had warned at the beginning of the play that it was all a story that never really happened. The postscript is ironic, of course, for *Zalmen* inspires belief in the possibility of belief. Within the play, one of the possibilities is Misha in

whom the flame of hope for Jewish survival has been kindled. Moreover, the existence of the play itself amounts to an eloquent demonstration of belief in contemporary drama as a vehicle for the expression of faith in the endurance of Judaism and as a powerful appeal to
the conscience and consciousness of being Jewish after Auschwitz.

Like Wiesel's play, the others we have looked at in this chapter
honor man's faculty for fashioning art out of grim human experiences. They have a common motivation, the desire to expose anti-
Semitism intensified to epidemic proportions. If one accepts the premise that literary investigation is an end in itself, these works respond
affirmatively to Abel Antokokoletz' question, "Can we return to the
places where fire is burning?" There is nothing novel about literary
portrayals of the Jew as the subject of persecution. What emerges as a
distinctly post-1945 dramatic concern is the probing of ways Jewish
identity responds to intolerance. The plays which investigate crises of
conscience and consciousness prompt several observations.

First, the postwar theatre affords a notably suitable medium for the
experiences treated in these plays. The historical records on which the
drama of disaster is based document man's inability to confront inhu-
man circumstances head-on and the consequent necessity of a mental
retreat to a vista from which empirical facts are more comprehensible.
The imperative to approach actuality on the oblique, to view reality
insulated by one remove or more is adroitly met by a stage already
conditioned by Pirandello, surrealism and German expressionism, and
dominated by the absurd.

The plays discussed here, like the characters in them, challenge
conventional values and repudiate orthodox principles. This is a theatre where everything is at once possible and impossible (Goldman
is/is not a German who murdered Jews), where there are no more
absolutes (Antokokoletz was/was not stoned to death). The reality of
the story within the story is more acceptable (Polish Jews who regard
a Dreyfus play as irrelevant), more ennobling (a Russian rabbi roused
to insurgency by unquenchable faith), and every bit as believable as
the outer reality of the plot (young Jews who look forward to fulfilling
their promise in Berlin in the 1930s; a synagogue from which Jews flee
in terror). Time is reckoned only by human perceptions of it: for
Kalisky's Jim, Hitler and his interchangeable factotums live on; Ilya
Moïssevitch inhabits the present and the past simultaneously; Grumberg's Simone lives in an eternal maybe.

For audiences, such ambiguities, unresolved dilemmas and relentless pain engender more than an intellectual challenge. These works

perturb. The horror and vulnerability they conjure up spill off the stage and overwhelm the beholder. This is drama that compels a personal response because it obliges us to reflect on what it means to be watching it, to be a citizen of the world that allowed the circumstances it depicts to happen. This is drama that calls out to Jews in the audience to consider what it means to be Jewish in the post-Holocaust world.

Which leads to a second observation. We have seen that as the protagonists of plays about modern crises confront their plights, they question who and what they are. Although they may become more keenly aware of themselves as Jews, they do not always find in Judaism all the reasons and reassurances they seek. So Eydoux's Captain Dreyfus and Marcel's Simon Bernauer face their destinies as Jews by behaving like Frenchmen, Ganzl's survivors search in vain for solace in the story of the Exodus, and Rumkowski, the most perversely faithful to tradition, pays a horrifying price for his obedience to an established precept. In none of these plays is there a "return to the Jewish condition" in any orthodox sense. Instead there are the "variations that that term implies," in the delineation of threatened, guilt-ridden, or disenfranchised Jewish characters who must be viewed primarily but no longer exclusively as Jews.

We have already seen ample evidence that Jews on the contemporary stage have far more dimension than their theatrical antecedents. That means of course that they bear stronger resemblance to life where Jews are rarely totally characterized by their Judaism. Soberingly, today's theatre rather accurately reflects a world where insofar as Jewishness is concerned, the "who" is at odds with the "what." It is a world where sometimes only Nazis can identify and rabbis define Jews with certainty, where "one has to be mad to believe in God and man." It is a world where Jews, even as they are crushed for being Jews, insist on the other allegiances that make them the people they are, without necessarily finding strength or consolation in these loyalties either. That the Jew's response to pain and oppression may not suffice to distinguish him from other men also acknowledges the fact that he lives in an age where prejudice, violence and estrangement are not unique to the Jewish experience. As Gatti's Manuel Rodriguez, wandering stateless after the second World War remarks, "Until the present, Jews were the only ones who died scattered to the four corners of the world. For twenty years now, the Spaniards have been trying to outdo them."[24]

One of the few feasible answers to the question "What is a Jew?" appears to be that he is someone whose psyche has been irreparably scarred by crises of conscience and consciousness. The nature of these crises compels many Jews to recognize how far they have strayed from their religious and ethical moorings and to despair of ever finding them again. Many doubt that the old principles can still operate. Those for whom some form of authentic Jewish life is not longer relevant or possible (e.g., Kalisky's Jim, Wiesel's Dr. Malkin, Shaw's Arthur Goldman) may be condemned to spend the rest of their lives searching.

The image of the disaffected, questing Jew falls into line with a preeminent concept of contemporary man whose essential self is thrown into question, who is, in René Kalisky's terms, "ambiguous" and "available." It is a concept illuminated by Albert Camus's observation that

> in a universe suddenly divested of illusions and lights, man feels an alien, a stranger. His exile is without remedy since he is deprived of the memory of a lost home or the hope of a promised land.[25]

The Jew who endures a crisis which leads him (and those who observe him) to understand that he is no longer defined or directed uniquely by his Jewishness takes his place on the postwar stage as a major representative figure. He actualizes Leslie Fiedler's prediction:

> Indeed, in this apocalyptic period of atomization and uprooting, of a catholic terror and a universal alienation, the image of the Jew tends to become the image of everyone. . . .[26]

It is not only in the pursuit of roots and identity in a hostile environment that the increasingly secularized image of the Jew has become an apposite symbol. In an impressive number of contemporary situations, the experience of the Jew is viewed as a comprehensive experience, and the figure of the Jew comes to stand as a metaphor for modern mankind.

8

The Jew as Metaphor

They say that tragedy makes us look better and comedy worse than we
are. But that is puzzling. In the first place, what are we? And in the
second place, what is worse?

—Saul Bellow

As the variety of theatrical roles and images examined in these
pages demonstrate, the "myths of the Jew" have earned increased
dramatic value because of their broad pertinence. On the one hand,
specific Jewish events, from biblical history to the reacquisition of a
homeland, from slavery to the Holocaust, have acquired widespread
relevance in a world where the Jewish experience suggests parallels
or involves consequences reaching deep into the lives of non-Jews. In
another sense, the "myths of the Jew"—his cultural ideas and in-
grained attitudes and responses—are seen to embody certain universal values. In using the Jew as a referent, dramatists have mined his
affinities with the rest of humanity. Chayefsky's Gideon and Miller's
Gregory Solomon affirm man's commitment to life. Wiesel's Zalmen
and Fry's Moses cry for freedom; Mankowitz' Fender and Pagnol's
Judas, for justice. Jewish personae illustrate the creative power of
the imagination (Wesker's Simmondses), as well as its destructiveness
(Pinter's Goldberg). Jews are depicted responding to fundamental
motivations: patriotism (Marcel's Esther Peyrolle), idealism (Hansberry's Sidney Brustein), loneliness (Grumberg's Simone), the pleasure principle (Kops's Solly Gold).

The demonstrable fact that on the postwar stage "the image of the
Jew tends to become the image of everyone" invites a reconsideration
of a question raised by Abraham Dreyfus in his 1889 lecture, "The Jew
in the Theatre." Perturbed by the tenacity and falseness of the formulaic stage Jew, Dreyfus wondered what would happen were more
lifelike Jews to appear. With caustic flippancy, he anticipated the objections: If the theatre were to depict Jews who are like everybody
else, they would not appear to be Jews. Indeed, why would they be

Jews?¹ A hundred years later, a well-established convention of humanized stage Jews allows a fresh appreciation of Dreyfus' skepticism. He
was right, though not for the reasons he had in mind. In the unlikely
instance that the Jew were to become indistinguishable from non-
Jews, he would surely lose his dramatic value. His worth is rooted in
his differences. A multitude of roles and images have their source in
some implication of his Jewishness.

So the question is no longer "Why should they be Jews?" but rather,
"To what extent does the Jew retain his Jewish identity as he represents people generally?" That inquiry provides the focus of this chapter which brings together plays built around the Jew as a metaphor
for all or a significant part of mankind.

No doubt the most popular prototype is the quintessentially Jewish
anti-hero, the *schlemiel*. He shares Camus's assessment of the incompatibility between man and his environment, except that from the
schlemiel's point of view, the incongruity is ridiculous. His sense of
humor provides the sword and shield with which he faces life. He is,
as Ruth R. Wisse says in her wonderful study *The Schlemiel as Modern
Hero*, "a challenge to the whole accepted notion of heroism." A number of variations of the *schlemiel* are examined here and his development is traced to its function as a metaphor in two plays by Victor
Haïm. The *schlemiel* protagonists in *Isaac and the Midwife* and in *Abraham and Samuel* operate according to a code of conduct in which essentially Judaistic values have been modified by oppression and slavery. In the first work, the Jew is a political entity, or more properly,
non-entity; in the second, Jews represent the class struggle between
labor and capital with the *schlemiel* in the former role, of course.

Less easily categorized is Saul Bellow's richly nuanced comic psy-
cho-philosopher in *The Last Analysis*. Curiously, the relevance of Bellow's generously proportioned Philip Bummidge to various quarters
of contemporary society derives from the character's solidly Jewish
substance.

While the metaphoric roles of characters in two other plays are
comparable, their images are vastly dissimilar. In his sensitive portrayal of aging, Arnold Wesker creates some of his most memorable
personae. They are lapsed Jews who retain enough of their heritage
to adapt it to their needs as they face their mortality. Unexpectedly,
they find consolation and reassurance in a religious festival and the
biblical text associated with it. The endearing humanity of Wesker's
people contrasts vividly with the post-modern doomsday types who
populate Bernard Kops's *The Lemmings*. These are cartoon caricatures
who have somehow managed to bring flesh-and-blood children in the
world—alas! Yet Kops's figures may be the most characteristic of all.

The impact of their religious tradition is simultaneously cause for laughter and despair and that is precisely what makes them typify Auschwitz-Hiroshima-conditioned mankind at the end of its tether.

This examination of the function of the Jew as metaphor begins with two works where gentiles declare themselves Jews and are accepted as such, forceful evidence that Jewishness can be separated from the Jew. In these plays, "Jew" becomes an ethical category. Although such a designation may appear to be an atavism of medieval drama's abstract Hebrew figurations of blindness or sinfulness (e.g., Archisynagogus, Synagoga), there is in fact only one significant parallel. Like the medieval playmakers, Arthur Miller and Marguerite Duras are interested in the Jew from a moral perspective. However, the modern dramatists incorporate social and historical truths into their iconoclastic definitions of the Jew. Moreover, unlike the negative connotations of the Jew in early theatre, the contemporary notions are held up as positive examples of morality, albeit disparate ones. In *Incident at Vichy*, Miller works out a special notion of the Jew to account for man's egoism and his capacity to behave inhumanly. In *Destroy, She Said*, Duras' concern is human solidarity and creativity. There is a degree of abstruseness in the play, but patience is rewarded by the author's ingenuity in completely reworking a number of received ideas, chief among which is the Jew.

Arthur Miller's inspired concept of the Jew as metaphor in *Incident at Vichy* (1965) deserves to be viewed as the result of long preoccupation with questions of identity and of personal and social responsibility. Two decades before *Incident at Vichy*, Miller treated in the novel *Focus* the interrelatedness of the Jewish and the non-Jewish persona. In *Focus*, an anti-Semite equivocally named Newman has to start wearing glasses and is suddenly mistaken everywhere for a Jew. The spectacles open his eyes to biases he himself had been perpetrating. Newman "atones" by willingly adopting Jewish identity with its attendant discrimination. However facile the premise of *Focus* that Jewishness is a façade that can be assumed voluntarily, the book states boldly two points Miller was to develop more substantially: anyone can be taken for a Jew and the implications are always dire.

In several plays which follow the novel, the author approaches human interconnectedness from another tack. *All My Sons* (1947) and, to a lesser degree, *Death of a Salesman* (1949) explore men's propensity for abdicating their responsibility to one another. Then in *The Crucible* (1952), Miller probes the individual's awareness of his contribution to evil and intolerance churned up to mass hysteria.

All these themes come together in *After the Fall* (1964) where it is impossible to miss Miller's obsession as a Jew with identity and with accountability for the madness in which millions of innocents were slaughtered. Gesturing toward the concentration camp tower that dominates the set of *After the Fall*, its protagonist Quentin cries, "Who can be innocent again on this mountain of skulls? I tell you what I know! My brothers died here . . . but my brothers built this place; our hearts have cut these stones!"[2]

In *Incident at Vichy*, Miller works these concerns through to a powerful conclusion. The work, which is based on an actual incident, is clearly inspired by the question of what it means to be a Jew after Hitler. It shows how man's recognition of himself vis-à-vis his fellows leads him to a new understanding of who he is and, equally noteworthy, what a Jew is.

Incident at Vichy takes place in 1942. The scene is the anteroom of a detention center where people rounded up by the Vichy police await interrogation and probable deportation. There is nothing to do but wait and talk, and the talkiness which sometimes weighs the play down succeeds in recreating the dismal world outside from which all humanizing values have disappeared. A gamut of annulled relationships is suggested. On the simplest level, the German Major withholds recognition from the French waiter who until the day before had been his favorite in a nearby café.

More notably, two years before, the same Major and Leduc, a Jewish psychiatrist then serving in the French Army, had faced one another at Amiens. At that time they were antagonists in the traditional sense, each convinced of the supremacy of the cause represented by his uniform. Such clear-cut distinctions have since blurred, leaving only a remnant of reluctant mutual respect and an insuperable barrier. The Major's German uniform has become the tool of Professor Hoffman's "science" of racial anthropology, and the soldier confides in the arrested psychiatrist that the devaluation of humanity bewilders him as much as its Jewish victims. "Tell me," the German pleads with Dr. Leduc, "how there can be persons any more. I have you at the end of this revolver—[the Professor] has me—and somebody has him. . . ."[3] Leduc's painful inability to cite a single reason to prove he is better for the world than the Major and hence worthier to live confirms both men's awareness that concepts like decency, honor, love and respect have become meaningless.

Not everyone in the anteroom wants to think about who he is or why he is there. Two of the Jews detach themselves from the situation mentally. The electrician Bayard escapes his present vulnerability by associating himself with the collective spirit of socialism he believes will triumph. A silent Old Jew also abnegates the present and takes refuge in the past. He rocks and prays, clutching a bundle. When it is torn from his stubborn grasp, the room fills with the contents of a feather quilt, remnants of a vanishing culture.

Imagination proves a retreat for two other Jews in the waiting room. The artist Lebeau refuses to look beyond the nose whose dimensions provided the Professor grounds for arresting him. He functions better in the world of illusion. "I knew I shouldn't go outside," he confesses, recalling the circumstances of his arrest. "But you get tired of believing in the truth. You get tired of seeing things clearly" (p. 80). Like Lebeau, the actor Monceau rejects the experientially real in favor of a reality he creates for himself. An inveterate performer, Monceau believes the Germans are a cultivated audience who could not "burn up actors in a furnace." The trick, he says, is to appear self-confident, "to make them believe you are who your papers say you are." None of the detainees' responses to imminent disaster is any more incredible than their doom itself.

Only two characters manifest the courage to think rationally. One is Wilhelm Johann Von Berg, an Austrian prince whose arrest confirms the capriciousness of Professor Hoffman's science. The second is the psychiatrist Leduc. The doctor sees that he has been deceiving himself about human nature, especially his own. His admission to the Major that he would not decline release even if the others were kept, and his confession to Von Berg that his leaving his hiding place to get codeine for his wife's toothache, the trip during which he was arrested, was insincerely motivated prove that he is neither selfless nor noble. Emotionally he tells the Prince:

> I am only angry that I should have been born before the day when man has accepted his own nature; that he is *not* reasonable, that he is full of murder, that his ideals are only the little tax he pays for the right to hate and kill with a clear conscience. I am only angry that, knowing this, I still deluded myself. (p. 104)

Leduc's fresh awareness of his own lack of rectitude and altruism leads him to question the authenticity of the Prince's protests against Nazism. There is no doubting the humane Von Berg's genuine revulsion of the "vile race of policemen and brutes," or his despair that the Nazis have created a world unfit for what used to be considered human beings. However, Leduc is convinced that the insight he has just gained into himself as an unregenerate egoist who balances himself on the backs of others applies as well to Von Berg—and of all mankind. The doctor contends that no one can call himself human until he puts himself in the next man's place and feels responsible rather than relieved that he is afflicted. Leduc rests his case on his professional experience which has taught him that all gentiles harbor some enmity for Jews. To the nobleman's contention that such animus is simply not part of him, Leduc responds with this forceful definition of "Jew":

> Until you know it is true of you you will destroy whatever truth can come of this atrocity. Part of knowing who we are is knowing we are not someone else. And Jew is only the name we give to that stranger, that agony we cannot feel, that death we look at like a cold abstraction. Each man has his Jew; it is the other. And the Jews have their Jews. And now, now above all, you must see that you have yours—the man whose death leaves you relieved that you are not him, despite your decency. And that is why there is nothing and will be nothing—until you face your own complicity with this . . . your own humanity. (p. 105)

This eloquent speech which a Jewish playwright puts in the mouth of a Jewish character in the context of the paramount Jewish event of modern times constitutes one of the most important statements made from the post-war stage. It explains the definitive expulsion from Eden to which *After The Fall* refers. After Auschwitz, innocence is impossible. Miller's redefinition of the Jew leaves all of us complicit in the vileness that corrupts and destroys. As long as we use the "Jew" to absorb the blameworthy effects of self-interest, we do not reckon with our identity or our responsibility. It is a harsh sentence that rings with truth.

Incident at Vichy ends with a stunning demonstration of the persuasive power of Leduc's argument. Given his pass to freedom, the Prince presses it on the psychiatrist and pushes him toward the door of the detention room. By suffering the fatal consequences of his act, Von Berg may redeem his thousand-year tradition of *noblesse oblige*. But Leduc, overcome with guilt, must search more urgently than ever for the answer to the Major's question as to why he is more deserving to live than the next man. Henceforth for Leduc, part of knowing who he is includes accepting his responsibility for the death of Prince Von Berg who has become his Jew.

Incident at Vichy is not the only contemporary play in which a gentile proclaims himself a Jew and is taken at his word. Marguerite Duras, also writing about responsibility and identity, uses the same device to entirely different ends. Strikingly, Miller's concept of the Jew as the other to whose pain man is insensitive runs counter to Duras' notion that the Jew is another self whose feelings one experiences as keenly as one's own. This sense of "Jew" is central to Duras' celebration of human vitality in *Destroy, She Said (Détruire dit-elle,* 1969). The play is a bizarre and difficult work animated by the rebellious sixties and composed of distorted conventions. Its very form is plastic, for it is simultaneously a poetic novel and a play whose scenic designations anticipate the film Duras ultimately made of it. Flexibility also marks the setting and the characters, guests at a strange hotel which resembles a convalescent home or an asylum.

Elizabeth Alione has come there to recover after a stillbirth. The place was recommended to Max Thor by a colleague because of its alluring forest whose significance is often asserted but never explained. Max is waiting for his wife Alissa to join him there. Stein comes back to the hotel every year to look for a woman he once knew there.

All the personae are caught up in the process of evolving. Stein claims that he is "on the way to becoming a writer." Thor teaches "the history of the future." Though happily married to Alissa, he is fascinated during her absence at the beginning of the play by the somnolent Elizabeth. She too seems to be unfolding in some way. Heavily tranquillized most of the time, she is particularly vulnerable to the influence of others. When Alissa Thor finally arrives at the hotel, her behavior suggests she is well en route to becoming something other than a typically eighteen-year-old who married her professor.

Stein introduces himself to Max abruptly: "My name is Stein. I am a Jew." One is at first led to believe that he is the only Jew. But eventually, he along with Alissa, whose background is unspecified, and Max Thor, who is French by birth, will all insist that they are German Jews. That claim becomes clear only in the subtext of the play and the social theory on which it rests, which we will come to shortly.

The relationships between the characters, like the personae themselves, are in a state of elaboration. Thor and Stein immediately become alter egos, then merge more and more into the same persona. They interpret one another's thoughts and act on each other's impulses. They are both Alissa Thor's lovers (though in light of her age it seems unlikely, Stein recognizes Alissa as the woman he has been searching for at the hotel). They are interchangeable as they relate to Elizabeth Alione and later to her husband Bernard. A similar coalescence takes place between the women. Standing before a mirror with Elizabeth, Alissa observes that they look alike. "Elisa," Max Thor calls tenderly from his dreams, the hybrid name a subconscious confirmation of the blending of his wife and Elizabeth.

The fusing of identities, the famous "Durassian gliding," results from the destruction referred to in the play's title. The notion of destruction is first among the concepts redefined here; the metaphor of the Jew depends upon it. Destruction is presented initially in the surge of desire Alissa feels for her husband who has just told her how happy he is that she has arrived at the hotel:

She turns toward him. She looks at him. Slowly. "Destroy," she says.

He smiles at her.

"Yes. We'll go up to our room before going out into the park."

"Yes."⁴

    The pleasurable merging of partners in sexual intercourse aptly symbolizes one of Duras' dominant ideas. "A progressive loss of identity is the most highly desirable experience one can know," she told Bettina Knapp in an interview. "It is in fact my own preoccupation: The possibility of being capable of losing the notion of one's identity, of being present at the dissolution of one's identity."⁵ Destruction is extended to include love which becomes both motive and means of destruction. It is a creative force, producing authentic human communication as well as physical and social well-being. Hence the absorption of individuality is not reductive (or destructive) but rather the source of vibrant concurrence in the people involved.

    Oddly, these convolutions serve as vehicles for Duras' social philosophy. In an interview with Jacques Rivette and Jean Narboni at the end of 1969, she explained that for her, destruction is the first step toward restoring Humanity: "I would like . . . to destroy in order to replace [consciousness] with the void. The complete unencumberedness of man."⁶ Such a neutral place, a "point zero," represents the seedbed for revisions of all social and political forms.

    Destroy, She Said draws not only on Duras' singular concept of destruction, but on her partiality for two special groups, madmen and hippies. The former have achieved a state she defines admiringly: "A madman is a being whose essential prejudice—the limits of the me— have been destroyed."⁷ The mounting number of mental disorders reassures her that the world is experienced as increasingly intolerable by sensitive people. The collective neuroses, she feels, will demand creative cures. Hippies earn Duras' respect because like the deranged, they are in their way disassociated from society. Her approval of their nonviolence, their use of the freedom they insist upon, and their flair for creating a vacuum works its way into the characterizations in *Destroy, She Said*. One can see a reflection of the hippies' tendency to present a uniform appearance to the world in the intermingling of identities in the play.

    Destroy, She Said was written soon after Marguerite Duras had participated in the Committee of Writers and Students in the tumultuous Paris of May 1968. Her respect for the potential of "les kids" illuminates Alissa Thor's character and role. As a student, Alissa used to fall asleep in Max Thor's lectures. Though Max marries her, it is Stein, arguably the most influential if the most enigmatic of all the personae, who fully recognizes Alissa's special attributes. "You didn't tell me Alissa was mad," he accuses Thor the first time he sees Alissa. Stein values the young woman's detachment ("She stares into space . . . It's the only thing she looks at. But well. She stares into space well" [p. 54]). He understands how her ability to commune with "point zero" qualifies her: "Capital destruction," says Stein, "will pass through Alissa's hands."

Once on the premises, Alissa loses little time exploiting Elizabeth's predisposition to creativity by "destroying" her. The procedure requires both eroticism and the clearing away of her former attachments so as to substitute the league formed by Alissa, Thor and Stein. Frightened, Elizabeth summons her husband to take her home. But Bernard Alione's arrival does not prevent his wife from being purged of her old values as she was of the stillborn child. Seized with nausea during a farewell lunch, Elizabeth excuses herself. When she returns, Alissa asks, "Did you throw up?"

"Yes."

"How was it?"

Elizabeth thinks about it. "Pleasant," she says.

"Good," says Stein, "good." (p. 107)

Although Elizabeth prevails upon her already intrigued husband to take her away, it is apparent that destruction is germinating in both of them.

Duras' reinterpretation of the word "Jew" is best demonstrated in Bernard's perceptions of Alissa, Max and Stein. Curious about his wife's new acquaintances, he asks, "Who are you?"

"German Jews," says Alissa.

"That's not what . . . I . . . , that's not the question . . ."

"It ought to have been," says Max Thor gently. (p. 100)

Alissa's affirmation and Max's mild insistence raise a couple of questions. During an early intimate scene with Elizabeth, Alissa wants to describe Max. "'He's a Jew,' she says. 'Do you recognize Jews?'" Elizabeth answers, "'Not very easily, but my husband does immediately, even when' . . . She stops, caught in a dangerous situation and realizing it" (p. 61). That Max Thor was born in Paris is unequivocally established early in the play. Alissa gives absolutely no clues to her origins. Why then should she identify herself, Stein and Max as

German Jews? And why to a man whose wife had alerted her to his biases?

A clue is suggested in the way Bernard's anti-Semitism is patiently defused by the "German Jews" who slyly confound the identity of his target. Bernard addresses Stein, no doubt sarcastically calling him by the wrong name:

"And you, Blum? What do you teach?" he asks.

"Nothing," says Max Thor. [He indicates Stein and Alissa.] "He, neither. And she, nothing either."

And then, this cryptic exchange with its probable Holocaust reference:

"Sometimes," says Alissa, "Blum teaches the theory of Rosenfeld."

Bernard reflects. "I don't know him," he says.

"Arthur Rosenfeld," says Stein. "He is dead." . . .

"At what age?" asks Elizabeth moaning.

"Eight years old," says Stein. "Alissa knew him." (pp. 110–11)

In her interview with Rivette and Narboni, Duras assessed the upheaval of the sixties in terms that illuminate her use of the Jew in *Destroy, She Said*: "We are all German Jews. We are all strangers. . . . strangers to your state, to your society . . ."[8] Her originality resides in reconstructing the words "strangers" and "German Jews." As with "destroy," she infuses them with unprecedented meaning and broad relevance.

The stranger is literally one least protected by society, a perch Jews have traditionally occupied. However, Duras' understanding of "German Jew" goes further. Asked by Bettina Knapp to explain her penchant for vulnerable, sensitive characters, Duras responded, "I like only vulnerable people. I think they are the only ones to be really alive. In my opinion, sensitivity begins the instant a person can suffer for another as much as for himself—and even more."[9] The playwright has chosen the German Jew as an obvious example of the watchful, susceptible stranger to serve not in the usual restricted sense, but as the representative of all who are turned out of the mainstream and participate in one another's plight. Using the same process that works within her play, the author "destroys" the primary sense of "Jew." She vacates it of its usual connotations. Into the word "glide" the formless energies and unrealized aspirations of Alissa, Max and Stein.

The shadow of the Holocaust is cast very differently on this play from on *Incident at Vichy*. Approaching the event more literally, Arthur

Miller depicts self-interest and fragmentation, a world where Jews are the people on whom guilt and anguish are projected. Marguerite Duras, reflecting figuratively the effect of the Holocaust on the chaos of the postwar world, posits a common sensitivity brought into existence just as the individuals involved have reached a "point zero" and the "limits of the me." Her intent is to dramatize the experiences of confronting the void and of sliding easily from "I" to "we." *Destroy, She Said* portrays the common soul state created through shared experiences and shared identity, not as a solidarity united against some prevalent enemy—a phenomenon conspicuously absent in the play— but as the climate most receptive to whatever unspecified new forms may arise.

In *Destroy, She Said*, the abstract "new form" comes as a Bach fugue which swells out of that formidable forest to uproot trees and smash walls. Smiling in her sleep, Alissa recognizes the force which has finally arrived and names it. "It's music on the name of Stein," she says. "Stein" is as subject to interpretation as the Bach fugue itself. Unlike Alissa, the play's audience grasps only that the emerging force, probably the consummation of the destroy-create process, is awesome, orderly and beautiful.

Marguerite Duras stretches "Jew" into a contemporary metaphor that subsumes ethnic particularities. Typical Jewish attributes—estrangement, sensitivity, vulnerability—are diffused in *Destroy, She Said* to identify those human beings who, alienated from society but in harmony among themselves, quietly but firmly recruit others to wait in the void for a new direction.

Duras' metaphor draws support from the proverbial Jewish aptitude for creating order out of chaos. From exactly the same faculty for synthesis comes a distinctly Jewish response to trouble—humor. In characterizing Jewish humor as "the solution of the powerless against the powerful," Sarah Blacher Cohen observes that East European Jews, the forefathers of Western Jewish humorists, saw themselves as "victims of a ludicrous irony: they were divinely designated to be Chosen People, yet they were treated like rejects. To fill the gap between glorious expectation and miserable reality, they wryly deprecated their persecutors and bittersweetly mocked themselves."[10]

Jewish humor is readily identified by its merciless irreverence, sardonic wit, and often eloquent disputations between fevered intellect and equally aroused id. The difficulty lies in explaining what makes this humor Jewish. Perhaps it suffices to posit a specific comic vision that finds expression in highly recognizable terms and to cite a few of the practitioners of the art writing for the theatre today: Bernard Kops, Woody Allen, Neil Simon, Carl Reiner, Elaine May, Herb Gard-

ner. The current wide appeal of Jewish humor attests to its relevance
beyond the specific culture that nurtured it. Jewish comic vision has
become representative because audiences share its perceptions of the
incongruities which make Jews laugh at the world and at themselves.

Such was not always the case. In the Paris of 1890, even the cos-
mopolitan playgoers and enlightened critics at Antoine's vanguard
Théâtre Libre were puzzled by two short comedies presented on the
same bill. The first was *Jacques Bouchard,* Pierre Wolff's nasty little
work in which a lovesick mason blandishes, then abruptly drops a
woman who had previously jilted him. *Bouchard* was followed by
Louis Mullem's *A New School* (*Une Nouvelle Ecole*), which deftly works
a sensational play within a play into its one-act structure. Today's
theatregoers would easily discern the irony in both works and the
joke of using the most naturalistic stage in Paris to mount pastiches of
naturalism.

Privileged by hindsight, we can trace the line of descent from the
intellectual humor and savage, double-edged laughter of Wolff and
Mullem. Its modern heirs include Jules Feiffer, for example, in *Knock,
Knock* (1976), where the bucolic existence of two middle-aged bach-
elors is demolished by a vaudevillian genie; or in *Little Murders* (1967),
in which the banal episodes of a situation comedy are nullified by
quotidian incidents of American-style violence. Among other exponents of the tradition there is Murray Schisgal in *The Old Jew* (discussed in Chapter Four), and *The Basement* (1967), whose hardworking
but incompetent protagonist martyrs his wife and abdicates all family
responsibilities in his obsession to resuscitate a dead chimpanzee.

Audiences who read or see these plays, unlike those at the Théâtre
Libre, have learned to appreciate Jewish humor. Indeed, many theatregoers may be scarcely conscious of its particular origins in an age
generally disenchanted with humanity, if not with life, where what
counts most is maintaining a precarious balance. While our era might
well be called the Age of the *Schlemiel,* its *mal du siècle* is generally
embodied in comic personae who lack such a precise Yiddish identity.
Even when their names and speech patterns sound Jewish, their ethnicity frequently goes no further (e.g., Abe and Cohen in *Knock, Knock*;
Zack and Minna in *The Basement*).

A more solid Jewish character makes jokes at the horrifying in
Lanford Wilson's *Talley's Folly* (1979). The articulate, appealing Matt
Friedman, a survivor of European persecution, dominates the two-
person play. Wilson makes excellent use of Friedman's first-hand
knowledge of man's destructiveness to account for his facetiousness,
his decision not to father children, and his need for love. The play
runs into trouble when it presumes an equivalence between Matt and

Sally, a thirty-one-year-old Southern spinster alienated from the narrow values of her background. Hurt and humiliation have made Sally fearful too, and she will never be able to bear children. However, it is not at all apparent that Sally should "see the world exactly as" Matt does. Nor does the play indicate what values missing in Matt's post-war life would be compensated by Sally's love. Surely a Jew as scarred and perceptive as Friedman has definite ideas about what he wants to make of the rest of his life. His characterization comes out oddly unbalanced: In terms of Matt's attraction to Sally, he is too Jewish; in terms of the relationship he hopes to establish with her, he is not Jewish enough.

Obviously it is no small task to create a character whose specifically Jewish background can be seen as thoroughly relevant to his function as metaphor. But at least two authors have brought it off. Moreover, Saul Bellow and Victor Haïm have devised comic personae of the first order.

Philip Bomovitch, now legally Philip Bummidge, commonly known as Bummy, is the overachiever at the center of Saul Bellow's *The Last Analysis* (1965). Bummidge represents several discrete groups. He is the first-generation American, raised behind a candy store in Brooklyn in terror of his father, a "humorless savage" committed to the belief that he could punish his son into becoming a *mensh*. What emerged instead was a comedian who "earned millions making people laugh—all but Papa." Next to the exemplar of rags-to-riches success, Bummy stands for the professional funny man. He evokes the image of the Jewish comedian (e.g., Jack Benny, Milton Berle, Groucho Marx, Phil Silvers) whose stock in trade is blocking pain by laughing at it. He has the unique perception of the stand-up comic who performs before audiences, "smelling like a swamp of martinis and half-digested steak," alert to the disappointments and inadequacies he is diverting them from.

While audiences love Bummy, his personal life is a shambles, especially now that he is down on his luck. A third paradigmatic image is the materialist whose fame and fortune net him only exasperation and betrayal. His estranged wife Bella, who seems to have all two million dollars Bummy settled on her firmly zippered in her patent-leather purse, revels in humiliating him. His only son Max resents his father epigrammatically: "You breathe all the air, eat all the food, and lay all the women."[11] Bummy's thoroughly corrupt sister, aunt and cousin revile him, meantime hoping for the return of the good old days when he lavished huge sums on them. Rich or poor, Bummidge is the center of a scene Bellow depicts with stunning accuracy. Glenn Loney aptly describes it as a world that "seethes with shrill

224 · THE NEW JEW

yentas and grasping, opportunistic males," a world in which "the insult has become the common currency of verbal intercourse."[12]

There is yet another widely representative facet of Philip Bummidge. He exemplifies the worshipper of vulgarized Freudian psychology, dedicated to analysis as the universal panacea. "I feel," he says, "like a museum of all the perversity, sickness and ugliness of mankind" (p. 74). Only one variation distinguishes Bummy from other devotees of psychotherapy: he serves alternately as the doctor and the patient.

All these elements of Bummidge's character come into play as he prepares a comeback whose sheer preposterousness at first discourages his hangers-on. He is putting together a closed-circuit television demonstration of his personal method, *Existenz*-Action-Self-analysis. The show is to be beamed to an invited audience from the American Psychiatric Association, leading universities and private foundations. Convinced of his "definitely higher purpose," Bummy has also asked artists and comedians to watch the broadcast because, "I want the comedians to see how the analysts laugh. I want the analysts to see how seriously the comedians take me. I must reach everyone. . . . I have something tremendous to say" (p. 15).

Bummidge's approach consists of wresting self-knowledge by "dragging repressed material into the open by sheer force of drama." His method has evolved from the fragmenting and distancing of the self he learned as a comedian. Bummy suffers from an emotional disease he has named Humanitis where the afflicted is overwhelmed by the human condition. He has also isolated and named Pagliacci gangrene, a condition in which self-pity, masochism, fear and passivity combine to cut off circulation. With all this experience, the ex-star wants to open a theatre of the soul where people will work with his *Existenz*-Action-Self-analysis.

When the parasites discover what their favorite eccentric is up to, they are scandalized and depressed. Unable to discourage him, they decide the part of wisdom is to exploit him. They invite media executives and "kingpin impresario" Fiddleman to join the audience watching Bummidge's demonstration. His son Max shrewdly observes:

> There's nothing so extreme or kookie that the mass media won't try to use it. We talk of atomic explosions and population explosions, but in the twentieth century there's also an explosion of consciousness. Society needs the imagination of its most alienated members. They want to defy it? It doesn't care. It pays them millions. Money reconciles all tendencies. (p. 68)

No doubt it is Bummidge's zeal for his undertaking rather than natural innocence that leads him to ignore the motives that have turned his critics into supporters. He accepts their cooperation and assigns them roles in re-enacting crucial scenes from his life as the cameras turn. There is a good deal of sado-masochistic exposing of the ghosts haunting Bummidge's psyche. Then a Greek chorus of his new-found collaborators participates in an extravagant playlet which combines elements of the ancient and the avant-garde to recreate Bummy's conception, gestation and birth. The broad humor of the parody does not quite mask the pain the protagonist relives as he re-experiences his initial encounters with loss and frustration. Now functioning as a spokesman of the generation born in the first decade of the twentieth century, Bummidge describes his early awareness of the "weight of suffering" in the world around him:

> Armistice Day, nineteen eighteen. From the abyss of blood, the sirens of peace. I have a vision of bandaged lepers screaming, "Joy, joy!" Twenty million mummy bundles of the dead grin as the child, Philip Bummidge, intuits the condition of man and succumbs for the first time to Human-itis, that dread plague. Being human is too much for flesh and blood. . . . (p. 95)

The drama is scarcely over when Fiddleman arrives. Although the sceptical associates regard the broadcast as a disaster, they are perfectly willing to accept the impresario's opinion and huge option checks hailing *Existenz*-Action-Self-analysis as a triumph. However, when its inventor makes his entrance, he is strangely aloof. It is apparent that he has transformed himself through his last analysis. He rebukes each of his hangers-on fittingly, tears up the contracts Fiddleman offers and throws the whole pack out. Then he bids his secretary usher in his "scientific colleagues" and optimistically makes plans to teach his method to "the sad, the bored and the tedious of the earth."

In the best traditions of comedy, *The Last Analysis* exposes the deficiencies, excesses and tinsel values of the civilization it depicts. Its protagonist, in terms of all the representative roles one can identify with him, stands for Making It Big in a society where "money reconciles all tendencies." Yet for Philip Bummidge, the price of success cannot be calculated wholly in terms of making and spending. While he denounces his family at last with great satisfaction and dances with glee when he extricates himself from their clutches, his jubilation at being done with them is shot through with regret. For one thing, he acknowledges his own contribution to their selfishness and amorality. For another, Bummidge reckons as the most exorbitant price of his success the alienation from his family, an extension of himself. His bitter clowning about his impossible father, his sarcastic banter with his own son, his witty cognizance that his family "dragged me down into affluence" fail to conceal his disappointment in himself and in them. "You came between me and my soul," he reproaches them collectively. His terminology is even more revealing when he accuses his lawyer cousin, "You made me change my name. Lead a false life." His regrets bespeak a Judaistic morality which stresses concern for other people's integrity and emphasizes the sanctity of respectful family relationships.

Like other Bellow protagonists, Bummidge is a veteran of "the lonely war of mind and heart." He represents those who are torn between the Romantic pursuit of self and crass materialism. Although his background, his experiences and what he has made of them certify his Jewishness, Bummidge finally takes a stance appropriate to all responsible men. It assumes that life asks each person to find himself, that having done so, his noblest goal is to help others accomplish the same, and that, in view of the bleakness and sadism in the world, in the last analysis it helps to laugh. Glenn Loney hardly overstates the case when he calls Bummidge "the prototype of the absurd man trying to come to terms with existence."[13]

The Jew is portrayed symbolically in several delightful works by actor-playwright Victor Haïm. *Isaac and the Midwife* (*Isaac et la Sage-Femme*, 1976) demonstrates the relevance to the modern world of a fanciful adventure during the reign of "Amenotestis V" in 3761 B. C. Isaac is a *schlemiel*, ensnared by forces beyond his control, but never abandoned by his sense of humor or his facility for talking beautifully and speculating endlessly on the reasons behind his terrible luck. Isaac lives on a wreck of a boat on the Red Sea, catching barely enough fish to stay alive. However precarious his life outwitting the maritime patrol, he finds it preferable to joining his coreligionists who are worked or starved to death in the Pharoah's Egypt. His running monologues addressed to God sound like Voltaire writing for the Yiddish theatre. "In countries where only the Pharaohs have enough to eat, because Thou hast willed it so, the children of the people are so worn out that they don't even know that they're hungry. Perfect!" observes the wretched fisherman. "How come the divine perfection of everything that happens here below didn't occur to me sooner?"[14]

Suddenly, Isaac feels his net is full. He pulls in a young Egyptian woman and promptly falls in love with her. She is the midwife, Lua, and she has thrown herself into the sea to escape punishment for disobeying the Pharaoh's command to suffocate all newborn Jewish males. Before her insubordination was discovered, she had cleverly managed to save a thousand Jewish babies. Lua embodies the life force and the eternal feminine in the comic manner of a nag who loses little time urging Isaac to attempt impossible measures to save them. When he refuses, Lua tricks him into rowing her to shore. She intends to take advantage of her favor with the Pharaoh's daughter whom she helped through a difficult childbirth. But the plan is only half successful. The princess Malika agrees to save the midwife, but not Isaac. His religion is against him, of course; besides, Malika, a young widow who has learned how love leads only to sorrow, counsels Lua to spare herself future heartbreak by killing the fisherman straight away. Lua, of course, is incapable of killing anyone. In a tragi-comic final scene, Isaac is again alone on his drifting boat. To shut out God, who might try to guide or console him, he clasps a pair of shells over his ears. His reveries and the earphones keep him from hearing Lua who has swum miles and clings exhausted to his boat. Not until her lifeless body drags on the net does Isaac become aware of her.

The first time Isaac brought Lua into his boat, she was starving. Because the fishing was so bad and her appetite so voracious, she eventually indulged in a bit of good-natured cannibalism, feasting on Isaac's arm. Now Isaac would give her his very breath. And finally he does give his life for her. He resolves to return to Egypt and bury Lua next to his parents, surely a fatal decision for him.

On one level, *Isaac and the Midwife* works effectively as a parable. Even without its anachronistic references to crematoria, genocide and an Egyptian fisherman killed in a particularly gruesome way because he looked Jewish, the parallels with centuries in which tyrants of one kind or another have menaced Israelites are plain. The mid-Eastern setting is eminently appropriate, as is the play's black humor. Observed one French critic, "Our laughter gets stuck somewhere between Auschwitz and the Yom Kippur War. We know only too well that Isaac has not yet found the Egyptian midwife who will help him bring forth peace."[15]

Haïm's play surpasses its Jewish references to work on another level. In a broader sense, Isaac, the self-styled "maritime bum" stands for modern man. Choosing to live adrift on an unfriendly sea that sends him signs but little sustenance (Isaac catches starfish which are inedible), abandoned by a God whom he maligns but can't quite dismiss, he resolves never to marry and bring children into a world where malefactors have a way of engendering other malefactors. Lua changes everything. Because Isaac responds in spite of himself, she coaxes hope out of his despair. So vigorously does Lua uphold life that the fisherman wishes she might advise God on the subject. That Isaac encourages her to feed on him makes a bold statement about his commitment to the life force she embodies. Lua understands that life sometimes involves making deals, hence her negotiations with Malika, death's associate. Although the stubbornly idealistic Isaac tries to isolate himself once again in his offshore limbo, he has been irrevocably won over by life. With his decision to bury Lua in the Pharaoh's land, he accepts the consequences of revering life in a society which devaluates it.

In another short play, *Abraham and Samuel* (*Abraham et Samuel*, 1974), Haïm makes devastating and wide-reaching observations on the ex-

Samuel reasons with his employer, the widow. Victor Haïm's *Abraham and Samuel*. Paris 1973. Photograph by Bernard, Paris.

ploitation of the weak by the powerful, a subject traditionally close to
Jewish hearts which often beat in unison with those of the world's
workers. The play's Samuel is a little Jew in the employ of a rich
widow of gigantic stature somewhere between Mae West and Gorgeous George. Samuel has worked for the woman, a diversified entrepreneur, for ten years. So poorly does she pay him that he has
survived only by stealing from her, an expedient adopted in fact by
all the workers on her estate. Unfortunately, it is Samuel who gets
caught.

The first half of the play has the flavor of a medieval farce. The
crafty little Jew insults and hoodwinks his boss so engagingly that he
almost makes her forget her determination to kill him. The widow
finds Samuel "the funniest Jew on earth." Even when his delicious
arrogance pushes her a bit too far, her "Don't make me laugh" sounds
more like an appeal than a rebuff. Cunningly, the Jew manages to
trap the widow in one of her own wine barrels which he pierces with
her sword. The crisis brings on the first of two *coups de théâtre*. Hoping
to extricate herself, the employer reveals her astonishing secret: she is
not a widow, or a woman, or a gentile. "She" is Abraham, a crafty
Jew who has adopted this disguise so as to exploit people he has
fooled into thinking that they were taking advantage of a woman.

Farce gives way to dialectic in the rest of the play. Abraham counts
on winning sympathy from his coreligionist, a benefit that is not
forthcoming. The employer lays claim to a fraternity between Jews
that is transparently expedient. For the underpaid worker, the fact
that he and his boss are of the same religion is far less consequential
than that Abraham is wealthy and powerful precisely because he uses
the poor and weak like Samuel. While their argument is lightened by
Abraham's bumbling hypocrisy (e.g., he accuses Samuel of lacking
respect for his religion by stealing from a Jew) and by the colorful
epithets the antagonists hurl at one another, the diversions do not
obscure the irreconcilable gap between them. Samuel speaks for all
workers imposed upon by the Abrahams of the world. How could
he face his companions having spared his employer's life? To their
charges that he had betrayed them, Samuel would have to answer,
"I had the choice between you, who resemble me because you can
hardly afford a loaf of bread or a piece of meat, and my boss who
proclaimed loud and clear that he was my brother."[16] The brotherhood
of Jews is overshadowed by the brotherhood of man.

As hostility mounts, the two come to blows. The enormous Abraham would easily finish off his frail opponent were it not for a second
coup de théâtre. Suddenly, miraculously, Abraham is turned into a
statue, his raised arm forever frozen over his head.

Samuel considers his options. He might assume the widow's role, but that would involve a life of truckling to society's morality and laughing at its anti-Semitic jokes. Or he could bravely adopt the widow's guise, defiantly transforming her into a self-assured Jewess who has acquired all the qualities of a gentile. More realistically, Samuel realizes he cannot act alone. He needs the advice and cooperation of his fellows. His final speech, addressed to a group dominated by conspicuously gentile names, makes clear his resolution. Jubilantly he calls his friends to come look at their former employer and to rejoice that the estate is theirs and that they will have a chance to use their various talents to run it. Samuel's joyful reaction makes the contrived "inheritance" seem less a quirk than a symbol of the working class triumph over the bourgeoisie. "Come everybody!" he exults. "The grass is ours! The sun is ours! The sky is ours! . . . Samuel is calling you. Samuel, Age: reasonable; Profession: proletarian; Race: human" (p. 46). There is nothing subtle about Haïm's personae as metaphors; what is especially original is making the Jew serve as both oppressor and oppressed.

Abraham and Samuel's vigorous portrayal of Jews in the socio-economic arena does not stand alone in treating the proletarian more sympathetically than the bourgeois. Haïm's Abraham, with his sword, tricks and unconscionable exploitativeness is perhaps too recognizable a descendant of Barabas. A less caricatured example of contemporary Jewish capitalists are the effete young business people in Arnold Wesker's *The Friends* (1970). No villains, they have built up a fine home decorating firm, only to lose all interest in it. Neither the sensible, loving advice of their business manager nor the lucidity of their devoted gentile associate succeeds in rousing them from their apathy. They are entirely engrossed in the lingering death of one of the partners. The play is subtle in its criticism of these eminently likable people whose failure in business implies a larger-scale squandering of talents and resources.

Although Wesker draws rather extensively on the Jewishness of his proletarians in *The Trilogy* (see Chapter Five), in *The Friends* the characters' heritage serves primarily to suggest the source of their aesthetic and political values, their intellectualism and their flair for business. By contrast, in his next play after *The Friends*, Wesker puts to explicit use Jewish values which work their way through his personae's lives and help endow them with transcendent meaning.

There is a prefatory note to the list of dramatis personae in *The Old Ones* (1972): "Everyone except Jack and the three youths happens to be Jewish; nevertheless, the play is essentially about defiant old age."[17] However, the religious background of the characters is not at all fortuitous as the central role the play assigns to Judaism makes clear.

Rather Wesker's note alerts us to the fact that the plucky characters in *The Old Ones* are generally representative of human persistence in the face of reversals and disappointments.

Tenacity is everywhere apparent in the titular Old Ones. Seven of them are between the ages of sixty-eight and seventy-one. Among the many challenges that the brothers Emanuel and Boomy defy are one another. Their running quarrel began over fifty years before. As youths, they emigrated from Lithuania, the remains of their father's fortune in a bag of diamonds. Already fired by the idealism which still rules his life, Manny got Boomy to agree that they should start out on their own. Then he tossed the diamonds in the Thames. Instead of going to university, the brothers became tailors. As they aged, each grew more zealous in his obsession, Emanuel with human perfectibility, Boomy with life's futility. Both voracious readers, they have feuded for a half-century through a ritual of vigorously exchanging exquisitely chosen literary quotations.

Manny's sources are typically Voltaire, Ruskin and Buber. Recently, dark intimations of his own waning vitality have increased his devotion to positive principles. At seventy, he decides to indulge a lifetime ambition to learn to sing. "And you know what?" he chortles, "I got a good voice." Although the optimistic citations he aims at Boomy are persuasive, Manny is at his most eloquent in a scene near the end of the play. Wrapped in a towel, he dashes out of the bath and back to the family gathering to enunciate his newest argument that the reasonable man must act on his rectitude irrespective of the foolishness and evil around him. Challenged by the clearly impressed Boomy to identify the author of this eloquent "quotation," Manny slyly admits it is he. Then he dances out of the room to the applause of his family, turning on the tape recorder of himself singing as he goes, and crowing jubilantly, "Me! Me! Meeeeee!"

The very antithesis of his brother, the dour Boomy cannot cope with human frailty, including his own. Embittered by an accumulation of thwarted projects, not the least of which was seeing his education sink into the Thames, Boomy finds advancing age intolerable. "I can't bear being defenceless," he confides to Manny's wife Gerda. "And now look at me, playing with T.V. sets in order to start understanding things. Now! Sixty-eight years old. Like a senile Doctor Faustus" (p. 164). Boomy's defiance seeks confirmation in literature of his conviction that happiness and fulfillment are vanities. His point of view is couched in extracts from Carlyle and especially from Ecclesiastes. Perhaps his most heartrending obstinacy is his refusal to permit himself to aid or even accept his only child Martin, a rebel whose values Boomy rejects as contemptible.

Each in her own way, the female Old Ones are equally resolute.

Manny, the tailor philosopher. Arnold Wesker's *The Old Ones*. London 1972.
Photograph by John Haynes, London.

Though Manny's wife Gerda argues with him, she stands behind her
husband in his ongoing battle with Boomy, but never gives up urging
the brothers to come to terms. Her most daring act of defiance occurs
in the Act I curtain scene where she almost dissuades three street
hoodlums from attacking her: "It's really *me* you want to bash? Little
bash-boys? *I'm* the biggest 'enemy' you can find? Look at me. Look at

yourselves. Three of you. That's brave? I'm the biggest conquest you can make? Go home. Brave boys, go home!" (p. 165)

Manny and Boomy's sister Sarah is dedicated to preserving the treasures of the past. One of her most tenacious attachments is to youthful mental acuity. "Make your mind think, think!" she admonishes her friend Millie, who is almost hopelessly senile. "Forget things and you'll go to pieces." An outspoken partisan of the working class, Sarah derives a mischievous pleasure from competing with her intellectual son-in-law, a soil expert. Vigorous plants fill her apartment, while at his house boxes of carefully mixed earth grow only mud.

Sarah's witty friend Teressa, still handsome and mentally vigorous, funnels her rage at the ravages of time into a heroic struggle with language ("Very important, language; without language, men think with their fists"). Her persistence is remarkably displayed in a scene—probably unparalleled in all dramatic literature—in which she wrestles with the translation of a line of poetry from the Polish.

The only Old One who doesn't "happen to be Jewish" is Sarah's neighbor, Jack. He is a strange old Cockney, given to hugging walls and ringing bells like an untouchable warning people away because he is a bastard and has been taught that that is a contamination. Perhaps his belief in his own wickedness makes him look to redeem himself by seeking out the society of Teressa and Sarah, who treat him kindly, and of Millie, whose dependence he finds irresistible:

But—I loves London and I loves England and I loves the little foreigners like you wot they let in to mix the blood a bit. Come, Missus, me arm. I'll escort you safe and sound to the other little Jewish lady wots my neighbour. ([Millie] takes his arm, shyly.) And wot a neighbour she is, she is. A fighter, a real little pellet of steel she is. Pellets of steel all you lot are. (p. 175)

Collectively, these protagonists put forth unforgettable images of advanced age and command our respect.

Wesker's claim that the play's subject is defiant old age may be too modest. For the behavior of the "young ones" (a relative term as the cousins' ages range from twenty-eight through forty) reveals patterns of familial resoluteness. Sarah's daughter Rosa persists until she gains control of a group of recalcitrant school drop-outs she's been assigned to counsel. Rudi, the son of Sarah's dead sister, is as serious a painter this year as he was a voice student last year. And although Boomy's activist son Martin cannot make his father understand why his political involvement is more important to him than the wife and child he has abandoned, he insists, "I'm not a delinquent and I'm not a fool, and I will, I will follow my conscience" (p. 153).

Quarrels provide an important motif in *The Old Ones*, but they are not its focal point. Rather the play seeks to depict both quotidian adversities (among them poverty, street crime, limited future prospects) and the conflicting claims of an extended family life whose participants, despite their preoccupation with their own problems, want to let others know they care about them. Wesker effectively dramatizes the dynamics which draw people together and pull them apart by using two devices. One is to substitute for a linear plot a series of twenty-four scenes which frequently comment upon one another indirectly and which in the aggregate convey major themes such as the fundamental isolation of the characters and the determination of all the Old Ones except Boomy to overlook their own disappointments in encouraging the younger ones to learn and aspire.

A second contrivance gives the play its dramatic focus and binds its diverse elements together in impressive dimension. The central event in *The Old Ones* is the family's almost unprecedented celebration of the autumn festival of Succoth and the construction of a succah.* The structure that rises on the balcony of Sarah's flat revives a custom the family has not observed since Sarah, Manny and Boomy were young. Martin and Rudi help their aunt build and decorate, while Rosa reads aloud from a guide to the festival celebration. But when Rosa reaches the specification that the roof of foliage must permit a view of the stars, for "the heavens declare the 'glory of God,'" Sarah makes plain that for her, the value of the holiday lies elsewhere. "Let the heavens declare the glory of God, we'll build the 'Succah' to declare the glory of man. . . . And to remember my father. . . . And for your Aunty Gerda who likes these things" (pp. 137–38). Though the celebrants are self-conscious about it, they follow the prescriptions in the festival guide for the procession with branches and citron. Then they relax at Sarah's traditional dinner to discuss their impressions of the holiday. When Manny observes that the succah is a symbol of joy, Boomy is quick to remind him that the biblical text that belongs to Succoth is Ecclesiastes.* "So! Go read Ecclesiastes and be joyful!" he challenges his brother.

Whatever Boomy's reservations and the liberties the family takes with established ritual, this Succoth celebration preserves the holi-

---

*A succah is a fragile hut erected outside and decorated with fruits and other symbols of the harvest. It is customary for observant families to take their meals in the succah during the eight days of the festival. The little booths have historical and agricultural significance. They recall Israel's wanderings after the Exodus as well as the rude shelters put up in the fields during the harvest season.

*Ecclesiastes is read in the synagogue during Succoth. Its eloquent pessimism reminds man of his finitude and suggests he modulate his behavior and expectations, remembering more barren days in the midst of the harvest celebration.

The Succoth procession in *The Old Ones*. London 1972. Photograph by John Haynes, London.

day's essential worth. Like their ancestors toiling in the wilderness, Sarah's people need the emotional warmth and temporary shelter her succah offers. Gerda is recovering from the street assault; Rosa's self-confidence has been badly shaken on the job; Rudi yearns to be with the family whom he sees too infrequently; Teressa is pathologically lonely; Millie, all but helpless. The holiday is an ingathering. Like the ancient Jews who relaxed in their makeshift huts after the harvest, Sarah's guests indulge in sharing their stored-up tales, dreams and passionately held opinions.

The Succoth observation restores to this family a tradition it had lost for at least forty years (the number itself has the biblical connotation of wandering in the desert). Although Sarah observes that the succah is wobbly, it is strong enough to shore up values important to these people which the rigors of daily life have tended to undermine. Sharing the holiday brings the Old Ones closer to the parents they remember as it tightens the bonds between the Old Ones and their own children. Strengthened family relationships are expressed in a lovely scene in which Rosa and Sarah execute a delicate Hasidic dance to Manny's Yiddish songs and the humming and clapping of the others.

The renewal of one generation's consideration for the next gives Manny fresh energy to chide Boomy for his "catastrophe-mongering." It is bad enough that Boomy makes his life's purpose the accumulating of pronouncements of doom, but unforgivable that he prematurely disillusions and disheartens the young. Manny does not try to quarrel with Ecclesiastes; his attitude seems an implicit acknowledgment of his awareness that Ecclesiastes is considered the work of Solomon in his old age. However Manny insists that "you have to earn the right to call the world a vain place," and that the greatest vanity is to abandon one's own potential. Of course Emanuel does not convince Boomy whose last lines quote Ecclesiastes on man's defenselessness in the face of death, but he helps Sarah make a convincing case for life. A family gathering (however infrequent) to observe a holiday (however irregularly) needs no apology. The torrent of pessimism in Ecclesiastes does not obscure its observations that life is for the living (e.g., 9:7–10; 11:8–9); or, as Manny puts it, quoting himself, "'All right! I said, 'so the world's got troubles, but someone's got to remember how to be happy. You mustn't lose the habit of joy.' I said. 'Someone's got to carry it around'" (p. 183).

Succoth is a perfectly chosen central metaphor for this sensitive play. The autumn holiday brings together the gaiety of the harvest with the somber reminder that winter will follow. The cycle of the seasons applies suitably to the assembly of young and old in the play.

The festival's mixed tone of rejoicing and melancholy corresponds specifically to the contrasting outlooks adopted by Emmanuel and Boomy and, by extension, to the other polarities in the work (e.g., love and estrangement, solitude and togetherness, impoverishment and plenty, intellectualism and action).

Paradoxically, the Jewish holiday and the Old Testament text associated with it function to give *The Old Ones* general relevance. Succoth has special significance as a universal feast. Traditionally during the festival sacrifices were offered for the welfare of the nations of the world, an act intended as "public expression of Israel's solidarity with all mankind."[18] Then too it is entirely appropriate for a play about defiant old age to be populated by descendants of an old people who have earned a reputation for persistence in finding ways and reasons to cling to life however imperfect or threatened. Finally, because the characters in *The Old Ones* maintain the right to affirm their own values even when the assertion puts them at odds with tradition or the wisdom of centuries, they become representative of all men, whether or not they "happen to be Jewish."

Old age, no matter how defiant, points in only one direction. Our last play takes place on the brink of death. It is, in fact, the end of humanity. Man's death wish has succeeded in destroying all possibility of life. Fortunately, this chilling premise is warmed by a crazy quilt of Ionescian absurdities, outrageous clichés and Freudian bromides. In its exaggerated subject, its grim world view and its wild humor, Bernard Kops's *The Lemmings* (1963) is a quintessentially Jewish play.

Word has gone forth from incontrovertible authority that "the Kingdom of God draweth water." On a universal seashore, the world's populace disports in enthusiastic, orderly self-destruction. What must pass for divine approval is transmitted via a Salvation Army band and choir—until their turn comes. A voice dictates the sequence ("Pregnant mothers and little toddlers will now march into the sea").

When the last of the suicides are hats floating on the waves, the Lemmings make their entrance. They are late because they got lost. Sarah Lemming is a *Yiddishe momma* who has somehow been conditioned Ionescianly; her greatest pleasure is stuffing bread into her son Norman. Her husband Harry is relieved he won't have to worry any more about the taxi business which hasn't been any too good. Seventeen-year-old Norman keeps asking *why* they have to walk into the sea; he is not particularly reassured by his father's "We're not going to die. We're only going to drown." Shortly, the Lemmings are joined by an upper-class family, Charles and Liz Jones and their sixteen-year-old daughter, Iris. There is an inverted platitude in the fact that the Joneses are the last to arrive.

Circumstances compel these final two families to postpone their deaths until the next day and force them to get acquainted. Their efforts at civility are hampered by mutual distrust. Mrs. Lemming anticipates prejudice ("Two sorts of people in this world. Jews and Jew haters") and is not disappointed, although she doesn't hear Mrs. Jones's outrage at having to share judgment day with the Jews. Mr. Jones admits sheepishly that he once knew one, "Rather nice, despite his obviously unattractive personality."[19] Before long, however, Jones declares stoutly to Lemming that some of his best friends. . . . Eventually, Jones even works up real enthusiasm for ending his days in the company of "God's chosen," although he keeps reminding himself that "Our Lord was of the Jewish persuasion," a turn of phrase that earlier prompted Harry Lemming to protest, "Believe me, we weren't persuaded."

Pure nosiness, or the adage that opposites attract, draws the couples together. After an impromptu party where Harry is coaxed into abandoning his customary abstinence, he tries to warm Liz Jones's blue blood, while Charles satisfies his curiosity about the exotic Jewess (no doubt he ends by believing Sarah's popping wads of bread in his mouth is a tribal custom). In their dotty dalliances, they reveal a profound ignorance about themselves and one another. When, for example, Jones asks the Lemmings to say what Jews have contributed to the world, their list begins with Eddie Cantor and cheesecake, and goes on to include Spinoza and Shakespeare. Asked the same question about their tradition, the Joneses propose crumpets and marmalade.

The younger generation has learned equally shallow concepts of identity. The Joneses have always assured Iris she was too good for other people; it has never occurred to her to question their criteria. Norman's boast that he is a Jew "hundred per cent" traps him in the embarassment of having to explain what he barely understands:

Iris: So what? What are Jews?

Norman: Who knows?

Iris: Who cares?

Norman: We're proud. We love life. We cover mirrors and sit on low chairs.

Iris: Why?

Norman: I forget.

Iris: Are Jews better than other people?

Norman: Yes.

Iris: Are they worse?

Norman: Yes. . . . Jerusalem's our home. That's why we say "Next year in Jerusalem."

Iris: What a lovely word. JERUSALEM! Where is it?

Norman: It's nowhere. It's next year. It's just a dream, I suppose. We're not connected to anything. We don't belong anywhere. (pp. 253–54)

The muddle-headed teenagers find it easier to relate physically. Iris teaches young Lemming the kiss of life, dealing his Oedipal complex a mortal blow. Discovering the couple in the grass brings out their parents' true natures. Sarah ignores her son's furious invective, throws bread at him and tries to lure him away with promises of hot soup and lullabies. Iris' parents feel more aggrieved. "He's a Jew," shrieks Liz Jones. "They drink blood. They're dirty. Look at his hands! How can you let them touch your body?" (p. 256). At the same time, she admits to herself that Norman is beautifully built and grinds her teeth with jealousy. As for Charles Jones, he curses Norman and nurses memories of little Iris promising she was going to marry her daddy when she grew up.

Norman and Iris' sexual initiation is only the first wrench for their parents. Tutored by Iris who wants to go on making love and have children, Norman reconsiders his former unquestioning acceptance of his parents' values. The young people decide to defy their elders and the world. They will not walk into the sea. Each set of parents blames the other for contaminating their children with life and hope. Soon Harry and Charles come to blows. But when Norman steps in to separate them, both fathers turn on him.

While Iris nurses Norman's bruises, the elders make final preparations to pay their debt. The Joneses set their camper ablaze and sing a chorus of "Keep the Home Fires Burning." Sarah does her laundry because she has always been an immaculate housekeeper and sees no reason to change now. Then they splash singing into the sea. Norman's exaltation in being free at last to fulfill his own ambitions is short-lived. Though Iris entices him and Norman dreams mighty dreams, it is clear he is not capable of making his own decisions. The sea exerts an erotic allure against which he is powerless. He rationalizes: he will give Iris everything when they get to the other side. What matter that neither of them can swim? Perhaps they can walk on the glassy surface of the silvery sea. Laughing, the last two people in the world dance into the water and disappear.

While mocking Sarah's facile dichotomy that divides society into

Jews and Jew haters, Kops's play makes good use of it to focus on the dearth of values in both groups. Careless heirs of an ancient tradition, the Lemmings preserve little pride in their heritage and, as the passages quoted above testify, even less understanding of it. It is shocking, for instance, that a Jew in the 1960s could say that Jerusalem was "nowhere" and that Jews "don't belong anywhere." Virtually all that remains of their Judaism is blind attachment to formulas which they have vulgarized almost beyond recognition and are unable to explain to their son:

Mrs. Lemming: Eat your bread and say a prayer. (She cuts the bread.)

Norman: I don't want to. (Mr. Lemming starts praying.)

Mrs. Lemming: Pray! Pray! Quickly pray.

Norman: I don't believe in prayer.

Mrs. Lemming: That's not the point. Pray!

Norman: I don't know any prayers. What shall I pray?

Mrs. Lemming: What was that one again? The Lord is my—

Norman: Yeah, I remember—what is he? (p. 242)

The Joneses are not any more certain about what they believe. As representatives of the elite, they are alert to such matters as size and source of income and who is admitted into their spheres of influence. But their principles and behavior hardly suggest nobility of spirit. "Tell me," Jones asks Lemming, "Is incest all that bad?" Neither the Joneses nor the Lemmings have ever taken the trouble to think about who they are or what they stand for. Their inanity is effectively demonstrated in the men's two fights. The first time, they vilify while tickling one another; the second, they trade compliments and murderous blows. It is at this point that Norman steps into the fight and that the older generation closes ranks to turn on the younger. One suspects Lemming and Jones sense Norman's budding will to survive and regard it either as an impertinence or as a threat.

The beating is no accident. The play finds several ways to say that children are the ultimate losers by their parents' vacuity. Norman had already attempted suicide three times; were it not for Iris, he would never have guessed that life was worthwhile. For a time, it appears that he might be able to build on the life force she signifies, casting off his parents' baneful influence and his own death wish. Unfortunately, Norman's spiritual deficiencies even more than his immaturity undo him in the end. One of the few touching moments in the play occurs when, prepped by Iris, he proclaims grandly to the parents, "We mean to survive—to profit from your experience." But then he falters, forgetting his carefully memorized lines and losing his nerve, "Here on the edge of death we want . . . to resolve . . . I forget" (p. 277). Significantly, at this point the parents cheer. Norman simply is not man enough to go his own way, and Iris, who doesn't want to be left alone, has no choice but to follow him into the sea.

It would be as unreasonable to blame all of Iris and Norman s shortcomings on their parents as to assume that the Lemmings and the Joneses were wholly responsible for what is happening to them. Early in the play, Charles Jones recalls a "wonderful" dream that suggests the context in which the play's mass suicide takes place. Jones describes hurrying to escape some sort of catastrophe. Just when he thinks he is safe, he runs into a blockade of men with machine guns. He suspects everyone is doomed. Sure enough, fighting breaks out and "people do such things to each other that I never could believe people could do such things." Just as the carnage reaches its peak, the sound of helicopters is heard:

And inside them I clearly saw the military heads and the Government and an Archbishop. A Lord and trade union leaders, and even a few film stars and then the Royal family. And then I heard someone shout "They're escaping to carry on the good work in our dominions beyond the seas." And guess what? They started waving at us! Everyone stopped fighting and we all sang the National Anthem with tears in our eyes, and even though we are all turning to ash, we slap each other on the back. And though we died, it didn't matter any more. (pp. 248–49)

Behind its blackly humorous façade, *The Lemmings,* whose deep pessimism Kops attributes to a trip he had recently made to Eastern Europe, depicts a world devoid of all that supports human life. Its population has become so destitute of principle and purpose that it can think only of migrating, like lemmings, in a vain search for sustenance which comes largely from within. Not finding it anywhere, they turn to the appeal of the sea where they are surely even less fit to survive. Nevertheless, they move toward death with the same compliant automatism and obedience to empty values by which they lived.

Kops's choice of caricatures to populate his macabre scenario makes excellent sense logically and artistically. Not only is their lack of human substance essential to explaining their acquiescence in their own destruction, it also makes them mechanical comic figures capable of performing the most outlandish acts. Like the English couples in Ionesco's *The Bald Soprano,* the Joneses and the Lemmings have lost all sense of proportion and propriety. Sarah and Harry, Liz and Charles are post-modern stereotypes who would be funny even if their situation were less critical.

The role of the Jew in this play grows slippery when one recalls that it is the Lemmings who give their name to the play. Generally speaking, all the characters are lemmings. Though they are not as bestial as Ionesco's rhinoceroses, like them they have lost their individuality and ability to think for themselves. But this is not true of Iris and Norman who are depicted, like Duras' characters, in the process of becoming and are thoroughly aware of what is happening, even though they are unqualified to resist. Says the last Lemming, "It's rotten that we weren't born some other time on some other planet where people have already found the secret of love and the secret of how to live forever. I feel cheated" (p. 267). *The Lemmings* declares that civilization ends not with a bang, but with spiritual bankruptcy. The degree of contemporary man's impoverishment is symbolized by this young Jew who ought to feel in the very prime of his life, but who instead cannot find the strength or support to continue it.

The Jewish personae who function as metaphors in these plays form a heterogeneous assemblage. As they represent humanity in one way or another, they also demonstrate that the question "What is a Jew?" invites as diverse a range of legitimate answers as "What is a human being?" In Roman comedy, characters from similar backgrounds were said to be as alike as drops of milk. Jewish personae on the post-1945 stage regularly seem more different from one another than curds and whey. Or, to borrow a more appropriate vocabulary, their only sure likeness is that all have "hands, organs, dimensions, senses, affections, passions." In that, they resemble—indeed, sometimes stand for—mankind in general.

The Kops play brings this study full circle. The Lemmings who walk into the sea as the last people on earth are the literary descendants of the occupants of the ark who survived the Deluge in *The Flowering Peach*. Neither Odets nor Kops was compelled by fidelity to any outside truth to make these key characters Jews. That each dramatist did so—Odets to add flavor to a Broadway production, Kops to represent a segment of the population that had a tradition to lose and lost it—evinces the suitability of contemporary Jewish personae to roles which run quite literally the gamut of the human experience.

9

Conclusion

A notion which has captured the imagination of our miracle-working era involves freezing people for revival under more auspicious circumstances. The concept (naturally already the subject of a Woody Allen filmscript) applies rather accurately to the life story of the stage Jew. For some eight centuries, dramatic literature preserved the Jew in immobilized shapes and circumstances. With the advent of the modern theatre at the end of the last century, the thaw set in. The Jew was finally delivered if not to a promised land, at least to a hospitable one. He was no longer routinely characterized by his profession (paid malefactor), his address (elsewhere) or his point of view (the antithesis of whatever is right this time). In the favorable climate of the twentieth century, and with noteworthy abundance since World War II, Jewish personae have been fruitful and multiplying. They have flourished because they lend themselves versatilely to the needs of Western dramatists interested in portraying life more or less realistically. For real life is inhabited by real people rather than by congealed stock types. Even the more stylized theatrical modes of mirroring nature allow the Jew normal vital signs.

Normality diminishes however. While the Jew on the contemporary stage has dimension, he lacks the stature of a Shylock or a Samson; though he is sentient, his passions do not rival those of the Racinian queens. He is an ordinary man among *ses semblables, ses frères* in a theatre for ordinary people. A telling measure of the development of the Jewish persona is that he gets woven into the fiber of his play exactly as he does into the fabric of the community the play reflects. In the instance where a Jew dominates a classical play (Marlowe's Barabas as an apt example), it is precisely because he is unique and detachable. In modern works, the Jew becomes a protagonist to the degree that he is generally representative of those around him. *The Jew of Malta* exists to make a sensational characterization; Sidney Brustein, Dave Simmonds, Esther Peyrolle exist as vehicles for what their plays have to say about society.

Still, however competently the stage Jew serves various roles as exponent of a social scene, he never melds entirely into the crowd. The Jew offers exactly the kind of paradox the theatre adores: he can be two things simultaneously—the specific and the general. The specific has occupied center stage throughout this demonstration of the expanded repertoire of Jewish roles and images. The general is more complicated.

No matter how calculatedly and precisely he has been created by his dramatist, the character who declares himself a Jew is susceptible to being perceived in terms of prevailing feelings about Jews. The characterization originated by the playwright is completed and colored by attitudes on both sides of the footlights. The same observation holds to some degree for all dramatis personae, yet obviously "Jew" is a more provocative designation than, say, "faded Southern belle." Amanda Wingfield is more likely to be viewed as Tennessee Williams intended her to be than is Gibson's Gittel Mosca, whatever the interpretations of the actresses in the roles. Audiences can be relied upon to have lively, preconceived notions which affect their understanding of stage Jews. Indeed, as we have seen, one of the most ingenious accomplishments of post-1945 drama is exploiting these preconceptions, notably by rendering them useless in understanding the character (e.g., *Jim the Temerarious; Destroy, She Said*). No matter how persuasively a dramatist may think he has designed his Jews, he incurs the risk of having them judged and found wanting on grounds difficult to dispute. Francine Szapiro in *The Basel Jewish Gazette* saw Haïm's Abraham and Samuel as "ex-Jews, superficial and inauthentic"; Hannah Grad Goodman observed in *Hadassah Magazine* that Matt Friedman (*Talley's Folly*) "doesn't think like a Jew."

Another special factor figures in the attitudes that inform Jewish characters on the contemporary stage. A fair number of Jewish dramatists are now writing for audiences of which Jews are faithful and enthusiastic constituents. Beyond whatever he may anticipate the reactions of gentile viewers to be toward his Jewish characters, the Jewish writer is certainly aware of his coreligionists' sensitivities to the image his personae may be held responsible for presenting. The bitter Jewish criticism that has been levelled at Budd Schulberg, Philip Roth and Mordecai Richler exemplifies the hazards. The denunciations were not aimed at the effectiveness of these authors' characterizations, accomplishments the brouhaha implicitly confirmed. Rather they questioned the ethics of Jewish artists' offering devastatingly unflattering portraits of Jews for public consumption. It is doubtful that in the West much support could be mustered to restore theatre's didactic function or that very many theatregoers genuinely believe that disseminating propaganda constitutes one of the stage's objectives. Nevertheless, there is little question that a traditionally harassed people's concern about its image must operate at several levels throughout the process of bringing Jewish-created Jews to the public stage. But if the phenomenon is undeniable, it is also hard to substantiate. Whether, for instance, a gentile would have rehabilitated Shylock as vigorously as did Arnold Wesker amounts to a moot question. Hence the central consideration in this book has been to investigate why a character in a given role is a Jew rather than to attempt to show the influence of his author's background or that of the prevailing social scene.

This much is clear, however: Jewish self-consciousness (or self-confidence) has altered the representation of Jewish characters and Jewish life in the theatre. Ironically, some rather accurate portrayals of Jewish particularity have ended by pointing up the universality of the Jew. For example, vague, mystifying references to worship ("Go, Tubal, and meet me at our synagogue") have given way to the staging of part of a synagogue service (e.g., *The Tenth Man*) or of religious observances in the home (e.g., Noah's family Shabbat in *The Flowering Peach*, shivah in *The Hamlet of Stepney Green*, the Succoth celebration in *The Old Ones*). That in each of the instances cited a Jewish playwright adapts the ritual to the requirements of his work does not invalidate the significant shift of viewpoint. If anything, the liberties enhance the authenticity of what audiences are shown. Here, say these plays, are some of the ways Jews perceive the cultural differences that set them apart.

The demonstration is not limited to ceremonies. It includes a number of attitudes toward being considered the chosen, from the total devotion to Judaism of the rabbi in *Zalmen, or The Madness of God*, to Jonah's finagling with his divine orders to go to Nineveh, to Gideon's preference of the glory of man to the glory of God. Challenging the prescribed code supplies an appropriate vehicle for dramatizing a Jew's defiance. Hence Philip Bummidge gets back at his tyrannical father by eating pork and Alexey and Nina assert their independence of her rabbi father by their refusal to train their son for Bar Mitzvah. It is not Jewish beliefs that these inside views endeavor to dramatize, but rather Jewish attitudes toward those beliefs. In proportion as the irregularities in stage observances (or nonobservances) of Judaism invalidate them as lessons in comparative religion, so the same deviations enhance the reliability of the scenes as indicators of human behavior. Precisely because Jewish characters question the authority or relevance of their tradition, they become representative of all contemporary men dissatisfied with time-honored customs, doctrine and values.

Depictions of the gap between the Jew and his tradition are not limited to the attenuated influence of religious tenets and practices. In *Black Opera,* the Jewish protagonist finds his niche only by leaving his own people to align his fate with that of another minority. The "agonizing availability" which explains why Kalisky's Jim is captivated by Nazi ideology results from his total detachment from his people. Nor is Jewish deracination exclusively a subject for Jewish playwrights. Jean Anouilh shades in a poignant side of Messerschmann's disorientation in high society by showing his unrealizable desire to return to the simple gratifications of a Cracow tailor shop. Phillip Hayes Dean portrays a Jew's isolation in a nowheresville between rejection of his parents' religion and incomplete acceptance into the non-Jewish world, despite his bobbed nose.

The dramatic portrait of the Jew as alien or marginal is as venerable as the persona himself. He has ever been—and, as many plays show, still is—excluded, suppressed or destroyed because he is a Jew. What is strikingly original is the image on the post-1945 stage of the Jew who is isolated not *because* of his Jewish identity, but *from* it. Dispossessed of the foothold which provided at least a frame of reference if not true consolation, the doubting or renegade Jew is as vulnerable as any other disillusioned, confused modern in confronting the "thousand nameless faceless vapors that are the evil of our time," as Sidney Brustein puts it.

The difficulties inherent in viewing dramatic literature as an index to rather than as a reflection of attitudes have already been noted here. There is no way of ascertaining how accurate the image of the alienated Jew may be. Still, one cannot fail to notice that in the world beyond the theatre, disaffection predominates even in the wake of the momentous identity-galvanizing phenomena of the Holocaust and Israeli statehood.

Fortunately, estrangement is not the only image that prevails on the post-war stage. Alongside all the variations of the disenchanted, the persecuted and the outsider, there persists another view of the Jew, more traditional and as vital as ever: In the midst of the anonymity of an American city there is Gittel Mosca, who makes jokes and love, six old men determined to gather a minyan to save a psychotic girl, and a dowdy woman on a park bench whose simple good will mitigates the seething discontent of a bright young black. In Stepney Green, the Levy family sings even when faced with deception and death, while not far away, a drunken tailor hurriedly sews a warm coat for his impoverished friend. At a strange hotel, three Frenchmen who call themselves Jews prepare for an ameliorated society, while in Maryland, a French Jewess demonstrates her loyalty to the homeland she cherishes.

On the Red Sea, a hapless fisherman nourishes life with his own blood. At seventy, a Jew mischievously wraps himself in a bath towel to deliver a tirade against pessimism. An eighty-nine-year-old invests in a houseful of furniture and, sitting in the midst of it, is overwhelmed by delicious laughter. The Promised Land may not seem any closer. Not all the Jews are even talking about Jerusalem any more. But an impressive number of them demonstrate that savoring life and loving the living are indispensable and dignifying attributes of the *mensh*. For in contemporary drama, as in the Yiddish theatre that helped to nourish it, the Jewish "hero" is the hero as *mensh*.

In that role, as in so many of the images he projects from the Western stage today, the Jew demonstrates that eight centuries of stereotyping did not atrophy his potential. He can play any role intended for a human being.

Notes

Preface

1. Jean-Paul Sartre, *Anti-Semite and Jew*, trans. George J. Becker (New York: Schocken, 1948), p. 69.

2. Henry Popkin cites with approbation George Ross's *Commentary* article which argues convincingly the Jewish elements in *Death of a Salesman*; see Popkin, "Arthur Miller: The Strange Encounter," in *American Drama and Its Critics*, ed. Alan S. Downer (Toronto: Univ. of Toronto Press, 1965), p. 221. Mary McCarthy faults Miller for insufficiently particularizing Willie and Linda Loman, giving them Jewish speech cadences, but not corroborating their ethnicity in any other way; see *Mary McCarthy's Theatre Chronicles, 1937–1962* (New York: Farrar, Straus and Co., 1963), pp. xix, xxi.

3. William Baker and Stephen Ely Tabachnick, *Harold Pinter* (New York: Harper and Row, 1973), p. 39.

1. Introduction: The Tradition of the Stage Jew

1. Heinz Pflaum, "Les Scènes de Juifs dans la littérature dramatique du moyen-âge," *Revue des Etudes Juives*, 89 (1930), 111.

2. *Ibid.*, p. 113.

3. Karl Young, *The Drama of the Medieval Church* (Oxford: Clarendon, 1933), II, 190.

4. *Ibid.*, p. 192. Similarly, the instructional purpose of *The Croxton Play* (c. 1470) is evident where it relates "the doubts of Jews concerning the flesh and blood nature of the Sacrament to the audience's own doubts on the matter." See Richard Axton, *European Drama of the Early Middle Ages* (London: Hutchinson Univ. Library, 1974), p. 198.

5. Pflaum, pp. 125–32.

6. Murray Roston, *Biblical Drama in England* (Evanston: Northwestern Univ. Press, 1968), p. 27.

7. Pflaum, p. 112.

8. Harold Fisch, *The Dual Image: The Figure of the Jew in English and American Literature* (New York: Ktav, 1971), p. 18.

9. Louis Réau, *Iconographie de l'Art chrétien*, I (Paris: Presses universitaires de France, 1955), 261.

248

10. Fisch, p. 18.
11. Roston, p. 30.
12. *Ibid.*
13. Axton, p. 114.
14. Pflaum, p. 115.
15. Luce Klein, *Portrait de la Juive dans la littérature française* (Paris: Nizet, 1970), p. 203.
16. According to Réau, it is impossible to be sure whether art inspired theatre, or vice versa; see Réau, *Iconographie de l'Art chrétien*, II, 2 (Paris: Presses universitaires de France, 1957), 744.
17. Réau, *Ibid.*, p. 746.
18. Young, II, 388.
19. Axton, p. 94.
20. Young, II, 243–44.
21. *Ibid.*, p. 244.
22. Klein, p. 19.
23. François-René de Chateaubriand, "Essai sur la littérature anglaise," *Oeuvres complètes* (Paris: Garnier, 1859), XI, 766.
24. The term is aptly coined by Harold Fisch to designate the Jew as the inspirer simultaneously of fear and hatred, and of reverence and devotion; see *The Dual Image*, p. 13.
25. Max L. Margolis and Alexander Marx, *A History of the Jewish People* (Philadelphia: Jewish Publication Society, 1945), pp. 384–91.
26. Cecil Roth, *A History of the Jews* (New York: Schocken, 1970), p. 210.
27. Bernhard Blumenkranz, ed., *Histoire des Juifs en France* (Toulouse: Edouard Privat), p. 24.
28. Although the evidence is scanty and contradictory, there does seem reason to believe that the coarse and grotesque image of stage Jews was not exclusively the product of Christian fancy and resourcefulness. Jewish dramatizations of the story of Esther and Mordecai form a traditional part of the Purim celebration. Israel Abrahams observes that because Purim coincides with Carnival, Jews may well have imitated Christian practices of mockery and buffoonery in the Purim plays. He records that French and German Jews in the fourteenth century infringed on Mosaic law by allowing men to impersonate women during the holiday when celebrants acted out not only the Book of Esther, but other subjects thematically less appropriate to Purim, e.g., the sale of Joseph, David's confrontation with Goliath; see Abrahams, *Jewish Life in the Middle Ages* (New York: MacMillan, 1896), p. 262.

Cecil Roth describes ghetto dramatizatons of the lives of the patriarchs as well as the story of Esther and adds, "Weddings and banquets were enlivened by professional jesters . . . , the broadness of whose witticisms sometimes scandalized devout opinion." See Roth, *A History of the Jews*, p. 291.

Abrahams, Roth and M. J. Landa all record forced participation of Jews in the most demeaning roles in Rome's Carnival celebrations. Landa, noting the history of Jewish involvement in the theatre dating to Talmudic times, supposes that Jews acted in the ancient Greek plays, though he does not specify what roles they may have played. Writing in 1926, Landa adds that the long connection of Jews with the theatre notwithstanding, they have been unable to counter the convention of the odious stage Jew, an observation that the present study is fortunately able to rectify; see Landa, *The Jew in Drama*, (1926; rpt. New York: Ktav, 1969), pp. 16–17.

250 · NOTES

29. Joshua Trachtenberg, *The Devil and the Jews* (New Haven: Yale Univ. Press, 1943), p. 43.
The fraternity of the Jew and the devil cannot always be dismissed as the invention of superstitious or miseducated minds. George Bernard Shaw uses this very association in Act III of *Man and Superman* (1903), where Mendoza, who "became leader, as the Jew always becomes leader, by his brains and imagination," turns up in Hell as the Devil, "the leader of the best society."

30. If only in passing, Marlowe's portrayal of the Jewess here is worthy of note because it completes the picture of Barabas' unmitigated maliciousness. Abigail is remarkably nuanced, especially by comparison with Jessica in *The Merchant of Venice*. Like Jessica, Abigail commits apostasy (or "sees the light"), but only after having been driven to it by her ruthless father to whom she had been devoted and obedient. Marlowe effectively demonstrates Barabas' monstrousness by the ease with which he casts aside his feelings for his "lovely daughter" and by his lack of scruples or remorse in poisoning her having incorrectly assumed that she had revealed him to be the murderer of her beloved. The disintegration of the father-daughter relationship which drives Abigail to the nunnery, the only refuge open to her, contrasts with Jessica's eagerness from the start to escape the shame of being her father's child.

31. Pflaum, p. 134.

32. M. F. Modder, *The Jew in the Literature of England* (Philadelphia: Jewish Publication Society, 1939), p. 15.

33. Landa, p. 47.

34. *Ibid.*, p. 49.

35. The intriguing history of usury and the participation of Jews in it has been exhaustively recorded and explained by numerous scholars, among them Cecil Roth, Salo Baron, Max L. Margolis and Alexander Marx, and Israel Abrahams. Interest rates which seem astronomical even in the 1980s were apparently the inevitable result of confiscatory laws, royal extortion, rapacious demand and, of course, unusually high risk.
History does not support the notion of usury as a Jewish monopoly. It was a widespread occupation, even among those whose religious law expressly forbade it. The Lombards and the Cahorsins became particularly well known in the practice. It is instructive to note that Jews sometimes served as "fronts" for gentile bankers.
Israel Abrahams reports that Jews were known to be more lenient than gentile creditors; see Abrahams, *Jewish Life in the Middle Ages*, pp. 242–43. We read in both Salo Baron and Cecil Roth that after the expulsion of Jews from the western European countries, Christian usurers demanded double the rate of interest the Jews had charged; see Cecil Roth, *A History of the Jews*, p. 195; Salo Wittmayer Baron, *A Social and Religious History of the Jews*, 2nd. ed. rev., XII (New York: Columbia Univ. Press, 1967), 144.

36. In his Introduction to Landa's *The Jew in Drama*, Murray Roston observes, "Almost every pogrom in history has been preceded by the charge that the Jews had murdered a Christian child" (p. x).

37. Edgar Rosenberg, "The Jew in Western Drama," essay introducing the 1968 reissue of Edward D. Coleman, *The Jew in English Drama* (New York: The New York Public Library and Ktav, 1968), p. 26.

38. Important representative titles include Théodore de Bèze's *Abraham Sacrificing* (1550), translated into English by Arthur Golding in 1577; Thomas Garter's *Godlye Susanna* (c. 1568); Jean de la Taille's *Saul Mad* (1572); Robert

Garnier's *The Jewesses* (1583); Thomas Legge's *The Destruction of Jerusalem* (1591); George Peele's *The Love of King David and Fair Bethsabe* (1599).

39. Edgar Rosenberg's observation that biblical drama constitutes a category all its own is borne out by such solid and widely different studies as Edward Coleman's *The Bible in English Drama, An Annotated List of Plays Including Translations from Other Languages from the Beginnings to 1931*, updated by *A Survey of Recent Major Plays* by Isaiah Sheffer in 1968 (New York: New York Public Library and Ktav) and Murray Roston's *Biblical Drama in England*.

40. Fisch, *The Dual Image*, p. 43. See also Roston, *Biblical Drama in England*, pp. 69–78, for a thoroughly documented discussion of this phenomenon which he appropriately calls "postfiguration."

41. Roston, pp. 160–61.

42. *Ibid.*, p. 157.

43. Samuel S. Stollman argues cogently for *Samson Agonistes* as a late work in which Milton makes the strongest case for his liberty versus bondage theme; see Stollman, "Milton's Dichotomy of 'Judaism' and 'Hebraism'," *PMLA*, 89 (1974), 105–12. In so doing, contends Stollman, Milton separated out the Judaic factor to represent the bondage which he opposed from the Hebraic element of the Samson story which stood for the freedom to which Milton subscribed. I do not think that Professor Stollman's distinction vitiates my point that Milton's Samson is a sentient, dimensional, and remarkably humanized character. Moreover, in literature as in life, the Jew frequently embodies just those antithetical elements Stollman identifies.

44. See Bettina Knapp, *Jean Racine: Mythos and Renewal in Modern Theatre* (University, Alabama: Univ. of Alabama Press, 1971), pp. 195 and 220–21; C. Lehrmann, *L'Elément juif dans la littérature française*, I (Paris: Michel Albin, 1960), 101. Both studies present valuable discussions of the Jewish elements in *Esther* and *Athalia*.

45. See, for example, Maurice Descotes, *Les Grands Rôles du théâtre de Jean Racine* (Paris: Presses universitaires de France, 1957), p. 175.

46. Roland Barthes, *On Racine* (New York: Hill and Wang, 1964), pp. 126 and 130.

47. See Knapp, pp. 201 and *passim*, pp. 223–30; Barthes, pp. 128–29, 132.

48. Perhaps he accomplished more than he himself realized. Lehrmann proposes a provocative analogy between Racine's and Shakespeare's treatments of traditional Jewish themes. Lehrmann feels that in both cases, the poet's genius took him deeper into his subject than he had projected, leading Shakespeare to a genuine appreciation of the tragic plight of Shylock, and Racine to the passion and religious poetry of Israel in *Esther* and *Athalia* (*L'Elément juif dans la littérature française*, I, 108).

49. Léon Poliakov, *The History of Anti-Semitism*, III, trans. Miriam Kochan (New York: Vanguard, 1975), 288.

50. Edward Coleman details the predominance of imports and the persistence of conventional Jewish villains and buffoons in them among plays shown on the American stage in the eighteenth and early nineteenth centuries; see Coleman, "Plays of Jewish Interest on the American Stage, 1752–1821," *Publications of the American Jewish Historical Society*, 33 (1934), 171–98.

51. René de Chavagnes attributes the tolerance Jews enjoyed "in town as well as on the stage" to the *esprit philosophique* which flourished in the eighteenth century; see Chavagnes, "Le Juif au théâtre," *Mercure de France*, 84 (1910), 22.

52. Solomon Liptzin, *The Jew in American Literature* (New York: Bloch Publishing Co., 1966), p. 24.

53. *Ibid.*, p. 25.

54. Both Coleman ("Plays of Jewish Interest," p. 195) and Landa (*The Jew in Drama*, pp. 145, 150 and *passim*) record the self-conscious apologies which began to appear in programs and on title pages or in prefaces of plays containing slighting references to Jews explaining that the work had not originally been intended for public performance, but the author's friends had prevailed, etc., an implicit and sometimes explicit acknowledgment that the author was aware of his impropriety and wished to go on record as broadminded.

55. *The Dual Image*, p. 47. See pp. 47–50 for Harold Fisch's insightful discussion of Sheva as embodiment of the age of reason's predilections and goals.

56. Quoted by A. M. Nagler, ed., *A Source Book in Theatrical History* (New York: Dover, 1952) p. 357.

57. Vigny's anti-Semitism has been amply documented by Léon Poliakov who shows how with all Jewish men, including Heine and Spinoza, the Frenchman "saw the Jew first, the man afterward." See Poliakov, *The History of Anti-Semitism*, III, 359–64.

58. Fernand Baldensperger, "Notes et Eclaircissements," *Oeuvres complètes d' Alfred de Vigny, Théâtre*, I (Paris: Conard, 1926), 286.

59. Landa, p. 148.

60. *Ibid.*

61. *Mary Tudor*, First Day, sc. 6, in Victor Hugo, *Dramas*, II (Boston: Estes and Lauriat, 1892), p. 24.

62. In *The Jew in English Drama*, Edward D. Coleman lists forty-five adaptations of *Ivanhoe*. Some of these plays take provocative liberties with their subject, e.g., the Brough brothers' "last edition of Ivanhoe, with all the latest improvements," a production starring "Isaac of York, principal partner in the eminent firm of 'Isaacs and Son,' cheap tailors, armourers, etc., Houndsditch, York" (p. 43). There are almost as many versions of *Oliver Twist* recorded in Coleman's listing. The enduring appeal of this work was demonstrated in the 1960s by Lionel Bart's "Oliver," well received as a musical comedy and a film. Here Fagin sings fetchingly about the possibility of abandoning his wicked life style, but perseveres in it anyway, because "life's one consolation's the money you may have put by."

63. *Torquemada*, II, 3, in Victor Hugo, *Dramas*, II, 395.

64. Moses Debré, *The Image of the Jew in French Literature from 1800 to 1908*, trans. Gertrude Hirschler (New York: Ktav, 1970), p. 35.

65. Chavagnes, "Le Juif au théâtre," pp. 246–47.

66. *Charles Dickens and His Jewish Characters* (London, 1918), quoted by Landa, p. 163.

67. Alexandre Dumas *fils*, Preface to *La Femme de Claude*, in *Théâtre complet* (Paris: Calmann-Levy, n.d.), V, 214.

68. Abraham Dreyfus, "Le Juif au théâtre," *Actes et Conférences de la Société des Etudes Juives*, 52 (1889), 52.

69. Scott is reported to have modelled his Rebecca on a lovely, philanthropic Philadelphian, Rebecca Gratz, described to him by Washington Irving—another instance of a literary Jew based on an actual person; see Edward D. Coleman, "Jewish Prototypes in American and English *Romans* and *Drames à Clef*," *Publications of the American Jewish Historical Society*, 35 (1939), 235–37.

70. *La Femme de Claude,* pp. 289–90.

71. In the first half of our own century, for example, a good Jewish woman, especially as defined by her female admirers, was one who could make a really satisfying pot of soup or bridge hand out of "nothing."

72. Maurice Donnay, *Le Retour de Jérusalem* (Paris: Charpentier et Fasquelle, 1904).

73. Albert Guignon's *Decadence* (1901), for example, unfolded in such an unsavory manner its tale of a self-serving marriage between a Jewish man and a gentile woman that the play was banned from the stage for three years. Oddly, Guignon's intent apparently was to pillory the nobility by putting them at odds with Jews almost as despicable as they.

74. Dreyfus, "Le Juif au théâtre," p. 53.

75. Max Beerbohm, "'Children of the Ghetto'," in *More Theatres, 1898–1903* (New York: Taplinger, 1969), p. 219.

76. One of the many expressions of this conviction comes from theatre critic Jules Lemaître, who in a characteristic digression in one of his reviews points out what he considers the defensive clannishness of Jews and offers a "remedy" to it: "I see no other solution than to please their women and marry their daughters. Doubless they are 'reducible' only in that way." See Lemaître, *Impressions de théâtre,* VIII (Paris: S. F. I. L., 1897), pp. 169–70.

77. Chavagnes, p. 252.

78. Henry Arthur Jones, *Judah* (1890), in *Representative Plays by Henry Arthur Jones,* ed. Clayton Hamilton (Boston: Little, Brown, 1925), I, 203.

79. *The Jew in Drama,* p. 272.

80 "'The Ghetto' and Other Plays," in *More Theatres,* p. 184.

81. *Les Débats,* April 15, 1901, quoted by René de Chavagnes, "Le Juif au théâtre," p. 248.

82. Chavagnes observed in 1910 that the theatre instead of mocking Jews now used them to scoff at others. What Guignon in *Decadence* and Savoir and Nozière in *The Baptism* were not quite able to bring off was accomplished with grace by George Bernard Shaw in Act II of *The Doctor's Dilemma:*

> SCHUTZMACHER: You see, when an Englishman borrows, all he knows or cares is that he wants money; and he'll sign anything to get it, without in the least understanding it, or intending to carry out the agreement if it turns out badly for him. In fact, he thinks you a cad if you ask him to carry it out under such circumstances. Just like the Merchant of Venice, you know. But if a Jew makes an agreement, he means to keep it and expects you to keep it. If he wants money for a time, he borrows it and knows he must pay it at the end of the time. If he knows he cannot pay, he begs it as a gift.
> RIDGEON: Come, Loony! do you mean to say that Jews are never rogues and thieves?
> SCHUTZMACHER: Oh, not at all. But I was not talking of criminals. I was comparing honest Englishmen with honest Jews.

83. Coleman, *The Jew in English Drama,* p. 86. Louis Harap identifies M. B. Curtis as a Jewish actor, Maurice Bertrand Strellinger, from Detroit; see Harap, *The Image of the Jew in American Literature* (Philadelphia: Jewish Publication Society, 1974), p. 230.

84. Landa, p. 201.

85. Murray Roston, Introduction to Landa, *The Jew in Drama,* p. x.

86. Coleman, p. xvii.

87. Sholome Michael Gelber, "The Image of the Jew in the Productions of the London Stage from 1919 to 1965," Diss. New York University 1967, p. 69.
88. John Galsworthy, *Loyalties* (New York: Charles Scribner's, 1932), p. 4.
89. *Ibid.*, p. 77.
90. Michel de Ghelderode, *Chronicles of Hell*, in *Seven Plays*, I (New York: Hill and Wang, 1960), p. 249.
91. *Ibid.*, p. 273.
92. Clifford Odets, *Awake and Sing!*, in *Masters of Modern Drama*, ed. Haskell Block and Robert G. Shedd (New York: Random House, 1967).
93. Dreyfus, "Le Juif au théâtre," p. 70.
94. Leslie A. Fiedler, "What Can We Do About Fagin?: The Jew-Villain in Western Tradition," *Commentary* (May 1949), p. 418.

2. Modern Heroes of Biblical Drama

1. Samuel Beckett, *Waiting for Godot* (New York: Grove Press, 1954), p. 35.
2. Laurence Housman, *Palestine Plays* (London: Jonathan Cape, 1942), pp. 5–6.
3. Cited by Murray Roston, *Biblical Drama in England* (Evanston: Northwestern Univ. Press, 1968), p. 260.
4. *Ibid.*, p. 241.
5. Paul Mankin, *Precious Irony: The Theatre of Jean Giraudoux* (The Hague: Mouton, 1971), p. 146.
6. Similarly, in Lanza del Vasto's ambitious *Noé* (Paris: Editions Denoël, 1965), Noah is referred to as "the king of wine." The biblical anecdote which inspires this image occurs after the Flood: "And Noah began to be a husbandman, and he planted a vineyard: And he drank of the wine, and was drunken" (Genesis 9:20–21).
7. Clifford Odets, *The Flowering Peach* (New York: Dramatists Play Service, 1954), p. 85. Subsequent citations will be noted in the text.
8. Christopher Fry, *The Firstborn*, in *Three Plays* (London: Oxford Univ. Press, 1960; rpt. 1968), p. 26. Subsequent citations will be noted in the text.
9. Paddy Chayefsky, *Gideon* (New York: Random House, 1961), pp. 71–72. Subsequent citations will be noted in the text.
10. Max L. Margolis and Alexander Marx, *A History of the Jewish People* (Philadelphia: Jewish Publication Society, 1945), p. 27.
11. René Kalisky, "Du surjeu au surtexte," essay published with *Dave au bord de mer* (Paris: Stock-Théâtre ouvert, 1978), p. 219. Subsequent references are noted in the text.
12. Lionel Abel, *Metatheatre* (New York: Hill and Wang, 1963), p. 118.
13. *Ibid.*, p. 113.
14. Lionel Abel, *Absalom*, in *Artists' Theatre: Four Plays*, ed. Herbert Machiz (New York: Grove Press, 1960), p. 150. Subsequent citations are noted in the text.
15. Abel has combined two biblical figures in the character of Achitofel. They are Bathsheba's father, Eliam, and David's advisor, Ahithophel, who conspired with Absalom against the king (II Samuel 15:31).
16. Wolf Mankowitz, *It Should Happen to a Dog*, in *The Penguin Wolf Mankowitz* (Harmondsworth: Penguin Books, 1967), p. 280. Subsequent citations are noted in the text.

17. Because Rabi incorporates the figure of the Wandering Jew into his *Judas*, that work will be discussed in Chapter III which treats stock types. Carlo Suares' *The Passion of Judas* (Berkeley: Shambala, 1973) is a polemic arguing that Jesus introduced Satan into Judas who "in humble obedience, goes out carrying the Light that will destroy his world."

18. Marcel Pagnol, *Judas* (Paris: Grasset, 1956), p. 28. Further references are included in the text.

19. *1965 World Book Year Book* (Chicago: Field Enterprises, 1965), p. 379.

20. Philip Birnbaum, *A Book of Jewish Concepts* (New York: Hebrew Publishing Co., 1964), p. 35.

3. Myths and Stock Types

1. Edgar Rosenberg, *From Shylock to Svengali: Jewish Stereotypes in English Fiction* (Stanford: Stanford Univ. Press, 1960), p. 191.

2. Arthur Miller, *The Price* (New York: Viking, 1968), p. 38. Subsequent citations are noted in the text.

3. Although *L'Invitation au château* has been translated into English by Christopher Fry as *Ring Round the Moon* (London: Methuen, 1950), the adaptation eliminates much of the Messerschmann component which is essential to the present investigation. For that reason, the original version is used here. All citations are to *L'Invitation au château* (Paris: La Table Ronde, Livre de poche, 1958) and pages are noted in the text. The translations are mine.

4. Harold Pinter, *The Birthday Party* (New York: Grove, 1961), p. 24. Subsequent citations are noted in the text.

5. I have explored this aspect of Meg and Stanley, among others, in "Pancakes and Soap Suds: A Study of Childishness in Pinter's Plays," *Modern Drama*, 16, 1 (1973), 91–101.

6. William Inge, *The Dark at the Top of the Stairs*, in *Four Plays by William Inge* (New York: Random House, 1958), p. ix. Future citations are noted in the text.

7. See Edgar Rosenberg, *From Shylock to Svengali*, especially Chapter VIII. Rosenberg's study of the genesis and evolution of the Wandering Jew, to which the present investigation is greatly indebted, is indispensable and fascinating.

8. Rosenberg, p. 196.

9. Hermann Sinsheimer, *Shylock: The History of a Character*, (1947; rpt. New York: Benjamin Blom, 1963), pp. 117–18.

10. *Ibid.*, p. 119.

11. Rosenberg, p. 189.

12. Rabi, *Anatomie du Judaisme français* (Paris: Editions de Minuit, 1962), p. 8.

13. Rabi, *Judas* (Gap: Ophyrs, 1951), p. 91. Citations are noted in the text.

14. Rosenberg, p. 190.

15. Toby Lelyveld, *Shylock on the Stage* (Cleveland: Western Reserve Univ. Press, 1960) provides an excellent guide to the history of the role on the British and American stages.

16. Mendel Kohansky, *The Hebrew Theatre: Its First Fifty Years* (New York: Ktav, 1969), p. 131.

17. Tristan Bernard, *Le Juif de Venise*, in *Les Oeuvres libres*, 182 (Paris: Fayard, 1936), 88–89.

256 · NOTES

18. Arnold Wesker, *The Merchant*, in *Adam International Review*, Nos. 401–403 (1977–78), p. 6. Subsequent citations are noted in the text.
19. Leslie Fiedler, " What Can We Do About Fagin?" *Commentary* (May 1949), p. 418.

4. The Jew as Other

1. Charles I. Glicksberg, "The Jewish Element in American Drama," *Chicago Forum*, 10, No. 1 (Fall 1951), p. 111.
2. Sidney Kingsley, *Detective Story* (New York: Dramatists Play Service, 1949), p. 24. Next citation noted in the text.
3. Morton Wishengrad, *The Rope Dancers*, in *Best American Plays*, 5th ser., ed. John Gassner (New York: Crown Publishers, 1963), p. 228.
4. Gabriel Marcel, *Rome n'est plus dans Rome* (Paris: La Table Ronde, 1951), p. 66. The next citation is noted in the text.
5. André Harris and Alain de Sédouy, *Juifs et Français* (Paris: Grasset, 1979), p. 344.
6. Kate Smith, a popular singer, became widely identified with the song "God Bless America."
7. Herman Wouk, *The Caine Mutiny Court-Martial* (New York: Samuel French, 1955), pp. 92–94.
8. Yvonne Mitchell, *The Same Sky* in *Plays of the Year*, ed. J. C. Trewin, vol. 6 (London and New York: Paul Elek, 1952), p. 237. Subsequent citations are noted in the text.
9. Paddy Chayefsky, *Middle of the Night* (New York: Random House, 1956), p. 107. Subsequent citations are noted in the text.
10. William Gibson, *Two for the Seesaw* (New York: Alfred Knopf, 1968), p. 169. Subsequent citations are noted in the text.

5. The Jew in a Jewish World

1. Israel Abrahams, *Jewish Life in the Middle Ages* (New York: MacMillan, 1896), pp. 267–72.
2. David Lifson, *The Yiddish Theatre in America* (New York: Thomas Yoseloff, 1965), p. 21.
3. Abrahams, pp. 253–55.
4. Quoted by Lifson, p. 18, from B. Gorin, *The History of the Jewish Theatre* (New York: Max N. Maisel, 1923) (in Hebrew). See also Abrahams, pp. 251–52.
5. Samuel J. Citron, "Yiddish and Hebrew Drama," in *A History of Modern Drama*, ed. Barrett H. Clark and George Freedley (New York: Appleton-Century Co., 1947), p. 602.
6. In addition to Lifson's *The Yiddish Theatre in America* and Citron's chapter in Clark and Freedley, the subject is treated delightfully and exhaustively by Nahma Sandrow in *Vagabond Stars: A World History of Yiddish Theatre* (New York: Harper and Row, 1977); see also Joseph Landis and M. J. Landa.
7. *The New York Times*, October 26, 1946, quoted by Lifson, p. 371.
8. Nahma Sandrow, *Vagabond Stars*, p. 278.
9. Hannah Grad Goodman in *Hadassah Magazine*, January 1981, p. 19.
10. *Vagabond Stars*, p. 110.

11. Lifson, p. 387.
12. *Ibid.*, p. 333.
13. *Ibid.*, p. 302.
14. Joseph C. Landis, ed. and trans., *The Great Jewish Plays* (New York: Avon-Equinox, 1972), p. ix.
15. Harold Clurman, *The Fervent Years* (New York: Hill and Wang, 1957), p. 4.
16. M. J. Landa, *The Jew in Drama*, p. 286.
17. Bernard Kops, *Four Plays* (London: MacGibbon and Kee, 1964), p. 9.
18. Citron, p. 617.
19. Joseph C. Landis, ed., *The Dybbuk and Other Great Yiddish Plays* (New York: Bantam Books, 1966), p. 6.
20. Rosten's and Landis' definitions serve to underscore the vicious irony in Goldberg's promise as he leads the catatonic Stanley away at the end of *The Birthday Party* (see p. 79), "You'll be a mensch."
21. Paddy Chayefsky, *The Tenth Man* (New York: Random House, 1960), p. 40. Subsequent citations are noted in the text.
22. Wolf Mankowitz, *The Bespoke Overcoat*, in *The Penguin Wolf Mankowitz* (Harmondsworth, Middlesex: Penguin Books, 1967), p. 253. Subsequent citations are noted in the text.
23. Bernard Kops, *The Hamlet of Stepney Green* in *Four Plays* (London: MacGibbon and Kee, 1964), p. 31. Subsequent citations are noted in the text.
24. Bernard Kops, *Enter Solly Gold* in *Four Plays*, p. 161. Further references are noted in the text.
25. Molière, *Tartuffe*, trans. Richard Wilbur (New York: Harcourt Brace Jovanovich, Harvest Edition, 1963), p. 25.
26. *Tartuffe*, p. 91.
27. Arnold Wesker, *I'm Talking About Jerusalem* in *The Wesker Trilogy* (Baltimore: Penguin Books, 1960), p. 186. Subsequent references to this play, *Chicken Soup with Barley*, and *Roots* are noted in the text.
28. See Tina Margolis and Susan Weinacht, "Introduction to Jewish Theatre Festival 1980," *The Drama Review* (September, 1980). This entire issue is devoted to Jewish Theatre.
29. For a generous representation of pertinent titles and descriptions, see *Catalogue of Plays of Jewish Interest*, 2nd ed., ed. Edward M. Cohen (New York: The Jewish Theatre Association and the National Foundation for Jewish Culture, 1981).

6. The Jew and Other Outsiders

1. Nahma Sandrow, *Vagabond Stars*, p. 182.
2. Elmer Rice, *Counsellor-at-Law*, in *Seven Plays by Elmer Rice* (New York: Viking Press, 1950), p. 239.
3. *Ibid.*, p. 248.
4. Rabi, in *La Terre retrouvée*, March 1948, cited in *Anthologie juive des origines à nos jours*, ed. Edmond Fleg (Paris: Flammarion, 1951), pp. 473–74.
5. *Ibid.*, p. 474.
6. Bettina L. Knapp, "Interviews avec Marguerite Duras et Gabriel Cousin," *French Review*, 44 (1971), 663–64.
7. Loften Mitchell, *Star of the Morning*, in *Black Drama Anthology*, ed. Woodie King and Ron Milner (New York: Columbia Univ. Press, 1971), p. 595.

8. Quoted by Doris Abramson, *Negro Playwrights in the American Theatre, 1925–1959* (New York: Columbia Univ. Press, 1967), p. 56.

9. Lillian Hellman, *My Mother, My Father and Me*, in *The Collected Plays* (Boston: Little, Brown and Co., 1971), p. 796.

10. Lorraine Hansberry, *The Sign in Sidney Brustein's Window* (New York: Random House, 1965), p. 66. Subsequent citations are noted in the text.

11. William Branch, *A Medal for Willie*, in *Black Drama Anthology*, p. 449.

12. Howard Sackler, *The Great White Hope* (New York: Dial Press, 1968), p. 55.

13. William Styron, *In the Clap Shack* (New York: Random House, 1973), p. 23. Subsequent citations are noted in the text.

14. Phillip Hayes Dean, *Thunder in the Index*, in *American Night Cry* (New York: Dramatists Play Service, 1972), p. 9. Further citations are noted in the text.

15. Author's manuscript.

16. Philip Birnbaum, *A Book of Jewish Concepts* (New York: Hebrew Publishing Co., 1964), p. 520.

17. Ed Bullins, *The Taking of Miss Janie*, in *Famous Plays of the 70s*, ed. Ted Hoffman (New York: Dell, 1981), p. 212. Subsequent reference in text.

18. Lewis John Carlino, *Sarah and the Sax*, in *Doubletalk* (New York: Random House, 1964), p. 61. Subsequent citations are noted in the text.

7. Crises of Conscience and of Consciousness

1. Jean Halperin, "Problèmes culturels," *La Vie juive dans l'Europe contemporaine*, Proceedings of the Colloquium Held at the Institute of Sociology of the Free Institute of Brussels, 19–21 Sept., 1962 (Brussels: Institut de Sociologie de l'Université Libre de Bruxelles, 1965), p. 158.

2. See Glenda Abramson, *Modern Hebrew Drama* (New York: St. Martin's Press, 1979) and Mendel Kohansky, *The Hebrew Theatre: Its First Fifty Years* (New York: Ktav, 1969).

3. Leon Bernstein, *Dark and Bright* (London: Lincolns-Prager, 1956), p. 49.

4. Sholom Aleichem, "Dreyfus in Kasrilevke," in *The Best of Sholom Aleichem*, ed. Irving Howe and Ruth Wisse (Washington: New Republic, 1979) p. 112.

5. Léon Blum, *Souvenirs sur l'Affaire* (Paris 1935), quoted in *Histoire des Juifs en France*, ed. Bernhard Blumenkranz (Toulouse: Edouard Privat, 1972), p. 353.

6. Edward D. Coleman, *The Jew in English Drama* (1943; rpt. New York: New York Public Library and Ktav, 1968), p. 68.

7. Blumenkranz, *Histoire des Juifs en France*, p. 381.

8. Emmanuel Eydoux, *Capitaine Alfred Dreyfus* (Marseilles: Roger Eisinger, 1967), p. 89.

9. "Dreyfus Case," *The Jewish Encyclopedia*, (New York, Ktav, 1901–06), IV, 666–67.

10. Jean-Claude Grumberg, *Dreyfus*, in *L'Avant-Scène Théâtre*, No. 543 (15 June 1974), pp. 35–36.

11. Marcel's play was first published in 1949. In 1953, he added an epilogue which he claimed gave the play "all its meaning," and it is this version that is considered here. It appears in *Cinq Pièces Majeures* (Paris: Plon, 1973). All citations are noted in the text.

12. George Wellers, *De Drancy à Auschwitz*, quoted in *Milieux juifs de la France contemporaine*, ed. Pierre Aubéry (Paris: Plon, 1957), p. 303.

13. Robert Shaw, *The Man in the Glass Booth* (New York: Grove Press, 1968), p. 9. Subsequent citations are noted in the text.

14. Author's manuscript. *Throne of Straw* will appear in *The Theatre of the Holocaust*, ed. Robert Skloot, forthcoming from the University of Wisconsin Press.

15. René Kalisky, "Le Théâtre climatisé," *Cahiers de la Compagnie Madeleine Renaud-Jean-Louis Barrault*, 77 (3ᵉ trimestre, 1971), 117.

16. René Kalisky, *Jim le Téméraire* (Paris: Editions Gallimard, 1972), p. 62. Subsequent citations are noted in the text.

17. Gruendgens became the subject of a book, *Mephisto*, by Klaus Mann, who was for a while his brother-in-law. In turn, Mann's book was adapted very successfully to the stage under the same title by Ariane Mnouchkine with her Théâtre du Soleil. See Mnouchkine, *Méphisto* (Paris: Editions Solin, 1979).

18. Jean-Claude Grumberg, *L'Atelier* (Paris: Editions Stock, 1979), p. 69.

19. Serge Ganzl, *Fragments* (Paris: Editions Stock, 1978), p. 191.

20. Tatenberg is a fictitious name, although Gatti situates the camp near identifiable locations in Austria that are important in the play. In "Armand Gatti's Carnival of Compassion: *La Deuxième Existence du camp de Tatenberg*," Richard N. Coe identifies Tatenberg as Mauthausen; see Coe, *Yale French Studies*, 46 (June 1971), 60–74.

21. Armand Gatti, *La Deuxième Existence du camp de Tatenberg*, in *Théâtre*, (Paris: Editions du Seuil, 1962), III, 257. Further citations are specified in the text.

22. Richard N. Coe, "Armand Gatti's Carnival of Compassion," p. 67.

23. Elie Wiesel, *Zalmen, or The Madness of God*, trans. Nathan Edelman, stage adapt., Marion Wiesel (New York: Random House, 1974), p. 45. In the introduction to this English-language stage adaptation of the play, published six years after the original (Paris: Seuil, 1968), Wiesel acknowledges changes in the Soviet Union in the interim. He pays tribute to the increased courage of Russian Jews engaged in proud demonstration of their faith and in nonviolent rebellion against repression. Although it is well beyond the scope of this study to assess the current situation in Russia, the daily press makes it reasonable to view the Jews depicted in *Zalmen* as distillates, as representative today as they were when the play was written. Page references are incorporated in the text.

24. *La Deuxième Existence du camp de Tatenberg*, p. 263.

25. Albert Camus, *The Myth of Sisyphus and Other Essays*, trans. Justin O'Brien (New York: Alfred A. Knopf, 1975), p. 6.

26. Leslie A. Fiedler, "What Can We Do About Fagin?" *Commentary* (May 1949), p. 418.

8. The Jew as Metaphor

1. Abraham Dreyfus, "Le Juif au théâtre," *Actes et Conférences de la Société des Etudes Juives*, 52 (1889), 70.

2. Arthur Miller, *After the Fall* (New York: Viking, 1964), p. 113.

3. Arthur Miller, *Incident at Vichy* (New York: Bantam, 1971), p. 88. Subsequent references are noted in the text.

4. Marguerite Duras, *Détruire, dit-elle* (Paris: Editions de Minuit, 1969), p. 30. Subsequent citations are noted in the text.

5. Bettina Knapp, "Interviews avec Marguerite Duras et Gabriel Cousin," *The French Review*, 44 (1971), 656.

6. Jacques Rivette and Jean Narboni, "Marguerite Duras la destruction la parole," *Cahiers du cinéma*, 217 (November 1969), 52.

7. *Ibid.*, p. 51.

8. *Ibid.*

9. Knapp, p. 655.

10. Sarah Blacher Cohen, ed., Introd., *Comic Relief: Humor in Contemporary American Literature* (Urbana: Univ. of Illinois, 1978), p. 8.

11. Saul Bellow, *The Last Analysis* (New York: Viking, 1965), p. 33. Subsequent references are noted in the text.

12. Glenn M. Loney, Headnote to *The Last Analysis*, in *Comedy: A Critical Anthology*, ed. Robert W. Corrigan (Boston: Houghton Mifflin, 1971), p. 670.

13. *Ibid.*, p. 671.

14. Victor Haïm, *Isaac et la Sage-Femme*, in *L'Avant-Scène Théâtre*, No. 600 (December 15, 1976), p. 8.

15. Emmanuel Haymann in *T. J. Hebdo.* (October 29, 1976), quoted in *L'Avant-Scène Théâtre*, No. 600, p. 22.

16. Victor Haïm, *Abraham et Sarah*, in *L'Avant-Scène Théâtre*, No. 548 (September 15, 1974), p. 44. The next citation is noted in the text.

17. Arnold Wesker, *The Old Ones*, in *Arnold Wesker*, Vol. 3 (Harmondsworth, Middlesex: Penguin Books, 1980). All citations to the play are noted in the text.

18. Yaacov Vainstein, *The Cycle of the Jewish Year* (Jerusalem: The World Zionist Organization, 1964), p. 120.

19. Bernard Kops, *The Lemmings*, in *Four Plays* (London: MacGibbon and Kee, 1964), p. 251. Subsequent citations are noted in the text.

Bibliography

The following list of titles constitutes a selected bibliography compiled for those who would like to pursue the study of the Jew in Western drama. While it includes most of the works cited in the text as well as relevant references to plays and secondary sources that lie outside its focus, it makes no claims to being comprehensive. Materials are divided into two sections: I. Plays; II. Background and criticism.

I. Plays

Abel, Lionel. *Absalom*. In *Artists' Theatre: Four Plays*. Edited by Herbert Machiz. New York: Grove Press, 1960.

Allen, Woody. *Death*. New York: Samuel French, 1975.

———. *Don't Drink the Water*. New York: Random House, 1967.

———. *God*. New York: Samuel French, 1975.

Anouilh, Jean. *L'Invitation au château*. Paris: La Table Ronde, 1968.

Anski, S. [Shloyme Zanvl Rappoport]. *The Dybbuk*. In *The Great Jewish Plays*. Edited and translated by Joseph C. Landis. New York: Avon-Equinox, 1972.

Bellow, Saul. *The Last Analysis*. New York: Viking, 1965.

Bernard, Tristan. *Le Juif de Venise*. Oeuvres libres, Vol. 182. Paris: Fayard, 1936.

Bernstein, Henry. *Israël*. Paris: Arthème Fayard, 1908.

Bernstein, Leon. *Dark and Bright*. London: Lincolns-Prager, 1956.

Boucicault, Dion. *London Assurance*. Edited by Ronald Eyre. London: Methuen, 1971.

Branch, William. *A Medal for Willie*. In *Black Drama Anthology*. Edited by Woodie King and Ron Milner. New York: Columbia University Press, 1972.

Bridie, James [Osborne Henry Mavor]. *Tobias and the Angel*. In *The Anatomist and Other Plays*. New York: Richard Smith, 1931.

Bullins, Ed. *The Pig Pen*. In *Four Dynamite Plays*. New York: William Morrow, 1972.

———. *The Taking of Miss Janie*. In *Famous American Plays of the 1970s*. Edited by Ted Hoffman. New York: Dell-Laurel, 1981.

Carlino, Lewis John. *Sarah and the Sax.* In *Doubletalk.* New York: Random House, 1964.

Chayefsky, Paddy. *Gideon.* New York: Random House, 1961.

———. *Middle of the Night.* New York: Random House, 1956.

———. *The Tenth Man.* New York: Random House, 1960.

Claudel, Paul. *L'Echange.* In *Oeuvres complètes,* Vol. 8. Paris: Gallimard, 1954.

———. *L'Otage, Le Pain dur, Le Père humilié.* In *Oeuvres complètes,* Vol. 10. Paris: Gallimard, 1956.

Cousin, Gabriel. *L'Opéra noir. Théâtre,* I. Paris: Gallimard, 1963.

Crowley, Mart. *The Boys in the Band.* In *Famous American Plays of the 1960s.* Edited by Harold Clurman. New York: Dell, 1972.

Cumberland, Richard. *The Jew.* In *British Theatre,* Vol. 18. London: Longman, Hurst, Rees and Orme, 1808.

Darzens, Rodolphe. *L'Amante du Christ.* Paris: Alphonse Lemerre, 1888.

Dean, Phillip Hayes. *Thunder in the Index.* In *American Night Cry.* New York: Dramatists Play Service, 1972.

DeAnda, Peter. *Ladies in Waiting.* In *Black Drama Anthology.* Edited by Woodie King and Ron Milner. New York: Columbia University Press, 1972.

Donnay, Maurice. *Le Retour de Jérusalem.* Paris: Charpentier et Fasquelle, 1904.

Dumas fils, Alexandre. *La Femme de Claude.* In *Théâtre complet,* Vol. 5. Paris: Calmann-Lévy, n.d.

Duras, Marguerite. *Détruire, dit-elle.* Paris: Editions de Minuit-10/18, 1969.

Erckmann [Emile]-[Alexandre] Chatrian. *Le Juif polonais.* New York: D.C. Heath, 1903.

Eydoux, Emmanuel. *Abraham l'hébreu* et *Samuel le voyant.* Geneva: La Baconnière, 1946.

———. *Capitaine Alfred Dreyfus.* Marseille: Roger Eisinger, 1967.

Feiffer, Jules. *Knock, Knock.* New York: Hill and Wang-Mermaid, 1976.

———. *Little Murders.* Harmondsworth, Middlesex: Penguin Books, 1971.

Fry, Christopher. *The Firstborn.* In *Three Plays.* London: Oxford University Press, 1960; rpt. 1968.

Galsworthy, John. *Loyalties.* New York: Charles Scribner's Sons, 1932.

Ganzl, Serge. *Fragments.* Paris: Stock-Théâtre ouvert, 1978.

Gatti, Armand. *Chroniques d'une planète provisoire.* In *Théâtre,* III. Paris: Editions du Seuil, 1962.

———. *La Deuxième Existence du camp de Tatenberg.* In *Théâtre,* III. Paris: Editions du Seuil, 1962.

Ghelderode, Michel de. *Chronicles of Hell* and *Pantagleize.* In *Seven Plays,* Vol. 1. New York: Hill and Wang-Mermaid, 1960.

Gibson, William. *The Seesaw Log with the Text of Two for the Seesaw.* New York: Alfred A. Knopf, 1968.

Goldberg, Isaac, ed. and trans. *Six Plays of the Yiddish Theatre.* Boston: John W. Luce, 1916.

Goodrich, Frances and Albert Hackett. *The Diary of Anne Frank.* New York: Random House, 1956.

Grumberg, Jean-Claude. *L'Atelier.* Paris: Stock-Théâtre ouvert, 1979.

———. *Dreyfus*. In *L'Avant-Scène Théâtre*, No. 543 (15 June 1974), pp. 7–36.

———. *Michu*. Paris: Stock-Théâtre ouvert, 1979.

Haïm, Victor. *Abraham et Samuel*. In *L'Avant-Scène Théâtre*, No. 548 (15 September, 1974), pp. 33–46.

———. *Isaac et la Sage-Femme*. In *L'Avant-Scène Théâtre*, No. 600 (15 December, 1976), pp. 3–21.

———. *La Visite*. In *L'Avant-Scène Théâtre*, No. 562 (15 April 1975), pp. 3–19.

Hansberry, Lorraine. *The Sign in Sidney Brustein's Window*. New York: Random House, 1965.

Hellman, Lillian. *My Mother, My Father and Me*. In *The Collected Plays*. Boston: Little, Brown, 1971.

Hennique, Léon. *Esther Brandès*. Paris: Tresse et Stock, 1887.

Housman, Laurence. *Palestine Plays*. London: Jonathan Cape, 1942.

Hugo, Victor. *Cromwell*. In *Dramas*, vol. 3. Boston: Estes and Lauriat, 1892.

———. *Mary Tudor* and *Torquemada*. In *Dramas*, Vol. 2. Boston: Estes and Lauriat, 1892.

Inge, William. *The Dark at the Top of the Stairs*. In *Four Plays*. New York: Random House, 1958.

Jones, Henry Arthur. *Judah*. In *Representative Plays*, Vol. 1. Edited by Clayton Hamilton. Boston: Little, Brown, 1925.

Kalisky, René. *Dave au bord de mer*. Paris: Stock-Théâtre ouvert, 1978.

———. *Jim le Téméraire*. Paris: Editions Gallimard, 1972.

Kingsley, Sidney. *Detective Story*. New York: Dramatists Play Service, 1949.

Kops, Bernard. *Enter Solly Gold, The Hamlet of Stepney Green* and *The Lemmings*. In *Four Plays*. London: MacGibbon and Kee, 1964.

Landis, Joseph C., ed. and trans. *The Great Jewish Plays*. New York: Avon-Equinox, 1972.

Levin, Meyer. *Anne Frank*. Privately published by the author for literary discussion.

Lieberman, Harold and Edith. *Throne of Straw*. In *The Theatre of the Holocaust*. Edited by Robert Skloot. Madison: University of Wisconsin Press, forthcoming.

Mankowitz, Wolf. *The Bespoke Overcoat* and *It Should Happen to a Dog*. In *The Penguin Wolf Mankowitz*. Harmondsworth, Middlesex: Penguin Books, 1967.

Marcel, Gabriel. *Le Signe de la Croix*. In *Cinq Pièces majeures*. Paris: Plon, 1973.

———. *Rome n'est plus dans Rome*. Paris: La Table Ronde, 1951.

Marlowe, Christopher. *The Jew of Malta*. In *Five Plays*. Edited by Havelock Ellis. New York: Hill and Wang, 1956.

Miller, Arthur. *After the Fall*. New York: Viking, 1964.

———. *Incident at Vichy*. New York: Bantam, 1971.

———. *The Price*. New York: Viking, 1968.

Milton, John. *Samson Agonistes*. In *The Portable Milton*. Edited by Douglas Bush. New York: Viking, 1949.

Mitchell, Loften. *Star of the Morning*. In *Black Drama Anthology*. Edited by Woodie King and Ron Milner. New York: Columbia University Press, 1972.

Mitchell, Yvonne. *The Same Sky*. In *Plays of the Year*, Vol. 6. Edited by J. C. Trewin. London and New York: Paul Elek, 1952.

Mnouchkine, Ariane, adapt. *Méphisto*. Paris: Solin, 1979.

Mullem, Louis. *Une Nouvelle Ecole*. Paris: Tresse et Stock, 1890.

Odets, Clifford. *Awake and Sing!* In *Masters of Modern Drama*. Edited by Haskell Block and Robert G. Shedd. New York: Random House, 1967.

———. *The Flowering Peach*. New York: Dramatists Play Service, 1954.

Pagnol, Marcel. *Judas*. Paris: Grasset, 1956.

Perr, Harvey. *Jew!* In *Collision Course*. Edited by Edward Parone. New York: Random House, 1968.

Peterson, Louis. *Take a Giant Step*. In *Black Drama in America: An Anthology*. Edited by Darwin T. Turner. Greenwich, Conn.: Fawcett, 1971.

Pinero, Arthur Wing. *Iris*. New York: R. H. Russell, 1902.

———. *Letty*. London: William Heinemann, 1904.

Pinter, Harold. *The Birthday Party*. New York: Grove Press, 1961.

Rabi [Wladimir Rabinovitch]. *Judas*. Gap: Ophyrs, 1951.

Racine, Jean. *Esther* and *Athalia*. In *The Complete Plays of Jean Racine*, Vol. 2. Translated by Samuel Solomon. New York: Random House, 1967.

Rice, Elmer. *Counsellor-At-Law*. In *Seven Plays*. New York: Viking, 1950.

Sackler, Howard. *The Great White Hope*. New York: Dial, 1968.

———. *Skippy*. In *A Few Enquiries*. New York: Dial, 1970.

Sartre, Jean-Paul. *The Condemned of Altona*. Translated by Sylvia and George Leeson. New York: Knopf, 1961.

Schisgal, Murray. *The Basement* and *The Old Jew*. In *Five One Act Plays*. New York: Dramatists Play Service, 1968.

Scribe, Eugène. *La Juive*. In *Oeuvres complètes*, Vol. III, 3. Paris: Dentu, 1875.

Shakespeare, William. *The Merchant of Venice*. In *The Riverside Shakespeare*. Edited by G. Blakemore Evans, *et al.* New York: Houghton Mifflin, 1974.

Shaw, George Bernard. *The Doctor's Dilemma*. In *Complete Plays with Prefaces*, Vol. 1. New York: Dodd, Mead, 1962. ·

Shaw, Robert. *The Man in the Glass Booth*. New York: Grove Press, 1968.

Skloot, Robert, ed. *The Theatre of the Holocaust*. Madison: University of Wisconsin Press, forthcoming.

Styron, William. *In the Clap Shack*. New York: Random House, 1973.

Suarès, Carlo. *The Passion of Judas*. Translated by Micheline and Vincent Stuart. Berkeley: Shambala, 1973.

Vigny, Alfred de. *Shylock*. In *Oeuvres complètes d'Alfred de Vigny. Théâtre*, I. Paris: Conard, 1926.

Wesker, Arnold. *The Friends* and *The Old Ones*. In *Arnold Wesker*, Vol. 3. Harmondsworth, Middlesex: Penguin Books, 1980.

———. *The Kitchen*. In *Arnold Wesker*, Vol. 1. Harmondsworth, Middlesex: Penguin Books, 1964.

———. *The Merchant*. In *Adam International Review*, Nos. 401–403 (1977–78), pp. 4–68.

———. *The Wesker Trilogy*. Baltimore: Penguin Books, 1960.

Wiesel, Elie. *Zalmen ou la Folie de Dieu*. Paris: Editions du Seuil, 1968.

———. *Zalmen, or the Madness of God*. Adapted for the stage by Marion Wiesel after a translation by Nathan Edelman. New York: Random House, 1974.

Wilson, Lanford. *Talley's Folly.* New York: Hill and Wang, 1979.
Wishengrad, Morton. *The Rope Dancers.* In *Best American Plays,* fifth series, 1957–1963. Edited by John Gassner. New York: Crown, 1963.
Wolff, Pierre. *Jacques Bouchard.* Paris: Tresse et Stock, 1890.
Wouk, Herman. *The Caine Mutiny Court-Martial.* New York: Samuel French, 1955.
Zola, Emile. *Les Héritiers Rabourdin.* In *Oeuvres complètes,* vol. 3. Paris: Cercle du livre précieux, 1969.

II. Background and Criticism

Abel, Lionel. *Metatheatre: A New View of Dramatic Form.* New York: Hill and Wang, 1963.
Abrahams, Isaac. *Jewish Life in the Middle Ages.* New York: MacMillan, 1896.
Abramson, Doris E. *Negro Playwrights in the American Theatre, 1925–1959.* New York: Columbia University Press, 1967.
Abramson, Glenda. *Modern Hebrew Drama.* New York: St. Martin's, 1979.
Aubéry, Pierre. *Milieux juifs de la France contemporaine à travers leurs écrivains.* Paris: Plon, 1957.
Axton, Richard. *European Drama of the Early Middle Ages.* London: Hutchinson University Library, 1974.
Baron, Salo. *A Social and Religious History of the Jews.* 2nd edition, revised and enlarged. 17 vols. New York: Columbia University Press, 1952–80.
Beigbeder, Marc. *Le Théâtre en France depuis la libération.* Paris: Bordas, 1959.
Biben, Augusta C. "The Jew in English Literature," *Jewish Ledger,* 67 (1928), 3 and 18–19.
Birnbaum, Philip. *A Book of Jewish Concepts.* New York: Hebrew Publishing Co., 1964.
Black Anti-Semitism and Jewish Racism. New York: Schocken, 1969.
Bloch, Maurice. "La Femme juive dans le roman et au théâtre." *Revue des Etudes juives,* 24 (1892), 28–39.
Blumenkranz, Bernhard, ed. *Histoire des Juifs en France.* Toulouse: Edouard Privat, 1972.
Bourdel, Philippe. *Histoire des Juifs de France.* Paris: Albin Michel, 1974.
Calisch, Edward N. *The Jew in English Literature, as Author and as Subject.* 1909; rpt. Port Washington: Kennikat Press, 1969.
Chamberlin, Roy B. and Herman Feldman, eds. The Dartmouth Bible. Boston: Houghton Mifflin, 1950.
Charles, Gerda. "Elizabethan Age of Modern Jewish Literature, 1950–1960: Decade of the Great Break-Through." *World Jewry,* Sept. 1961, pp. 15–17.
———. "Trends in Anglo-Jewish Writing." *The Jewish Quarterly,* Spring 1963, pp. 11–13.
Chavagnes, René de. "Le Juif au Théâtre." *Mercure de France,* 84 (March 1, 1910), 16–34; (March 16, 1910), 245–260.
Citron, Samuel J. "Yiddish and Hebrew Drama." In *History of Modern Drama.* Edited by Barrett H. Clark and George Freedley. New York: Appleton-Century, 1947.

266 · BIBLIOGRAPHY

Claudel, Paul. "La Figure d'Israël." In *Cahiers Paul Claudel*, Vol. 7. Paris: Gallimard, 1968.

Clurman, Harold. *The Fervent Years*. New York: Hill and Wang, 1957.

Coe, Richard N. "Armand Gatti's Carnival of Compassion: *La Deuxième Existence du camp de Tatenberg*." *Yale French Studies*, 46 (June 1971), 60–74.

Cohen, Edward M., ed. *Catalogue of Plays of Jewish Interest*. 2nd ed. New York: The Jewish Theatre Association and the National Foundation for Jewish Culture, 1981.

Coleman, Edward D. *The Bible in English Drama: An Annotated List of Plays Including Translations from Other Languages from the Beginnings to 1931*. 1931; rpt., with Isaiah Sheffer, "A Survey of Recent Major Plays." New York: New York Public Library and Ktav, 1968.

———. *The Jew in English Drama: An Annotated Bibliography*. 1943. Reprint, with Edgar Rosenberg, "The Jew in Western Drama: An Essay and a Check List," and Flola L. Shepard, "Addenda to the Jew in English Drama." New York: New York Public Library and Ktav, 1968.

———. "Jewish Prototypes in American and English *Romans* and *Drames à Clef*." *Publications of the American Jewish Historical Society*, 35 (1939), 227–80.

———. "Plays of Jewish Interest on the American Stage, 1752–1821." *Publications of the American Jewish Historical Society*, 33 (1934), 171–98.

Corbin, John. "Drama and the Jew." *Scribner's Magazine*, 93 (Jan.–June 1933), 295–300.

Danson, Lawrence. *The Harmonies of the Merchant of Venice*. New Haven: Yale University Press, 1978.

Debré, Moses. *The Image of the Jew in French Literature from 1800 to 1908*. Translated by Gertrude Hirschler. New York: Ktav, 1970.

Dreyfus, Abraham. "Le Juif au théâtre." *Actes et Conférences de la société des études juives*, 52 (1889), 49–71.

Driver, Tom F. *Romantic Quest and Modern Query: A History of the Modern Theatre*. New York: Dell, 1970.

Drumont, Edouard. *La France juive*. Paris: Marpon et Flammarion, 1886.

Fiedler, Leslie A. "What Can We Do About Fagin? The Jew Villain in Western Tradition." *Commentary*, May 1949, pp. 411–18.

Fisch, Harold. *The Dual Image: The Figure of the Jew in English and American Literature*. New York: Ktav, 1971.

Fleg, Edmond. *Anthologie juive des origines à nos jours*. Paris: Flammarion, 1951.

Gassner, John. *Theatre at the Crossroads*. New York: Holt, Rinehart and Winston, 1960.

Gelber, Sholome Michael. "The Image of the Jew in the Productions of the London stage from 1919 to 1965." Diss. New York University 1967.

Glazer, Nathan. *American Judaism*. Chicago: University of Chicago Press, 1957.

———. "Negroes and Jews: The New Challenge to Pluralism." *Commentary*, December 1964, pp. 29–34.

Glicksberg, Charles I. "The Jewish Element in American Drama." *The Chicago Jewish Forum*, 10, No. 1 (Fall 1951), 110–15.

Guttman, Allen. *The Jewish Writer in America: Assimilation and the Crisis of Identity.* New York: Oxford University Press, 1971.

Haft, Cynthia. *The Theme of Nazi Concentration Camps in French Literature.* The Hague: Mouton, 1973.

Harap, Louis. *The Image of the Jew in American Literature: From Early Republic to Mass Immigration.* Philadelphia: Jewish Publication Society of America, 1974.

Hardison, O. B., Jr. *Christian Rite and Christian Drama in the Middle Ages.* Baltimore: Johns Hopkins University Press, 1965.

Harris, André and Alain de Sédouy. *Juifs et Français.* Paris: Grasset, 1979.

Hertzberg, Arthur. *The French Enlightenment and the Jews: The Origins of Modern Anti-Semitism.* New York: Schocken, 1970.

The Holy Bible. King James Version. Cambridge: Cambridge University Press, n.d.

The Holy Scriptures According to the Masoretic Text. Philadelphia: Jewish Publication Society of America, 1955.

Hyman, Paula. *From Dreyfus to Vichy.* New York: Columbia University Press, 1979.

The Jewish Encyclopedia. New York: Ktav, 1901–06.

"The Jewish Writer and the English Literary Tradition, A Symposium." *Commentary*, Part I, September 1949, pp. 209–219; Part II, October 1949, pp. 361–70.

Kalisky, René. "Le Théâtre climatisé." *Cahiers de la Compagnie Madeleine Renaud–Jean-Louis Barrault*, 77 (1971), 112–23.

Karpeles, Gustav. *Jewish Literature and Other Essays.* Philadelphia: Jewish Publication Society of America, 1895.

Kienzle, Siegfried. *Modern World Theatre: A Guide to Productions in Europe and the United States since 1945.* Translated by Alexander and Elizabeth Henderson. New York: Frederick Ungar, 1970.

Klein, Luce. *Portrait de la Juive dans la littérature française.* Paris: Nizet, 1970.

Knapp, Bettina L. "Interviews avec Marguerite Duras et Gabriel Cousin." *The French Review*, 44 (March 1971), 653–64.

————. *Jean Racine: Mythos and Renewal in Modern Theatre.* University, Alabama: The University of Alabama Press, 1971.

Kohansky, Mendel. *The Hebrew Theatre: Its First Fifty Years.* New York: Ktav, 1969.

Lalou, René. *Le Théâtre en France depuis 1900.* Paris: Presses universitaires de France, 1965.

Landa, Myer Jack. "The Jew and the Drama." *The Jewish Chronicle*, August 27, 1920, p. 21.

————. *The Jew in Drama.* 1926; rpt. New York: Ktav, 1969.

Leftwich, Joseph. "Anglo-Jewish Literature." *The Jewish Quarterly*, Spring 1953, pp. 15–24.

Lehrmann, C. *L'Elément juif dans la littérature française.* Vol. 1: *Des Origines à la Révolution*, 1960; Vol. 2: *De la Révolution à nos jours*, 1961. Paris: Albin Michel.

Lelyveld, Toby. *Shylock on the Stage.* Cleveland: Western Reserve University Press, 1960.

Lifson, David. *The Yiddish Theatre in America*. New York: Thomas Yoseloff, 1965.

Liptzin, Solomon. *The Jew in American Literature*. New York: Bloch, 1966.

Marcus, Jacob R. *The Jew in the Medieval World*. 1938; rpt. New York: Harper and Row, 1965.

Margolis, Max L. and Alexander Marx. *A History of the Jewish People*. Philadelphia: Jewish Publication Society of America, 1945.

Mersand, Joseph. *The American Drama Presents the Jew: An Evaluation of the Treatment of Jewish Characters in Contemporary Drama*. New York: New York Public Library, 1939.

————. *Traditions in American Literature: A Study of Jewish Characters and Authors*. 1939; rpt. Port Washington: Kennikat, 1968.

Modder, Montagu Frank. *The Jew in the Literature of England to the End of the Nineteenth Century*. Philadelphia: Jewish Publication Society of America, 1939.

Orcibal, Jean. *La Genèse d'Esther et d'Athalie*. Paris: Librairie Philosophique J. Vrin, 1950.

Petit, Jacques. *Bernanos, Bloy, Claudel, Péguy: Quatre Ecrivains catholiques face à Israël: Images et mythes*. Paris: Calmann-Levy, 1972.

Pflaum, Heinz. "Les Scènes de Juifs dans la littérature dramatique du moyen-âge." *Revue des Etudes Juives*, 89 (1930), 111–34.

Poliakov, Léon. *The History of Anti-Semitism*. 3 vols. New York: Vanguard Press, 1965–75.

Popkin, Henry. "Jewish Writers in England." *Commentary*, February 1961, pp. 135–41.

Rabi [Wladimir Rabinovitch]. *Anatomie du judaïsme français*. Paris: Editions de Minuit, 1962.

Réau, Louis. *Iconographie de l'art chrétien*. 3 vols. in 6. Paris: Presses universitaires de France, 1955.

Rosenberg, Edgar. *From Shylock to Svengali: Jewish Stereotypes in English Fictions*. Stanford: Stanford University Press, 1960.

————. See also Coleman and Van der Veen.

Rosten, Leo. *The Joys of Yiddish*. New York: McGraw-Hill, 1968.

Roston, Murray. *Biblical Drama in England from the Middle Ages to the Present Day*. Evanston, Illinois: Northwestern University Press, 1968.

Roth, Cecil. *A History of the Jews: From Earliest Times through the Six Day War*. Rev. ed. New York: Schocken, 1970.

————. *A History of the Jews in England*. 3rd ed. Oxford: Clarendon Press, 1964.

Rovit, Earl. "Jewish Humor and American Life." *The American Scholar*, 36 (Spring 1967), 237–45.

Sandrow, Nahma. *Vagabond Stars: A World History of Yiddish Theatre*. New York: Harper & Row, 1977.

Sartre, Jean-Paul. *Anti-Semite and Jew* (translation of *Réflexions sur la question juive*). Translated by George J. Becker. New York: Schocken, 1948.

Serreau, Geneviève. *Histoire du "Nouveau théâtre."* Paris: Gallimard, 1966.

Shillman, Bernard. "Legends of the Jews in English Literature." *The Reflex*, February 1929, pp. 17–24.

Shunami, Shlomo, ed. *Bibliography of Jewish Bibliographies*. Jerusalem: Magnes, 1965.

Sinsheimer, Hermann. *Shylock: The History of a Character*. 1947; rpt. New York: Benjamin Blom, 1963.

Surer, Paul. *Cinquante Ans de théâtre*. Paris: S.E.D.E.S., 1969.

The Drama Review. Jewish Theatre Issue, 24, No. 3 (1980).

Trachtenberg, Joshua. *The Devil and the Jews: The Medieval Conception of the Jew and Its Relation to Modern Anti-Semitism*. New Haven: Yale University Press, 1943.

Vainstein, Yaacov. *The Cycle of the Jewish Year*. Jerusalem: The World Zionist Organization, 1964.

Van der Veen, Harm R. S. *Jewish Characters in Eighteenth Century English Fiction and Drama*. 1935; rpt. with Edgar Rosenberg, "Tabloid Jews and Fungoid Scribblers," and appendices, New York: Ktav, 1973.

Versini, Georges. *Le Théâtre français depuis 1900*. Paris: Presses universitaires de France, 1970.

La Vie juive dans l'Europe contemporaine. Proceedings of the Colloquium Held at the Institute of Sociology of the Free University of Brussels from 19 to 21 September, 1962. Brussels: Institut de l'Université libre, 1965.

Wisse, Ruth R. *The Schlemiel as Modern Hero*. Chicago: University of Chicago Press, 1971.

Young, Karl. *The Drama of the Medieval Church*. 2 vols. 1933; rpt. Oxford: Clarendon Press, 1951.

Index

DATE DUE

GAYLORD